THE NEW TERRITORY

THE NEW TERRITORY

Ralph Ellison and the Twenty-First Century

Edited by Marc C. Conner and Lucas E. Morel

UNIVERSITY PRESS OF MISSISSIPPI • JACKSON

www.upress.state.ms.us

Every effort has been made to locate and credit the copyright holders of material reprinted in this book. Intellectual property rights remain with the original authors, their estates, or representatives. The editor and publisher will be happy to correct any errors or omissions in a future edition.

The University Press of Mississippi is a member of the Association of American University Presses.

Copyright © 2016 by University Press of Mississippi
All rights reserved
Manufactured in the United States of America

First printing 2016

∞

Library of Congress Cataloging-in-Publication Data

Names: Conner, Marc C., editor. | Morel, Lucas E., 1964– editor.
Title: The new territory : Ralph Ellison and the twenty-first century / edited by Marc C. Conner and Lucas E. Morel.
Description: Jackson : University Press of Mississippi, 2016. | Based on papers presented at a 2012 symposium held at Washington and Lee University, Lexington, Virginia, on Ralph Ellison and the twenty-first century. | Includes bibliographical references and index. | Description based on print version record and CIP data provided by publisher; resource not viewed.
Identifiers: LCCN 2016010326 (print) | LCCN 2015050081 (ebook) | ISBN 9781496806802 (epub single) | ISBN 9781496806819 (epub institutional) | ISBN 9781496806826 (pdf single) | ISBN 9781496806833 (pdf institutional) | ISBN 9781496806796 (cloth : alk. paper)
Subjects: LCSH: Ellison, Ralph—Criticism and interpretation—Congresses. | Literature and society—United States—History—21st century—Congresses. | African Americans in literature—Congresses. | Race relations in literature—Congresses.
Classification: LCC PS3555.L625 (print) | LCC PS3555.L625 Z77 2016 (ebook) | DDC 813/.54—dc23
LC record available at http://lccn.loc.gov/2016010326

British Library Cataloging-in-Publication Data available

ionized visible with a grant

FIGURE FOUNDATION

To my father, Louis Terrence Conner. —*MC*

To my youngest daughter, Natalie Luna Morel. —*LM*

CONTENTS

ACKNOWLEDGMENTS   XIII

ABBREVIATIONS   XV

INTRODUCTION: The New Territory
Ralph Ellison and the Twenty-First Century
    MARC C. CONNER AND LUCAS E. MOREL   3

PART ONE: *Invisible Man* Sixty Years Later
Revisiting Ellison's Masterpiece in the Twenty-First Century

INVISIBLE MAN AND THE POLITICS OF LOVE
    ROBERT BUTLER   39

THE BODY AND *INVISIBLE MAN*
Ralph Ellison's Novel in Twenty-First-Century Performance and Public Spaces
    PATRICE RANKINE   55

THE NOISY LOSTNESS
Oppositionality and Acousmatic Subjectivity in *Invisible Man*
    HERMAN BEAVERS   75

INVISIBLE MAN IN THE AGE OF OBAMA
Ellison on (Color) Blindness, Visibility, and the Hopes for a Postracial America
    BRYAN CRABLE   99

PART TWO: *Three Days before the Shooting . . .*
Ellison's Ongoing Epic of America

RALPH ELLISON IN HIS LABYRINTH
ERIC J. SUNDQUIST   117

THE POLITICS OF FATHERHOOD IN *THREE DAYS BEFORE THE SHOOTING...*
LENA HILL   142

FATHER ABRAHAM
Ellison's Agon with the Fathers in *Three Days before the Shooting . . .*
MARC C. CONNER   167

RALPH ELLISON'S *THREE DAYS*
The Aesthetics of Political Change
TIMOTHY PARRISH   194

RALPH ELLISON'S *THREE DAYS BEFORE THE SHOOTING* . . . AND THE IMPLICIT MORALITY OF FORM
GRANT SHREVE   218

PART THREE: Ralph Ellison and American Culture
Ellison Past, Present, and Future

"IN A STRANGE COUNTRY"
The Challenge of American Inclusion
LUCAS E. MOREL   245

INVISIBLE MAN'S GRANDFATHER AND THE AMERICAN DREAM
STEVEN D. EALY   260

MOURNING AND MELANCHOLY
Explaining the Ellison Animus
ROSS POSNOCK   285

"HOW MANY LIGHTBULBS DOES IT TAKE TO SCREW IN A BLUES SINGER?"
The French Revolution, King Louis Armstrong, and the Futuristic Jungleism of Jazz
STEVEN C. TRACY   294

CONCLUSION: Ralph Ellison in the Twenty-First Century

"THAT PAUSE FOR CONTEMPLATION"
A Centennial Meditation on Ralph Ellison
   JOHN CALLAHAN   313

WORKS CITED   329

ABOUT THE CONTRIBUTORS   343

INDEX   346

ACKNOWLEDGMENTS

This book has been a collaborative effort from its first conception. We want first and foremost to thank the fourteen contributors, whose enthusiasm for investigating the meanings of Ralph Ellison to the twenty-first century has been so provocative and inspiring. This project grew out of the 2012 symposium at Washington and Lee University, "Ralph Ellison and the Twenty-First Century," and we are grateful to the many figures who supported that effort: Bob Strong, provost at Washington and Lee; Hank Dobin, dean of the college, and Larry Peppers, dean of the Williams School; Barbara Mollica and Mary Woodson; and the Lenfest Endowment for Faculty Summer Support. The Ralph Ellison Trust has strongly supported this project, and we thank in particular John Silberman and Donn Zaretsky. Alice Birney and George Chiassion at the Library of Congress have been extremely helpful to all Ellison scholars, and we thank them in particular for their help with the two Ralph Ellison seminars we held at the Ralph Ellison Reading Room at the Library of Congress. The Ralph Ellison Society, founded in 2011, has been a wonderful community of Ellison scholars and we are grateful to this group as well as the American Literature Association for all their support of the rich growth in Ellison studies in recent years. John Callahan has been a constant inspiration, resource, living archive, and inexhaustible trove of information and insight about Ralph Ellison, and every Ellison scholar today is in his great debt. Certainly this book owes much of its quality to John's work. The University Press of Mississippi has embraced this project and helped give it shape, and we particularly thank Vijay Shah, Katie Keene, Anne Stascavage, Anne Rogers, and Walter Biggins. Finally, we express our heartfelt gratitude to our families, whose love and support make possible all that we do.

ABBREVIATIONS

CERE: *The Collected Essays of Ralph Ellison.* John F. Callahan, ed. Preface by Saul Bellow. Rev. and enlarged ed. New York: Modern Library, 2003.

CRE: *Conversations with Ralph Ellison.* Maryemma Graham and Amritjit Singh, eds. Jackson: University Press of Mississippi, 1995.

IM: *Invisible Man.* New York: Vintage, 1989.

TD: *Three Days before the Shooting . . . .* John F. Callahan and Adam Bradley, eds. New York: Modern Library, 2010.

THE NEW TERRITORY

THE NEW TERRITORY
Ralph Ellison and the Twenty-First Century

MARC C. CONNER AND LUCAS E. MOREL

"A TERRITORY OF HOPE"
Ralph Ellison's Meaning for the Twenty-First Century

One century ago, Ralph Ellison was born in Oklahoma City, Oklahoma, in a state that just a few years earlier had still been a territory. He described the land of his birth as "a relatively unformed frontier state" that offered to "the descendants of the freed slaves ... a territory of hope, and a place where they could create their own opportunities" (CERE 607, 605). The concept of "the territory" would form one of the most potent emblems for the American character in Ellison's thought, synonymous ultimately with hope, possibility, the interaction of art forms and discourses, the site of the vernacular, and the place where one would have the opportunity to forge what he would call "that condition of man's being at home in the world" (CERE 154). Here the artists and musicians could "bring together and make possible an interaction of art forms, styles, and traditions" that expressed the power of "the vernacular as a dynamic *process*" of "play-it-by-eye-and-ear improvisations" that ultimately points us toward "the homeness of home" (CERE 610, 612, 615).

The homeness of home remained for Ellison the elusive grail that he restlessly sought his entire life. That sense of home was torn from him by his father's death when Ellison was only three years old, leaving him with the sense *"that by his death I was fatally flawed and doomed"* (CERE 36). Ellison spent the bulk of his life in an unrelenting effort to return to that sense of "homeness" through his carefully crafted fiction and essays; what Henry James would call the "house of fiction" became precisely that for Ellison, the ideal dwelling place he sought and could never quite locate again. For Ellison, this struggle became in effect a struggle with time itself. His never-completed second novel was begun perhaps as early as 1953, right after the publication of *Invisible Man,* and Ellison continued to work on it right up to within a few months of his death on April 16, 1994. This protean work of fiction also resisted a single setting in time; while Ellison claimed its time was the mid-1950s (in one note he begins the main narrative with "On the day of April, 1953"[1]), he gradually expanded the time of its setting: "Action takes place on the eve of the Rights movement but it forecasts the chaos which would come later . . . reach[ing] beyond the frame of the fiction [and] look[ing] forward to the reassertion of the Klan and the terrible, adolescent me-ism of the '70's" (139/5). Much of the material seems strikingly contemporary, particularly in the computer sequences—the long sections of narrative drafts that Ellison composed on his computer from the mid-1980s onward—and yet other parts seem to look backward, evoking a rich sense of African American culture of the early twentieth century or even the late nineteenth century, such as the evocative sermon that Bliss and Hickman preach together at the Juneteenth revival meeting. One wonders if Ellison, in his ongoing battle with history, was trying to create a book that would both define, and transcend, its own time, its own historical moment.[2]

What then can we say about Ralph Ellison now, as we move further into the twenty-first century, twenty years removed from Ellison's death, in the age of Obama and the markedly new territory of technological change that Ellison himself glimpsed near the end of his life? Put differently, how does Ralph Ellison speak to us here, in our position in and of the twenty-first century? And what purchase does his concept of "the territory" have on our world today? Our claim is this: Ralph Ellison has never been more relevant to American thought than he is today; indeed, Ellison looks more and more like the cultural prophet of twenty-first-century America. As Ross Posnock has stated, "If in our global, transnational age the renewed promise of cosmopolitan democracy has emerged as an animating ideal of popular, political, and academic culture, this is a way of saying that we are only now beginning to catch up with Ralph Waldo Ellison" (1). Timothy Parrish makes a similar claim for Ellison's relevance, not just to his own day, but to future days: "Ellison was forever addressing an America that is still unrealized. His ideal readers most likely never knew the world he knew and live closer to the future America he addressed" (*Genius* x). Parrish claims that Ellison belongs less to his own time, and more to the time that he intuited would follow from it: "Ellison, not Richard Wright or James Baldwin or Amiri Baraka, was the black intellectual who could envision an America that would, within a generation of Martin Luther King, Jr.'s death, elect and celebrate the election of a black president" (6). In his post–*Invisible Man* writing—his magnificent essays and the long, unfinished work that became *Three Days before the Shooting*...—Ellison "indicated that he wanted that novel to portray and perhaps define the postsegregation era" (9).[3]

Indeed, Ellison explicitly saw his mission as a writer to be to chronicle the America that could be, the America that is always promised and still unrealized. As he argued in so many of his essays, and throughout *Three Days before the Shooting*..., America is a land of contradiction between profession and practice when it comes to fulfilling the promises of its "sacred documents," the Declaration of Independence, the Constitution, and the Bill of Rights. He defined the role of the "novelist of minority background" to be precisely the gadfly to the nation: "So while remaining true to his own group's unique perception of experience, he is also goaded to add his individual voice to the futuristic effort of fulfilling the democratic ideal," for "we're only a partially achieved nation, and I think this is good because it gives the writer of novels a role beyond that of entertainer" (CERE 470, 763). Consequently the role of the American novelist—and perhaps particularly the African American novelist, who is most acutely aware of America's promise and also its betrayals—is to craft his fiction toward the realization of what America can become in the unglimpsed future: "I'll close by reminding my fellow writers, as I frequently remind myself, that you're doing far more than creating interesting tales based on your individual view of the American experience. Underneath your efforts you're helping this country discover a fuller sense of itself as it goes about making its founders' dream a reality" (CERE 856). This is the drive toward the new territory that America is only now achieving. Thus Parrish, Posnock, and other recent scholars[4] put before us a Ralph Ellison who certainly was not caught in the past or somehow out of step with his time, as Arnold Rampersad insinuates in his often troubling biography of Ellison,[5] nor an Ellison who is defined by his present, but rather an Ellison who saw more clearly and more penetratingly where America would go culturally and politically in the decades that followed the civil rights era. They put before us the Ralph Ellison of the twenty-first century.[6]

This is an opportune moment to reconsider Ralph Ellison's centrality to our own time, for we seem to be in need of new concepts and structures to understand America, and particularly African America, today. In a major revisioning of the narratives African Americans have long told and been told about themselves, the novelist and philosopher Charles Johnson argues that we need to recognize that the long-standing narrative for making sense of African American experience, a narrative of victimization and oppression, no longer applies to the America of the twenty-first century. Johnson writes, "This unique black American narrative, which emphasizes the experience of victimization, is quietly in the background of every conversation we have about black people, even when it is not fully articulated or expressed. It is our starting point, our agreed-upon premise, our most important presupposition for dialogues about black America" ("End," *American Scholar* 33). This narrative had great explanatory power for African American life from the time of the Jamestown colony up to the civil rights era, when the African American condition could well be described as one of "thinghood," defined first by slavery, then by segregation and legal disenfranchisement. Yet, Johnson argues, in our current era, "40 years after the epic battles for specific civil rights in Montgomery, Birmingham, and Selma, after two monumental and historic legislative triumphs—the Civil Rights Act of 1964 and the Voting Rights Act of 1965—and after three decades of affirmative action that led to the creation of a true black middle class ... a people oppressed for so long have finally become, as writer Reginald McKnight once put it, 'as polymorphous as the dance of Shiva'" (36–37). The result of this long process of historical transformation is that African America can no longer be thought of as a single entity, nor can a single narrative about African America in any way express the diversity, heterogeneity, and, to invoke Ralph Ellison's favorite term, "the complexity of American experience" (CERE 460).[7]

For Ellison, revealing this complexity was a specifically African American vocation: "No one else in this country can tell it as well as we can if we ever have the will to tell it in its fullness and complexity, with all of its comic overtones and tragedy" (CERE 460). Ellison's understanding of American complexity formed the foundation of his sense of the responsibility of the (black) American artist, who betrays that complexity, and the "stern discipline" of art, if he reduces American experience to easy sociological statements: "If a Negro writer is going to listen to sociologists—as too many of us do—who tell us that Negro life is thus and so in keeping with certain sociological theories, he is in trouble because he will have abandoned his task before he begins" (CERE 726). These "ideological formulas" seemed to Ellison—in an argument that is strikingly similar to Johnson's, though twenty-five years earlier—"reductive [because] they overemphasized the negative aspects of our condition while leaving unnoticed the tragic-comic transcendence through which we had survived and remained hopeful, both as individuals and as a people. Most of all, such ideological formulas sought to reduce our complex American identity to the single aspect of race" (CERE 834). There is much in these ideas to incite controversy, to elicit a strong response, to inspire an artist to move beyond the accepted boundaries of expression—indeed, Johnson himself, upon becoming the first African American writer since Ellison to receive the National Book Award for fiction, stated in his acceptance speech (with Ellison in the audience) that what most inspired him in Ellison's work was "the intellectual expansiveness and artistic generosity of his novel." Johnson credited Ellison with providing precisely the broad multiplicity of narratives about African American life that he sought as a self-proclaimed philosophical black novelist: "[Ellison] envisioned a black American personality as complex, multisided, and synthetic as the American society that produced it" ("Acceptance Speech" 208–9).

For Ellison, this is precisely the role of the artist, whose audience, embodied for Ellison in the little man behind the stove at Chehaw Station, expects (and will accept) no less:

> The little man feels no urge to impose censorship upon the artist. Possessing an American-vernacular receptivity to change, a healthy delight in creative attempts at formalizing irreverence, and a Yankee trader's respect for the experimental, he is repelled by works of art that would strip human experience, especially American experience, of its wonder and stubborn complexity. (CERE 497–98)

Ellison's view of the truth-telling warrant for African American experience is renewed in Johnson's argument for new narratives of that experience. As Johnson explains, "No matter which angle we use to view black people in America today, we find them to be a complex and multifaceted people who defy easy categorization. *We challenge, culturally and politically, an old group narrative that fails at the beginning of this new century to capture even a fraction of our rich diversity and heterogeneity*" ("End," *American Scholar* 37; emphasis added).

Johnson, like Ellison, certainly acknowledges and grapples with the ongoing injustices of race and class throughout his writings, and nowhere suggests that America has somehow healed itself of outrageous wrongdoing, particularly against its black populations. Yet he insists that this old narrative of victimization has become ahistorical, a fixed ideology that no longer matches the ever more complex realities of black American life.[8] What is needed are new narratives, much more provisional and humble and subject to reinterpretation—what Ellison described many times as the improvisational give-and-take of the jazz soloist and the group, his penetrating metaphor for the American experiment of the one and the many, the *E pluribus unum* invoked by Sunraider in the early pages of *Juneteenth*, as the "prayer and promise" of the American project (TD 242).[9] Johnson concludes, in wording that is remarkably consonant with Hickman's descriptions of the American reality in *Three Days before the Shooting . . .* , "In the 21st century, we need new and better stories, new concepts, and new vocabularies and grammar based not on the past but on the dangerous, exciting, and unexplored present, with the understanding that each is, at best, a provisional reading of reality, a single phenomenological profile that one day is likely to be revised, if not completely overturned" ("End," *American Scholar* 42).[10]

Johnson's argument resembles nothing more than Ellison's famous rejoinder to Irving Howe in his 1963–64 essay "The World and the Jug." Rejecting Howe's argument that the authentic black writer is capable only of protest fiction rooted in social realism, Ellison eloquently argues for (and demonstrates) the broad, rich possibilities inherent in black life, a life that always exceeds the limiting definitions put upon it by others—be they other black writers, sociologists, or neo-Marxist literary critics. "There is also an American Negro tradition," Ellison explains, "which teaches one to deflect racial provocation and to master and contain pain. It is a tradition which abhors as obscene any trading on one's own anguish for gain or sympathy; which springs not from a desire to deny the harshness of existence but from a will to deal with it as men at their best have always done. It takes fortitude to be a man, and no less to be an artist" (CERE 159). Like Johnson a half-century later, Ellison, far from complaint or victimization, points to the fortitude and stoic heroism of African American life. For that life is not, contrary to Howe's erroneous assertion, "an abstract embodiment of living hell." Rather, "American Negro life [is] also a *discipline*—just as any human life which has endured so long is a discipline teaching its own insights into the human condition, its own strategies of survival. There is a fullness, even a richness here—and here *despite* the realities of politics, perhaps, but nevertheless here and real" (CERE 159–60). Between Ellison's exposition of the rich discipline of African American life and Johnson's call for an end of the narrative of victimization and complaint, we have the civil rights struggle, the emergence of Black Power, the increase of urban blight, the rise of gang warfare in the inner cities, and the gradual establishment of African Americans in all areas of science, the arts, the military, business, and eventually the White House with the election of the first American president of African descent. Yet the similarity of vision of the two writers is evident. Ellison, like Johnson after him, insists upon the rich, complex, tragicomic humanity of African Americans. Those critics, he argues, who deny such a complex view serve "not only to deny us our humanity but to betray the critic's commitment to social reality. Critics who do so should abandon literature for politics" (CERE 160).

EXPANDING THE ELLISON CANON
New Understandings of Ellison in and for the Twenty-First Century

During the past decade, a number of scholars have found Ellison's thought and writing to have enormous currency, not least his ideas about the complexity of American culture, the heterogeneity of its parts, the rich potential of its stories, and the need for a criticism that can match the complexity of Ellison's work. In many ways this scholarship runs counter to the major scholarly trends in humanistic studies of the late twentieth and early twenty-first centuries, when identity politics, racial essentialism, and neo-Marxist perspectives often dominated cultural criticism. Ellison himself predicted such ideologies of thought, warning as early as 1978 of "the newly fashionable code word 'ethnicity' [and its] heady evocations of European, African and Asian backgrounds accompanied by chants proclaiming the inviolability of ancestral blood. Today blood magic and blood thinking, never really dormant in American society, are rampant among us" (CERE 504–5). In one of the most insightful of recent studies of Ellison, Ross Posnock in 2005 argues that Ellison "conceives democracy and art not simply as doctrine, or knowledge, or contemplation, but as strenuous, risky ways of acting in the world." Consequently, Ellison's writings provoke Americans "to come alive to the fact that the nation's population and cultural life has always been a vibrantly miscegenated affair, mirroring the 'fluid, pluralistic turbulence of the democratic process'" (CERE 504; Posnock 2–3). Posnock views Ellison as articulating the vibrant opposite of the "various ideologies of American purity—be it Adamic innocence, 'nature's nation,' American exceptionalism, Jim Crow racism and Jim Crow (separatist) multiculturalism" (7). Against such purity, Ellison insists on the always improvisational, always masked, always mongrelized complexity of our identities. "Our cultural wholeness," he writes, "offers no easily recognizable points of rest, no facile certainties as to who, what, or where (culturally or historically) we are. Instead the whole is always in cacophonic motion" (CERE 508). Posnock comments that "before this spectacle of barely controlled chaos which 'eludes accepted formulations' [CERE 512], proponents of ethnic and racial identity stand flatfooted, refusing to enter into the cacophonic rhythm, or slip into the breaks and look around" (7).

The story of Ellison's own victimization by identity politics is well known. In the 1960s, as Black Power, Black Nationalism, and the Black Aesthetic became ascendant, Ellison was frequently decried as an integrationist or accommodationist, and, in the most spectacular case, he was confronted at a reception at Grinnell College and called an Uncle Tom (Rampersad 439–40). As previously noted, throughout Rampersad's biography this condemnatory view of Ellison persists: Rampersad frequently implies that the main reason Ellison could never finish his second novel was because of the "growing distance between himself and the black social reality about him" (315). Rampersad asserts that, by the mid-1970s, "Ralph was bedeviled by too rigid ideas about culture and art, myth and symbol, allusion and leitmotif. His inability to create an art that held a clean mirror up to 'negro' life as blacks actually led it, especially at or near his own social level, was disabling him as a writer. As a novelist, he had lost his way. And he had done so in proportion to his distancing of himself from his fellow blacks" (513). Many Ellison scholars have taken issue with Rampersad's thesis.[11] A major flaw in his argument consists of the fact that Ellison, while he never completed his ongoing second novel, was nevertheless enormously productive, creating throughout the forty-year period of its composition thousands of pages, including some of the most accomplished and stirring prose ever written by an American.[12] But the crucial point to make here is that, as Posnock argues, Ellison's rejection of racial essentialism is not a simple, conservative desire for "the sanctity of American unity"; rather, "Ellison's complaint is that blood thinking is an anxious, defensive response to the radical challenge of American democracy" (6). Ellison's conception of American culture insists on the complexity of that culture, a complexity that cannot be reduced to simple slogans or easy political posturings. He writes, "It would seem that for many our cultural diversity is as indigestible as the concept of democracy in which it is grounded," and repeatedly insists that "the most agonizing mystery sponsored by the democratic ideal is that of our unity-in-diversity, our oneness-in-manyness" (CERE 507).

This understanding of Ellison's contemporary relevance, of how presciently he seems to speak to us in our twenty-first-century moment, is surely a major part of the boom in Ellison studies over the past several years. Much of this boom is fueled by the posthumous publications of Ellison's own writings, made possible by the dedicated editorial work of his close friend and literary executor, John Callahan. Callahan has brought out since Ellison's death a wealth of material that was either unpublished or uncollected and hence nearly unavailable to the general reader. First came *The Collected Essays of Ralph Ellison* in 1995, which combined Ellison's two published volumes of essays (*Shadow and Act* [1964] and *Going to the Territory* [1986]) with eleven previously published but uncollected essays (including the astonishing 1965 essay "Tell It Like It Is, Baby," which has emerged in recent years as a crucial piece for understanding Ellison's work[13]), two crucial interviews, and nine previously unpublished pieces. The essays have become essential material for understanding Ellison and more broadly American culture writ large, confirming Ellison, along with his namesake Ralph Waldo Emerson, as perhaps the greatest essayist in the history of American letters.

Callahan then discovered a sheaf of both published and unpublished short stories in a box in the Ellison apartment. He collected and arranged these stories—written mostly in the early 1940s, as Ellison was honing his craft and preparing to commence work on what would become *Invisible Man*—and published them in 1996 as *Flying Home and Other Stories* (the introduction to which is itself a major biographical study of Ellison). In 1999, Callahan published *Juneteenth*, a version of the Book II typescript of the second novel and without a doubt the strongest and most central narrative in that book. (We discuss the anatomy of the second novel in more detail in the following pages.) In 2000 Callahan and Albert Murray published *Trading Twelves: The Selected Letters of Ralph Ellison and Albert Murray*, which includes the extraordinary correspondence between these two men of letters in the mid- to late 1950s, right when Ellison was making his initial progress on the second novel and observing the burgeoning civil rights movement from Rome. Finally in 2010, Callahan and Adam Bradley brought out *Three Days before the Shooting . . .* , the 1,101-page compilation of the main parts of the second novel, to which scholars have begun to respond with vigor. (Several essays have appeared in the past four years treating this work; the current volume is the first book to address *Three Days* in detail.[14]) Currently in progress, Callahan and Conner are editing *The Selected Letters of Ralph Ellison*, which will reveal Ellison as perhaps the last great letter writer of the twentieth century. Ellison's letters are virtually essayistic, and here one can discern the voice of Ellison the essayist and also Ellison the novelist, particularly the voices of the second novel. The letters will also constitute a powerful addition to the biographical understanding of Ellison—to be sure, Ellison's own voice and words are likely to counter and complicate some of the biographical studies published to date.

Thus, whereas Ellison published in his lifetime one novel and two books of essays, we now have readily at hand thousands of pages of his fictional work, from spare short stories that predate *Invisible Man* to the final computer typescripts on which he was working within months of his death. We also have an enlarged corpus of his nonfiction essays, and soon a significant body of his correspondence. Scholars are only now seeing the depth of insight and the keen understanding of American history, culture, literature, and politics contained in those essays and letters. As Posnock remarks, "Ellison's achievement in criticism and in fiction is virtually unique among postwar American prose writers; for precedents one must turn to the creative and critical work of T. S. Eliot and Ezra Pound in the early decades of the century" (2). Or, to quote Tim Parrish, Ellison's legacy "is as complex and rich as any in the canon of American literature—as if the same mind had written *Moby-Dick* and 'The American Scholar'" (*Genius* 5). And of course, with the publication of the most substantial parts of his ongoing second novel, we are able to read, teach, study, and grapple with the epic of America on which Ellison labored for over forty years.

Three Days before the Shooting . . . is a tremendous work of literature, but it is unlike anything else in the American canon. Even the title is an educated guess—Ellison never indicated what he would call his "second novel," and Callahan and Bradley employed the opening lines of what Ellison intended to be the prologue to the entire work: "Three days before the shooting, a chartered planeload of Southern Negroes swooped down upon the District of Columbia and attempted to see the Senator" (5). We choose to call this work "Ralph Ellison's unfinished epic of America," a concept that acknowledges the essentially unfinished nature of the work—and ultimately Ellison knew, on some level or lower frequency, that it *had* to be unfinished, as the American project itself is unfinished. This description of the second book also underscores that this work is not a novel, it is an epic, bearing all the qualities of epic, from its flawed but spectacular hero to its quest to establish the nation to its ongoing search for home. Finally, as our appellation suggests, the work is quintessentially about America—America is Ellison's great obsession, his muse and his Calypso, his lover and temptress.

Ellison considered publishing the work in parts, perhaps as three separate novels, but wanted to be sure the pieces had sufficient harmony and integrity. To be sure, he was utterly unwilling to publish anything less than a supreme fiction, and we might speculate that this very ambition, this refusal to compromise his artistic vision, was a key factor in his final inability to complete the book. McPherson reported in 1970 that Ellison had "enough typed manuscripts to publish three novels, but is worried over how the work will hold up as a total structure." He conveyed the story, first promulgated by Fanny Ellison, that "she hears him in his study at night, turning pages and laughing to himself. He enjoys the book so much that he isn't in a hurry to share it with the public" (CERE 387). Yet for another near-quarter of a century, Ellison continued to revise, refine, expand, and explore this fictional world, never bringing it to completion. Upon his death, Callahan found "thousands of handwritten notes, typewritten drafts, mimeographed pages and holographs, dot-matrix and laser printouts," all constituting "a series of related narrative fragments, several of which extend to over three hundred manuscript pages in length, that appear to cohere without truly completing one another" (TD xv–xvi). What then did Callahan and Bradley publish in the 1,101-page book that they brought out in 2010?

The anatomy of *Three Days before the Shooting . . .* is as follows. There are two central narratives: the first focuses on the white reporter, Welborn McIntyre, and his efforts to understand the attempted assassination of a racist New England senator; and the second focuses on the assassination story itself. Senator Sunraider is gunned down on the floor of the Senate (his assailant leaps to his own death) and in the hospital the dying senator insists that the old black preacher who had mysteriously arrived in Washington the day of the shooting be brought to his deathbed—and this is Hickman, who, it turns out, was Sunraider's surrogate father, raising him from his birth in an all-black community in rural Georgia, training him to be a preacher too, until one day the young boy, named Bliss, ran away from this loving community to become a filmmaker and con artist, and ultimately a New England senator. Along the way he fathered a child who, ultimately, is the young man who shoots him down on the Senate floor. This is the central part of the entire epic, and remarkably, Ellison had these pieces all in place by the late 1950s. He knew the basic story almost from the beginning.[15]

These two central narrative strands form the two "typescripts" in the Library of Congress, which Ellison had largely finished by 1972, and which he labeled as only "Book I" and "Book II." (These are published as "Book I" and "Book II" of *Three Days*.) Book I contained McIntyre's story; Book II the Bliss-Hickman-Sunraider story. Both were eminently publishable. The McIntyre story is less compelling, and it has some side stories that Ellison should have trimmed out, but he seemed to think they would connect with the other narrative at some point. The Book II material is what Callahan published in 1999 as *Juneteenth*, with only minor editorial changes. This is what Conner has called, borrowing a phrase from Yeats, the "deep heart's core" of Ellison's epic. The central narrative is right here in the young boy Bliss, of uncertain race—his mother is certainly white, but was his father black or not? Ellison never reveals this. He is raised by Hickman, a jazz trombonist who turns to preaching the word of God after he encounters the infant Bliss. Hickman is the father to Bliss and he raises him in love, but two pressures weigh on Bliss: first, the pressure of the ministering vocation that Hickman puts upon him; and second, the pressure of not knowing his mother and of desiring, desperately, to find his mother and regain that essential oneness of mother-love that has been denied him. These pressures drive Bliss to leave the black community, pass for white, become a scam artist and moviemaker dealing in mere surface images, and ultimately to rise in the political world as a virulently racist white senator. When he is shot down and Hickman comes to him in the hospital, the two men commence a remarkable call-and-response narration in which they recall, reconstruct, and reimagine their past lives. Here they work out the traumas that separated them and that, by extension, separate America. This is absolutely brilliant writing, on a level with, say, Faulkner's finest work. This Book II material, the Juneteenth story, may well be Ellison's greatest accomplishment.

The great question is, what happened after 1972? Ellison could have published these two books as separate novels. They were all but finished. True, Book I was not a completely successful narrative, and Ellison wanted to do more with Book II. But for whatever reason, and surely there were many, both conscious and deeply subconscious, Ellison could not release this work. He continued to add to it and revise it. And then in 1982 he bought a home computer, and soon he was working on the second novel on this computer. Thus he created what we now call "The Computer Sequences," massive text files that endlessly expand the scope of the novel. What is odd about the computer files is that they do not add very much new material to the novel—rather, Ellison embellished, revised, and usually expanded previous episodes, almost obsessively working over material that he had already produced in an earlier era. The prime example of this expansion is the transformation of what was a seven-page prologue in the 1972 typescript, describing the arrival of Hickman and his congregation to DC, into a 157-page narrative by the 1990s, filled with fascinating asides and picaresque passages and marvelous vernacular riffs, but getting us no further into the action nor closer to the resolution of the main story.[16]

What Callahan and Bradley brought out in 2010 is Books I and II, with a crucial insertion, the narrative titled in Ellison's hand "Bliss's Birth," a separate piece that narrates how Bliss was born and the profound alteration to Hickman's life that results. (This is an integral part of the second novel, without which one cannot understand the whole project; and it is an incredibly moving piece of writing, perhaps Ellison's finest piece of sustained narrative.) Following these two parts, they included the three longest strands of narrative composed on the computer: "Hickman in Washington, D.C."; "Hickman in Georgia & Oklahoma"; and "McIntyre at Jessie Rockmore's." These three narrative sections constitute 463 pages of printed text, or as much as Books I and II and "Bliss's Birth" combined. Finally the published book concludes with a selection of Ellison's voluminous notes about the project, and the eight excerpts that he published during his lifetime, between "And Hickman Arrives" in 1960 and "Backwacking, a Plea to the Senator" in 1977. The editors include substantial introductions and notes that describe the manuscript status of the material as well as how each segment fits into the whole, and place the material in the context of Ellison's life. The sum of this work is to bring into relief the ways in which Ellison, between *Invisible Man* and *Three Days*, shifted from the yearning for identity (a distinctly American preoccupation, according to Ellison) to the evasion of identity as a democratic people struggles to live up to its civic or political proclamations.

The *Three Days* material is going to require many years of study, and already Ellison scholars are reevaluating his achievement in light of this material. And all of this newly available work also partly explains the surge in critical, biographical, and interpretive studies of Ellison that have emerged in the past decade and more. Since 2000, at least 140 essays, articles, and book chapters have been published directly related to the study of Ellison's work.[17] Interestingly, there have been nearly as many pieces published on Ellison from 2000 to 2014 as in the period from the first piece written about him—the short notice in 1953 in the NAACP's *Crisis* titled "Ralph Ellison—Fiction Winner" about his receiving the National Book Award—up to 2000. In short, the attention paid to Ellison in the twenty-first century has equaled all the work done on Ellison in the five decades leading up to this moment.

Since 2002, at least sixteen book-length studies about Ellison have appeared, ranging from biographical studies to collections of critical essays to monographs pursuing particular interpretive elements in Ellison's work. The range and depth of this work is impressive. Several seek to explore the contexts and backgrounds informing Ellison's life and work, such as Steven Tracy's *A Historical Guide to Ralph Ellison* (2004), John Callahan's *Ralph Ellison's "Invisible Man": A Casebook* (2004), and Lena Hill and Michael Hill's *Ralph Ellison's "Invisible Man": A Reference Guide* (2008). Others bring together a range of scholarly views to explore interpretive issues in all of Ellison's work: Lucas Morel's *Ralph Ellison and the Raft of Hope: A Political Companion to "Invisible Man"* (2004) explores the multiple political implications of Ellison's writing; and Ross Posnock's *Cambridge Companion to Ralph Ellison* (2005) features a number of exceptional essays that seek to reassess Ellison and to explore areas of his work—such as religion—that had heretofore been insufficiently investigated. Two major biographical studies appeared: Lawrence Jackson's *Ralph Ellison: Emergence of Genius* in 2002 explored Ellison's life from his birth through the publication of *Invisible Man*; and Arnold Rampersad's *Ralph Ellison: A Biography* in 2007 offered the first full exploration of the entirety of Ellison's life. In addition, the PBS documentary *Ralph Ellison: An American Journey* by Avon Kirkland aired in 2005 and a three-act play adaptation of *Invisible Man* by Oren Jacoby and Christopher McElroen toured several major cities in 2012.

At the same time, a series of focused studies of Ellison have brought our understanding of his complexity and achievement much further along: Kenneth Warren's *So Black and Blue: Ralph Ellison and the Occasion of Criticism* (2003) explored what he terms the "multiple guises" of Ellison to understand how "Ellison's work continues to resonate in our post-segregation era" (19, 20). William Rice, in *Ralph Ellison and the Politics of the Novel* (2003), examined the political and formal elements in all of Ellison's work, from *Invisible Man* and the essays up to *Juneteenth*. In a complex and multifaceted book, John Wright's *Shadowing Ralph Ellison* (2006) studied a wide range of Ellison issues, aiming "to profile Ellison's intellectual career as novelist, cultural critic, and man of letters" throughout his career (though Wright did not discuss the second novel in detail); Patrice Rankine's *Ulysses in Black: Ralph Ellison, Classicism, and African American Literature* (2006) examined Ellison's work in the context of the classical tradition and its implications for African American writers; and in Japan Konomi Ara brought out *Ralph Ellison and Individuality* (2008), assessing Ellison as an exemplar of what she terms "the various elements and ideas that constitute the 'American spirit' Ellison depicts in *Invisible Man*" (17). Barbara Foley, in *Wrestling with the Left: The Making of Ralph Ellison's "Invisible Man"* (2010), performs a careful audit of the manuscripts of *Invisible Man* and argues that Ellison's connections to radical leftist politics in the years leading up to his first novel were more complex and deep than readers had perhaps realized; and Bryan Crable's *Ralph Ellison and Kenneth Burke: At the Roots of the Racial Divide* (2012) offers a powerful evaluation of the friendship and cross-influences between Ellison and Burke and what this relationship tells us about race relations in America even in our present day. Adam Bradley's *Ralph Ellison in Progress: From "Invisible Man" to "Three Days before the Shooting . . ."* (2010) also turns to the Ellison archive to study Ellison's composition of both of his major fiction projects. Bradley begins with *Three Days* and then reads backward into the major "nodes of time in Ellison's life and literature." This method of "reading both novels in the process of their becoming" reveals the protean nature of all of Ellison's work and reinforces Bradley's conviction that "Ellison's second novel is the best means by which to measure Ellison's literary legacy" (4, 5). Finally, Timothy Parrish, in *Ralph Ellison and the Genius of America* (2012), offers a series of studies of Ellison in the contexts of other major American writers and cultural figures. Placing Ellison in conversation with Philip Roth, Richard Wright, Robert Penn Warren, C. Vann Woodward, Martin Luther King Jr., and Barack Obama, Parrish elucidates the depth and complexity of Ellison's thought and its place within the American intellectual currents of the late twentieth and early twenty-first centuries. Writing specifically to counter the negative and reductive portrait of Ellison that Arnold Rampersad draws in his biography, Parrish aims "to re-imagine Ellison's career in terms of what he achieved rather than what he did not achieve" and "to show what a truly revolutionary, wide-ranging intellectual figure he was" (ix). All of this work is employed and interrogated in the essays of this current book, as the multiple perspectives of these essays engage with the material that precedes us. Indeed, we view this collection as a culmination of the wave of Ellison scholarship that has emerged so plentifully over the past decade and more; and in its serious focus on the *Three Days* project, this work is unique among Ellison studies to date.

RALPH ELLISON AND OUR CONTEMPORARY MOMENT

What does all of this activity and interest tell us about Ralph Ellison and the new territory of the twenty-first century? In short, our argument is that we are already in the new territory that Ralph Ellison began mapping for us in the previous mid-century. There has been no more accurate nor succinct statement about Ellison's importance than the one offered in 2012 by Timothy Parrish:

> The true tragedy of Ralph Ellison is not that he never published another novel but that the scope of his extraordinary and arguably singular achievement as an American intellectual still goes unrecognized. When one actually confronts the body of Ellison's work, his fiction and nonfiction, the work he published and the work he left for others to publish, one confronts a legacy that is as complex and rich as any in the canon of American literature.... William Faulkner, along with Henry James, wrote more "great" novels than any other American novelist, but no one, including Ellison's namesake Ralph Waldo Emerson, has ever told us more than Ellison did about what it means to be an American and to be committed to democracy as a living civic ideal. (*Genius* 5)

Parrish argues that Ellison, more than any other American writer, understood and even foresaw the post–civil rights era. He was "the black intellectual who could envision an America that would, within a generation of Martin Luther King Jr.'s death, elect and celebrate the election of a black president." Parrish continues, "The election of Barack Obama does not by itself justify Ellison's vision, but it does suggest the prescience and vitality of that vision" (6).

The affinities between Barack Obama and Ralph Ellison have been noted with increasing frequency, and it is well worth reflecting on what these affinities might mean, of what they might consist, and how they bear upon our focus on Ellison and his importance to the twenty-first century, because Obama could well be described as the first "Ellisonian" American president. Obama's affinity to Ralph Ellison was noted even before his 2008 election to the presidency. In an article titled "Invisible Man: How Ralph Ellison Explains Barack Obama," David Samuels argued that "the literary model for Obama's narrative self is Ellison's *Invisible Man*." Samuels claims that Obama learned from *Invisible Man* that he could leverage his invisibility as a black man in America "in a strategic way if he wishes to lead" (Samuels, "Invisible" 23).[18] But for Samuels there are limits to what Obama, at least publicly, has determined to learn and convey about the influence of Ellison's view of himself and the world: "Where Ellison and Obama differ is that Ellison sees group identity as bunk and Obama sees it as a component of psychological health, at least in his own particular case" (Samuels, "Changeling" 37).[19]

The similarity between Ellison's observations about being black in America and Barack Obama's personal journey was captured by Jerry Kellman, one of Obama's early mentors: "Barack has always had to deal with the way people react to him, which has nothing to do with him, but, rather, with the fact that he is black, or looks black. A lot of the struggle for him was to figure out who he was independent of how people reacted to him" (qtd. in Remnick 136). Anyone familiar with *Invisible Man* can readily identify this with the narrator's quest for identity: "All my life I had been looking for something, and everywhere I turned someone tried to tell me what it was" (IM 15). Obama admitted as much in his quasi-autobiography, *Dreams from My Father*: "Away from my mother, away from my grandparents, I was engaged in a fitful interior struggle. I was trying to raise myself to be a black man in America, and beyond the given of my appearance, no one around me seemed to know exactly what that meant" (*Dreams* 76).[20] For that, Obama would turn to books, especially by canonical black authors, which included Ralph Ellison.

While his memoir lauded the "self-creation" and "sheer force of will" of Malcolm X for inspiring him "down the road to self-respect," the preponderance of evidence shows that not Malcolm X but Ralph Ellison became Obama's muse as a writer and politician.[21] As a college friend of Obama's relates, during Obama's two years at Columbia University "for a period of two or three months" he "carried and at every opportunity read and reread a fraying copy of Ralph Ellison's *Invisible Man*. It was a period during which Barack was struggling deeply within himself to attain his own racial identity, and *Invisible Man* became a prism for his self-reflection" (Maraniss 453). The narrative structure of *Invisible Man* and *Dreams from My Father* shows many similarities, and the influence of Ellison's novel and learned commentary on the black American experience appears throughout Obama's memoir. Obama credited his white mother with providing example after example of black Americans worthy of admiration, but his reflections on her tutorials in black American history bear the imprint of Ellison: "To be black was to be the beneficiary of a great inheritance, a special destiny, glorious burdens that only we were strong enough to bear. Burdens we were to carry with style" (*Dreams* 51).[22] Ellison in numerous writings makes the same assertion:

> If you have a society in which all men are declared equal . . . then it seems to me that you must act out of an assumption that any people which has not been destroyed after three hundred years of our history, and which is still here among us, is a people possessing great

> human potentialities and strengths which its members have derived from their background. And it follows that those potentialities are to be respected. (CERE 551)

For example, Ellison once highlighted the courage of the Little Rock Nine and the youth who engaged in nonviolent protests in the modern civil rights movement: "How do you account for Little Rock and the sit-ins? How do you account for the strength of those kids? You can find sociological descriptions of the conditions under which they live but few indications of their morale." Citing this as "a further instance of man's triumph over chaos," he commented that "the skins of those thin-legged little girls who faced the mob in Little Rock marked them as Negro, but the spirit which directed their feet is the old universal urge toward freedom. For better or worse, whatever there is of value in Negro life is an American heritage, and as such it must be preserved." Stanley Ann Dunham preserved it for her son, and Barack not only learned those early-morning lessons, but also drew from that history when he applied his talents to public service.

Early in Obama's political career, he displayed an Ellisonian fidelity to what Ellison called "the sacred principles of the democratic faith" and "our sacred documents of state" (CERE 413, 412).[23] At the 2004 National Democratic Convention, in a keynote speech that catapulted a little-known state senator into the political stratosphere, Obama cited the principles of human equality and individual rights from the Declaration of Independence as central to "the greatness of our nation" and "the true genius of America" (*American Story* 99–100). In 2006 he would give a more comprehensive account of his understanding of the principles of the American founding in his second book, *The Audacity of Hope: Thoughts on Reclaiming the American Dream*, calling those principles "not only the foundation of our government but the substance of our common creed" (53–56).[24] Similarly, Ellison maintained that "these principles—democracy, equality, individual freedom and universal freedom—now move us as articles of faith" and "prod us ceaselessly toward the refinement and perfection of those formulations of policy and configurations of social forms of which they are the signs and symbols" (CERE 505).[25]

But instead of waxing nostalgic on that national stage in 2004, Obama asked Americans "to reaffirm our values and commitments" in order to "hold them against a hard reality and see how we are measuring up, to the legacy of our forbears, and the promise of future generations" (*American Story* 100). Ever the pragmatist, Obama restated this obligation of measuring our practice by our principles in *Audacity of Hope*: "We hang on to our values ... so long as we understand that our values must be tested against fact and experience, so long as we recall that they demand deeds and not just words" (69). This gap between American profession and practice was an abiding theme of Ellison's, as was his insistence that it had long been black Americans who, regardless of their precarious position in American society, reminded majority-white America of its highest ideals. In a 1976 *Time* magazine essay he originally titled "The Fantasy of a Blackless America," Ellison declared, "Today it is the black American who puts pressure upon the nation to live up to its ideals. It is he who insists that we purify the American language by demanding that there be a closer correlation between the meaning of words and reality, between our assertions and our actions" (CERE 587).

Obama also drew upon the national motto, *E pluribus unum* ("Out of many, one"), to tie the Declaration of Independence's emphasis on the rights of the individual to another American principle—that of union: "Alongside our famous individualism," there is the "belief that we are connected as one people," as "a single American family." Anticipating a divisive campaign season in 2004, he declared to raucous applause that "there's not a liberal America and a conservative America—there's the United States of America. There's not a black America and white America and Latino America and Asian America; there's the United States of America" (*American Story* 102–3). The parallels to the epilogue of Ellison's *Invisible Man* are striking: "Our fate is to become one, and yet many—This is not prophecy, but description" (577).[26] Both Ellison and Obama acknowledge the diversity of the American experience, social and political, while emphasizing the underlying humanity that enables the various strands to be woven into a harmonious whole.

For Obama, empathy does that weaving (*Audacity* 66–69). But he insists that for our common humanity to be affirmed not only in word but also in deed requires political action. As Obama concludes near the end of *Dreams from My Father*, "What is our community, and how might that community be reconciled with our freedom? How far do our obligations reach? How do we transform mere power into justice, mere sentiment into love?" (*Dreams* 438). This echoes Invisible Man's plaintive cry at the heart of *Invisible Man*: "And could politics ever be an expression of love?" (452).[27] According to both Ellison and Obama, love is necessary for community to manifest itself out of the chaos of modern life.

During Obama's first campaign for the presidency in 2008, an opportunity for love to unify Americans occurred when the divisive issue of race arose over the controversial statement of his former pastor, the Reverend Jeremiah Wright.[28] Obama criticized Wright's "profoundly distorted view of this country—a view that sees white racism as endemic, and that elevates what is wrong with America above all that we know is right with America" (*American Story* 58). Wright's rant against America rankled Obama because "he spoke as if our society was static; as if no progress had been made." But "what we know—what we have seen—is that America can change. That is the true genius of this nation." Of course, a different sermon of Wright's became the inspiration of the title of Obama's second book, *The Audacity of Hope*.[29] It was that sermon Obama essentially quoted back to Wright when he reminded him and the rest of the nation that America was not "irrevocably bound to a tragic past" regarding race: "What we have already achieved gives us hope—the audacity to hope—for what we can and must achieve tomorrow" (*American Story* 65).

Obama challenged Americans to believe that to form "a more perfect union" (which was the title of his Philadelphia speech) "requires all Americans to realize that your dreams do not have to come at the expense of my dreams" (*American Story* 65).[30] This is a dominating theme of both of Ellison's novels. *Invisible Man*'s narrator put it this way: "America is woven of many strands; I would recognize them and let is so remain. It's 'winner take nothing' that is the great truth of our country or of any country" (577). Similarly, Hickman observes the following regarding his former protégé Senator Sunraider: "Just listen to him down there; he's making somebody mighty uncomfortable because he's got them caught between what they profess to believe and what they feel they can't do without" (TD 1101).

"To form a more perfect union" is Obama's signature description of America's modus operandi. Quoted from the preamble to the US Constitution, which he described as "ultimately unfinished," it both hearkens to the past while highlighting its most progressive feature—that our nation is a work in progress, its federal Constitution "not a static but rather a living document" to be "read in the context of an ever-changing world." Obama declared, "What would be needed were Americans in successive generations who were willing to do their part . . . to narrow that gap between the promise of our ideals and the reality of their time" (*American Story* 255; *Audacity* 90).[31] This is strikingly similar to Ellison's thought: he described America as "the extension of the democratic process in the direction of perfecting itself." Given America's history of white supremacy, "the most obvious test and clue to that perfection is the inclusion, *not* assimilation, of the black man" (CERE 586). On election night, November 4, 2008, when president-elect Barack

Obama declared that "change has come to America," the nation took a major step forward in passing this Ellisonian test (*American Story* 319).

Exactly fifty years before America elected its first black president, Ellison had predicted that a black American president would be shaped more by the office than by his skin color: "The demands of state policy are apt to be more influential than morality. I would like to see a qualified Negro as President of the United States, but I suspect that even if this were today possible, the necessities of the office would shape his actions far more than his racial identity" (CERE 300–301). As President Obama approaches the end of his second term, the debate continues regarding his impact on the presidency as its first self-consciously black occupant. Clearly Ellison and Obama share a determination to help Americans honestly face the complexity of their American history. In the words of Ellison: "I just feel that we are called upon to do a big job, not because someone is going to give us a star on the report card, but because this is America and our task is to explore it, create it by describing it. . . . We've got a big country. Here it takes more doing, but it'll be new" (CRE 53).

THE NEW TERRITORY
Exploring Ralph Ellison in Our Time

The fourteen essays in this volume are divided into three major sections. In the first group, we offer fresh readings of Ellison's classic first novel, *Invisible Man*, focusing in particular on how that novel speaks to us in the twenty-first century. The second group of essays focuses on *Three Days before the Shooting . . .*, providing the first sustained, multi-perspective analyses of that landmark literary work. Finally, the third group of essays examines Ellison's work and achievement in terms of culture, politics, and social implications for the twenty-first century. Taken as a whole, these chapters offer a thorough and penetrating assessment of Ellison at this crucial historical moment, and the most comprehensive interpretive study of Ellison to date.

Robert Butler, in "*Invisible Man* and the Politics of Love," takes issue with the critique of Ellison as insufficiently engaged politically and alienated from authentic black culture, a critique that has been voiced most recently in Rampersad's biography and Barbara Foley's *Wrestling with the Left: The Making of Ralph Ellison's "Invisible Man"* (2010). Butler argues that this view of Ellison misreads the extent of Ellison's authentic political commitment, a commitment that is far more rigorous and complex than Foley's reductive treatment of his so-called flight from leftist extremism into "mythic individualism." Butler explores what he calls Ellison's commitment to Christian love and integration, bringing into relief a political vision that is far more harmonious with the civil rights activism of Martin Luther King Jr. than the outmoded Marxism that Ellison abandoned in the early 1940s. In Butler's view, Ellison's political concept of integration and mutual love is strongly attuned to the needs of America in the twenty-first century.

Patrice Rankine's "The Body and *Invisible Man*: Ralph Ellison's Novel in Twenty-First-Century Performance and Public Spaces" contrasts the artistic uses of physicality in *Invisible Man* the novel with its 2012 play adaptation. Rankine argues that the stage performance sixty years after the novel's first publication enables the novel to speak beyond Ellison's original intentions. The stage version's "focus on the corporeal reality of race," Rankine observes, complements what the novel can do to facilitate social or political progress; in short, "there is therapeutic value in 'staging' or reliving such experiences." Staging *Invisible Man* extends Ellison's relevance in an age where, although the United States has a black president, the very novelty of the black body illustrates how infrequently that body is seen and hence integrated into society. This takes on increased significance insofar as the novel insists that race is an aspect of one's identity that is imposed from without and not a marker that inherently carries any significant meaning. Given the new context for the novel, as it is performed in the twenty-first century, the meaning of race as a performative aspect of life becomes much more clear than on paper. Rankine distinguishes the novel form as an appeal to reason in contrast to theater, with its emotional or visceral draw, but without privileging the novel over its adaptation to the stage.

In "The Noisy Lostness: Oppositionality and Acousmatic Subjectivity in *Invisible Man*," Herman Beavers interrogates Ellison's complex analyses of jazz and bebop music, situating Ellison's views in the larger context of modernism. Beavers draws upon the nascent discipline of sound studies and emphasizes the quality of "oppositionality" in such jazz greats as Louis Armstrong to interpret *Invisible Man* as an instance of oppositional, as opposed to revolutionary, narrative. Beavers views the novel as a study of the disruption of the feedback loop between listening and speaking, in which Ellison uses noise as a disruptive, "acousmatic" presentation of the black body. By showing how the narrator shifts from the prison of sight to the freedom of sound, and thus from regulation to improvisation, Beavers argues that the narrator finally moves from a misguided trust in false systems of protection to a tactical realization of the security of chaos.

Bryan Crable's "*Invisible Man* in the Age of Obama: Ellison on (Color) Blindness, Visibility, and the Hopes for a Postracial America" offers a bold view of the implications of Ellison's work on the enduring American questions of race and color. Crable takes up the discourse of Barack Obama's 2011 reelection campaign to see how that discourse reveals the influence of Ellison's analysis of appearance, of visibility and invisibility. He asks, in the age of Obama, does the problem of the color line still persist? Have we entered into a postracial America? By pursuing the crucial connections between these two paradigmatic American writers, Crable concludes, "The discourse surrounding Obama's first term (and his quest for reelection) simply reminds us that *Invisible Man*'s work is not yet done; it remains as important for us today as it was for readers in 1952."

The cluster of essays that focuses on *Three Days before the Shooting...* begins with Eric Sundquist's "Ralph Ellison in His Labyrinth," which focuses on the elusive figure of Bliss and his descent from Bliss Proteus Rinehart in *Invisible Man* through his many incarnations in the second novel project. Drawing upon the extensive evidence in the Ellison archive, Sundquist views Bliss as a version of R. W. B. Lewis's American Adam—a trope that was highly influential on Ellison when he read Lewis's work. Yet, unlike the Proteus of Homer's *Odyssey*, who served as Ellison's prototype of the American novelist, Bliss cannot be grappled into submission. Moving through a dazzling survey of the signifying characters in *Three Days* and the litany of verbal artists in the novel (such as Mother Smathers, Heapachange Hudson, and especially the sublime vernacular artist Leroy), Sundquist eventually argues for the two-faced, Janus nature of Bliss/Sunraider—making him representative of the nation itself and placing the figure in the genealogy of signifying tricksters at the crossroads of time, including Oedipus, Eshu-Elegba, Peter Wheatstraw, Louis Armstrong, and ultimately Ralph Ellison himself. Reading the second novel through the multiple lenses provided by Ellison's luminous essays, Sundquist examines Ellison's use of the Icarus myth in *Three Days*, comparing the myth to the figures of flight and transcendence in African American and world mythology that always fascinated Ellison even in his early stories from the 1940s. Ultimately, Sundquist suggests that the many trickster figures that populate *Three Days* are all avatars of Sunraider himself, constituting a mystery of identity and history as profound as the Trinity, as Ellison states in one of his many notes about the novel.

Lena Hill's "The Politics of Fatherhood in *Three Days before the Shooting* . . ." examines Ellison's use of fathers and sons to explore the role of African Americans in US history. Hill focuses on the use of visual art in *Three Days* to present a sophisticated response by African Americans to their ambivalent place in America's political development. In particular, she shows how the novel's protagonist, the Reverend A. Z. Hickman, appreciates and reflects upon visual art, thereby embodying what Ellison believes black Americans contribute to the land of their birth: an astute, self-reliant judgment of the nation's practices in light of its professions. Even as a flawed father, Hickman represents "the possibility that imperfect men may best serve the nation as they honestly acknowledge their personal failings." In contrast with sociologically reductive accounts of black victimhood or pathology, with its corollary of white political paternalism, Hill reads Ellison as interpreting American history, even back to the slave era, as involving significant black American agency and influence that belies African Americans' status as second-class citizens.

Marc Conner, in "Father Abraham: Ellison's Agon with the Fathers in *Three Days before the Shooting* . . . ," places Ellison's seminal essay "Tell It Like It Is, Baby" alongside the second novel project to examine the role of fathers throughout Ellison's thought and writing. This approach brings into relief an array of father figures that challenged Ellison to confront and become reconciled with his many absent fathers—biographical, historical, literary, biblical—in the very process of writing the ongoing, unfinished second novel. By viewing *Three Days* through the lens of Ellison's struggle with the defining influence of fathers, we see why Alonzo Hickman, the great father figure within the novel, fails in rearing the child Bliss as a savior of his people; and we see why Bliss's own flight from his community and home is doomed to fail, resulting in his fragmentation of identity and tragic loss of coherent self. This father-struggle reveals Ellison's highly self-conscious efforts to position himself in relation to both American literary traditions and modernist world literature. Consequently, Conner argues against the overdetermined and simplistic relations between Ellison and Wright and Ellison and Faulkner, and turns instead to the far more complex signifying relations between Ellison and the work of Fitzgerald and Joyce. Ellison saw in Fitzgerald's work the patterns of American tragedy that he would anatomize in Bliss/Sunraider; and he saw in Joyce's work the redemptive patterns of modernism that offer the regenerative model that he sought, the affirmative "yes" to the past, to human relations, and ultimately to American history itself. This affirming urge pushes against and balances the tragic impulse of *Three Days* and ultimately defines Ellison's own tragicomic vision—the vision that pervades and defines the *Three Days* project.

In "Ralph Ellison's *Three Days*: The Aesthetics of Political Change," Timothy Parrish claims that we have yet to understand Ellison properly. Parrish examines the unfinished second novel and argues that Ellison transcends the novel form, becoming an epic poet writing in a prose form that took on the contours of fiction, history, and myth simultaneously, creating what he calls Ellison's "Book of America," an evolving canon unto itself. As a true modernist artist, kin to Louis Armstrong and James Joyce, Ellison understood that the modern novel is never truly finished; like Robert Musil's *The Man without Qualities*, another novel whose aesthetic premise depended on its not being finished, Ellison's second novel both rejects and creates history in its very writing. Parrish terms Ellison, in what will become a memorable phrase, "the great modernist redactor of African American experience." He argues that in ways that Ellison himself could not recognize, Ellison did not finish the second novel because he was writing a book that could not be finished. Like the civil rights movement out of which the novel emerged, *Three Days* is an incomplete project: "The novel cannot end until the story of America and its struggle to realize its Edenic promises ends too."

In a profound meditation on the tragic structures of Ellison's second novel, Grant Shreve, in "Ralph Ellison's *Three Days before the Shooting . . .* and the Implicit Morality of Form," describes an underlying tension between sacrificial violence and literary form that becomes the central problem of the work. Like Parrish, Shreve brings into relief the relations between the civil rights movement, especially the momentous *Brown v. Board of Education* (1954) decision, and Ellison's aesthetic and ethical aims for the novel. Shreve examines the second novel as a classical tragedy but one in which the final catharsis and resolution is denied, as the conclusion of Bliss's plot is left incomplete. Bliss is the tragic scapegoat figure, but Ellison is unable to kill him off and thereby achieve the tragic catharsis. Yet in the computer sections that occupied Ellison over the last twenty years of his life, we see a profound and substantive reorientation to the form of the novel itself and its moral capacities. Shreve argues that for Ellison, catharsis can be achieved only through integrative, not divisive, methods. We see such a catharsis in Hickman's ethical and religious adherence to a tragicomic democratic sensibility and an immersion in dialogue, rather than the aesthetics of revenge.

The final section of essays focuses on issues of culture and politics, asking what concepts Ellison emphasizes in American politics and history, and what Ellison can teach us about our own cultural moment. The section begins with Lucas Morel's "'In a Strange Country': The Challenge of American Inclusion," which interprets Ellison's 1944 short story as a civics lesson for a nation struggling with the legacy of race in a professedly free society. "In a Strange Country" follows a black merchant marine, Mr. Parker, during World War II as he recovers from a mugging by white American servicemen while on shore leave in Wales. Morel finds in Ellison's ironic mode an apt register to negotiate the gap between American principle and practice. Ellison teaches a lesson about civic inclusion or membership by showcasing "a black Yank" being rescued by foreigners (Welshmen). When Mr. Parker is invited to a private singing club, Morel sees this as analogous to the private club that is the modern nation-state. Mr. Parker witnesses how the Welsh transcend occupational differences as opposite as mine owner and mine worker through a common devotion to music, which he likens to the racially mixed "jam sessions" he experienced back in America. If music or culture can perform this integrating function, could politics do so as well? By closing the story with "The Star-Spangled Banner," which the Welshmen sing in honor of their American guest, Ellison depicts Mr. Parker singing the national anthem without irony for the first time. Morel finds in this short story an account of both the obstacles and pathways to black American citizenship—a reminder that those living in "the land of the free" need to be not only "brave" about how they react to the misuse of freedom, but also good-humored, self-disciplined, and hopeful in their efforts to participate fully in the American regime.

In "Invisible Man's Grandfather and the American Dream," Steven D. Ealy focuses on the grandfather in *Invisible Man*, an enigmatic figure from whom the narrator learns despite his doubts about any wisdom coming from a former slave. Highlighting Invisible Man's identification with a hibernating bear (at least while he hides out to write a memoir that eventually compels him to surface), Ealy examines what the narrator or "Jack-the-Bear" discovers about his grandfather's deathbed advice. The grandfather offers Frederick Douglass and Booker T. Washington as key figures for the narrator's instruction. The central insight Invisible Man gains from his grandfather is what he calls "the principle on which the country was built." By leaving this principle undefined, however, the narrator (and his creator, Ralph Ellison) invites the reader to wrestle with the meaning and implications of human equality in a world that will always fall short of aligning its practice with this ideal. But Ealy spells out one implication by connecting the grandfather's "principle" with the South African concept of *ubuntu*, where love becomes the means by which each person's humanity is acknowledged in the public sphere.

In "Mourning and Melancholy: Explaining the Ellison Animus," Ross Posnock investigates the "animus" or sense of resentment and criticism that has dogged Ellison since *Invisible Man* first appeared, but that has taken on a new intensity during the past decade. Citing Rampersad's 2007 biography and Foley's 2010 book *Wrestling with the Left*, Posnock argues that the long-standing Ellison animus has become a generational sense of grievance, mixed with melancholy, reflecting a disappointed, idealized sense of Ellison. Rampersad's study is dominated by a desire for Ellison to have been a different sort of black man than he was, a simultaneous idealization and frustration that is clearly Oedipal in nature. This sense of immense promise unfulfilled dominates Foley's approach as well, particularly in her heroicization of the figure of Leroy, the proletarian revolutionary manqué who appeared in the drafts of *Invisible Man* but was eventually cut from the book by Ellison. For Foley, *Invisible Man* becomes only the evidence of Ellison's failure to live up to his promise as a radical leftist writer—the sort of black writer that Foley wishes he had been. For both Foley and Rampersad, the resentment at Ellison's betrayal (to them) of what he should have been remains palpable and powerful. Like Obama, Ellison becomes the locus of a curious dynamic of idealism and hostility. Posnock concludes by suggesting that one way to reject this melancholic view of both men is to realize their flawed humanity and their refusal of easy affirmation and ideal reflection. Instead, each man insists upon a similar self-reliance of thought on the part of their audience, a self-reliance that rejects political creed and racial essentialism and instead examines the ideas of the writer. Such self-reliance might well be the cure for the unresolved mourning that breeds melancholy.

In "'How many lightbulbs does it take to screw in a blues singer?': The French Revolution, King Louis Armstrong, and the Futuristic Jungleism of Jazz," Steven C. Tracy interprets *Invisible Man* to reveal a futuristic mode hidden beneath seemingly primitive or backward elements. He explains that the "jungleism" of the novel, whether represented by the narrator's basement apartment on the border of civilized society or the allegedly primitive music of jazz, operates in an ironic mode to express how black Americans have exercised greater agency and worked toward liberation despite their oppressive environment. Exemplified in the artistry of Louis Armstrong, Tracy examines his adaptation of the Andy Razaf song "(What Did I Do to Be So) Black and Blue?" to show the genius of blackness and bluesness. Through virtuoso trumpeting and an inversion of lyrics, Armstrong transforms a song whose surface meaning serves as a lament by blacks for their plight in a white-supremacist society to show off the heights of musical artistry that even an oppressed people can produce. These motifs inform Ellison's novel through its major concerns with revolution and liberation. Ultimately, Tracy explores how Ellison reconsiders the nature of purity, seeing it as "illusory and oppressive," and countering with its opposite, not so much impurity as hybridity and heterogeneity, which Tracy sees as emblematic of the postmodern world.

In the book's final chapter, John Callahan—Ellison's literary executor and the dean of Ellison studies—looks back upon Ellison's life and work from the perspective of the Ellison centennial, asking what Ellison's accomplishment looks like one hundred years after his birth, as this new century proceeds in his wake. Beginning with the "thought experiment" of a young Barack Obama jogging past Ralph Ellison in New York in the 1980s, Callahan meditates on Ellison's sustained investigation of the relationship between the individual search for self-identity and America's pursuit of democratic equality. Drawing upon Ellison's wealth of posthumously published material—the short stories, essays, interviews, and of course his unfinished second novel—Callahan emphasizes Ellison's relentless pursuit of the novel form as his means of interrogating the fluid, improvisational, always-evolving form of American identity. The essay ultimately probes the omnipresent father figures that dominate Ellison's work after *Invisible Man*—Lewis Ellison, Abraham Lincoln, Alonzo Hickman, and others—as Ellison worked to understand his own relation to his father and indeed to all fathers in both his life and his writing.

Taken as a whole, these fourteen essays represent the most far-reaching and original assessment of Ralph Ellison's entire career and body of work ever published. Fully informed by and building upon the surge in Ellison studies over the past ten years, this book simultaneously reassesses Ellison's extraordinary importance to American letters, and also brings into relief Ellison's prescient vision of American culture in the twenty-first century. With the publication of *Three Days before the Shooting*... we now have a full portrait of Ellison's achievement, which transforms the way we understand the entirety of his work and the significance of his influence on his own era and on the era that follows.

Charles Johnson has stated that Ellison's great achievement was "the intellectual expansiveness and artistic generosity" of his writing. Johnson praises in particular the way in which Ellison "envisioned a black American personality as complex, multisided, and synthetic as the American society that produced it" ("Acceptance Speech" 208). Ellison's always-expanding understanding of the form of the novel, his insistence on never reducing the complexity of American culture to fashionable statements or empty postures, and the generative, tragicomic, yet ultimately affirming ethos of his writings reveal him to be perhaps the most significant American writer in the post–World War II period. In these essays we hope to show the full complexity and brilliance of this quintessential American writer and to bring to the fore what Callahan has described as the defining qualities of Ralph Ellison: "The courage, the defiant mind, the generosity, the moral, intellectual, and personal curiosity, the humor, and above all the complexity" (Wolven 314).

NOTES

1. This note is contained in the Library of Congress Ellison archives, part 1, box 140, folder 4. Subsequent archival materials are noted by box and folder numbers in parentheses (e.g., 140/4).

2. Adam Bradley notes that Ellison's very use of a personal computer as his mode of composition, beginning in 1982 when he purchased his Osborne 1, marks him as a revolutionary figure in the history of the novel. "Ralph Ellison was a literary pioneer for the digital age," he remarks. "In composing his novel in progress on the computer he was among the first authors enlisted, whether consciously or not, in a grand experiment measuring the effects of digital technology on the craft of fiction" (32–33). This is another way in which Ellison's text, set in the past, bears the marks of his contemporaneity.

3. Focusing on the question of the contemporary relevance of just *Invisible Man*, Adam Bradley poses this question of Ellison's relevance in 2000 and beyond: "As the circumstances of race relations in the United States improve, could it be that the utility of Ellison's technique of dilated realism and, with it, the social relevance of *Invisible Man* might diminish as well?" (175). Kenneth Warren has argued that this might well be precisely the hope implied in Ellison's thought and writing: "Taking seriously Ellison's democratic hopes may be to imagine a world in which *Invisible Man* no longer speaks immediately to us or for us as a way of investigating contemporary American identity" (*So Black* 23). Yet Bradley ultimately rejects this direction, arguing instead that Ellison offers the paradigms that are most accurate, predictive, and hopeful for precisely the future that he envisioned so clearly: "Ellison's writing is not simply proscriptive or documentary but paradigmatic. *Invisible Man* is relevant today not because we have failed to move beyond Jim Crow logic but because Ellison saw beyond Jim Crow himself to a future of new possibilities" (175).

4. In addition to the many writings referenced later in this introduction, see also, for example, Brian Edwards, who argues for the evolving internationalism of Ellison's writings.

5. A lurking implication of Rampersad's biography is that Ellison had lost touch with the tenor of American life, and particularly black American life, from the mid-1960s onward. Rampersad writes of "the growing distance between [Ellison] and the black social reality about him" (315) and claims that "as a novelist, [Ellison] had lost his way. And he had done so in proportion to his distancing of himself from his fellow blacks" (513). Rampersad invokes quotes from a private interview with Toni Morrison to imply that the second novel project was backward-looking, a "'dead'" and "'senile'" story and "'not really a story anybody needed to hear again'" (359). Clearly the present book takes issue with Rampersad's

positions. For responses to Rampersad's implications about Ellison, see Timothy Parrish, *Ralph Ellison and the Genius of America,* and Marc Conner, "Reading Ralph Ellison." Many of the essays in the current volume engage Rampersad's arguments in detail; see especially Ross Posnock's essay.

6. Lawrence Buell, in his magisterial 2014 book *The Dream of the Great American Novel,* reinforces Ellison's standing among the definitive American novelists. He considers Ellison's work as a key model in the "Aspiration in America" script, ranking it among "the most notable Great American Novel projects by hyphenated American writers ... that revisit and reframe the up-from script" (176). As much as Ellison looked backward in *Invisible Man* to its precursors, particularly Melville and Twain, the novel itself turned out to be strikingly prescient in its model of portraying the "imaginative space of psychological interiority" as its central and defining agon. Buell cites Ellison's novel as the major influence on a wide range of novelists to follow. Nabokov, Salinger, Warren, Bellow, Kerouac, Vonnegut, and Roth each pursued the narrative Ellison created: "The alienated, wounded first-person's quasi-confessional, quasi-evasive headlong monologue, often in a distinctive subcultural idiom (ethnic or otherwise), its tonalities a rich admixture ranging from comedic-playful to meditative-philosophical to manic-impassioned" (180). Buell's consideration of *Three Days* is brief and merely skims the surface of that work; yet, here too he recognizes that Ellison aspires to a kind of classic, representative text that speaks to and for its entire era. Indeed, both of Ellison's novels reach toward the "Great American Novel" (GAN) status, though by defining that achievement in different ways: "Ellison's life-long labor on that second project reinforces the suspicion that the GAN must either be a premature crystallization or a never-ending work in progress" (182).

7. In 2011, Kenneth Warren published his important study, *What Was African American Literature?,* which argues a parallel position to Johnson's, though with greater historical detail. Warren's defining claim is that what we think of as "African American literature" effectively began in the 1920s and ended with the 1960s: "African American literature as a distinct entity would seem to be at an end, and ... the turn to diasporic, transatlantic, global, and other frames indicates a dim awareness that the boundary creating this distinctiveness has eroded" (*What Was* 8). This claim is consonant with the arguments of Posnock and Parrish that suggest that Ellison's vision in effect looked beyond his current period and foretold our own contemporary age.

8. As Marc Conner has argued elsewhere, Johnson's own representations of the horrific suffering experienced in African American history are profound and powerful, even more graphic and detailed, particularly in their representations of the suffering black body, than the depictions in the novels of Toni Morrison. Morrison certainly aligns more precisely with the older narrative of black victimization in her novels. She has famously stated, "We are all of us, in some measure, victims of something" (CRE 40), and we might say that this ethos dominates her powerful fictions"; see Conner, "To Utter the Holy," 80. For a further elaboration of Johnson's concepts of racial and cultural pluralism and possibility, see his "A Phenomenology of the Black Body," "The King We Need: Teachings for a Nation in Search of Itself," and especially "Whole Sight: Notes on New Black Fiction."

9. There are many examples of Ellison comparing the sublime give-and-take of the jazz soloist and the group to the complex processes of American democracy: "The delicate

balance struck between strong individual personality and the group during those early jam sessions was a marvel of social organization" by which the jazz artist, and, we might infer, the democratic leader, "reduced the chaos of living to form" (CERE 229). See also CERE 228–29, 244–49, 266–67, 325, 492–93, and 509–10. For a discerning discussion of these ideas, see Horace Porter, *A Jazz Country*.

10. In the "Hickman in Washington, D.C." section of *Three Days*, Hickman describes the endless story-telling modes of African American culture, modes that refuse any single narrative and any single ethical content:

> For now they strolled along telling anecdotes which ranged from their grandparents' memories of slavery, the Civil War, and Emancipation to their own adventures during the Spanish-American and First World Wars. And listening to tale after tale unfold, he could hear that unmistakable blend of truth and fiction, tragedy and comedy, which marked it as uniquely their own, as Negro; a triumphant note which sounded in most of their accounts of difficult experiences that had been transformed in memory by the passage of time and the sheer wonder of their endurance. (TD 572)

The very form of *Three Days,* with its ever-changing, poly-voiced, improvisational experimental mode and its astonishing array of stories, tales, and verbal performances, is itself testimony to Ellison's conviction that American reality is what he elsewhere describes as "the mixture, the improvised form, the willful juxtaposition of modes" (CERE 507).

11. See in particular Parrish, "Ralph Ellison, Finished and Unfinished"; Butler, "Review of *Ralph Ellison*"; Conner, "Reading Ralph Ellison." Conner confronts Rampersad's covert thesis, arguing that Rampersad depends upon a concept of "black authenticity" that "is equivalent to leftist, race-defined politics, and an aesthetic of social realism," a reductive view of black culture that mirrors the arguments of Irving Howe in the early 1960s:

> Thus, the reader realizes in this biography that Rampersad is squarely in the camp of Irving Howe, the white critic who in the early 1960's criticized Ellison for not being sufficiently protest-oriented, for not decrying racial injustice the way Wright did. In his brilliant response to Howe, "The World and the Jug," Ellison shows with scrupulous care the racist assumptions behind Howe's critique and the limiting and limited view of African-American intellect and artistry that Howe reveals. That essay also is the format for Ellison's eloquent and stirring defense of his own proud and consciously willed identification with African-American culture and history, and his refusal to simplify or reduce that culture in order to please critics of whatever racial or political stripe. ("Reading" 149)

Consequently, Rampersad's view of Ellison's cultural, political, and racial ideas seems backward-looking, as opposed to the forward-looking perspectives that Ellison himself stood for.

12. It is noteworthy that Rampersad never refers to the *Juneteenth* book, brought out by John Callahan in 1999, directly. His main references to the second novel are confined to the short excerpts Ellison published in the 1960s and 1970s, further implying that Ellison was barely writing during the last twenty years of his life—a clearly false impression, as the archives at the Library of Congress demonstrate. Although Rampersad had full access to these archives during the composition of the biography, he gives no evidence of having grappled with the substantial body of work that forms the second novel. The present volume, with its powerful focus on *Three Days before the Shooting . . .*, works to correct this under-reading of Ellison's life.

13. See, for example, Conner, "'Leaving the Territory,'" which employs "Tell It" to interpret Ellison's remarkable, unpublished memoir, "Leaving the Territory," and Warren, "Chaos Not Quite Controlled," which views "Tell It" as "a window onto the task that Ellison set for himself in writing the second novel" (197). The Second Ralph Ellison Seminar in the Library of Congress, an international gathering of Ellison scholars in the Ellison Reading Room for the purpose of interrogating his work, chose "Tell It" as one of their three key texts for the May 22, 2014, seminar. See the Ralph Ellison Society website for details: http://ellisonsociety.wordpress.com.

14. For probing essay-length discussions of *Three Days*—beyond the initial book reviews, many of which were disappointing in their failure to grapple in an informed way with the work—see Purcell, "Enigma of Arrival," and Szalay, "Ralph Ellison's Unfinished Second Skin."

15. The long section of narrative published in Saul Bellow's journal *The Noble Savage* in 1960 contained the key scenes of Hickman's arrival, the senator's speech and shooting, Hickman's coming to his hospital bedside, and their antiphonal, call-and-response memories of the key events in Bliss's boyhood. See TD 1004–34 for this excerpt. (TD contains all eight of the excerpts published during Ellison's lifetime.)

16. The strongest scholarly grappling with the computer sequences is certainly Bradley's *Ralph Ellison in Progress*, particularly the introduction, "1993," and first chapter, "1982."

17. This figure is based on an MLA International Bibliography search on August 21, 2014. By way of context, this represents roughly one-third the number of pieces published on Toni Morrison during this time, and roughly one-half the number of pieces published on William Faulkner, the two most oft-researched writers in the American canon.

18. Similarly, Parrish interprets Obama's political strategy as more necessity than choice: "As a politician Obama is obligated to manipulate to his political advantage other's misperceptions of who he seems to be" (*Genius* 230).

19. Samuels goes on to assert, "Where Ellison sees the invisibility imposed by the social category of race as subjecting individuals to a state of tragic isolation, Obama sees his father's race as a source of personal freedom and strength" ("Changeling" 37).

20. Obama would later conclude, "You might be locked into a world not of your own making, . . . but you still have a claim on how it is shaped. You still have responsibilities. . . . My identity might begin with the fact of my race, but it didn't, couldn't, end there" (*Dreams* 111). He attributed this epiphany to his conversation with a college friend he called "Regina," but Ellison taught that lesson explicitly in *Invisible Man*. See the discussion of responsibility in the prologue of *Invisible Man* (esp. 14), in light of Invisible Man's ultimate conclusion,

which he draws after recounting his experience, in twenty-five chapters, in the epilogue (esp. 574–81).

21. His dismissal not only of Ralph Ellison but also James Baldwin, Langston Hughes, Richard Wright, and W. E. B. Du Bois, in deference to Malcolm X, he attributed to their supposed offering of "the same anguish, the same doubt; a self-contempt that neither irony nor intellect seemed able to deflect" (*Dreams* 86). Obama claimed that despite their literary achievements, they found themselves personally "in the same weary flight, all of them exhausted, bitter men, the devil at their heels." Yet Obama's reservations grew regarding Malcolm X's black nationalism as the route to black *American* self-respect, as he realized "that traveling down the road to self-respect my own white blood would never recede into mere abstraction. I was left to wonder what else I would be severing if and when I left my mother and grandparents at some uncharted border" (86, also 197–98).

22. Later in his memoir, Obama expanded the potential beneficiaries of this black American legacy to all people regardless of race or nationality: "Our trials and triumphs became at once unique and universal, black and more than black. In chronicling our journey, the stories and songs gave us a meaning to reclaim memories that we didn't need to feel shame about—memories that all people might study and cherish, and with which we could start to rebuild" (294).

23. See also CERE 154, 458, 461, 469, 761, 777–78, and 844. Of course, the epilogue of *Invisible Man* includes the narrator's reverie about "the principle upon which the country was built" (574).

24. For a critique of Obama's interpretation of the founders, see Kesler, *I Am the Change*, esp. 212–26.

25. Ellison added that these principles "interrogate us endlessly as to who and what we are; they demand that we keep the democratic faith" (CERE 506).

26. Ellison would hasten to add that getting *unum* from *pluribus* is no small task, let alone accomplished once and for all: "I see a whole chaotic world existing within the ordered social pattern—with the cops on the corner, the busses running on schedule, the subways on schedule and so forth—everything that it takes to keep a big city operating—and I can see a million contradictions to that order" (CRE 26). Ellison virtually foresaw the protests, civil as well as disruptive and even violent, that have sprung up in response to the deaths of unarmed blacks by white police officers that have rocked the nation in recent years. Prefigured in the tragic death of *Invisible Man*'s Tod Clifton, the violent conflict between whites in authority and blacks feeling under siege has marked too much of America's history; nevertheless, for Ellison these encounters have not and would not justify black violence as a means of righting the scales of justice: "But violence as a means of achieving freedom in the United States has not been practical for Negroes. . . . We do want our rights now. But you don't get rights by destroying them. No, when violence occurs, violence will be answered in some way, but if you are playing the long game . . . you've learned the necessity of discipline" (CRE 81). Similarly, he says of violent change: "You cannot challenge a great nation on that level. And you certainly can't challenge the United States that way, because there are too many violent people who want to do nothing but kill blacks! There's a *tradition* for that. Our parents knew it. They weren't afraid. They were afraid of getting white folks afraid!" (O'Meally, *Living* 281).

27. Ellison turned up the volume on this fundamental query in his unpublished novel: "I say, HOW THE HELL DO YOU GET LOVE INTO POLITICS OR COMPASSION INTO HISTORY?" (TD 392). See also his letter to Albert Murray, where he states, "I've had occasion to point out, that democracy is, or should be, the most disinterested form of love" (*Trading* 175). He said this, as well, upon accepting the National Book Award for *Invisible Man*: "The way home we seek is that condition of man's being at home in the world, which is called love, and which we term democracy" (CERE 154).

28. Wright's April 13, 2003, sermon "Confusing God and Government" contained the now-infamous imperative: "The government gives [young black men] drugs, builds bigger prisons, passes a three-strike law and then wants us to sing 'God Bless America.' No, no, no! Not God Bless America. God *damn* America—that's in the Bible—for killing innocent people. God *damn* America for treating her citizens as less than human" (Remnick 518–19).

29. For Obama's first impressions of the Reverend Jeremiah Wright, see *Dreams from My Father,* 280–95. He mentions Wright's sermon and the phrase "audacity of hope" in the epilogue of *Audacity of Hope,* 356.

30. Obama would note that the controversy over Wright's sermon and the diverse American responses to it "reflect the complexities of race in this country that we've never really worked through—a part of our union that we have yet to perfect" (*American Story* 260–61).

31. See also *Audacity of Hope* regarding the need "to bring promise and practice into closer alignment" (22).

PART ONE

INVISIBLE MAN SIXTY YEARS LATER
Revisiting Ellison's Masterpiece in the Twenty-First Century

INVISIBLE MAN AND THE POLITICS OF LOVE

ROBERT BUTLER

Although Ralph Ellison's *Invisible Man* has been carefully studied over the past sixty years by literally hundreds of critics, scholars, and cultural historians, much important work needs to be done if we are to gain a fuller, more comprehensive knowledge of this extraordinary novel. We need not only to build upon this large body of research and criticism but also step clear of it for a while and develop a fresh look at the book. But this task has been made difficult by a critical bias against Ellison that began with a few initial reviews of *Invisible Man* from disgruntled leftists who were unhappy with its portrayal of the Communist Party and has in the past twenty years calcified into a strange kind of literary grudge against Ellison and his work. Books such as Jerry Gafio Watts's *Heroism and the Black Intellectual* (1994) and Barbara Foley's *Wrestling with the Left: The Making of Ralph Ellison's "Invisible Man"* (2010) have portrayed Ellison and his novel in such a blindingly negative light that it has been difficult for many scholars and critics to see either of them in a fair, clear, and objective way. Many years ago, Donald Gibson complained that "the difficulty for most critics who write about Richard Wright's *Native Son* is that they do not see Bigger Thomas. They see him with their outer eyes but not with their inner eyes." (729) A similar claim might be made today about *Invisible Man*. Many established critics filter their reading of the novel through "mirrors of hard, distorting glass" (IM 3), in the form of narrow critical theories, political biases, and personal prejudices. As a result, they fail to see either Ellison or his masterwork.

One of the most important tasks facing Ellison scholarship today, therefore, is to clear our minds of myths, stereotypes, and personal animosities that have produced a hardened narrative that makes it difficult, perhaps impossible, to clearly perceive Ellison's complex, richly nuanced vision of American experience. What is most troubling about this critical blindness is the fact that Ellison's fiction and critical writings are especially relevant today because they open our eyes to complex problems in twenty-first-century America that have been obscured by political and cultural blindness that bears a strong resemblance to the literary myopia that has plagued so much of the recent critical thinking about *Invisible Man* and its creator.

The case against Ellison has solidified into a full-fledged narrative that calls into question not only the cultural and literary value of his work but also his integrity as a man and artist. This narrative, which has become a standard assessment in some scholarly circles, has the following parts:

1. First, Ellison began his career in the late 1930s behaving admirably as an authentic African American writer and activist. He was politically engaged in a number of radical causes, was deeply sympathetic to Communist ideology and practice, and was apprenticed to Richard Wright. His first stories greatly resembled the pieces in Wright's *Uncle Tom's Children*, securing Ellison as a writer operating in the tradition of black protest literature.

2. Second, Ellison eventually "sold out" as an African American writer when he was composing *Invisible Man*, bowing to the pressures of the white critical establishment and the ideological pressures of Cold War America. He cut his ties with leftist organizations, aggressively attacked the Communist party, and sharply criticized Wright's work in particular and all protest literature in general. *Invisible Man*, which was begun in 1945 as a vibrant work of social protest in the manner of *Native Son*, had become by its publication in 1952 a tamed, antipolitical book, celebrating the narcissism of its central character and fraudulently celebrating the "magical fluidity" of American life to garner favor with the white establishment.

3. The third part of this narrative alleges that Ellison consciously falsified the story of his life of growing up in hardscrabble Oklahoma,

minimizing its racism and poverty. In essays collected in *Shadow and Act* and *Going to the Territory*, Ellison promoted a myth that he was the product of a frontier society that provided him with the independence and freedom he needed to take advantage of the rich possibilities of American life. In this way, he could separate himself from his mentor Richard Wright, who was raised in the brutally racist, segregated world of Mississippi, which compelled him to write politically engaged fiction that was deeply critical of American society. All this was done, Ellison detractors claim, to make himself more palatable to white audiences who were weary of the proletarian literature of the Depression and favored literary work that would portray post–World War II American life in more affirmative terms.

4. The fourth major complaint against Ellison is that he curried favor with white writers and intellectuals such as R. W. B. Lewis, Stanley Elkin, Saul Bellow, and Richard Chase while consciously distancing himself from young black novelists and critics. This was done to promote his own career and turn his back on cultural and political issues that were important to black Americans involved in both the civil rights and Black Power movements. Arnold Rampersad's *Ralph Ellison: A Biography*, while celebrating many of Ellison's achievements as a writer, nevertheless speculates that his failure to publish a second novel can be explained by his identifying himself too closely to the white critical establishment and thus distancing himself too much from current black life and black literary tradition. He regards Ellison as a high modernist who swam too far out into the mainstream of American culture, creating "a growing distance between himself and the black social reality around him" (315).

Very few, if any, American or African American writers of the past sixty years have had to labor under the weight of such an assault on one's work and character. Frank Yerby, who chose to write "raceless" novels, was indeed criticized for this by some critics but was generally left alone to do his own thing. Zora Neale Hurston's antipolitical aesthetic and her ultimate embrace of Southern segregation was largely forgiven when she was rediscovered as a feminist writer in the late 1960s. Langston Hughes's hesitance to engage in civil rights marches during the 1950s and 1960s went largely unnoticed. And Richard Wright's surprising lack of support for the great Southern protest movements of the fifties was never held against him. And when Wright turned away from overtly political themes in his later fiction such as *The Outsider* and *Savage Holiday*, he was never accused of currying favor with the white critical establishment or bowing down to the pressures of Cold War ideology. But with Ellison it has been a very different matter. Perhaps put off by Ellison's sometimes irascible temperament or stung by his unwillingness to compromise his independence as a writer and critic or perhaps even jealous of his literary success on a national and global scale, an increasing number of scholars and critics have gone after Ellison with an intensity that is difficult to understand.

It is time now to examine these complaints against Ellison in order to clear our minds of unfair judgments created by such rigid and outdated critical agendas so that we may see his work more clearly and understand what it means to us as twenty-first-century Americans. Perhaps one of the best ways of beginning to develop a fair assessment of Ellison is to put him in a useful historical context with other writers such as James T. Farrell, John Dos Passos, John Steinbeck, and Richard Wright, each of whom was deeply committed to the ideals and practices of the radical left in the 1930s but who was forced by the evidence provided him by historical events to seriously modify or even reject such commitments by the 1940s and early 1950s. After discovering the gruesome facts of the Stalin show trials and purges of the late 1930s, most American novelists who had earlier endorsed radically leftist ideology recoiled from Communism for very good reasons. And if this were not enough, the Soviet overtaking of much of Eastern Europe after World War II would make it nearly impossible to continue to hold doggedly to the extreme positions held by the American left during the early and mid-1930s.

Farrell, Dos Passos, Steinbeck, and Wright were never seriously disparaged by literary scholars and critics for abandoning shopworn ideologies that history had discredited. However, for reasons that are still not altogether clear, Ellison continues to be pilloried for abandoning the ideological commitments he made as a young writer. Wright was justly praised for not making *Native Son* a political tract and for his rejection of Communism in *Black Boy/American Hunger* and "I Tried to Be a Communist." And Wright's *The Outsider*, published a year after *Invisible Man*, makes the same attack on programmatic leftist politics made in Ellison's novel. Both *Invisible Man* and *The Outsider* are centered in very similar existentialist ideas that are deeply suspicious of political ideology and practice. But Wright's work has never suffered from the sustained attacks Ellison's book received for its alleged antipolitical individualism. By the end of Wright's career, his haiku poems and novels such as "Island of Hallucinations," *Savage Holiday,* and *A Father's Law* clearly established the fact that he had despaired of the utility of organized, ideologically dominated politics, but this has never been an issue for Wright scholars, many of whom fiercely attack Ellison for his reputed abandonment of politics in favor of what they regard as a self-indulgent individualism.

Barbara Foley's recent study of the composition of *Invisible Man, Wrestling with the Left,* makes the case against Ellison and *Invisible Man* in the fullest possible way. Examining various drafts of the novel from its inception in 1945 to its publication in 1952, she argues in considerable detail that it began employing "proletarian realism" (83) to protest the injustices of American racism but eventually lost its way and became an expression of what she characterized as "depoliticized mythic individualism" (83). For Foley, this represents a failure of nerve on Ellison's part, a kind of literary sellout to win the approval of white liberal critics such as Stanley Edgar Hymen, R. W. B. Lewis, and Lionel Trilling. Foley also indicts Ellison for aligning himself with white novelists like Saul Bellow, Philip Roth, and William Styron who were drawing increasing amounts of praise from the white critical establishment. As she studies Ellison's revisions of *Invisible Man,* she detects a consistent pattern of toning down and eventually eliminating its radical protest in favor of what she describes as Cold War liberalism that required him to celebrate American individualism and freedom. For Foley, the novel concludes with its protagonist speaking like a "Cold War liberal" (340) who embraces a naive vision of "American exceptionalism" (341) and democratic possibility that is at variance with the racial, social, and economic injustices that the novel dramatizes. The radically leftist political vision that, for Foley, originally energized the novel, was gradually watered down and eventually discarded by Ellison in order to position himself more advantageously with the critical powers controlling American criticism during the 1950s.

Such criticisms are certainly not new. Over the years, similar complaints have been made about Ellison's writing. Several initial reviews of *Invisible Man* objected to the novel's attack on radical leftist politics and its alleged valorization of modern alienation and individualism. Abner Berry, for example, in *The Worker* in 1953 faulted the novel for what he believed was a simplistic vilification of the Communist Party, and Lloyd Brown in *Masses and Mainstream* in 1954 accused Ellison of being a kind of "Judas" who betrayed the masses of black people by aligning himself with elitist white writers such as T. S. Eliot and failing to suggest ways in which blacks could be liberated from an oppressive capitalistic system. Most famously, Irving Howe, in a much-discussed essay, "Black Boys and Native Sons," chided Ellison for abandoning the protest tradition of African American literature centered in Richard Wright's work and retreating into an excessively individualistic vision of American life. Howe argued that *Invisible Man* was "literary to a fault" (100) and was "marred by the ideological delusions of ... the fifties" (101), which valorized "unconditioned freedom" (102) of the individual rather than protesting against racial and economic injustice. And Jerry Gafio Watts, in a book-length indictment of Ellison published in 1994, went even further, accusing Ellison of "establishmentarianism" (146) that separated him from the plight of the African American masses. Like Howe, he contrasted Ellison with the politically engaged Wright and found Ellison wanting, diagnosing him as suffering from "a rather typical black intellectual disease," which he characterizes as "the elitism of heroic individualism" (119).

Because our view of Ellison has been so distorted by the cultural agendas of critics who have constructed such a blinding narrative about Ellison, we have real difficulty seeing and understanding the richly nuanced political vision that is such an important part of *Invisible Man*. Foley is wrong when she argues that Ellison was a writer who finally "avoid[ed] the dull certainty of political commitment" (344). Quite to the contrary, Ellison's novel is deeply rooted in the values of a political movement that was beginning to shift into high gear when *Invisible Man* was published in 1952: the American civil rights movement. Although it rejects the power-hungry politics of Jack and the fantasy-based politics of Ras, it expresses in very lucid and compelling ways the Black Freedom movement that would transform post–World War II American life and continues to inspire meaningful political action. When Ellison's protagonist asks, "Could politics ever be an expression of love?" (452), it is neither a rhetorical question nor an ironic gesture. This novel, published on the cusp of the modern American civil rights movement, is centered in a deeply political vision that is altogether consistent with the nonviolent revolution that would succeed where earlier movements sponsored by radically leftist ideologies failed. Ellison's novel clearly upholds and vividly dramatizes the three core values that Martin Luther King Jr., C. T. Vivien, Fred Shuttleworth, James Farmer, and many others stressed: (1) nonviolence, (2) Christian love, and (3) integration.[1]

Arnold Rampersad's biography of Ellison carefully documents his sustained interest in the civil rights movement. Ellison never became what might be called an activist because he wanted to protect his independence and integrity as a writer and was acutely aware of how many writers of the

1930s compromised their art by substituting political ideology for artistic vision. Moreover, he knew he could better serve the movement by fulfilling his role as a writer rather than by taking to the streets as an activist. As he revealed to Irving Howe in 1963 when Howe questioned his commitment to African American politics, his commitment to the "Freedom Movement" was unequivocally strong and he was "enlisted for the duration." But he stressed that there was "a certain division of labor among members of the tribe" in these matters and his writing was a vitally important way to serve the movement. His rebuttal of Howe concludes brilliantly when he states, "My reply to your essay is in itself a small but necessary step in the Negro struggle for freedom" (CERE 188).

Ellison was clearly much more involved with the civil rights movement of the 1950s and 1960s than were other black writers such as Richard Wright and Langston Hughes. He was profoundly moved by the 1954 Supreme Court decision, *Brown v. Board of Education,* and regarded it as a major turning point in American history. In a letter to Morteza Sprague he exclaimed, "What a wonderful world of possibilities for the children" (Rampersad 28). He engaged in a much-publicized and spirited debate with Hannah Arendt after she questioned the wisdom of the parents of the nine black children who integrated Central High School in Little Rock, Arkansas, in 1957. In an interview with Robert Penn Warren, he praised these parents for helping their children to learn a valuable lesson in "self-confidence, self-consciousness, and self-mastery" (Rampersad 421). Rampersad also points out that Ellison was deeply affected by the 1961 student sit-ins in Nashville, Tennessee, and Greenville, North Carolina, both of which "rocked his idealistic notions about the likelihood of voluntary change in the South" (375). In 1960 Ellison wrote an article on the Freedom Riders that was rejected by *Esquire* as "too radical" (Rampersad 379). He testified before two US Senate committees investigating the urban riots of the mid-1960s. And he was a longtime member of the NAACP, working with Thurgood Marshall, William Hastie, and Jack Greenberg to develop its Legal Defense Fund. After the Selma demonstrations in 1965 he was very active in helping the NAACP strengthen its fund-raising activities. Far from being politically disengaged in the 1950s and 1960s, Ellison was meaningfully involved in the black freedom movement and this clearly left its mark on *Invisible Man, Juneteenth,* and several of his most important essays.

In a recent study of Richard Wright's political commitments in the 1950s, Leonard Cassuto has argued that "Wright was a restless thinker, not a movement politician. An admirer of 'those who can stand alone' (qtd. in Rowley,

"Exile"), he declared himself 'a rootless man'" (Wright, *White Man* 47). Given these assertions, it is perhaps not surprising that Wright largely ignored the American civil rights movement, even as it gained visibility in the fifties (Cassuto 51). Wright and Ellison were strongly involved in radical leftist politics during the Great Depression but were eventually disillusioned with the ideals and practices of Communism and developed an understandably keen suspicion of the effects of ideological demands on their writing. But whereas Wright's late fiction such as *The Outsider* (1953), *Savage Holiday* (1954), and *A Father's Law* (2008) are centered in existential ideas that are completely at odds with Wright's earlier political faiths, Ellison was able to recover a belief in a "politics ... of love" (IM 452) that could provide him with an imaginatively compelling alternative to his earlier proletarian fiction such as "A Party down at the Square." Cassuto perhaps overstates his case when he asserts that Wright "largely ignored" the civil rights movement but it is clear that he never was able to make literary use of it. Ellison, on the other hand, was indeed "stirred by the civil right struggles in America" (Rampersad 348). His letters to Albert Murray offer consistent proof of his strong commitment to the freedom movement in America and his attempts to represent this in his writing. These letters often record his impatience with conservative black leaders for not being sufficiently militant, and he continually praises the work of black demonstrators in Montgomery and Nashville. In a March 16, 1956, letter to Murray, Ellison observes,

> Mose is fighting and he's still got his briarpatch cunning; he's just been waiting for a law, man, something solid under his feet; a little scent of possibility. In fact, he's turned the Supreme Court into the forum of liberty it was intended to be, and the Constitution of the United States into a briarpatch in which the nimble people, the willing people, have a chance. (*Trading* 116–17)

Ellison not only was strongly committed in his personal and public life to the civil rights movement but made powerful use of its core values in his masterwork, *Invisible Man*.

Two of these core values, nonviolence and Christian love, are powerfully dramatized in the prologue when the narrator describes his near killing of a white man. This episode artfully signifies on the death of Mary Dalton in *Native Son*, echoing Wright's scene but transforming its meanings. The

Invisible Man is overwhelmed by a "frenzy" (IM 4)—not unlike Wright's Bigger Thomas, who is dominated by an emotional "frenzy" (Wright, *Native Son* 85) triggered by his racial fear and anger when he is insulted by the white man's racial slurs. Like Bigger, he initially responds to this situation with reflexive violence, knocking the man to the ground and preparing to slit his throat. But unlike Bigger, whose conscious thoughts are completely blocked out by his "hysterical terror" (Wright, *Native Son* 85) and who continues to regard his victim as an anonymous force rather than an individual person, Invisible Man's human consciousness is awakened when the lights of a passing car illuminate his victim's face and he sees him as "a man who had not seen me" (IM 4). The white man continues to function in terms of the way a racist environment has programmed him, inhabiting "a walking nightmare" (4) as he writhes on the ground, screaming racial insults, his lips "frothy with blood" (4). But Invisible Man wakes up from his environmentally induced nightmare of violence and calmly states: "And I stopped the blade, slicing the air as I pushed him away, letting him fall back into the street. I stared at him hard as the lights of a car stabbed through the darkness. He lay there, moaning on the asphalt, a man almost killed by a phantom" (4–5). Drawing upon emotional and moral resources that Bigger is unable to call upon, he does not make the white man another Mary Dalton, a stereotyped symbol that activates animalistic acts of uncontrollable violence. Instead, Invisible Man sees both himself and the white racist in deeply human, essentially Christian terms. Realizing that his attacker is "a man," not a demonized representative of a whole race, he also rejects the stereotype that his attacker has applied to him, refusing to act the role of the "bad nigger," a "phantom" (5) inside the white man's "thick head" (5). Moreover, he finally perceives the man with the same kind of Christian love that Martin Luther King Jr. extended to those who persecuted him. He regards the man with "sincere compassion" (5) rather than hatred, perceiving him as a "poor blind fool" (5) to be understood and pitied rather than murdered.

Dr. King in *Why We Can't Wait* described nonviolence as "a sword that heals" (16), a political strategy that pragmatically creates the possibility of true integration because it reveals the humanity of both the black victim and the white victimizer, thus opening the door to reconciliation. Invisible Man is healed when he resists the reflexive desire to strike violently against his oppressor and then recognizes a common humanity with him. Both have been turned into "fools" by a racist society but Ellison's protagonist can transcend this with consciousness and love. (He certainly has to realize that he too has been a "poor blind fool," like his white attacker, in most of the important episodes of the novel but that he now has the human resources necessary to overcome this condition.)

Violence is portrayed at all points in *Invisible Man* as a revelation of cultural and personal sickness but, as the narrator stresses in the epilogue, "you can either make passive love to your sickness or burn it out and go on to the next conflicting phase" (576). In 1952, the "next phase" of development for Americans was the civil rights movement, which demanded a higher form of consciousness that rejected violence and centered on Christian love. Invisible Man's most traumatic moments occur when he is threatened by violence or tempted to engage in acts of brutality. But his moments of healing take place when he can experience compassion and love that integrate him with other people.

The physical and emotional beating he takes in the battle royal reduces him to a stereotyped "boy" who must accept the dehumanizing roles imposed upon him by Southern racists. When he thinks of striking back at them with retaliatory violence, matters get worse because his actions will only increase their attacks on him. Likewise, when he agrees to fight his fellow blacks in the ring he is simply confirming the degraded image that Southern society has imposed upon him. But when he establishes eye contact with the stripper, he recognizes their common humanity. As a woman, she is humiliated by the sexism that in many ways originates from the same sick drives of a dehumanizing society. Nearly all of the novel's major scenes expose Invisible Man to a wide assortment of violence and Ellison stresses in each of these episodes that he must rise above it with deepened consciousness. His desire to "fight" (141) Bledsoe, for example, only results in making his situation worse. (He should certainly be more careful with a person who threatens to have "every Negro hanging on a tree" [143] if that is what it takes to maintain his power.) And his decision to engage in a fistfight with Lucius Brockway also works out badly for him since he is no real match for the wily old man who nearly kills him. His desire at the end of the novel to participate in the Harlem riot almost results in his death as he narrowly misses being shot. It turns out that the "good fight" (16) that his grandfather urges him to undertake is psychological, political, and moral rather than physical. It is the same "fight" that civil rights leaders of the '50s and '60s engaged in, a "battle" that required one to use the sword that heals rather than the gun that kills.

It is for this reason that Invisible Man's most meaningful moments occur when he rejects his impulses toward violence and responds to people with deepened consciousness leading to Christian love. Midway through the book, when he is sent to the hospital after his ill-advised fight with Brockway, he comes to the angry realization that the iron lung in which he is trapped is a symbol of the society that has imprisoned him throughout his life. Although his first thought is to destroy the machine as a way of liberating himself, he soon realizes that short-circuiting the machine will only result in electrocution: "I had no desire to destroy myself even if it destroyed the machine. I wanted freedom, not destruction" (243). He realizes, as all civil rights leaders understood, that violence is pointless self-destruction and that true freedom could be attained only through deepened consciousness, pragmatic action, and love.

In the scene that follows, he finds all three. After passing out on the streets of Harlem, he awakens with "wild infant's eyes" (251) and becomes the beneficiary of Mary Rambo's unselfish love and wise practicality. She is the first person in the novel to respond to him with genuine human care rather than a manipulative scheme. As her name indicates, she is a figure of Christian motherhood who treats him like her "son" (252). Mary, described as a person who is "always helping somebody" (253), physically revives him with shelter and food but, more importantly, she regenerates him morally and spiritually by shaking him out of his narcissism that has driven him up to this point in the book and challenging him to help others. She reminds him of his responsibilities to assist his fellow black people by stressing that "you got to lead and you got to fight and move us all up a little higher" (255). From this point onward, Ellison's protagonist moves steadily beyond the self-absorption that has limited his growth and he develops the capacity to love. His encounter with the yam vendor helps him regain a respect for African American culture and a love of his fellow blacks. When he exclaims at the end of this episode, "What a people *we* were" (264; emphasis added), it contrasts sharply with his earlier response to Peetie Wheatstraw when he exclaimed, "God damn . . . *they're* a hell of a people" (177; emphasis added). In the eviction scene that directly follows the yam episode, he identifies closely with the evicted couple and feels great compassion for them. For the first time in the novel, he sacrifices himself for others by rebelling against the authorities and risking arrest when he speaks up for Primus Provo and his wife. As he awakens to the needs of this old couple, he connects himself lovingly to black people from whom he earlier would have distanced himself. He sees the men protesting the eviction as his "Black Brothers" (275) and the Provos inspire in him a "vision" of his "mother" (273).

As his eyes open and his consciousness deepens in the second half of the novel, he is able to experience Christian love in fuller, broader ways. One of his motives in joining the Brotherhood is to work toward achieving a more just society and become part of a movement that creates "the possibility of being more than a member of a race" (355). He develops a father-son relationship with Brother Tarp, who bestows upon him his leg shackle that provides another "link" (389) between him and his fellow blacks as well as other oppressed minorities. The eulogy he gives at Tod Clifton's funeral "wasn't political" (457) but is instead a deeply felt expression of both personal loss and his strong identification with the audience whom he sees "not as a crowd but the set faces of individual men and women" (459). And when he finally gets an opportunity to exact revenge upon white people by taking sexual advantage of Sybil, he responds to her compassionately, refusing her offer of sex and being careful to take her to a place where she can be safe from the riot developing in Harlem. Near the end of the novel, when he has a dream that is an epiphany of how he has been manipulated by Jack and several other authority figures, he does not respond with self-destructive anger that would lead him to violence. He realizes now that he is "through with them at last" and that he might "kill himself" (568) psychologically by brooding over them or angrily retaliating against them. Significantly, when he later encounters Norton, who asks for directions to Center Street, a locus of outward power in New York, he responds to him with amused irony rather than an angry verbal attack.

Invisible Man ultimately realizes that the real "soul sickness" (575) is located not only in the external social world that men like Norton control but "at least half of it lay within me" (575). And he understands that the only way to treat this sickness rooted in hatred and violence is to counter it with love:

> In spite of all I find that I love. In order to get some of it down I *have* to love. I sell you no phony forgiveness. I'm a desperate man—but too much of your life will be lost, unless you approach it as much through love as through hate. So I approach it through division. So I denounce and I defend and I hate and I love. (580)

For Ellison, the best way to resolve the tensions created by these sharp divisions is through a process of integration, what Dr. King described at the end of *Why We Can't Wait* as "a vision of total interrelatedness" (190). In a 1973 interview with Holly West, Ellison declared "The imagination is integrative. . . . I am unabashedly an American integrationist" (CRE 3). On a personal level, Invisible Man must use his imagination to become a writer who can harmonize the various parts of his identity and thus develop a coherent sense of self, capable of pragmatic action in the above-ground world. This is clearly "the next phase" (IM 576) of his growth. On a political and cultural level, Ellison declares the need for the United States to reinvigorate "the principle upon which the country was built" (576) and which is clearly formulated in its founding documents, the Constitution and the Bill of Rights.[2] These are the same documents that Dr. King cited in *Why We Can't Wait* to validate the claims of the civil rights movement. The principles of the founding fathers harmonized individual freedom with social responsibility, thus balancing "the one" with "the many." In the same way, Ellison's protagonist must play "a socially responsible role" (581) while constructing a robust self. He therefore has to reject both the anarchy of a Rinehart and the conformity of his earlier self. All of the leaders of the civil rights movement strongly argued for achieving the same balance of self and society, warning against anarchic violence and numb allegiance to the status quo of a segregated society.

One of the most important results of this cultural balance for Ellison is the racially integrated society that the civil rights movement strove to achieve. *Invisible Man* begins with the word *I*, which asserts the voice of a unique black individual, but it concludes with the word *you*, declaring a kinship with even the whites who have caused him such pain. *Invisible Man* can ultimately "affirm the principle" that "we were linked to all the others in the loud, clamoring semi-visible world" (574) of modern America. For Ellison understood, as Martin Luther King Jr. frequently acknowledged, that "sin is separation" ("Letter from Birmingham Jail" 90) and that "on the lower frequencies" (IM 581) we share a common humanity that makes possible both American democracy and racial integration.

In recent years a number of scholars, critics, and writers have argued that, given the important transformations of much of black life over the past forty years, new directions in African American literature are needed to represent accurately racial reality in contemporary America. For example, Kenneth Warren has called for "broader work" (*What Was* 120) to be done by black American writers that transcends the rigid ideological assumptions and political agendas of much previous black literature. He urges black writers to break away from the tradition of narrow protest literature, which was premised upon the idea that monolithic racial oppression required African American literature to be a "collective undertaking" (113) centered in a uniform racial protest. Warren instead urges black writers to develop a literature that grants them the freedom to explore American reality in much more complex, open, and comprehensive terms.

The African American novelist and philosopher Charles Johnson, in a 2008 essay published in *The American Scholar*, makes a very similar point, questioning "the truth and usefulness of the traditional black American narrative of victimization," which is rooted in the assumption that black people in America are "culturally homogenous" ("End," *American Scholar* 37). He calls for new narratives that can express the full complexity and diversity of current African American experience. The "new and better stories" that Johnson desires will not be shackled by outdated ideologies or shopworn political faiths that can only blind us and "short-circuit direct perception of the specific phenomena before us" in the twenty-first century. Quite to the contrary, these new narratives must be "open-ended, never fixed," providing a liberatingly "provisional reading of reality" that makes no "claim to be absolute truth" (39). For Johnson, such stories come much closer to the truth of contemporary black experience than the "dated narrative" (39) that imagines black life in monolithic terms as a uniform protest against a massively segregated society. *Invisible Man*, which is centered on an individual who ultimately transcends victimization by cultivating the supple, penetrating consciousness that frees him from all forms of "absolute truth" that had earlier trapped him, offers a powerful model for the kind of black American narrative that Johnson advocates.

Given the arguments that Warren and Johnson make, Ralph Ellison is clearly not the obsolete Cold War ideologue that Barbara Foley and others have made him out to be. Instead, Ellison's writings, both fictional and critical, offer a rich and compelling vision of American and African American life that can serve as an inspiration for the new black literature emerging in recent years. Ellison's insistence that black experience is much more complex and interesting than narrowly conceived "protest" literature is able to describe sets a liberating example for young African American writers. And his deep suspicion that preconceived abstractions and stereotypes will only blind us to the full richness of human experience is shared by many outstanding black writers such as Colson Whitehead, ZZ Packer, and Michael Thomas. Not surprisingly, the only twentieth-century novelist whom Charles Johnson cites as a model for twenty-first century black writers is Ralph Ellison, whose masterwork, *Invisible Man*, continues to probe "the mysterious, untamed life that forever churns beneath widely accepted interpretations of 'history' and 'culture'" ("End," *American Scholar* 39).

Ellison's politics of love, far from being a dated account of values that were relevant in the '50s and '60s but no longer serve the needs of twenty-first-century Americans, are especially relevant to us today.[3] For Ellison's political vision is not controlled by the narrow ideology that blinds people like Ras, who then try to separate blacks, thus prolonging racial injustice. Ellison's finely nuanced political vision also avoids the other extreme: Jack's fraudulent plan to "integrate" African Americans into a vast totalitarian system that will also betray them. Instead, Ellison proposes a politics of love that is protean, always open to change as America evolves into a more democratic and truly integrated society. By operating "on the lower frequencies" (IM 581) of political consciousness where understanding arising from love is possible, Ellison's politics of love can distill universal human values, which contemporary American discourse has largely forgotten. These values bind us together, making genuine integration possible. We, therefore, in the twenty-first century have much to learn from Ellison's wise political vision, which stresses the need for the *I* to lovingly engage the *you*, thus regaining the balance between individual freedom and social responsibility for which both the founding fathers and the leaders of the civil rights movement called.

NOTES

1. Although much attention has been devoted in recent scholarship to Ellison's involvements in radically leftist politics in the 1930s when he was emerging as a writer, relatively little has been written about his interest in the civil rights movement and how this has helped to shape his mature work. But two essays in *Ralph Ellison and the Raft of Hope* (Morel) make strong and revealing connections between Ellison and the Freedom Movement. Alfred Brophy's "*Invisible Man* as Literary Analogue to *Brown vs. Board of Education*" suggests that Ellison's novel "signaled—and perhaps propelled—the changes that were coming in American law and custom" (119), culminating in the *Brown* decision. He argues that *Invisible Man* is thematically consistent with the Supreme Court's decision to ban racial segregation in America's schools, stressing that both are grounded in similar moral visions and reject similar moral evasions. For Brophy, both Ellison and the Supreme Court "drew upon a common reservoir of thinking" (119). Kenneth Warren's "Ralph Ellison and the Problem of Cultural Authority: The Lessons of Little Rock" explores Ellison's impassioned support of the nine black students who integrated Little Rock Central High School and examines Ellison's argument with Hannah Arendt, who sharply criticized the parents of these children for exposing them to the dangers of forced integration. Ellison strongly disagreed with Arendt, viewing the actions of both the Little Rock Nine and their parents as heroic activity in the main tradition of African American history. Warren points out that the crisis in Little Rock "reflected some of the concerns that shaped the writing of *Invisible Man*" (146). For Warren, the nine black students were faced with the same challenge that confronts Ellison's central character—how to discover "legitimate authority" (151) for his actions by balancing "individual personality" (153) with "a larger group context" that was "Negro, American, or some combination of the two" (154).

2. Ellison stressed the importance of these cultural documents in several speeches and essays. For example, in "Hidden Name and Complex Fate," an address delivered at the Library of Congress in 1964 and included in *Shadow and Act*, he argued that the United States was not formed "through the accidents of race or religion or geography" but instead was founded on "quite sacred papers" (CERE 206) that defined core American values. The Constitution, the Bill of Rights, and the Declaration of Independence pledged Americans to "certain ideals of justice" as well as "a system which would guarantee all of its citizens equality of opportunity" (CERE 206). In "Society, Morality, and the Novel," published in *The Living Novel* and later included in *Going to the Territory*, he argued that classic American writers such as "Hawthorne, Melville, James, and Twain" grounded their work in "the moral imperatives of American life" that were "implicit in the Declaration of Independence, the Constitution, and the Bill of Rights" (CERE 706). Ellison aims for this same politically engaged and idealized writing.

3. The continued relevance of Ellison's vision of American culture can also be seen in how his careful balancing of individualism and community harmonizes with numerous important cultural studies that have emerged in America over the past thirty years. *Habits of the Heart* (Bellah et al.), which deplored the "cancerous" (vii) individualism of late twentieth-century American life and argued that American self-reliance "must be balanced by a renewal of commitment and community" (227), is altogether consistent with Ellison's integration of self and society. And Ellison's Invisible Man would have no trouble agreeing with Robert Putnam's conviction in *Bowling Alone* that "we Americans need to reconnect with each other" (28). After experiencing the narcissism of Rinehart and nearly being killed in the Harlem riot, Ellison's protagonist would also understand what Amitai Etzioni's *The Spirit of Community* (1993) means by "the anarchic drift" (11) of American life, and he would certainly concur with Etzioni's claim that "free individuals require a community" (15). Charles Wallace's essay "The New American Divide" (2012), which builds a compelling argument that "America is coming apart" (1) because it offers "too few shared experiences" (2), bears strong resemblance to the stern warnings made in *Invisible Man* that the alternative to genuine integration is cultural fragmentation and dissolution.

THE BODY AND *INVISIBLE MAN*
Ralph Ellison's Novel in Twenty-First-Century Performance and Public Spaces

PATRICE RANKINE

"For Tamir Rice, Eric Garner, and our countless other Hopes Shot Down."

A disconnect between what actually happened and how the media reported it is palpable in *The Riots* (a theatrical presentation of the 2011 London riots by Gillian Slovo). As the fires blazed, real stories got lost amid the rush to condemn rioters. While politicians squabble and journalists continue to pontificate, what can theater contribute to the debate? "The advantage we have is space," argues Slovo. "We have two hours to deal with one issue.... You read a newspaper on your own ... but we need to create a space in which people can think about what has happened together" (Allfree).

The cultural significance of Ralph Ellison's *Invisible Man* in the twenty-first century is not simply a matter of the novel's place within the canonical American "great books," or its permanence globally among literary masterpieces from the time of its publication in 1952.[1] As if its satirical and profoundly intelligent treatment of American identity during segregation were not enough, *Invisible Man* graced the American stage in 2012 with Oren Jacoby's adaptation, which Christopher McElroen directed.[2] The Court Theatre's three-hour-plus performance—meriting two intermissions—gives audiences another perspective on the novel. In *Invisible Man* a young college student meets disappointment in the South when he is kicked out of a segregated school for a mistake he makes; similar to the slaves of a previous generation, he travels to New York in hope of a better future, but he faces disappointments there as well.[3] My interest here is not in writing a review article about the performance of *Invisible Man*. Rather, the theatrical production of *Invisible Man* provides an opportunity to revisit Ellison's writing from two distinct vantage points: namely, the novel as a literary genre, and the performance of race in contemporary theaters, whether a staged production or within a spontaneous (unstaged), social drama, such as twenty-first-century city streets.[4] In this latter context, the riot with which the novel closes is pivotal.

It is noteworthy that during his lifetime, Ellison resisted adaptation of *Invisible Man* for the stage.[5] Perhaps he saw and disliked the theatrical version or the film adaptation of other novels, such as *Native Son*, which his literary rival and sometimes friend Richard Wright brought to the stage with the help of playwright Paul Green. Ellison's resistance to the staging of a novel that he also criticized on formal grounds would not be out of character.[6] Everything he ever said about artistic form, whether in interviews or in his essays, amounted to an insistence upon distinctions between and among genres. Ellison's dogged protestation approached the level of a kind of artistic purity, despite the wise advice of his character Mr. Emerson Jr. in *Invisible Man* to resist purity. In the novel, Emerson comes to Invisible Man's aid and tells him that the letters the protagonist thinks will allow him entry into a job in New York City are in fact damning. He seeks to comfort the protagonist and assures him, whether soothingly or cynically, that "all our motives are impure" (IM 186). Within this context, the performance of *Invisible Man* is an ironic, cautionary tale about the pitfalls of such artistic purity. Such irony is of value to Ellison criticism because of what many continue to treat as the writer's "failure" to produce a second novel within his lifetime, itself a reflection of a kind of purity, at least in the context of criticism, an inability to hold Ellison to any other standard but that which he himself established, that of novelist.[7]

In addition to the reflection on Ellisonian thought that it allows in general, the performance of *Invisible Man* also calls attention to something that the novel cannot do, if we hold the genre to the formal standards that Ellison and others proclaimed. To be specific, the novel cannot—in fact, must not—focus on the corporeal reality of race, whereas performance, by its very nature, would call attention to such a fact, no matter the reaction to this phenomenon on the part of particular audience members.

Ellison never describes the protagonist of *Invisible Man* as black, even though *other* characters in the novel see him as Negro, to use the nomenclature of the social framework of Ellison's mid-century novel. Certainly Invisible Man evokes Louis Armstrong's invocation of "what did I do to be so black and blue" from the start of the novel, in the prologue, even if blackness and the blues can be metaphorical (IM 14). And a white Southerner refers to him as a "ginger colored nigger" during the violent battle royal scene (IM 21), where black boys are pitted against one another to the bloody finish. So the reader knows that the protagonist is black. Nevertheless, despite the strong narrative framework and description of what amounts to a fictional version of segregated America, Ellison—remarkably—describes race as a kind of external imposition on the individual and on American life, a truth that is always there though often not directly addressed, part of a larger set of social concerns, including class, sex, Communism, and democracy. While the novel can *describe* race from various perspectives, through embodiment the *performance* of race in *Invisible Man* must be visceral and inescapable, physical rather than intellectual, whatever the audience's reaction to race's corporeality. Performance reveals what race really is—performance. As tautological as this sounds, the stage version of *Invisible Man*, where race is shown to be a corporeal presence dependent upon physical and verbal gestures, allows the material to interact with the twenty-first-century global environment in somewhat unexpected ways.

THE NOVEL FORM

Ellison articulated his theory of the novel in a number of essays and interviews, in particular in "The World and the Jug," published in *Shadow and Act*; "Society, Morality, and the Novel" and "The Novel as a Function of American Democracy," published in *Going to the Territory*; and in a roundtable discussion for the Southern Historical Society, with William Styron, Robert Penn Warren, and C. Vann Woodward, where comparisons between fiction (through the novel) and history emerge (CRE). While other articles show Ellison's sustained interest in the American novel, these essays best characterize his dedication to a particular formal approach, which he derived mainly from Georg Lukács. Ellison directly cites Lukács in the Southern Historical Society discussion. He calls attention to Lukács's observations on the "increasing concreteness of the novel" (CRE 150). The novelist "move[s] about inside of his subject" and possibly brings a "new outlook" to his readers, whatever their previous "prejudices" (CRE 150, 151). The understanding of Lukács that Ellison demonstrates in the discussion would only be sharpened in his later essays.

Some consideration of Lukács's formal approach to the novel is worthwhile here in order to contextualize Ellison's comments. Lukács's treatise, first published in 1920, anticipates Mikhail Bakhtin's distinction between the epic and the novel. According to Lukács, the epic conveys the "heaviness" of life, "an inability to liberate oneself from the bonds of sheer brutal materiality" (57–58). The novel, in contrast, has "seekers" as its heroes, those who will not accept the heaviness of life but construct out of the brutal materiality their individual approach: "The epic gives form to a totality of life that is rounded from within; the novel seeks, by giving form, to uncover and construct the concealed totality of life" (Lukács 60). Lukács draws distinctions between inside and outside, the material world and the containers (forms) through which artists forge meaning—Ellison's "world and the jug," the latter the container that is crafted, holds a shape, and serves a purpose. That is, the novel is the jug, the written material, the fluid it holds. To use another metaphor, Lukács defines artistic form in terms of home, but society (the world) cannot define home for the individual. Lukács hits upon a general existential problem that Ellison will take up in specific, local terms; namely, that a novel, as a formal structure of process, of individual "seekers," *cannot* define people in static terms. The novel's material is fluid, whereas the epic is static. Thus, for Ellison, race, as a social construct, cannot ultimately hold any fixed meaning for the novelist because it is part of the fluid material that he must manipulate.

For Lukács, "every art form is defined by the metaphysical dissonance of life which it accepts and organises as the basis of a totality complete in itself" (71). Whatever enters the novel, however fragmented and dissonant it is, comes out on the other end of the process. The novel is something "complete in itself," what might be called a narrative whole. For Ellison, the novel form allows for an optimism regarding race in America. The writer's responsibility is "to the unfettered and replenishing power of his own imagination" (CRE 152). While the historians in Ellison's conversation at the Southern Historical Association return, time and again, to the material realities of race and segregation in America, Ellison shifts focus from "the dead baggage of facts" (152). How can history explain that Ellison hears firsthand "from Negro students that I attended college with at Tuskegee" (153) positive things about certain white racists? Shouldn't these students hate their ostensible oppressors? There is for Ellison something incongruous about lived experience when it is set against raw facts. Although history does not tell the entire story, the novel form, as defined by Lukács and embraced by Ellison, can contain these "incongruous juxtapositions."[8] The novel insists on crafting a complete, fictive entity out of the brutal materiality that is the fact of life. What comes on the other end of the narrative experience is an individual invention, unique and separate from anything that came before, and from the facts of history.

As Lukács had it, the novel must move toward "disillusionment" (Lukács 144). That is, chaos, not the "conventional world" (144), is where a novel's protagonist ends up, but this chaos is a laboratory of creative possibility, "the novel's ability to forge images which would strengthen man's will to say no to chaos and affirm him in his task of humanizing himself and the world" (CERE 701). Here again, the muck with which one enters into the abyss, the underworld of creative possibilities that is the material of lived experience, is only the stuff out of which the individual crafts Lukács's "totality." The novelist is "committed to optimism" (CERE 706), whereas the reality of race can be grueling. The "inherent ambiguity" of the novel benefits from a psychological and emotional distance. This is why the protagonist of *Invisible Man* is *retelling* his story, once he has organized its narrative structure, after the fact, as it were, rather than as he undergoes the existential crises he experiences. In the end, Ellison advances Lukács's ideas to the extent that he sees the novel, and no other artistic form, as having reached a particular pitch in America where it becomes the place for working out the democratic process itself, a site of "maximum freedom" of expression (CERE 763).

Ellison's approach to the novel is a useful contrast to theater and performance. Early in "The Novel as a Function of American Democracy," Ellison directly contrasts how the novel functions to theater, wherein the former is "a literary form which could project the shiftings of society with a facility and an intimacy that had not existed before, either in the theater or in romantic poetry" (CERE 755). Whereas performance can be visceral and emotional in its display of experiences, a good novel, in Ellison's estimation, cannot afford to be. Lack of a certain kind of intelligence—that is, an emotional appeal rather than an appeal to reason—was Ellison's ultimate problem with *Native Son*. This is not to say that performances fail to be logical or considered, but they depend on emotional reactions, whereas novels, as defined here, cannot. Ellison certainly understood racial categories as cultural distinctions, but he thought that the novel was the means by which Americans could transcend these material realities. Within this context, the fault with *Native Son* was the extent to which it beat its reader over the head with the poverty and degradation of Wright's character, Bigger Thomas. Bigger is not a novelistic hero who crafts his own sense of the world out of the chaos that surrounds him. Rather, he is a symbol of that chaos, as James Baldwin argued in "Everybody's Protest Novel." Such a character could never appeal to Ellison, and in the end *Native Son* is branded "protest fiction," rather than a novel by Ellison's or Lukács's definition.

THE STAGE

Of course, every art form and literary genre has a claim to uniqueness, exceptionalism, and an ability to do what other forms cannot. The American stage has certainly been a place for unparalleled responses to the material realities of life in the United States. Through costume and set design, theater had an indelible place in American modernism, setting forth the rubric of modern style in ways that poetry and fiction could not, even in the hands of T. S. Eliot or Ezra Pound (Walker). Throughout the twentieth century, the American stage was a place where antiestablishment rhetoric and modes of life could be tried on, as plays like *Waiting for Lefty* make apparent (Krasner). The American stage was also instrumental in the penetration of the racial subject into the modern American imagination. Eugene O'Neill's *Emperor Jones*, published in 1920 and starring Paul Robeson in the lead role, certainly was not realistic theater, but it put a black actor in a serious role on Broadway for the first time. What theater can do in a specific way is bring corporeal realities to bear on audience members, whatever their reactions to these realities. As performance theorist Harvey Young argues in *Embodying Black Experience*, the reality of "the black body" as a phenomenon, a thing-in-the-world, is perhaps best couched in terms of history and memory, whereas Ellison was perhaps interested in fiction and creative forgetfulness.

When Ellison presents such events in *Invisible Man* as the battle royal, the bloody contest that white racists set up to have black boys compete in a group boxing match for scraps of money, the key is ambiguity. In the scene, the white woman with the American flag tattooed on her body is as much a focal point as any, as Sandra Adell has argued in *Double-Consciousness/Double Bind*. Performance of this scene onstage, however, calls for precision and presence: the director might make choices about what the scene means, fix upon those choices, and present the actors whose bodies will play the role. The same is the case with the eviction scene later in the novel, or with the riots with which the novel closes. The novelist can play with ambiguity and move his reader from individual experiences toward the totality of the form. Not so for the theater director. Lack clarity here and lose your theater audience!

At the same time, performance does, as Young argues, allow for presence and historical repetition. An event such as a riot happens once. As will be evident, Ellison's attempt to move beyond the historical reality of such an event as a riot through the novel is one of his contributions beyond the 1950s, as these events recur. In this case, the novel and performance work in tandem, the latter reliving the events, the former imagining a world without them. The enactment of a riot can act on the mind in therapeutic ways. By seeing the events onstage, audiences can relive the traumatic events again and again, perhaps discussing those events together in "talkbacks," in a controlled environment.

Theater played this role in 2011 in London with Gillian Slovo's *The Riots*, where performers acted out skits derived from the real-life riots, which began in Tottenham and spread across the United Kingdom during the fall of 2011.[9] The facts, such as they were, are worth recounting.[10] On August 6, 2011, police officers killed Mark Duggan. Friends say Mark was unarmed; officers say he shot at them first. An independent commission later corroborated that Mark was unarmed at the time of his murder, although he did possess an illegal firearm. Beginning in Tottenham, young adults damaged property and threw their bodies in the way of buildings, automobiles, and police. The riots began on August 6, 2011, but by the end there were 3,100 arrests, over 1,000 charges, and 3,443 crimes committed.[11] Such repetition as what was staged in *The Riots* allows audiences to relive the terrible events but with the purpose of discussion and healing. Given the uncontrolled chaos of riots, it is not surprising that Ellison would seek to master the riots he lived through, in the novel form. Ellison's private "intimacy" (CERE 755), which the novel form allows, contrasts with what Slovo sought to achieve with her play *The Riots*; namely, to "think about what happened together" (quoted in the epigraph at the beginning of this chapter). Further comparisons between the London riots and the historical riots in Harlem as they are represented in *Invisible Man* follow. Most important for the moment is the fixity of the event as the novelist represents it, as opposed to the way in which such an event can be relived and repeated onstage. In the novel as Ellison conceives it in 1952, the individual reads and reflects silently upon the events. (This isolation is certainly not the case at other points in the history of reading. Ancient Greeks and Romans, for example, always read aloud and mostly in groups.) In a theater, individuals must confront one another's reactions to the staged event, even if in silence. Living bodies are seated next to one another in a theater space, and there are bodies onstage.

THE BODY AND JACOBY'S *INVISIBLE MAN*

The body is a focal point in performance and the instrument through which individuals enact a number of dramas (Schechner). Individuals enact these dramas in formal and informal theaters.[12] For the context with which I am concerned, the performance of scenes from *Invisible Man* onstage, it is worth focusing on two theaters, the street, where riots and conflict take place, and the dramatic stage, where conflicts can be relived and further dramatized— heightened, as it were. The differences between these theaters are important to my discussion here. The street, if one thinks in terms of such acts as a mugging or a demonstration, can be chaotic and overtly political, at times improvisational, and given to a set of rules independent of the home, a courtroom, or other public and private spaces. The other theater, the dramatic stage, is structured, primarily sanitized (and perhaps sacred),[13] and has its own rules of engagement. The potential sterility—sanitized, sacred—of theater is why Richard Schechner and others pushed for an "environmental theater" in the 1960s and 1970s (Schechner). This environmental theater would be a theater more spontaneous, closer to the ritual and communal origins of the practice. The street and the theater, as Schechner's approach demonstrates, have much in common and a great deal that separate them, but conceiving of them together brings focus to a unifying factor that makes them different from a novel—the body. The novel can, in fact, call the reader's attention to corporeal realities, but performance is another matter entirely, evoking visceral and immediate reactions. As is clear from the very opening of *Invisible Man,* the body can move through streets in invisible, undetected ways. The white man that the protagonist bumps into at the novel's opening does not see him. The protagonist contemplates this lack of recognition in terms of conflict. He can choose to react violently, or peacefully. That is, his body can be a factor in disorder and disruption, or it can in certain ways remain unseen. Bodies bring to life not the totality to which the novel moves, but rather the potential civic conflict that might underpin particular moments of materiality, to borrow again from Lukács's language.

Perhaps Ellison rejected theater because the presence of the body onstage—its present*ness*—was too complicated, too unwieldy, for him to control the outcome. Onstage, the body is the site of dramatic action, the focal point of the audience's attention, usually finely adorned so as to emphasize its beauty and orderliness, but also at times wracked and haggard, if that is what the role requires. The dramatic stage can call attention to the body in ways that everyday interactions do not. Everyday conflicts might be relived on stage, whereas in the novel form, such conflicts are brought to narrative order. Put otherwise, Ellison wanted *his* approaches to blackness—"what did I do to be so black and blue"—to linger in the reader's mind, not the quotidian realities of race as it was lived in segregated America of the 1950s.

It would have been hard to ignore the body during Jacoby's adaptation of *Invisible Man*. The reader of the battle royal scene in *Invisible Man* might imagine the violence and bloodshed that Ralph Ellison describes; seeing the blood spew from the boy's mouth, his guts a gallery of dysfunction and misuse, even in the make-believe setting of a play, involves other senses. Phillip Zarrilli talks about the body to which the *viewer's* attention is being called, as in the staged version of *Invisible Man,* the "latent body" (Zarrilli 656). The actor's body is a surface phenomenon, an "aesthetic body" that, under normal circumstance, does not feature physical pain, unless the role calls for that (Zarrilli 656). Under normal circumstances, the body in which blood circulates and food digests is latent because we do not pay attention to it. At times of pain or discomfort, when we bleed, digest food, or shit, the unseemly functioning of our bodies becomes more apparent:

> The normative disappearance of both surface and recessive bodies is reversed when we experience pain or dysfunction. In pain, sensory intensification in the body demands direct thematization. Pain is an affective call which has the "quality of compulsion," i.e., the pain seizes and constricts our attention. I must act now to the body to relieve the discomfort. (Zarrilli 661)

The distinction between the aesthetic body and the latent body, the "surface" and "recessive," allows the black body onstage to serve a civic function. Audience members see the aesthetic body onstage (dressed, composed, and, at times, even decorous) transform into the latent body (guts, pain, and unseemly functions), and the blackness of this body does not go unnoticed. At some point, Teagle F. Bougere's black body in the role of Invisible Man is not his own, but it is rather the theoretical black body that Young describes, the "second body" that "shadows or doubles the real one" (Young 7). Audience members who perhaps do not normally come into contact with the black body might now view it, as they did with *Emperor Jones*, ostensibly suffering pain, unnecessarily in the case of *Invisible Man*, due to its dehumanization at the hands of others.

Without real parallel in the novel, the body onstage calls for a visceral reaction; it cannot be put down, as a novel can, though one might turn away. For the audience members in the theater watching Invisible Man onstage bleeding during the battle royal scene, perhaps their own latent bodies become more sensitive to what might have been the experience of blacks in America during the period with which the novel is concerned, the 1950s. The reality of Jim Crow America, where Ralph Ellison himself once sat for a job interview in a chair that was wired for electricity, bearing the discomfort and shock at how someone could be entertained by this harm to his body, is made phenomenon again, through the performance of the novel (Jackson, *Ralph Ellison* 79–80). There was apparently little connection between young Ralph Ellison's black body and that of his white interviewer, but this is only through a mistake of dehumanization, the travesty of segregation and Jim Crow.

The intensity of the performance adds to the corporeal experience. The body onstage is unmistakably wracked, not so much by the staged blows and fake blood that gushes from the actor's mouth, even if for a moment the audience is caught up in its suspension of disbelief. Rather, Bougere hurls his body into the role of Invisible Man for the 205 minutes of the play. Bougere is able to transform the intensity of performance, the discomfort to his latent body, into his embodiment of a segregated American experience of the 1950s. Theater critic Chris Jones describes the experience of viewing Teagle's performance as follows:

> It's a hugely empathetic performance from an actor who clearly understands he's playing an African-American everyman, buffeted by forces, switching endlessly from positive to negative, without regard to the care of the influencer. Bougere shows us a man who finally learns he cannot control the acts of others, even as the lesson comes with great personal pain.[14]

Invisible Man depends on Bougere to shoulder the load, as it were. There are of course other actors onstage throughout *Invisible Man*. They take on multiple roles. *Chicago Sun-Times* reviewer Hedy Weiss calls A. C. Smith's performance in his roles "blistering,"[15] and she argues that Smith calls to mind Idi Amin (or even Forest Whitaker's incantatory rendition). Smith plays the college administrator Bledsoe, whose expulsion of Invisible Man from college, along with his damning letters, hurls the protagonist in a downward spiral.

The adaptation of the novel is by no means seamless. It is not necessarily clear, for example, how Smith's role as Bledsoe connects to the less developed ones later in the performance. The inability to tie together all the loose strands is, in fact, one of many places where performance differs from the novel form. As Jacoby develops the play and brings it to the stage in Washington, DC, and elsewhere, he—or others who bring it to stage—might be able to rewrite and refocus his adaptation. (The final version of this essay was completed before many of the productions subsequent to that of Chicago's Court Theatre.) Reviewers all point to the challenge of bringing the novel to stage. As Lauren McEwen puts it, "the novel is lengthy, forcing Jacoby to skim over some parts."[16] Early critical responses to the Boston run in 2012–13 reveal that the space of theater remains a challenging one for the novel's surrealism. As reviewer Bill Marx puts it, "An adaptor has to make choices, and the approach here is to focus on the novel's most straightforward narrative strand."[17]

Whatever comes of subsequent performances, the weight of *Invisible Man* was primarily on Bougere's shoulders at Chicago's Court Theatre. An otherwise fit man, the paunch he shows from the beginning of the play, the staged version of the novel's prologue, is suggestive of the place where he has held the rigors of his role. By the end of the performance, there is no doubt where the gut comes from, both for Bougere and, possibly, for Invisible Man. The gut is the materialization of difficult experiences, evidence of the latent body. Performance allows Teagle to enact the guts of a segregated body in ways that the reader of a novel can only imagine. In Weiss's words, "you could feel the sheer weight of it all as Bougere visibly exhaled at the close of Saturday's opening night performance. He was understandably exhausted beyond all reckoning after his journey as the superhuman Everyman who is no longer invisible, at least to himself."[18]

EMBODYING THE RIOTS

While Bougere's performance calls attention to the individual black body, race is often a collective experience made real in relation to others; in no place is shared, civic pain clearer than in the riot at the end of the novel. The riot onstage is, of course, the act of an ensemble. The riot onstage represents the actual, civic theater in which groups often act—the streets. As was the case as the novel *Invisible Man* comes to a close, there is an attempt onstage to prepare the audience for what comes at the end, even if it is ultimately an unsuccessful one. That is, the scene does not fully translate to the stage because the writer and director have not given it enough motivation; the links that might seem apparent to a reader are lost in the translation to stage. From the early reviews, this is as much the case in the later performances of the play as it was in Chicago. As Marx puts it,

> Given that theater audiences are uncomfortable with abstraction, the emphasis on the book's realism is understandable: photographs of the period are projected throughout the show. But predictably, as the novel becomes increasingly surreal, especially during the climactic race riot, the adaptation loses considerable steam and impact. The conflagration flies by on stage in an incomprehensible few minutes (if you haven't read the book, I am not sure you will know what is happening) leading to an abrupt and somewhat confused dramatic wrap-up.[19]

Marx concurs that some aspects of the staging are successful. Throughout the performance, as Marx describes, McElroen uses old photographs, some harkening to the daguerreotypes of the mid-1800s, to contextualize the individual experience of the protagonist within a familial, collective frame. The photographic panels provide an architectural structure for such scenes as the eviction of a family in Harlem, which shapes the context for the riot that comes later. In the novel, Invisible Man stumbles upon this family as he walks through the streets of Harlem. Items from their lives and their family history are sprawled across the street, as police officers enforce their eviction: slave papers, old photographs, family letters, and so on. The protagonist does not know the family personally, but he acts on their behalf by uttering an impromptu speech that draws the attention of members of the Brotherhood. The incident moves the novel to its final third, the protagonist's experiences in Harlem, which culminates in the riot with which this third ends (although the novel itself closes with an epilogue). The Brotherhood, the quasi-Communist organization that pretends to transcend race in favor of universal humanity, is shown to be itself a sham. In the staged version, the framework of the photographs helps to draw attention to the communal aspect of the family's experience, the idea that these people are not alone in their suffering but are part of a group, members of which have similar experiences daily—a shared drama.

Some further background is necessary to establish the riot's significance to the novel. In some ways, as Marx asserts, McElroen fails to convey the importance of the events that lead to the riots in the novel, which include the Brotherhood's abandonment of "the Harlem district." When the Brotherhood counts Harlem a strategic loss and leaves the area, despondency sets in for many of the local leaders left in the wake. Having seen the death of a significant black member of the Brotherhood, Tod Clifton, Invisible Man thinks the riot is for Tod. Here again, actual riots—the Harlem riots of the first half of the twentieth century, the London riots of 2011—help to convey what is at stake in Ellison's novel. Similar to Mark Duggan in the riots throughout the United Kingdom in 2011, Tod ("Death") Clifton is a type of catalyst, a symbol that will be repeated in other personages. Some time prior to the riot, Invisible Man spots Tod downtown, near Bryant Park (Forty-Second Street), selling Sambo dolls, when the protagonist himself leaves Harlem to purchase shoes downtown (retail therapy, as it were, to compensate for the chaos he sees in Harlem, which results from the Brotherhood's departure). As Tod is selling merchandise without a license, a police officer comes to chase him away, and he kills Tod. As with so many incidents involving bodies on city streets, both in the United States and internationally, the killing is ultimately inexplicable, and yet painfully familiar: an armed officer shooting an unarmed citizen, the State reaches into—or beyond?—its proscribed role in policing bodies that we once thought were our own, and lives are lost or traumatically disrupted. Was Mark Duggan armed? Was Tod Clifton a lawbreaker or an upstanding citizen? Whatever the answers, the person provides the catalyst for the events that ensue.

Some bit of Ellison's sublime prose is worth lingering on; it is a scene that would have to be staged in slow motion, given its complex movement, and so it was:

> They were coming my way, passing a newsstand, and I saw the rails in the asphalt and a fire plug at the curb and the flying birds, and thought, You'll have to follow and pay his fine . . . just as the cop pushed him, jolting him *forward* and Clifton trying to keep the box [with the Sambo dolls] from swinging against his leg and saying something over his shoulder and going *forward* as one of the pigeons swung down into the street and up again, leaving a feather floating white in the dazzling backlight of the sun, and I could see the cop push Clifton again, stepping solidly *forward* in his black shirt, his arm shooting out stiffly, sending him in a head-snapping *forward* stumble

until he caught himself, saying something over his shoulder again, the two moving in a kind of march that I'd seen many times, but never with anyone like Clifton. (IM 329; emphasis added)

While this is not the place for extended prose analysis, the passage in *Invisible Man* is truly remarkable. Ellison conveys the urgency in so many ways that the scene feels surreal. The sentence marches "forward" with little punctuation, no break, as the officer pushes repeatedly, moving "forward," in "a kind of march" that the narrator is not alone in having "seen many times" before. (The word *forward* is repeated four times just in the cited passage.) The scene feels surreal, like someone else's, but it is not. No one would expect "anyone like Clifton," a clean-cut, upright, and beautiful black man, to succumb to such an experience. And yet, there it is, time and again. Lives are lost or traumatically disrupted.

To return momentarily to distinctions previously made about the novel form, particularly its difference from epic poetry, it would not be inconsistent to describe this scene in *Invisible Man* as epic. The scene is trapped, momentarily, in the "sheer brutal materiality" of the murder (Lukács 58), although Ellison seems to want to race "forward," outside of the moment. Part of the scene's epic "heaviness" is in its similes. As has been noted, Sandra Adell presents part of Ellison's power as his ability to capture various subject-perspectives, and this passage is no exception. Clifton is gone, but the cop must now deal with the trauma of his hasty act, the learned and unconscious responses: "I looked back to Clifton, the cop was waving me away with his gun, sounding *like a boy* with a changing voice" (IM 330; emphasis added). The cop, the "boy," has taken a life and must deal with the consequences, and here Ellison rises to the level of a Homeric simile not unlike that deployed when Patroclus enters battle on behalf of Achilles in the *Iliad*: "Meanwhile the armed band that was about Patroclus marched on till they sprang high in hope upon the Trojans. They came swarming out *like wasps* whose nests are by the roadside, and *whom silly children love to tease,* whereon anyone who happens to be passing may get stung" (passage from Homer, *Iliad* 16, Samuel Butler translation; emphasis added).[20] Just as war is—painfully—child's play in Homeric epic, the violence of the street involves players who are no more than children at the proverbial end of the day. But the genre of the novel does not stop here. It moves forward, from brutality to dissolution, pain to resolution, epic to the formal attributes of the novel.

The riot in *Invisible Man* is representative of actual civil disturbances in Harlem during the twentieth century; namely, the Harlem riots of 1935 and

1943. Ellison recorded firsthand versions of the former for the Federal Writers' Project. As is the case of the historical riots, Ellison's fictive representation of *riot* presents a kind of autopsy of civil unrest itself, but what is more, he is interested in the symbolic value given to individual lives during disruptive events. Always walking a tightrope between sociology and psychology, the group and the individual, society and its fictions, Ellison understood the anatomy of civil unrest, where bodies momentarily disrupt the prescribed norms. A perceived injustice done to a member of the local community ignites each of the Harlem riots. Here again is Mark Duggan, and even Tod Clifton. In his reflections on the riots, Ellison would have had his own account and that of leading social scientists and philosophers. Alain Locke describes the touchstone event of the 1935 riot in his article "Harlem: Dark Weather-Vane":

> Its immediate causes were trivial,—the theft of a ten-cent pocketknife by a Negro lad of sixteen in Kresge's department store on 125 Street. It was rumored that the boy had been beaten in the basement by store detectives and was gravely injured or dead; by tragic coincidence an ambulance called to treat one of the Kresge employees, whose hand the boy had bitten, seemed to confirm the rumor and a hearse left temporarily outside its garage in an alley at rear of the store to corroborate this. As a matter of fact the boy had given back the stolen knife and had been released through the basement door. But it must be remembered that this store, though the bulk of its trade was with Negroes, has always discriminated against Negroes in employment.[21]

The triviality of the cause of the 1935 riot is echoed in 1943, when a police officer shot a black US Army soldier who tried to help a woman arrested for disturbing the peace at Braddock Hotel (Knopf). The man was shot in the shoulder, but rumor spread through the street that he had been killed. Here again, as was the case with Mark Duggan in 2011, rumor overshadows the facts of the event. A black boy, a black soldier, Tod Clifton: Tod, "death," born to die, but still not trivial or meaningless.

In *Invisible Man*, the cause of the riot is as potentially meaningless and trivial as its historical counterparts. The hero, however, ever in search of meaning, constructs a higher cause: "Clifton, I thought. It's for Clifton. A night for Clifton" (IM 408). The protagonist credits Clifton. The touchstone, however, in the minds of many, is shockingly trivial. Invisible Man overhears the looters: "About eight o'clock down on Lenox and 123rd this paddy slapped a kid for grabbing a Baby Ruth and the kid's mama took it up and then the paddy slapped her and that's when hell broke loose" (IM 408). Versions of the story proliferate, but on all counts, the community gives value to the individual life; the life takes on ritualistic, symbolic meaning. Order and disorder follow: a funeral, civil unrest, ritualized violence.

Perhaps McElroen was not daring enough in his staging of the novel, but the significance of the riot was indeed lost in performance. There is something even more haunting, more riveting about Ellison's imagined body of Clifton and the rioters than the performance conveyed. In this case as well, *The Riots* provides a worthwhile contrast in that Slovo takes on the corporeal reality of civic spaces directly.[22] For *Invisible Man*, perhaps because the actor who plays Tod, Chris Boykin, does not move through his multiple roles as fluidly as A. C. Smith did, his presence as Tod, "our hope shot down" (IM 450), remains shadowy.[23] Jacoby and McElroen fail to connect effectively the death of Clifton to the riot that follows a number of episodes later. As *Tribune* reviewer Chris Jones puts it, "One of the key emotional moments in the piece, the death of a Harlem organizer named Tod Clifton, does not carry enough focus."[24]

Jacoby and McElroen shy away from what a riot onstage might signify. The chaos of such an experience would call for therapeutic intervention, if staged with the immediacy of what an actual riot might evoke. The London riots, staged in *The Riots*, are only the most recent example of a phenomenon for which *Invisible Man* provides a meaningful autopsy.

THE MUCK OF GENRES AND THE PERSISTENCE OF RACE

Ellison once wrote, in his essay "Change the Joke and Slip the Yoke," that between archetypes and literature "there must needs be the living human being in a specific texture of time, place and circumstances" (CERE 101). Between sociology and fiction stands the incident; *Invisible Man* resonates uncannily with the events of August 2011 in the United Kingdom. Even Ellison would have found the apocalyptic scale staggering. Prime Minister David Cameron proved to be at a total loss as to how to deal with the riots, which he called "sickening" and characterized as "criminality pure and simple."[25] Cameron was not alone in his simple-minded condemnation; a survey of comments from ministers of Parliament and Nick Clegg's coalition government affirms that few leaders in 2011 in the United Kingdom had the foresight of New

York's mayor, Fiorello La Guardia, in 1935, whose commission and report Locke discusses in his essay. The riots in 2011 certainly were sickening, but not for the reasons Cameron states in his August 9 message. They were certainly not "criminality pure and simple."

Addressing the cause and finding the means to redress such social ills as race and its link to class and poverty calls for deep reflection and thoughtful responses. Cameron was not up for the task, but he was not alone in his shortcomings. Though a work of fiction, *Invisible Man* contains some of the genius with which citizens in London in 2011 might come to terms with these circumstances. Yet, in the end, perhaps there is some relevance to Rampersad's criticism of Ellison, his sense that Ellison himself, though brilliant, sometimes hid behind fiction, and specifically the novel form, in order to avoid his own responsibility regarding the social dramas through which he lived. It is true that Ellison avoided certain theaters of racial enactment, barely speaking publically about the civil rights movement or the violence that ensued in the 1960s in its wake. But this is not to say that Ellison avoided the issue of race. Race is an American reality through which Ellison hoped to work, a brutality for which he sought resolution. He thought that the novel form was the best genre to come to terms with race because of its optimism. That is, the novel, in and of itself, moves beyond materiality toward something transcendent. As such, the novel form is a culminating American genre. The optimism reflected in it is akin to the democratic process and, specifically, the openness of the American constitution. As Ellison puts it in "Society, Morality, and the Novel,"

> One might deliberately overemphasize and say that most prose fiction in the United States—even the most banal bedroom farce or the most rarefied, stylized, and understated comedy of manners—is basically "about" the values and cost of living in a democracy (CERE 702).

At the end of *Invisible Man*, the protagonist famously "affirm[s] the principle on which the country was built and not the men, or at least not the men who did the violence" (IM 574). That is, to account for the cost of democracy, one emphasizes the values upon which that democracy was built. Such an approach might not make it all worthwhile, but for the optimism of the novel form, there is really no other way forward.

At the same time, race remains a reality.[26] Even the beauty of the aesthetic body evident in black dance is a result of toil, a bluesy attempt to make poetry out of pain (Manning). Blackness is an embodied experience that is individual and collective. Individual and group experiences can be enacted on stage in a way entirely foreign to the novel. Riots might be the most unwieldy example of a collective action that amounted to material realities that Ellison would rather have distilled to mythic significance than relived as they occurred. At the same time, there is therapeutic value in "staging" or reliving such experiences, as Slovo points out in the emphasis on the value of watching the enactment of riots as a community. Ellison recognized this, which is perhaps part of the reason he thought the novel form was the best, most controlled form of analysis.

By aligning Ellison's approach to race to what he had to say about the novel as a literary form, it becomes clear that some of the biographical objections to Ellison as a person, such as that of Rampersad, go a bit far. As is evident here, Ellison had a particular approach to the artistic form of the novel, which he, as a self-proclaimed novelist, valued above all other artistic forms. The genealogy of Ellison's approach to the novel can be traced directly (and primarily) to Lukács, who saw the novel as a culminating form in which the materiality of lived experience might be, at least momentarily, worked out. The novel was the "jug" in which Ellison poured the "world" of real experiences. Ellison's elevation of the novel (to a point of ill-advised purity) meant his rejection of other artistic forms, such as theater, especially as it pertained to the particularly mucky and unresolved reality of race in America. The recent stagings of *Invisible Man* reveal a number of things. In the first place, the stage versions of *Invisible Man* help to highlight their difference from the novel. Live performance reveals how visceral the experience of race in America can be, and this is true of both the past of segregation and of the reality of America in the early twenty-first century, where the phenomenon of a black president only points to an as-yet unrealized integration of American lives. In this difference between page and stage, the extent to which the reality of black bodies remains a rarity in certain corners of American life is striking. The disturbing event of a riot unveils disturbances beneath the seemingly calm surface. If there was any question as to the relevance of Ralph Ellison's *Invisible Man* in the twenty-first century, or that of his broader artistic vision, the challenging attempts to stage the novel should, for quite some time to come, serve as a resounding answer in the affirmative. During a time when riots can—seemingly inexplicably (to David Cameron)—erupt in poor and ethnic neighborhoods across London and the United Kingdom, Ellison's concerns and worldview remain urgent.

NOTES

1. On Ellison's work being among "great books," see, for example, Bloom, *How to Read and Why*. For Ellison's place in a black American literary canon, see Gates, *Figures in Black*.

2. The play's Chicago run was from January 12 through February 19. A survey of the relevant reviews appears on the "Theatre in Chicago" website at http://www.theatreinchicago.com/invisible-man/4749/ (accessed 23 December 2014), and on the Court Theatre's website, http://www.courttheatre.org/ (accessed 4 February 2014). The Studio Theatre run in Washington, DC, was in September and October 2012 and moved to Boston (through the Huntington Theatre Company and the Boston University Theatre) in December 2012 through the beginning of February 2013. This chapter focuses on the play's debut at Court Theatre in Chicago, where I attended one of the performances.

3. For a review of scholarship, see Patrice Rankine, *Ulysses in Black*, as well as the work of the writers in this volume.

4. On everyday life or "social drama" as theater and performance, see Victor Turner, *From Ritual to Theatre*.

5. See Chris Jones's January 22, 2012, review in the *Chicago Tribune*, "Invisible Man, Visibly in Pain," and Hedy Weiss's *Sun-Times* review of the same date, "Hypnotic 'Invisible Man.'"

6. For Ellison's subtle critique during Wright's lifetime, see "Richard Wright's Blues," in 1953, published in *Shadow and Act*, and upon Wright's death, "Remembering Richard Wright," published in 1986, in *Going to the Territory*. In a 1968 interview, Ellison could assert that "something is missing" in Wright's novel (CRE). The contrast extends back to the publication of *Invisible Man* in 1952. For more, see Gates, *Figures in Black*, and Rampersad, *Biography*.

7. See, most recently, Rampersad, *Biography*.

8. Ellison found such "incongruous juxtapositions" to be the norm in American society. See the essay "Going to the Territory" in the collection of the same name (120–44).

9. See Ester Addley's article in the *Guardian* from November 22, 2011.

10. My summary here is derived from Richard Adams's August 9, 2011, article in the *Guardian* and Simon Rogers's August 11, 2011, report in the *Guardian*.

11. Numbers are taken from British Broadcasting Company reports of August 15, 2011, and August 25, 2011.

12. See Turner, *From Ritual to Theatre*.

13. For theater as a sacred space, see Mamet, *Three Uses of the Knife*, and Woodruff, *Necessity of Theater*, although these are only two of many to make the claim.

14. Jones, "Invisible Man, Visibly in Pain."

15. Weiss, "Hypnotic 'Invisible Man.'"

16. *Washington Post*, August 9, 2012, available at http://www.washingtonpost.com/blogs/therootsdc/post/invisible-man-play-on-its-way-to-dc/2012/08/09/e54b29fa-db50-11e1-bd1f-8f2b57de6d94_blog.html (accessed 23 December 2014).

17. At http://artsfuse.org/75350/fuse-theater-review-seeing-the-invisible-man/ (accessed 23 December 2014).

18. Weiss, "Hypnotic 'Invisible Man.'"

19. At http://artsfuse.org/75350/fuse-theater-review-seeing-the-invisible-man (accessed 23 December 2014).

20. A copy of Homer's *Iliad* and *Odyssey* from Ellison's library are in the Library of Congress's Ellison Reading Room. One salivates at the marginalia that might be contained in them.

21. Locke's report, "Harlem: Dark Weather-Vane," is available online at http://newdeal.feri.org/survey/36457.htm.

22. Slovo apparently had some fifty-four hours of interviews on the riot, from various perspectives: police officers, rioters, bystanders, neighbors, and so on. See Dominic Cavendish's article "The Riots: Duo Who Turned a Crisis into a Drama" for the *Telegraph* on August 11, 2011.

23. It is worth noting that certain roles that might be deemed as key to the novel are not even listed along with the actors, who each play various roles. Tod Clifton, for example, is not listed as a role. Next to Boykin's role are listed "Tatlock, Sylvester, Ensemble." The choice of what constitutes a key role (and the process toward that choice) is of interest here.

24. Jones, "Invisible Man, Visibly in Pain."

25. See the August 9, 2011, video on the *Guardian* website, http://www.guardian.co.uk/politics/video/2011/aug/09/david-cameron-riots-criminality-video (accessed 23 December 2014).

26. Living with race—that is, the daily enactment of race—which is embodied, takes its toll on the latent body. See, for example, studies on health discrepancies between blacks and whites in America, some of which seem to be epiphenomena—that is, experiential rather than genetic differences—in the *Washington Post,* "Race Gap Persists in Health Care, Three Studies Say," August 18, 2005 (Stein).

THE NOISY LOSTNESS

Oppositionality and Acousmatic Subjectivity in *Invisible Man*

HERMAN BEAVERS

> Perhaps in the swift change of American society in which the meanings of one's origins are so quickly lost, one of the chief values of living with music lies in its power to give us an orientation in time. In doing so, it gives significance to all those indefinable aspects of experience which nevertheless help to make us what we are. In the swift whirl of time music is a constant, reminding us of what we were and of that toward which we aspired. Art thou troubled? Music will not only calm, it will ennoble thee.
> —RALPH ELLISON, "LIVING WITH MUSIC" (CERE 236)

I

Anxious to make a break from what they considered a past fraught with compromise, bebop musicians often resorted to negative characterizations of the career of Louis Armstrong. In his 1959 essay, "Golden Age, Time Past," Ralph Ellison observed that "they were resentful of Louis Armstrong, whom (confusing the spirit of his music with his clowning) they considered an Uncle Tom" (CERE 247).[1] This is a point echoed in "On Bird, Bird-Watching, and Jazz," where Ellison notes that

> when they fastened the epithet "Uncle Tom" upon Armstrong's music they confused artistic quality with the questions of personal conduct,

> a confusion which would ultimately reduce their music to the mere matter of race. By rejecting Armstrong they thought to rid themselves of the entertainer's role. And by way of getting rid of the role, they demanded, in the name of their racial identity, a purity of status which by definition is impossible for the performing artist. (CERE 259)

Given the fact that beboppers were expressing their disenchantment with Armstrong during the same period that Ellison was writing *Invisible Man,* it is noteworthy that his protagonist declares that Armstrong's playing indicates his ability to make "poetry out of being invisible," and marvels at his ability to bend the trumpet "into a beam of lyrical sound," comments that show that Ellison conceived Armstrong and his music as the novel's symbolic pivot and that he was distrustful of the assumptions underlying bebop musicians' motives.[2]

What interests me here is not whether we can resolve the dispute regarding the efficacy of the bebop "revolution" or if the younger generation of musicians' display of "bad manners" exemplified a newfound political consciousness. Rather, what the dispute suggests is that the history of jazz is "noisy," full of divergent perspectives that can never be reconciled. Further, the "static" that inheres between Ellison's privileging of the swing musician's role as entertainer over what he determined as the bebop generation's aspiration to become politically conscious aesthetes engaged in acts of revolutionary change is noteworthy. It invites us to remember Scott DeVeaux's observation that the "disjunction may be accounted for by the rhetoric of modernism, which by its insistence on the necessity of ongoing, radical innovation suggests that the process of growth in an artistic tradition is likely to be punctuated by many such 'revolutions'" (4).

In debunking the notion that bebop constituted a total rethinking of modernism's call to "make it new," Ellison situates himself at a critical intersection, where he can insist that the adherents of bebop were blinded by their own "myths and misconceptions" that assumed

> that theirs was the only generation of Negro musicians who listened to the classics; that to be truly free they must act exactly the opposite of what white people might believe, rightly or wrongly, a Negro to be; that the performing artist can be completely and absolutely free of the obligations of the entertainer, and that they could play jazz with dignity only by frowning and treating the audience with aggressive contempt; and that to be in control, artistically and personally, *one*

must be so cool as to quench one's own human fire. (CERE 247–488; italics mine)

Ellison contrasted this ethos with the "exuberant and outgoing lyricism of the older [musicians]," who embodied the performative heat synonymous with "hot" bands and the "hot" time that occurs when dance and music coincide; one thinks, for example, of how the Lindy Hop, with its signature swoops, spins, and lifts performed at breakneck speeds, is synonymous with swing music. But in asserting the efficacy of maintaining a quiet reserve, the younger musicians insisted that their notion of "cool" was, contrary to Ellison's interpretation, the result of finding a middle ground between extremes of emotionality and humble submission.[3] As Ted Gioia notes, one of the constitutive concepts of *cool* can be traced back to the Renaissance courtier, Baldassare Castiglione, who described *sprezzatura* as "the art of doing difficult things, but making them look easy. This state of mind merged neatly with the tenets of African American life, especially the notion that appearance and reality formed a duality that could be utilized in the service of stylistic innovation and verbal fluency."[4] Cool notwithstanding, bebop musicians tended to press their claims in defense of bebop, unwilling to concede. Dizzy Gillespie declared, "The say you have to bend; if you wanna make money you have to bend. As a very young man, I busied myself trying to create and I didn't have no time for bending at all" (230). By Ellison's lights, this kind of inflexibility meant that bebop musicians were treading on dangerous turf; the belief that their posture was a "corrective" one, meant to relocate the musician to his rightful place as artist rather than entertainer, ignored the manner in which jazz had so often assumed a stance of both/and rather than either/or. Ellison's skepticism regarding bebop's insistence on "cool" constituted the abandonment of an approach to performance that valued the exchange of information between musician and audience, the act of creating a space of equality, where musician and audience member alike *shared* in the creation of a good time.

Ellison's objections to bebop gain purchase when we shift the terms of the discussion away from revolution and toward oppositionality. As he makes clear in "Golden Age," at least a portion of the motivation for bebop musicians was the product of the "non-musical pressures affecting jazz," where "the greatest prestige and economic returns were falling outside the Negro community" (CERE 248) because of the popularity of big bands led by musicians like Benny Goodman, Artie Shaw, and Glenn Miller (and before that, Paul Whiteman) "whose popularity grew from the compositions and arrangements of Negroes," which meant the larger portion of the financial spoils went "to white instrumentalists whose only originality lay in the enterprise with which they rushed to market with some Negro musician's hard-won style" (248). By the time he had written both "Golden Age" and "On Bird, Bird-Watching, and Jazz," Ellison had imagined the machinations of Dr. Bledsoe and read Norman Mailer's "The White Negro," which means that Ellison was wary of what it would mean for an artist to locate identity at the uneasy nexus of race and profitability as the precursor to being credited as a genius.[5]

Ellison understood Armstrong's musical legacy as one whose most prominent commitment was to oppositionality, an attitude embodied by the public persona he cultivated over the course of his long career. So that even as musicians like Dizzy Gillespie could reject Armstrong's particular approach, he could nonetheless assert, "Hell, I had my own way of Tomming" (296). We begin to ascertain the importance of this ability by turning to *Room for Maneuver: Reading Oppositional Narrative,* in which Ross Chambers draws a distinction between revolution and opposition, defining the former as "a mode of resistance to forms of power it regards as illegitimate . . . as a force that needs to be opposed by a counterforce" (1). Oppositional behavior, by contrast, "consists of individual or group survival tactics that do not challenge the power in place, but make use of circumstances set up by that power for purposes that power may ignore or deny" (1). Hence, Gillespie concludes, "Every generation of blacks since slavery has had to develop its own way of Tomming, of accommodating itself to a basically unjust situation" (296).

Though Armstrong's presence in *Invisible Man* makes it possible to claim that Ellison, too, was seeking a way to imagine his novel as an oppositional narrative, I began to recognize the inherent difficulty of plotting a critical approach that could substantiate such a claim. Following on the heels of his distinction between oppositionality and revolution, I became most intrigued by Chambers's declaration that although it is clear that oppositional behavior is "ultimately conservative," it nonetheless represents an instance in which there exists "a particular potential to change states of affairs, by changing people's 'mentalities' (their ideas, attitudes, values, and feelings, which [are] ultimately manifestations of desire), a potential that is not available to 'other' forms of oppositional practice" (1). It would not be a stretch to insist that *Invisible Man* constitutes an extended rumination on the nature of oppositional narrative. Hence, my decision to use Ellison's term "the noisy lostness" as the title of this essay was not an effort to reprise Ellison's sardonic description of "bebop," but rather to link space and oppositionality. So when I assert opposition as a "noisy" practice, I do not mean to suggest that opposition is simply the equivalent of creating a racket, but rather that its deeper intent lies in the simultaneous production of uncertainty and confidence in the status quo, as if its existence turns on the belief that self-assurance and volatility are synchronous states. If oppositionality is akin to what sixties radicals referred to as "containing the contradiction," it shares some of the qualities of what Ellison terms "the true jazz moment," where the "cruel contradiction" of the music lies in the fact that "the jazzman must lose his identity even as he finds it" (CERE 267). When viewed through this description, we come to understand that Ellison's jazz musician resides in the realm of both/and, where the musical subject functions in the service of jazz's implementation of "thick description" where as soon as the proverbial house is complete, its builders set about the task of destroying it in order to build anew, as if to reject the idea of the "definitive" outright. Which is to say that jazz music is constantly being written and rewritten until it is an art form whose most salient feature is not composition, but rather, as Nathaniel Mackey proposes in *Bedouin Hornbook,* composting.[6] Indeed, DeVeaux's assessment of Armstrong's stature as a foundational figure in jazz music has more to do with Armstrong's abilities as a "compos[t]er," whose stylistic innovation was a by-product of his ability to sift through the figurative mountain of discarded musical ideas and recycle them.[7]

II

As an interdisciplinary project, sound studies has sought to problematize auditory space, ranging from interrogating noise as a creative practice to trying to distinguish the point when noise can break through the cultural barriers that separate it from music. Thus, in conjunction with information theory, which has long foregrounded noise as a necessary aspect of self-organization, sound studies has allowed us to investigate listening in ways that situate it alongside visual cultural practices like reading. Though it is clear that African American literary and cultural studies have long been aware of the ear as an interpretive instrument,[8] the conceptual link between hearing and space is a more recent development. For example, anthropologist Paul Carter's concept of "auditory space" requires us to pay heed to the distinction between hearing and listening. "Hearing," he states, "*can* be conceptualized (like looking) as a detached registration and classification of external phenomena" (43; italics in original). But Carter characterizes *listening* as "engaged hearing," and he continues:

> Its social equivalent in the visual sphere is the experience of eyes meeting and the sense that this produces of being involved in a communicational contract. Indeed, in an environment attuned to listening, the idea of *hearing* cultures might never have arisen.

So that in "hearing cultures [like the one inhabited by the Borono of Brazil], to be 'heard' socially depends upon mastering a feedback loop between listening and speaking" (43). The hero's "hibernation," then, is not only a writerly enterprise, but an auditory one, in which he seeks to understand how to create a feedback loop between the ear and the (writerly) voice. The hero's "compulsion to put invisibility down in black and white," his "urge to make music of invisibility" (IM 14), constitutes what artist Brandon LaBelle terms *auditory knowledge*. As LaBelle explains, "Auditory knowledge is a radical epistemological thrust that unfolds as a spatio-temporal event; sound opens up a field of interaction, to become a channel, a fluid, a flux of voice and urgency, play and drama, of mutuality and sharing, to ultimately carve out a micro-geography of the moment" (xvii). Thanks to the emergence of sound studies, I have been able to complicate the ontological and political aspects of noise, which leads me to observe that *Invisible Man* is a novel deeply concerned with the cultural work—as well as the cultural politics—of listening. And we come to understand the significance Ellison places upon listening by paying heed to the observations of philosopher Jean-Luc Nancy's *Listening*, in which he states:

> To be listening is always to be on the edge of meaning, or in an edgy meaning of extremity, and as if the sound were precisely nothing else than this edge, this fringe, this margin—at least the sound that is musically listened to, that is gathered and scrutinized for itself, not however as an acoustic phenomenon (or not merely as one) but as a resonant meaning, a meaning whose *sense* is supposed to be found in resonance, and only in resonance. (7; italics in original)

Nancy's comment provides an important conceptual framing of the narrator's declaration of his desire to listen to "(What Did I Do to Be So) Black and Blue" constantly, and we must conclude that by acknowledging the song's resonant meaning, his "hole" realizes Carter's notion of auditory space. Moreover, the narrator's achievement in the prologue and epilogue is that he occupies LaBelle's "micro-geography of the moment" and thus conceptualizes a culturally specific notion of the underground. Though we most often associate the "hole" in *Invisible Man* with two source texts—Dostoevsky's *Notes of the Underground* and Richard Wright's "The Man Who Lived Underground"—I submit that we can think of Ellison's underground more productively as

> a space of creaks and murmurs, a slow shifting of acoustical particles that hover on the threshold of perception, which carry the possibility of threat, danger, and inversion, suggesting that what lies underneath surreptitiously mirrors what lies above in full view. . . . The underground is a space of repressed guilt, a zone full of secrets. (LaBelle 5)

Further, LaBelle sees the underground as "a space of . . . hyperbolic sounding" where we find

> an acoustics that brings together the inherent potentiality of sound to echo, expand, and disorient while being interwoven with forces of struggle, hope, and resistance. The underground is where sound carries as physical matter, a mass of energy billowing out along long passageways and tunnels, caverns, and tombs, to pinpoint the intensities of secrets and anger, terror, and criminality. (4)

The conceptual framing of the novel's prologue and epilogue in a space underground, its indeterminate qualities notwithstanding, likewise points to the hero's quest for acoustic integrity. While the hero's "hole" might recall a tomb, Hades's underworld, or the belly of Jonah's whale, ultimately it represents a space in which, like Trueblood, he can listen to Armstrong's gravelly vocal and conclude that he is nobody but himself. Occupying the underground, the hero's speech comes to us uncensored. This is in sharp contrast to the Smoker, where he quickly discovers the act of replacing the phrase "social responsibility" with "social equality," a moment when black speech shifts away from humility to disaffection and thereby mobilizes white supremacy's regulatory machinery with its not-so-veiled threat of violence. Carter's feedback loop between listening and speaking is revealed to be a negative feedback loop in which the hero discovers that black public utterance is heavily policed, a circumstance reflected across a range of public speech acts in the novel, most notably Trueblood's narration of his dream, the eviction speech, Tod Clifton's Sambo doll spiel, and the eulogy for Clifton.

Realizing this led me to try to think practically about how I might make my way toward a new set of critical insights through which I could foreground the epistemological aspects of noise. To that end, I eschewed rereading *Invisible Man* from beginning to end, from prologue to epilogue as it were, in favor of reading the novel backward, excluding the framing aspects of the novel, from chapter 25 to chapter 1. I did so hoping, on the one hand, to defamiliarize the novel and also de-emphasize the centrality of the protagonist's pilgrimage. But I was also seeking to parse what it would mean to reverse the well-established ritual pattern in which the narrator moved from purpose to passion to perception, to isolate those moments when the protagonist moved in and out of spaces where he devoted—or failed to devote—his attention to matters involving acoustic literacy. Working backward from those moments in the novel where the hero achieves a new level of understanding, I found that those moments were often preceded by the dislocation of voice and intent or the disembodiment of the voice altogether, instances where the feedback loop between listening and speaking is either disrupted or corrupted.

In the practical sense, thinking about Ellison's novel as a "noisy" text is not difficult. The novel is rife with scenes that feature cacophonies of sound: explosions, riots, public speeches, subway rides, and steam-powered machines. But reading from chapter 25 back to chapter 1, I proceeded from such questions as the following: what creates the narrator's desire to listen to Louis Armstrong's "(What Did I Do to Be So) Black and Blue" on five radio-phonographs? What sort of auditory knowledge does Armstrong represent for the hero? And how will this knowledge serve him after he decides to reenter social relations above ground? I find LaBelle's concept of acoustic territories to be a most useful way to think through these questions. In LaBelle's thinking, acoustic territories "should not be exclusively read as places or sites, but more as itineraries, as points of departure as well as arrival." He defines them "as movements between and among differing forces, full of multiplicity" (xxv). In light of the ways that sound "creates a relational geography that is most often emotional, contentious, fluid, and which stimulates a form of knowledge that moves in *and* out of the body," the narrator's desire to overcome the "acoustic deadness" of his hole with music, "to *feel* its vibration, not only with my ear, but with my whole body" (IM 8; italics in original) suggests that his hibernation occurs in "acoustic territory." Further, remembering that LaBelle talks about auditory knowledge as a "spatio-temporal event," we come to understand what it means for the hero to conduct his "hibernation" underground. In making the transition from "ranter to writer," the narrator uses Armstrong to create a subterranean realm of both/and, a turbulent space that is, in the way of all noisy spaces, rife with both information and mystery, "a space of darkness and threat, [that] pivots to function as potential haven, sanctuary, or site for resistance, itself often tied to the reality of war" (LaBelle 27). By finally paying heed to his grandfather's observation that "our life is a war" (IM 16), the hero finds a refuge in sound.

But such a conclusion requires that we engage the question of what it means for the hero to listen to five records at once. As I have written elsewhere (in *Ralph Ellison and the Raft of Hope,* which celebrates the fiftieth anniversary of *Invisible Man*):

> If the records were played simultaneously, it would mimic the effects of a chorus. However, because we are talking about machines that have the potential to malfunction, the slightest drop in speed on the turntable would mean ... that the "system" would eventually become a cacophony. With "What Did I Do to Be So Black and Blue" playing at different speeds, its lyrics—which constitute the narrator's ability to engage in a perpetual act of signifying—would no longer be discernible. It would become, in other words, white noise. (Beavers 209)

Though I remember being very pleased with myself for reaching this conclusion, I must now admit, sadly, that I was wrong. A portion of my error lay in the fact that I interpreted the narrator far too literally, while the other portion was that I had not considered the effect of playing the records on people living in the building; the impact of playing five radio-phonographs has the potential to become the proverbial thorn in the sides of the building's inhabitants. Even if the record players are playing at different speeds, the effect, before the sound degrades into indecipherable noise, is that there would be an echo effect, where Armstrong's voice would achieve a kind of verbal stuttering that would intensify the signifying power of "(What Did I Do to Be So) Black and Blue" exponentially.

Hence, if the narrator is living in a "building strictly rented to whites, in a section of the basement that was shut off and forgotten during the nineteenth century" (6) in what he terms "a border area" to Harlem, then the impact of playing five radio-phonographs is that what had been an exclusively "white" space is now a white space with a difference. The negative feedback loop created by the social policy of racial exclusion remains intact, but the narrator's auditory posture of playing the record over and over, on multiple record players, means that the feedback loop between listening and speaking achieved when whites believe they are talking among themselves, a condition that assumes the exclusion of the black body as a constant, is now infiltrated by a black and disembodied voice.

If, as William Paulsen suggests, no message sent from one channel to another arrives free of distortion, then those instances when social discourse involves transactions across discursive boundaries are especially fraught with "static" that compromises the signal's integrity.[9] The history of US race relations is fraught with exchanges "distorted" by the static produced by race ritual. And just as there have been members of the majority for whom race-baiting and antagonistic rhetoric is the order of the day, there have been black leaders who understood the need to mollify white supremacy, a reflection of the exigency created during the nadir that straddles the end of the nineteenth century and the beginning of the twentieth century. But we might also consider what it means to build a social persona around the desire to be *the* conduit through which black/white exchange is conducted. Booker T. Washington personifies this mode of leadership, as demonstrated by the literary tactics he employs to describe the impact of his Atlanta Exposition speech in 1898. The chapter in *Up from Slavery* that chronicles the moment is titled "The Secret of Success in Public Speaking," where Washington opens with the following declaration: "As to how my address at Atlanta was received by the audience in the Exposition building, I think I prefer to let Mr. James Creelman, the noted war correspondent, tell. Mr. Creelman was present, and telegraphed the following account to the New York *World*" (Washington 168). Several aspects of Washington's social agenda are accomplished here: he avoids blatant self-congratulation while authenticating his narrative via an exterior source; but in a manner that distinguishes him from his predecessor, Frederick Douglass, he incorporates Creelman's account into his tale, but not in the form of a testimonial. In this instance, Creelman, the "noted war correspondent," portrays Washington's address as "a new epoch of the South," marking the occurrence as "the first time that a Negro has made a speech in the South on any important occasion before an audience composed of white men and women." Although Creelman has adopted the rhetorical posture of a witness to a historical event, Washington opts to utilize it because he seeks to demonstrate the address as *newsworthy*, which in Washington's view is infinitely more valuable than simply making history.

However, this move is not without its complications, as Creelman's description of Washington's delivery imputes:

> There was a remarkable figure; tall, bony, straight as a Sioux chief, high forehead, straight nose, heavy jaws, and strong determined mouth, with big white teeth, piercing eyes, and a commanding manner. The sinews stood out on his bronzed neck, and his muscular right arm swung high in the air, with a lead-pencil planted squarely in the clenched brown fist. His big feet were planted squarely, with the heels together and the toes turned out. (Washington 169)

The account is hyperbolic, its reliance on racist stereotypes undeniable. Without question, Creelman was working from the sources embedded in a cultural imaginary in which the everyday experiences of his readership would lead them to decipher the black male body as a distorted grotesque.[10] Washington's "heavy jaws . . . big white teeth, piercing eyes," along with his "big feet" with "the toes turned out," evoke the black male body as excessive, a small step beyond bestial. Though Washington's manner is described as "commanding," Creelman's use of the adjective signals the extent to which the rules governing Southern race relations have been temporarily suspended so that Washington's speech can be lauded as a landmark event.

And finally, Creelman's description of Washington's address incorporates an unintended effect when he notes, "Within ten minutes the multitude was in an uproar of enthusiasm—handkerchiefs were waved, canes were flourished, hats were tossed in the air. *The fairest women of Georgia stood up and cheered. It was as if the orator had bewitched them*" (170; italics mine). It takes a moment to realize that Creelman is describing white women who, in the presence of husbands and sweethearts, are standing up and cheering for a black man giving a speech, captured in a breach of public decorum. Washington's voice is cast as mystical, but this moment anticipates the manner in which the black body is overdetermined in the public sphere as being both performative and erotic. One explanation could be that Washington's address constitutes an instance where the carnivalesque trumps the social conventions of Jim Crow. But we could just as easily understand Creelman's journalistic account as "noisy" in the sense that the account depicts a black body that achieves a measure of social instability: at one moment grotesque, at another erotic, at yet another mystical.[11] At the same time, though, Washington's decision to include Creelman's account serves to ratify his investment in a politics of accommodation. The feedback loop between listening and hearing is one that portrays white social dominance as being sufficiently unstable so that a tactical approach to public discourse can yield positive results.

This moment bears a distinct relation to Ellison's novel because the hero imagines his role as leader of his race within the space of public addresses, which occur at various intervals in the novel, with the stakes for each address increasing in each instance. In chapter 17, as the hero is learning the Brotherhood's ideological positions, he concludes that his training has been "mainly a time for listening" (358). Jack's encouragement is telling: "The ideal is to strike a medium between ideology and inspiration. Say *what the people want to hear, but say it in a way that they'll do what we wish*" (358; italics mine). Interestingly, the narrator notes that Jack looks at him "as though he did not see me." What comes through here is that whenever the hero tries to assert himself through his cultural identity, there are institutional forces that seek to rein him in. Hence, in chapter 16, when the hero delivers the speech, several key features emerge. First, the speech takes shape because of the call and response between the narrator and a member of the audience he cannot see. When he establishes this contact, the narrator feels as if the "voice was that of them all." Unable to remember "the correct words and phrases from the pamphlets," the narrator returns to familiar rhetorical territory: "I had to fall back upon tradition and since it was a political meeting, I selected one of the political techniques that I'd heard so often at home: the old down-to-earth, I'm-sick-and-tired-of-the-way-they've-been-treating-us approach. I couldn't see them so I addressed the microphone and the cooperative voice before me" (342). When the speech ends, the response from the audience is deafening applause, but the speech is critiqued by the Brotherhood leadership, who characterize it as "a most unsatisfactory beginning," "irresponsible and dangerous," and finally, "incorrect." Though Jack tries to defend the speech, the others determine the speech is "the antithesis of the scientific approach" (348–51). As they see it, the main problem is that "the audience isn't thinking, it's yelling its head off." Because they associate the mob with noise, the Brotherhood's strategy is to dominate it with scientific rhetoric. The Brotherhood speech is successful because it draws on the narrator's knowledge of the sermonic tradition, but his approach is denigrated as being "un-scientific," a catalyst for noise; in essence, the narrator is chastised for speaking in a manner that might be deemed "too colored."

Taking the Brotherhood leadership's critique of his first speech at face value, as a credible source of guidance, the narrator's voice becomes the instrument of his blindness. However, moving backward through the novel, we come to understand, first, that the narrator's inability to see the audience is suggestive of the well-lit hole he will occupy in the prologue and epilogue and it anticipates the "irresponsible" voice he will become upon taking up residence there. Second, the techniques he utilizes to structure the speech are techniques that precede him; antiphony is a performative tactic that can be traced back to West Africa, which means that it is impossible for him to claim ownership of the technique; he is engaged in an act of "composting." Finally, as we read toward the beginning of the novel, we see at least two more iterations of sermonic discourse. In chapter 5, the narrator draws a contrast between the white Southerners who revel in intimidating the student body "with innocent words as they described to us the limitations of our lives" (112) and the sermon directed at Miss Susie Gresham. The fact that the sermon comes to us in italics denotes it to be free, indirect discourse. But reading the passage leading to the sermon, we find that the narrator has imagined the sermon as the echo of his own voice directed "at the highest beams and farthest rafters, ringing them ... and echoing back with a tinkling, like words hurled to the trees of a wilderness" (112–13). And in the prologue, of course, there is the sermon "The Blackness of Blackness," which the narrator discovers while moving down through the depths of Armstrong's recording. In each of these instances, the source of the sermon is difficult to discern (the narrator is only able to reference "The Blackness of Blackness" while under the influence).

But this points to an important trope that runs through the novel: acousmatic sound. Brandon LaBelle describes the acousmatic as "sound heard whose origin we do not see." In essence, the audience listening to the narrator is hearing a sound whose origin it cannot discern, but the fact that the speech is delivered through a microphone points to what LaBelle suggests is a deeper resonance when he claims, "The acousmatic forms the beginning of electroacoustic composition allowing a sound to be removed from its contextual and indexical source to acquire other meaning." Acousmatic sound, according to LaBelle, "is split from its visual source and brought into an auditory field to participate in the making of a more concentrated listening experience" (14). He concludes: "The 'acousmatic' carries forward the tracings of a voice that leaves behind the material world, to appear as if from the shadows. From this perspective, the underground echo is an acousmatic sound; it makes every sound a voice that breaks from its source to become something greater, more powerful and suggestive, a sound no longer bound to earth" (15). The problem for a protagonist striving to achieve visibility through public displays of oratorical skill is that he seeks to register the response to his voice on a visual grid, assuming that seeing where he is "aiming" the message will ensure that it makes its way through the channels of cultural exchange free of distortion. But as he intimates in the prologue, this produces an unwanted result: "Like the bodiless heads you see sometimes in circus sideshows, it is as though I have been surrounded by mirrors of hard, distorting glass," which for my purposes is meant to echo the forces distorting Washington's body. What he finally recognizes is that his body disappears behind the "noise" that is always already synonymous with a black body entrapped within the white cultural imaginary. So that when he states, "When they approach me they see only my surroundings, themselves, or figments of their imagination—indeed, everything and anything except me," he speaks from the awareness that the black body is analagous to a "noise" polluting the public sphere's visual field.

At numerous points in *Invisible Man*, the hero's dilemma is foreshadowed by his decision to privilege information he acquires from the visual sphere, despite the fact that visuality is compromised. Hence, before he is to give his speech at the Smoker, the hero is blindfolded in preparation for the battle royal. Before discovering that Dr. Bledsoe's letters have nullified any opportunity for the protagonist to find employment that will facilitate his return to the college, he must penetrate the illusion of Bledsoe's enthusiastic support of his efforts. But opening the envelope, he finds that Bledsoe's disembodied voice articulates the note from his dream that states, "To Whom it May Concern: Keep This Nigger-Boy Running." Upon the protagonist's arrival at the Brotherhood office in Harlem, there is also the visual information of the note containing the warning, "Do not go too fast." And we might also include here Tod Clifton's Sambo doll, which constitutes visual information meant to articulate Clifton's realization that his service to the Brotherhood is nothing more than racial ventriloquism.

What Ellison suggests over the course of the novel is that the acousmatic figures prominently with his narrator's enactments of oppositionality. According to Ross Chambers, "no oppositional behavior can be *fully* acknowledged, in any society, under pain of being perceived as resistance" (8–9). More to the point, he insists invisibility "is a rule of the oppositional; its *modus operandi* is disguise." And he goes on to state:

> So invisible may the oppositional be that its practitioners themselves are frequently unaware of it. . . . Opposition is most generally an involuntary and unexamined response to structures that, although alienating, are not themselves perceived in "loose" societies to be nor-

mal. For that reason, the general category of oppositional practices itself tends to go unrecognized; and people are surprised when it is pointed out to them how much of their own and other peoples' daily behavior consists of the creative adaption of dominating systems to uses for which they were not intended. (8–9)

It is here that we see the prescience in Ellison's use of Armstrong as the novel's symbolic pivot; the hero concludes that he likes Armstrong "because he's unaware that he *is* invisible" (8). The narrator stumbles into oppositionality when he slips Brother Tarp's chain link over his knuckles, prompting the old man to state, "Now there's a way I never thought of using it" (389). The narrator is in the midst of oppositionality when he encounters the three boys wearing zoot suits and wonders, "What if history was not a reasonable citizen, but a madman full of paranoid guile and these boys his agents, his big surprise? His own revenge?" (441). The narrator's recognition of the boys' embodiment of oppositionality becomes clear when he states: "For they were outside, in the dark with Sambo, the dancing paper doll . . . running and dodging the forces of history instead of making a dominating stand" (441).

When Ellison's narrator/hero comes to consciously occupy a posture of oppositionality, he arrives at the epiphany that his grandfather's deathbed advice to "live with his head in the lion's mouth" is also an effort to "affirm the principle," and thereby adopt an oppositional consciousness, not a revolutionary one. Despite all that has happened to him, he does not call for the system to be abandoned, a position he can embrace because he abandons his pretensions to leadership. By ceding the pretense of control, the narrator can accept himself as "one of the most irresponsible beings that ever lived," and thus constitute a revision of Lucius Brockway's claim that "we the machines inside the machine," for where the old man is content to function in service of making the "right white," the narrator's brightly lit hole "gives birth to [his] form," as his oppositional posture calls the very idea of form into question.

III

But there is yet another way to relate the narrator's trajectory to information theory. By accepting the invitation to speak at the Smoker, to reprise what had been his graduation speech, a moment in which he seeks to demonstrate that "humility was the secret, indeed, the very essence of progress," Ellison's hero reveals the relationship between verbal dexterity and flow. The choice of the "Atlanta Compromise Speech" reflects his belief that Washington's achievement as an orator turns on mastering the ability to maintain a steady flow of social discourse between blacks and whites. Hoping to satisfy his aspiration to be a leader of his people, the narrator conflates opportunity and audience. As information theory might conceive it, his aspiration is to be the next among his people to be able to speak to whites in a manner that is free of distortion. In seeking to generate "flow," the hero seeks to eliminate the static, the informational drag, which garbles a message traveling from one channel to another. Ellison underscores this by depicting the inherent difficulties that accompany a circumstance featuring a black speaker and white listeners. "I spoke automatically and with such fervor that I did not realize that the men were still talking and laughing until my dry mouth, filling up with blood from the cut, almost strangled me" (30). The actual performance of the speech, which seems "a hundred times as long as before," is shaped by the narrator's belief that he "could not leave out a single word," and that "all had to be said, each memorized nuance considered, rendered" (30). In a moment where Ellison communicates the severity of the moment by creating a comic gloss, his narrator must contend with an audience accustomed to hearing black voices circumscribed by social decorum and thus he states, "Whenever I uttered a word of three or more syllables a group of voices would yell for me to repeat it" (30). When he reaches the words "social responsibility," the coherence of the speech begins to break down:

> "What's that word you say, boy?"
> "Social responsibility," I said.
> "What?"
> "Social . . ."
> "Louder."
> ". . . responsibility."
> "More!"
> "Respon—"
> "Repeat!"
> "—sibility." (30–31)

The disruption of the speech's rhythms creates a drastically different effect. Where the narrator will, at later moments, discover the power of call and response, in which audience and speaker collaborate to produce meaning, here racial hierarchy asserts itself as a form of blockage that prevents the speech from achieving flow. Mihaly Csikszentmihalyi's book, *Flow: The Psychology of Optimal Experience*, describes *flow* as "optimal experience," an instance when the subject feels at one with the universe. The optimal experience that was the graduation speech vanishes in a wave of distortion, the "flow" is nullified and the narrator finds himself in peril.

Although the briefcase presented to the narrator after the speech should be a token of his value, it symbolizes the instance when the narrator was devalued, and also suggests the constant pressure exerted on blacks living under Jim Crow. As Csikszentmihalyi states, "One of the major functions of every culture has been to shield its members from chaos, to reassure them of their importance and ultimate success" (11). Such thinking, Csikszentmihalyi insists, is integral to the individual's belief that his or her actions constitute "the fast track to the future" (11). However, the briefcase serves as a reminder that the feedback loop formed between blacks and whites engaged in acts of listening and speaking is purely regulatory. What complicates this circumstance is the narrator's assumption that verbal information and visual information remain synchronous as they travel across racial lines, an assumption that should have been eclipsed when the white men at the Smoker refer to the hero and the other black boys in the boxing ring as "little shines." No matter how well the narrator speaks, as a "credit to his race," he will never be a light—only a "shine," which, after all, only occurs when light is reflected. Csikszentmihalyi is quick to advise against an "unrealistic trust in the shields, in the cultural myths, [which] can lead to equally extreme disillusion when they fail" (11) and thus he effectively summarizes the central predicament of *Invisible Man*, a novel in which the nameless protagonist, time and again, must suffer the consequences of his "unrealistic trust" in faulty systems of belief. He quickly comes to realize that his is a life largely characterized by the illusion of protection; he finds that he is trapped in a negative feedback loop that consists of raised expectations that create a false sense of security that inevitably lead to a rude awakening (11), requiring him to restore his optimism and start anew.

Among the many reasons that we find Ellison's novel so compelling, one of the most important is that the protagonist stumbles onto (or perhaps more rightly, *tumbles into*) a way to break the cycle of disillusionment in order to embrace wholeheartedly the security to be found in chaos. It could be said that the hero moves from a sensibility that emphasizes strategic thinking to one that values tactical thinking. Though it would seem on its face that the boundary we use to distinguish strategy from tactics is a permeable one, in fact, as Michel de Certeau takes care to remind us in *The Practice of Everyday Life*, there is a crucial distinction to be made. He notes that a strategy is the calculation (or manipulation) of power relationships that becomes possible as soon as a subject with will and power (a business, an army, a city, a scientific institution) can be isolated. It postulates a *place* that can be delimited as its *own* and serve as a base from which relations with an *exteriority* composed of targets or threats (customers or competitors, enemies, the country surrounding the city, objectives, and objects of research) can be managed. (Kindle edition loc. 130 of 3288; italics in original)

Where Ellison's protagonist runs afoul, of course, is in his mistaken belief that the power relationships he covets will incorporate his interests into their overall agenda if he accedes to their organizing logics. Believing that his destiny lies in creating a viable affiliation with the avenues of mainstream power, as he believes Booker T. Washington has done before him, the protagonist dismisses all those instances when he sees the tactical sensibility either hold at bay or defeat outright strategic forms of power. As de Certeau argues, strategic power is built on three essential assumptions regarding what he calls "the proper" and "place": (a) The proper is a triumph of place over time; (b) is also constituted through a mastery of places through sight and (c) its ability to transform the uncertainties of history into readable spaces. So, for example, Dr. Bledsoe's authority, what he describes as a "power set-up," rests on his ability to both control and contour the illusion that is the college, to create an instance where "[h]e show[s] them what [h]e want[s] [whites] to see." Unfortunately, in order to sustain the illusion, Bledsoe is required to internalize the rhetoric of oppositionality when he states, "I didn't make it, and I know that I can't change it." However the fact that it is at his disposal does not prevent him from aligning with the idea of force when he declares his allegiance to a corrupt system. "I've made my place in it," he declares, "and I'll have every Negro in the country hanging on tree limbs by morning if it means staying where I am" (143).

Following readerly convention and moving through the text from beginning to end leads us to emphasize Bledsoe's power at the expense of seeing the power of the acousmatic subject as it assumes the form of the statue on the college campus. The protagonist's description of the statue is worth quoting at length:

Then in my mind's eye I see the bronze statue of the college Founder, the cold Father symbol, his hands outstretched in the breathtaking gesture of lifting the veil that flutters in hard, metallic folds above the face of a kneeling slave; and I am standing puzzled, unable to decide whether the veil is really being lifted, or lowered more firmly into place; whether I am witnessing a revelation or a more efficient blinding. (36)

What we discover, reading from chapter 1 to chapter 25, is that the statue verifies Bledsoe's status as the perpetrator of an illusion that works in the service of his personal agenda. But reading the novel in reverse, we come to understand that the Founder's use of the veil is only effective if we privilege visual knowledge over auditory knowledge, which neither requires the visual to verify received information nor constitutes an instance of disempowerment for the kneeling slave—which is to insist that Ellison places the reader in the position of valuing the visual over the auditory because we are forced to rely on a narrator who, in the novel's early stages, has not yet learned the value of auditory knowledge. The "disordered history" that emerges is one in which the kneeling slave becomes a symbol for the acousmatic subject. Despite the presence of the "veil," the acousmatic subject would understand the value of assuming a listening posture in the proximity of enactments of power. This is by no means to suggest a *passive* response to power, but rather to insist on an understanding of power that is mindful of the ways the "weak" can use the power imbalance to their advantage.[12]

In light of this, we might think of Ellison's hero as the embodiment of the parasite, who, as Dagmar Buchwald points out, "does not transcend the dichotomy of structure and anti-structure," but instead "sits on the relation between two points of a system."[13] From this location, they "never fight directly or up front: they intervene, interfere, intercept" (76). Using his grandfather's advice as a blueprint, Ellison's acousmatic subject adopts a tactical posture that he associates in the prologue with being "irresponsible." Here, it is useful to remember Michel de Certeau's definition of a *tactic* as "a calculated action determined by the absence of a proper locus." According to de Certeau, the tactical is a posture assumed by the downtrodden and oppressed because no "delimitation of an exteriority . . . provides it with the condition necessary for autonomy. The space of a tactic is the space of the other" (Kindle edition loc. 704 of 3288). By abdicating on the desire to be the definitive source of or location for safety, the acousmatic subject is characterized by her or his tactical use of auditory knowledge. Although the narrator's use of the term *invisibility* is meant to suggest that much of what takes place in the novel is a struggle over how to interpret events in a visual register, I would urge us to think about the ways that invisibility privileges the ear over the eye.

By novel's end, the hero's enlightened posture rests on his realization—and thus the grandfather's realization before him—that being a "spy in the enemy's country" is grounded in tactical enactments of knowledge. Though one could certainly imagine espionage as a purely visual practice, it is equally reliant on listening because it seeks to uncover the enemy's secrets, which can occur in the acoustic territory of national imperative. If the narrator's desire in chapter 1 of *Invisible Man* is to achieve the kind of persuasive rhetoric that can contest the physical presence of institutions like the college (and recall Mr. Norton's comment that he is proud of the assistance he rendered in the realization of the Founder's "vision") or Liberty Paints, or the scientific rationality of the Brotherhood with its distrust of call and response, then he must utilize the acoustic territory of his "hole" to embody a consciousness that assumes a radically different posture toward his adversaries. Whereas Bledsoe's identity rests on "staying where [he is]," because he believes that "after you win the game, you take the prize and you keep it, protect it" (143), Ellison's acousmatic subject, having discovered the value of tactical behavior, understands that whatever he wins, he will not keep, and that he must constantly manipulate events in order to turn them into opportunities (Certeau, Kindle edition loc. 708 of 3822). The narrator declares as much when he states, "It's winner take nothing that is the great truth of our country or any country. Life is to be lived, not controlled" (IM 577), and it suggests that Ellison's acousmatic subject rejects the regulatory in favor of an improvisatory posture that eschews the desire for a definitive version of the text.

Remembering that the hero is living rent free and that he powers the 1,369 lights in his hole by tapping a power line from Monopolated Light and Power, we come to understand the parasitic relationship he has fashioned toward institutional knowledge. Circling back to where this essay began, to Ellison's disenchantment with bebop musicians, it occurs to me that part of his objection lay in the fact that he felt, by posturing as revolutionaries, bebop musicians were asserting their music as counterforce to racism's force. Their disapproval for Armstrong, he proposed, ultimately resulted from a conscious disconnect between the eye and the ear, where, as Albert Murray insists, what they believed they were *seeing* was an Uncle Tom, even as they were borrowing heavily from what they were *hearing* from his trumpet (Murray 71). As Albert Murray puts it in *The Blue Devils of Nada*:

> As for his response to caricatures of himself in the media (mostly early on) and misguided attacks by the ever sensitive brotherhood of proper black behavior in front of white folks, what must not be

forgotten is the fact that along with his incredible orientation to elegance and soaring magnificence, Louis Armstrong was also endowed with an irrepressible sense of humor and merriment, not to mention an acute awareness and profound appreciation of the ridiculous, the absurd, and the downright outrageous. (70)

And Murray reminds us that for all his enactments of public mirth, Armstrong stood firm in the face of folly. "He preferred merrymaking to conflict," Murray writes, "but could be devastating when crossed. He publicly rebuked one president of the United States over civil rights and angrily refused an invitation from another to be honored at the White House" (70). In short, Armstrong's appeal to Ellison lay in his embodiment of oppositionality; for Ellison, Armstrong's is the ultimate oppositional subjectivity whose performance of "(What Did I Do to Be So) Black and Blue" models a form of behavior that is instructive in light of Murray's observation that "when he made mistakes, he made corrections, not excuses" (71).

What I am finally proposing is that *Invisible Man* is a novel that argues for the acousmatic subject, the product of a moment when we cannot visually account for a sound's point of origin, an instance in which the narrator's "disembodied" voice, having been loosed from a cultural politics that places value on messages sent from a visually verifiable source, achieves the credibility to speak for us. Though critical orthodoxy has insisted that what transpires in chapters 1 to 25 is framed by the prologue and epilogue, reading the novel backward leads me to a different conclusion: we must look to the book's chapters to see how they frame the narrator's achievement of an acousmatic subjectivity in the underground. The narrator's disembodiment suggests that his voice can be seen as an echo, which LaBelle determines is "a sound that expands according to the acoustical dynamics of a given space, [which] can be heard as a proliferating multiplication—a splintering of the vector of sound into multiple events" (40). For Ellison's hero, the prospect of readers hearing an echo, signaling the act of the narrator speaking for them, was likewise an instance where the reflection of sound "mirrors back while also fragmenting any possibility of return" (40) to his previous life. Reading *Invisible Man* in reverse, it is indeed the case that the "end is in the beginning," not only because Ellison put such conscious thought into his novel's design, but also because, by deploying Louis Armstrong's recorded voice as the harbinger of the acousmatic moment, it is revealed that the path to the lower frequencies could only be traversed by recognizing that in matters of uncertainty, the answer must always be a very noisy *yes*.

NOTES

1. It needs to be pointed out, in all fairness, that Louis Armstrong was equally dismayed by the attitude of bebop musicians, whom he often characterized as "angry," which reflected emotional baggage Armstrong felt little obligation to shoulder. In his autobiography, *To BE, or Not . . . to BOP,* Dizzy Gillespie relates, "Louis Armstrong never played our music, but that shouldn't have kept him from feeling or understanding it. Pops thought that it was his duty to attack! The leader always attacks first; so as the leader of the old school, Pops felt that it was his duty to attack us." And he continues, "Pops really had no interest in learning any new music; he was just satisfied to do his thing" (296).

2. In his timely history of bebop, Scott DeVeaux seeks to complicate the divergent assessments of the music by pointing out that "jazz enjoyed no privileged status as high art before 1945," and he continues:

> As a music created for immediate consumption through commercial channels, it had depended directly upon audience approval. Suddenly, with bebop, the terms of the relationship seemed reversed: artists, acting on their own initiative, force radical and disorienting innovations upon a reluctant and bewildered audience, in this way guaranteeing a minority role in American culture for jazz as "avant-garde" art. (8)

Ellison's objections to the adherents of bebop music—and he was very clear in his disapproval of the talents of both Miles Davis and John Coltrane—are grounded in what DeVeaux characterizes as the *authority* of musicians like Armstrong, Duke Ellington, and Charlie Parker. In our reverence for these musicians, what we are valuing is "their ability to create artworks that embody their expressive intent, and their freedom to do so without interference from external restraints. We treat them, in short, as composers" (9).

3. Cf. Ted Gioia, *The Birth (and Death) of the Cool,* 44–56. Ellison seems, like other musical commentators of the previous generation, to associate speed and the bebop musician's approach to chord progressions with an excess of emotionality, with anger. While one could term bebop "volatile," that would suggest not a singular emotion, but rather a complex mélange of emotions, ranging across an entire spectrum of emotional weather.

4. What seems to have been superimposed onto *sprezzatura* is the African American response to what Gioia describes as "the especially tricky and dangerous conflict between inner and outer imperatives [they] constantly encountered in the New World" (51). The result, Gioia proposes, was the cultivation of a "middle ground" between brutal honesty and meek acceptance that could proceed from the realization that black life often rested on a profound paradox and thus required one to be able to hold a series of questions in a state of active suspension in one's consciousness:

> How could you speak your mind while appearing to remain quiet? How could you express deep inner emotions with honesty while apparently holding them in check? How could you assert your individuality while living in a community that demanded the utmost conformity and subservience? How could you exist outside

the scope of oppressive social rules and imperatives while also following them to the letter? (52)

As Gioia and others would have it, the behaviors that developed as a way to contain the contradictions of these questions came to be known as *the cool*.

5. Ellison relates the moment when drummer Art Blakey was asked the question of what Charlie Parker meant to Negroes and his reply, "They never heard of him" (CERE 228). Rather, Bird was "a 'white' hero," whose greatest significance "was for the educated white middle-class youth whose reactions to the inconsistencies of American life was the stance of cutting off its education, language, dress, manner, and moral standards; a revolt, apolitical in nature, which finds its most dramatic instance in the figure of the solitary white hipster" (228). He saw, rightly, that in those moments when whites looked to blacks for a way to escape the narrowness of their existence, the result was a fetishization of black life (see Mailer, "White Negro."). According to Mailer, the hipster was a white youth who looked to black culture as a way to evade the moral and institutional collapse of a mainstream society living in fear of nuclear annihilation. As a "psychopath," the hipster based his behavior on African Americans whose confrontation with a society that wished them dead led to the adoption of an attitude that emphasized physical pleasure and immediate gratification.

6. In Mackey's epistolary novel *Bedouin Hornbook*, his protagonist, who goes by the designation N, writes to his collaborator and intellectual sparring partner, the Angel of Dust, and states, "I awoke to the even more radical realization that it's not enough that a composer skillfully covers his tracks, that he can erase the echo of 'imposition' composition can't help but be haunted by." As Michael Jarrett sees it, N listens to John Coltrane and "hears in Coltrane's improvisations . . . the sound of songs composting. Or rather, he smells shit. Composters, both those who play music and those who write theory, *maneuver* their basic materials into a kind of textual heap from which other texts can grow. . . . Hence, *decomposition* is here contrary to *destruction* (Barthes 63; italics in original). Decomposers are saphrophytes; they regenerate by feeding 'off the decay of tradition'" (Jarrett 19–20). See also Mackey, *Bedouin Hornbook*, 78–79.

7. In *A Right to Sing the Blues: African Americans, Jews, and American Popular Song*, Jeff Melnick recounts a performance by Armstrong of "Ain't Misbehavin'" in which he "playfully incorporates an instantly recognizable bit of Gershwin's *Rhapsody in Blue*." While Melnick is commenting on "the porous boundaries which existed between African American and Jewish musicians," I see Armstrong's performance as an example of "composting." Cf. Melnick 56–57.

8. One thinks, for example, of the distinction Robert Stepto makes between storytellers and "storylisteners"; or, in my own work, trying to understand the aural politics informing Langston Hughes's poem "The Weary Blues." Cf. Herman Beavers, "Dead Rocks and Sleeping Men: Aurality in the Aesthetic of Langston Hughes," *Langston Hughes Review* 11, no. 1 (1992): 1–5, and also Stepto, *From behind the Veil*, whose second edition features an afterword titled "Distrust of the Reader in Afro-American Narrative."

9. What characterizes the communication between Ellison and musicians embracing bebop as the "new sound" is the fact that once their respective positions traveled from one

channel to another, they were garbled to the point where neither could make their position clear to the other. I am suggesting that Ellison's preference for swing music, and the way that he invokes it in contrast to bebop, points to a larger imperative, one in which a discussion about expressive culture substitutes for a rumination on racial conduct.

10. Certainly one of the images Southern audiences would have had was that of the blackface minstrel. The hyperbole we find in Creelman's account, then, has what must be regarded as a kind of comedic bent whose unintentionality nonetheless reveals his sense of racial superiority.

11. Located as they were on the pedestal constructed by white men to consolidate their power in the wake of Reconstruction, the image of white women standing and cheering for Washington, and Creelman's attribution of this effect to Washington's ability to call on forces beyond the realm of scientific understanding, suggests that he was figuratively deaf to Washington's tactical posture and equally blind perhaps to the kind of erotic desire identified by Ida B. Wells-Barnett.

12. As Dagmar Buchwald puts it, "In most cases the best and most radical tactic will be to refuse to engage in spectacular violence, to *withdraw* from the area of stimulation, to disappear." By recognizing the advantages of invisibility, the hero likewise opens "up the prematurely closed system of his own precarious subjectivity"; Buchwald, "'Let 'em Swoller,'" 84, 89.

13. Buchwald's argument is grounded in Michel Serres's notion of the parasite (Serres, *Le parasite* [Paris: Grasset, 1980]), which he posits as a manifestation of disorder (or noise) in a system, where, as Paulsen notes, "they place themselves in relation to order that they have not produced, and their presence brings disorder to the systems in which they appear" (37).

INVISIBLE MAN IN THE AGE OF OBAMA
Ellison on (Color) Blindness, Visibility, and the Hopes for a Postracial America

BRYAN CRABLE

In 1903, W. E. B. Du Bois famously warned that "the problem of the twentieth century is the problem of the color line" (*Souls* 23). Reflecting the imperialist dynamics—and pluralistic conception of race—common to his time, Du Bois's analysis was not limited to domestic matters, but included conflicts stretching beyond US soil: "The relation of the darker to the lighter races of men in Asia and Africa, in America and the islands of the sea" (*Souls* 23). However, by the mid-1930s, as Matthew Jacobson (and others) have argued, the complexities of turn-of-the-century racial identity had been narrowed down to a simple binary: white versus black. This powerful way of speaking and thinking about race, "racial binarism," deepened throughout the 1930s and 1940s, and conspired to make Du Bois's views seem especially prophetic.[1] This was the period of time when "race relations" grew to represent a significant field of study, and a notable public concern; indeed, by the mid- to late 1940s, the divide between white and black Americans was described by public figures and politicians as one of the nation's gravest, and most intractable, sources of conflict.[2]

By 1952, when Ralph Waldo Ellison's *Invisible Man* was published, racial binarism seemed a natural, even inevitable, framework for categorizing racial identities. Indeed, Americans reading Ellison's novel were provided daily and concrete reminders of this "racial divide," from the struggles over segregation, to the systematic (and institutionalized) efforts to deny voting rights to black Americans, to the earliest stages of the civil rights movement. Recognizing both the symbolic sources and consequences of this bitter division, Ellison crafted a politically charged narrative of one man's transformation, from childhood to self-illumination—touching, along the way, upon some of the central points of conflict shaping the relationship between white and black Americans. The complexity of his treatment of the subject, and the quality of his artistic achievement, earned him accolades (even, or especially, from white critics) and the National Book Award for 1952 (Rampersad 168–70). As the essays comprising this volume clearly attest, critical appreciation of and praise for the work has only increased in the decades since its publication. Here I would echo Ross Posnock's assessment from the celebration of *Invisible Man*'s fiftieth anniversary: "Of all American writers, Ellison most forcefully took up the challenge of thinking beyond the imprisoning reductiveness of race and of liberating the cosmopolitan energies of democracy" (1).

Yet, although Ellison might have been able to envision, in 1952, an America unmarked by the discourse of racial binarism, the same was not always true of his fellow citizens. As a result, decades elapsed without any significant transformation of this deep and enduring social division. For many commentators, such as John Hope Franklin, Du Bois's words thus appeared as relevant and incisive at the dawn of the twenty-first century as when they were first penned: "I venture to state categorically that the problem of the twenty-first century will be the problem of the color line. This conclusion arises from the fact that by any standard of measurement or evaluation the problem has not been solved in the twentieth century, and this becomes a part of the legacy and burden of the next century" (Franklin 5).

A decade after Franklin's pronouncements, some saw the nation poised to prove him wrong; a relative political newcomer was hailed as a sign that the new century would ease the divide between black and white that has characterized so much of American life. When a little-known state senator from Illinois, Barack Obama, rose to address the 2004 Democratic National Convention, few in the television audience were prepared for the powerful message he had for the Democratic Party, and for audiences across the country:

E pluribus unum: "Out of many, one."

Now even as we speak, there are those who are preparing to divide us—the spin masters, the negative ad peddlers who embrace the politics of "anything goes." Well, I say to them tonight, there is not a liberal America and a conservative America—there is the United States of America. There is not a Black America and a White America and Latino America and Asian America—there's the United States of America. (Obama, "Keynote Address" par. 31–32)

This speech catapulted Obama, the son of a black Kenyan and white Kansan, into the national spotlight and, subsequently, into the 2008 presidential campaign.[3] Given his inclusive rhetoric and biographical blending of white, black, and immigrant, the early success of his candidacy raised hopes that the "problem of the color line" was one that could be, and perhaps would be, finally solved. As commentator Juan Williams observed in late 2007, "If black and white voters alike react to Mr. Obama's values, then he will really have taken the nation into post-racial politics" ("Obama's Color Line"). The *New York Times* similarly announced, in their lead story on the 2008 election, "Barack Hussein Obama was elected the 44th president of the United States on Tuesday, sweeping away the last racial barrier in American politics with ease as the country chose him as its first black chief executive" (Nagourney). Or, in the words of a Georgia woman quoted by CNN, because of Obama's victory "we're now a United States of America, not a black America or a white America" ("Inaguration").

Such optimistic pronouncements of a "post-racial America" made in the wake of the 2008 election soon gave way to new, and decidedly less rosy, assessments of the impact of Obama's win. Within a few days, news outlets were reporting hundreds of troubling incidents apparently spawned by Obama's victory, ranging from racist graffiti and online threats to vandalism, cross burnings, and assaults (e.g., Jonsson, "After Obama's Win"). Other stories reported a dramatic rise in national gun and ammunition sales in the wake of the election—purchases made by white gun owners fearful of what an Obama presidency would mean for them (e.g., Bohn; National Public Radio, "Gun Shop"; Thomas). Within a year of the 2008 election, discontent with Obama had spread beyond the margins; news outlets featured stories on black leaders' dissatisfaction with Obama and on his declining support among white Americans (e.g., Ewers; Winant). By early 2010, polls reported that whites and blacks alike were increasingly pessimistic about Obama—and, specifically, about his ability to improve "race relations," to "heal" the American racial divide.[4]

The "next phase" of the age of Obama, his second term as president of the United States, is (as of this writing) still unfolding. For the purposes of this chapter, though, I wish to focus less upon his second term (or his second electoral triumph) than upon the discourse surrounding his bid for reelection. According to many observers of the campaign, there was a significant "enthusiasm gap" separating the president Obama of 2012 from the candidate Obama of 2008 (e.g., Fenn; Garrido; Krebs). In the months and weeks leading up to the general election, many felt that widespread disillusion with Obama would strip him of the young and progressive voters whose support (and grassroots efforts) had initially carried him into office. Although pundits expended many words and much energy upon the causes of this "enthusiasm gap," I believe that some measure of disillusion with Obama's presidency was inevitable. The breathless declarations of a "post-racial" America were an example of the kind of symbolic action that Ellison's friend and "ancestor," Kenneth Burke, termed "prayer."[5] According to Burke, "prayer" represents less an accurate assessment of a situation (what he calls "chart") than an instance of that tactic whereby "'would that it were' is stylistically rephrased: 'it is'—as when the dreamer, desiring to be rid of a certain person, dreams that this person is departing" (*Philosophy* 4). To put it bluntly, one cannot simply proclaim America "post-racial," and expect it to be so.

But that, I take it, is part of what draws us, as readers and as cultural critics, to study the work of Ralph Ellison. The discourse surrounding Obama's first term (and his quest for reelection) simply reminds us that *Invisible Man*'s work is not yet done; it remains as important for us today as it was for readers in 1952. Ellison's novel, sixty years after its publication, provides powerful resources for the interrogation of American racial identity in the early decades of the twenty-first century. Indeed, I believe that *Invisible Man* offers an unmatched perspective upon the still-alive, still-pressing discourse of racial binarism that, as Ellison told Burke in 1945, "has warped our culture, [and] truncated our ability to think deeply and broadly" (Burke, "Letter" n.p.). Given the constraints of this chapter, I shall focus upon only one dimension of this problematic: *the invisibility of our most visible man of color, the discourse of (color) blindness in the Age of Obama*. To that end, this essay draws upon *Invisible Man* to offer an analysis of Barack Obama as an object of public perception and symbolic action. I use this analysis to interpret the postracial depictions of Obama as reinscriptions of our characteristically American racial divide. Yet, rather than ending with cynicism or bitterness, I recall Ellison's hopeful vision for America within *Invisible Man*, his reminder to us that freedom lies in possibility, and in division. To that end, I reaffirm the kind of American social order that Ellison's novel, even today, calls us to symbolically enact—the only kind of postracial America that, Ellison tells us, is worth having.

"BEHOLD THE INVISIBLE" (IM 496)

When Obama defeated John McCain and became the forty-fourth president of the United States, the moment was celebrated as a victory not just for Obama, but also for the country as a whole. Obama had, as expected, received overwhelming support from black voters, had done surprisingly well with Latino/Latina voters—and had also managed to gain the support of more than 40 percent of white voters (e.g., "Inside"; Kuhn). This appeal to a significant portion of the white electorate appeared to validate Juan Williams's sentiments, prompting many pundits to join him in announcing the arrival of "post-racial politics" in America.[6] More than a year later, some of them, such as MSNBC host Chris Matthews, were still fixated on the "post-racial" implications of Obama's presidency—and, moreover, of Obama himself. Following the 2010 State of the Union address, Matthews memorably remarked, "I was trying to think about who he was tonight. It's interesting: he is post-racial, by all appearances. I forgot he was black tonight for an hour."[7] Let us unpack this a bit. Obama is, Matthews tells us, "post-racial"—*by all appearances*. How, we might ask, does one "appear" to be "post-racial"? Matthews implicitly provides an answer—that is, Obama "is" black, but that blackness can disappear, at least for an hour.

One might celebrate such sentiments, contending that they indicate the kind of "color blindness" necessary for the transcendence of racial difference—that the only problem with Matthews's statement is that he did not *completely* lose sight of Obama's race. By "forgetting" that Obama is nonwhite, on this reading, Matthews would be demonstrating our increasing acceptance of an ethic of equality; he would be simply asserting that racial categories determine little that is important in judging the quality or ability of another person. One might, alternatively, agree with Michael Eric Dyson that the studied inattention to race masks a conservative, antiblack, anti-affirmative action agenda—by "forgetting" that Obama is black, here Matthews subtly reinscribes his essential blackness while simultaneously reinforcing the belief that racism is no longer a problem in American life (Dyson 22–29).[8]

Though not disagreeing with Dyson—or similar analyses from critical race scholars—for present purposes, I would take a different tack in addressing this discourse. Matthews's remarks (and those made by countless others in the public sphere) indicate something crucial to us, as Americans and as Ellisonians—they point us toward the significance of Obama's *appearance*. It is here, I contend, that we see the vital, and continued, relevance of Ellison's *Invisible Man*, sixty years after its public unveiling. Indeed, I believe that we can best address the complexities of race and the reaction to Obama through Ellison's meditations upon the vicissitudes of visibility. As Ellison explained in his introduction to the thirtieth-anniversary edition of the novel, one of the ironic dimensions of black American life is that "'high visibility' actually render[s] one un-visible—whether at high noon in Macy's window or illuminated by flaming torches and flashbulbs while undergoing the ritual sacrifice that was dedicated to the ideal of white supremacy" (CERE 478). Or, we might add, at the helm of the ship of state, illuminated by the voracious lights of television cameras and the ever-present glow of smart phones.

There is no question that Obama is a "highly visible" American, that the coverage of him—as both presidential candidate and, later, as president of the United States—has been highly personalized. But even that description is insufficient; since his first appearance on the national political stage, coverage of Obama has been tightly, and consistently, focused upon his *features*. A 2007 profile of Obama in the *Atlantic* offers a striking illustration of this point: "It isn't about his policies as such; it is about his person.... If you are an American who yearns to finally get beyond the symbolic battles of the Boomer generation and face today's actual problems, Obama may be your man. What does he offer? First and foremost: his face" (Sullivan). This statement, like Matthews's, reflects one common theme of public discourse about Obama: that one need simply *look at Obama's face* to understand the transformative, transcending potential of his presidency. This position is both countered and echoed by opponents of Obama; although their caricatures and images of him are racially charged and coded, they similarly suggest that Obama's face reveals the nature of his presidency.[9] But as twenty-first-century Americans, whether friend or foe, gaze upon Obama's well-lit visage; what do we see?

A *Time* magazine profile, appearing late in the 2008 campaign, included a telling (for Ellison scholars) description of Obama: "He has been called a window into the American psyche. Or you might say he's a mirror—what you see depends on who you are and where you stand. Obama puts it this way: 'I serve as a blank screen on which people of vastly different political stripes project their own views'" (Drehle). A recent analysis of Obama's "high visibility" includes a similar passage: "It is important to recognize the extent to which his image is, before any positive content of, say, visible racial marking, a highly ambiguous blank slate on which popular fantasy could be projected. Obama noted this himself in numerous speeches, calling himself a receptacle for the projection of hope and insisting that his meteoric rise was 'not about me, but about you'" (Mitchell 126).

The strikingly optical terms featured in these two pieces—*window, mirror, screen, projection*—suggest the Ellisonian notion that Obama's substance arises from those who perceive him, that it is constituted by the meanings attributed to him by his audience. In other words, Obama's identity is not to be found in what he says or does, but in the significance others see in (or bring to) him. To describe him as a "blank screen" or "blank slate" is, I contend, to imply that what others *take him to be* is far more important than *who he describes himself to be*. This, I suggest, is the quintessential Ellisonian problematic: *the invisibility of one so visible*. However, in order to interrogate this statement further, let us return to Ellison's novel, and to the specific understanding of invisibility that it provides us.

"LOOK AT ME! LOOK AT *ME!*" (IM 505)

When we first meet Ellison's famous protagonist, he both describes himself as invisible and diagnoses the root cause of his predicament: "I am invisible, understand, simply because people refuse to see me" (IM 3). In terms that resonate with the passages on Obama quoted previously, Invisible muses that "it is as though I have been surrounded by mirrors of hard, distorting glass. When they approach me they see only my surroundings, themselves, or figments of their imagination—indeed, everything and anything except me" (IM 3). The parallel is quite striking: Obama is a mirror, while Invisible is surrounded by mirrors. Invisible's interlocutors see only "figures of their imagination," while Obama serves as a handy screen for the projection of others' fantasies. With both Ellison's protagonist and Obama, in other words, we are offered a description of a surface that reflects or receives rather than reveals, one that diverts the gaze away from the perceptual object, and toward the perceiver.

As powerful as such a description might be, Ellison immediately tells us that it is but a playful approximation, and a somewhat misleading one at that. It tempts us to focus on the object of perception—as though Invisible or Obama himself generates this kind of reaction in others. Indeed, the previously quoted descriptions of Obama certainly suggest that this is the case, through their focus on him or his features. However, Ellison reminds us that the source of invisibility, in both cases, lies within the *perceiver,* not the *perceived*. As Ellison's narrator informs us, despite what we might think, his invisibility is not "exactly a matter of a biochemical accident to my epidermis" (IM 3). On the contrary, "that invisibility to which I refer occurs because of a peculiar disposition of the eyes of those with whom I came in contact. A matter of the construction of their *inner* eyes, those eyes with which they look through their physical eyes upon reality" (3). Here, in this contrast between physical eyes and "*inner* eyes," Ellison artistically explores the symbolic foundations of our perceptions. However, in order to fully appreciate the intellectual work done by Ellison's novel, it is important to contextualize it—to identify its relationship to Kenneth Burke's early work on the linkages between language, perception, and reality.

Although scholars have often noted Ellison's explicit invocation of Burkean concepts, few have fully recognized the depth of Ellison's intellectual debt to Burke. To put it simply, the reason that Ellison drew upon Burke's work in *Invisible Man* is because Ellison had carefully studied Burke's perspective on symbolic action—and, indeed, had adopted a largely Burkean framework for the study of race in America. Dissatisfied with vocabularies that would simply trace the origins of racism to material life (as in Marxism) or to psychic disorders (as in Freudian psychoanalysis), Ellison found Burke's emphasis upon the symbolic, upon the human need for *meaning*, the key to understanding the role of race in American society. As he wrote Burke in 1945, "I suppose that is why I feel really indebted to you. Essentially the Negro situation is irrational to an extent which surpasses that of the rest of the world—though God knows that sounds impossible. Your method gave me the first instrument with which I could orientate myself—something which neither Marx alone nor Freud alone could do" (Burke, "Letter" n.p.).

After first hearing Burke speak (in 1939, at the Third American Writers' Congress), Ellison spent the 1940s studying Burke's corpus of writings. While working on *Invisible Man*, though, Ellison extensively studied two books in particular: *Permanence and Change* (1935) and *Attitudes toward History* (1937).[10] These texts devote a great deal of attention to the interpretive nature of vision, the symbolic resources driving our perception of the world around us. As Burke writes in *Permanence and Change*, "Stimuli do not possess an absolute meaning.... Any given situation derives its character from the entire framework of interpretation by which we judge it" (35). What we perceive, then, is a product of more than physiological processes: "A ringing bell is in itself as meaningless as an undifferentiated portion of the air we are breathing. It takes on character, meaning, significance (dinner bell or door bell) in accordance with the contexts in which we experience it" (Burke, *Permanence* 7). Burke's companion volume—a text that Ellison relied upon in crafting the prologue and epilogue to *Invisible Man*—develops this point even more specifically in relation to *vision*: "The eyes are the 'remotest' of the senses. They lack the immediacy that goes with experiences of taste or contact. They have been called a protrusion of the brain" (*Attitudes* 211). Yet, to emphasize the brain, for Burke, is not to reduce seeing to neurological processes. On the contrary, Burke consistently emphasizes that the "mind" is formed of symbolic materials: "Our minds, as linguistic products, are composed of concepts (verbally molded) which select certain relationships as meaningful.... These relationships are not *realities*, they are *interpretations* of reality—hence different frameworks of interpretation will lead to different conclusions as to what reality is" (*Permanence* 35).

According to Burke, then, our perceptions of the world are a product of the linguistic categories that we have internalized as part of the learning of language—a process tied to a specific cultural group, at a specific point in time: "We discern situational patterns by means of the particular vocabulary of the cultural group into which we are born" (*Permanence* 35). We are deemed successful symbol users by our interlocutors precisely to the extent that we are able to carve the world of sensation into the objects and relationships that are recognized by our community. Such training, though, comes at a cost; as Burke warns us, the power unleashed by our interpretive frameworks—as our perceptions fuel our responses to situations—tends to distract our attention from alternate ways of symbolizing (and thus perceiving) the world around us. Or, as Burke memorably writes: "A way of seeing is a way of not seeing—a focus upon object *A* involves a neglect of object *B*" (*Permanence* 35), which means that "*every* insight contains its own special kind of blindness" (*Attitudes* 41).

When Ellison's narrator distinguishes the fleshy from the "inner" eye, we can recognize his invocation of this Burkean conceit. What prevents Invisible from being seen is not his skin, his face, his body, but "a matter of the construction" of others' powers of vision—in Burkean terms, the system of meanings that directs their view of, and response to, him. Ellison underscores the terministic structure of these "inner" eyes by emphasizing that there is no physical malady, no physiological defect, prompting these others' lack of vision. Invisible similarly underscores the linguistic dimension of his invisibility in the novel's epilogue, when he tells us that "I have also been called one thing and then another while no one really wished to hear what I called myself" (IM 573). Invisible is unseen, in other words, because the symbolic framework that others use to "see" him does not, ultimately, allow them to perceive him in his humanity. All that they see when they look upon him is the insubstantial, stereotypical, two-dimensional object that their racially charged vocabulary *prepares* them to see. As he wryly notes, though, this means that he can tell the reader everything about his illicitly light-filled hole, "since you never recognize me even when in closest contact with me" (IM 13).

Readers of Ellison are quite familiar with these passages, and with the narrator's conspicuous invisibility. However, I would suggest that this understanding of language, vision, and visual object also offers a powerful way of addressing the significance of Barack Obama's appearance (in every sense of that word) within American public discourse. Obama's similarity to Invisible does not rest with the visual metaphors catalogued earlier. He "appears," we recall, "post-racial." Given the discussion of invisibility offered within *Invisible Man*, this description takes on a new significance—since it points to the ambiguous relationship between seer and seen in Obama's "post-raciality." Is this postraciality to be located in Obama? Or in the eyes gazing upon him?

Drawing upon Ellison's novel, I would argue that many in our nation have collapsed the terms of this key distinction—thus confusing a change in perceived *object* with a change in perceptual *apparatus*. We certainly see this in the descriptions that ascribe Obama's invisibility to something about *him* or his face—that *he* prompts these unusual reactions from his fellow citizens. But more importantly, the collapse of object and apparatus means that those who declared America "post-racial" following the 2008 election implicitly hoped that *who* we saw would fundamentally change our entrenched *way* of seeing. They talked about the election as though Obama's face, the subject of fascination and much discussion, would itself induce changes in our "inner" eyes. Ellison, of course, would suggest the obstacles to such efforts. He reminds us of the tendency of the blind to remain stubbornly so, the sleepwalker to avoid wakefulness—even at the moment of death. This is why Ellison's protagonist emphasizes that his invisibility is no accident, but is the product of a deliberate (and continuous) choice—that he is not seen precisely because "you refuse to see me" (IM 14).

In similar fashion—and despite early headlines to the contrary—the "post-racial" figure of Obama has been perceived through the stubbornly entrenched terms of the American "racial divide." That is to say, popular and news media have overwhelmingly used a familiar interpretive framework to describe him, a familiar perceptual apparatus to view his countenance. These media outlets have projected the language of racial binarism onto Obama's "blank screen"—seeing in his face the reflections of a society deeply divided between white and black. Given his now-famous personal history, and his (at times) transgressive statements about race, Obama could be a very unsettling figure, one whose efforts and visage could unsettle our habitually binaristic racial discourse—our "problem of the color line." But, by and large, he remains unseen, invisible; stories map the polarity of blackness and whiteness onto Obama, using his "blank screen" to implicitly confirm racial binarism rather than interrogate it. In part, this can be seen in the unending quest to define who Obama "is"—where, that is, he fits along the "color line." Such, I suggest, is also the underlying message of the stories that have repeatedly, almost obsessively, asked whether he is too white for blacks, or too black for whites.[11]

Although other stories have avoided asking such indelicate questions, they have been no less interested in Obama's proper racial "placement." Some of the media attention paid Obama (subtly or otherwise) has emphasized his whiteness (Smith, "Obama's Whiteness" 129–30); more common, though, are stories that remind the public of Obama's blackness. Though this frame was placed upon many of the watershed moments of his 2008 campaign and election, coverage of Obama's first inauguration was especially notable for its strong visual (and verbal) definition of Obama as black—a message that trumped any contained within Obama's address.[12] Yet efforts to subtly incorporate Obama into the comfortable terms of racial binarism were not limited to the inauguration; to the dismay of many multiracial or biracial observers, aspects of his identity that could challenge this black-white binary were consistently reduced to fit it (e.g., Arana; "He's Not Black"). For example, in 2010, when Obama reported his answers to the United States census, the headlines said it all: "It's Official: Obama Is Black" ("It's Official").

A similar dynamic unfolded during the 2008 campaign when Obama introduced his maternal great-uncle during his nomination acceptance speech at the Democratic National Convention. The elderly white man, hailed by Obama as a close relative, could have triggered a debate about our racial "trained incapacity," our limited ways of thinking and speaking about race in America. Accounts of the event, however, recaptured this moment within the confines of racial binarism by underscoring the distinction between white and black, even as they appeared to celebrate Obama's fusing of the two sides of this divide. Here is the episode as described by National Public Radio: "Charles Payne, his grandmother's brother. Michelle Obama clasped his hand. A niece with dark skin, holding the hand and kissing the cheek of her husband's granduncle, who is white" (National Public Radio, "Democractic Convention"). This family portrait, though touching, creates its emotional effect by first sharpening the distinction between the white (Charles Payne) and black (Michelle Obama) figures involved. Forefronting the visible (and racial) differences between the two, this account of this moment represents it—like Obama's kinship with Payne—as the fleeting contact of (visually) evident opposites. By underscoring this dramatic difference in race, the story implicitly prohibits, even as it celebrates, Obama's close relationship to Payne.[13]

As a consequence, regardless of his own intentions, beliefs, actions, or statements, when viewed in terms of this black-white opposition, Obama could never represent the transcendence of the American racial divide so powerfully described by Ellison. The invisibly visible face of Obama, the object (and product) of his observers' "inner" eyes, reflects less the *undoing* of our racial hierarchies than the endless possibilities for their *resignification*. Far from making or marking us postracial, viewers of Obama's appearance instead see the embodiment of our partisan discord; he is our characteristic national opposition made flesh. To say this, though, is to side neither with the foes of Obama, who find him abhorrent or cynical (or both) on matters of race, nor with his admirers, who find him a sign of radical change; instead, I believe, it is to side with Ellison. It is to emphasize that the needs of our twenty-first-century rhetorical situation are fully met not by a nonwhite president, but by a new way of talking about whiteness and blackness, a new set of "inner eyes." As *Invisible Man* makes clear, without a vocabulary that rejects binaristic opposition, Obama will remain our most prominent unseen figure.

"MUST I STRIVE TOWARD COLORLESSNESS?" (IM 577)

At a pivotal moment toward the end of *Invisible Man,* Ellison's narrator is struck by a sudden realization, a product of his newly broadened perspective on American social life. Rather than being trapped within his familiar, limiting and limited perspective upon the world, Invisible tells us (appropriating a key Burkean phrase) that "It was as though I'd learned suddenly to look around corners" (IM 508).[14] After peering around the corner of his usual perspective, Invisible recognizes both the blindness of those surrounding him and his own invisibility: "Here I had thought they accepted me because they felt that color made no difference, when in reality it made no difference because they didn't see either color or men" (IM 508).

In this important scene, and throughout the novel's epilogue, Ellison emphasizes that color blindness is *not* a sign of improved vision—that it is a form of blindness, not a form of sight. Indeed, *Invisible Man* suggests that the erasure of race is not the sign of progress it is all too often taken to be in our public discourse. Even at the beginning stages of his work on the novel, Ellison discussed this point in a letter to Burke. Referring to a recent conversation between the two of them on the topic, Ellison remarked, "I certainly agree with you that universalism is desirable, but I find that I am forced to arrive at that universe through the racial grain of sand" (Ellison, Letter to Kenneth Burke). Rather than viewing universality as the *elimination* of race, as Burke had apparently argued, Ellison insisted that race was its foundation: "To throw away the concern with racial ... emphasis would for me be like cutting away the stairs leading from my situation in the world to that universalism of which you speak. For in the dialectical sense the two are one." He added, "And I would say that it is not a concern with race that has harmed American Negroes, but that they were not concerned with it enough" (Ellison, Letter to Kenneth Burke).

Invisible Man, accordingly, does not call for the elimination of racial identity—Ellison is not directing us, like Matthews, to "forget" that Obama is black, *even* for an hour. Nor is he promoting the leveling of difference, as though we should strive to eliminate the diversity that shapes our varied performances and narratives of identity. Here recall Invisible's rhetorical question: "Whence all this passion toward conformity anyway?—diversity is the word. Let man keep his many parts and you'll have no tyrant states" (IM 577). But Ellison does not simply see diversity to be a guard against the bland, homogenous society of Orwell's *1984*. He also connects diversity—as both a value and a project—to American democracy. As Invisible asserts in the novel's epilogue, "America is woven of many strands; I would recognize them and let it so remain" (IM 577).

So, we might ask, when we gaze upon the now-famous face of Barack Obama, what is it that Ellison would have us see? But that is not the correct question. Instead, I believe that we should ask: *How* is it that Ellison would have us see? Or, in other words, what kind of perceptual apparatus, what kind of symbolic framework, should we cultivate in ourselves and in our fellow Americans, if we are to move away from the sedimented discourse of racial binarism? *Invisible Man* suggests some of the characteristics that such an apparatus would display. It would cultivate an appetite for ambiguity, for uncertainty, for possibility—and would reject the comforting, but ultimately destructive, "assumption that the world [is] solid and all the relationships therein" (IM 576). With such a symbolic framework driving our perception, there would be little mystery in (but much celebration of) the whiteness of blackness, the blackness of whiteness, the darkness of light, and the silence of sound. It would cultivate an appreciation for difference, for diversity, celebrating Invisible's realization that "all life is divided and that only in division is there true health" (IM 576).

Most importantly, this diversity would be viewed as part and parcel of the project of democracy; the cultivation of difference would be seen as inseparable from the work of unification. This is the point that Ellison's narrator underscores during the course of the novel. The American racial divide, he tells us, diverts our attention from a more profound, more primordial unity. After seeing (around the corner of) the blindness of those surrounding him, Invisible realizes, "I had no longer to run for or from the Jacks and the Emersons and the Bledsoes and Nortons, but only from their confusion, impatience, and refusal to recognize the beautiful absurdity of their American identity and mine" (IM 559). This comic insight reappears in the epilogue, when Invisible muses at the futility of white Americans' efforts to separate from black Americans: "Here's the cream of the joke: Weren't we *part of them* as well as apart from them and subject to die when they died?" (IM 575).[15] This, Ellison's novel reminds us, is the nature of democracy, of our characteristically American unity-in-difference: "Life is to be lived, not controlled; and humanity is won by continuing to play in face of certain defeat. Our fate is to become one, and yet many—This is not prophecy, but description" (IM 577).

I think we can agree that these are more than the "buggy jive" musings of a man hibernating in an underground lair. They are an appeal—a call to us to adopt them as the foundation for our own terministic schemes, our own frameworks for interpreting and acting within a complex social world. It is also, as Ellison's narrator makes clear, a call to community with others, to mix hate with love. To put it (deceptively) simply, Ellison challenges us to *see* the other. He artistically presents us with the choice to adopt a new perceptual apparatus, a symbolic edifice capable of bearing the responsibility of recognizing our fellow Americans as the persons that they say they are—and show themselves to be. I suggest that the widespread acceptance of this perceptual apparatus, this symbolic framework, would signify the only kind of "post-racial" America worth working toward. This might not provide fodder for a touching feature story, it might not be easily achieved, but it would represent the kind of America that, sixty years ago, Ralph Ellison's *Invisible Man* presented to its readers.

NOTES

1. For persuasive accounts of racial binarism and its rise, see Guterl, *Color of Race*, and Jacobson, *Whiteness of a Different Color*. For a fascinating analysis of other forgotten aspects of Du Bois's famous statement—"the *visual* meanings of the color line"—see Smith, *Photography on the Color Line*.

2. The current understanding of the term *race relations* first emerged in the early 1940s, thanks to the consolidation of whiteness (the shift away from 1920s "Nordicism," with its attendant hierarchy of European races) and the widespread acceptance of racial binarism. Prior to this point, "the categories of distinct races and the presumed moral-intellectual *content* of these distinctions were thought to govern the social and historical details that made up the story of 'race relations.' . . . In the 1930s and 1940s this link was dramatically reversed" (Jacobson 104). Further, although technically "race relations" might refer to any number of races, it is almost exclusively used in American public discourse to indicate the current state of the relationship between whites and blacks.

3. Though occurring in 2004, it is hardly an exaggeration to say that this speech made Obama's candidacy possible; as one reporter later wrote, "The first impression Obama crafted that night still forms the basis of his presidential campaign" (Saslow, "17 Minutes").

4. One poll measured Americans' optimism about race relations in the country as a result of Obama's election. It showed a decline of 20 percent among whites, and nearly 25 percent among blacks—in just over a year's time (Agiesta and Cohen, "Fewer Americans").

5. For more on the ancestral relationship between Burke and Ellison, and the intellectual significance of their long-standing personal relationship, see Crable, *Ralph Ellison and Kenneth Burke*.

6. Mainstream news outlets such as CNN were among the strongest voices proclaiming the new, postracial era (e.g., Dimaggio, "Transcending Racism"), but were not the only ones to do so. The approving use of the term even spanned traditional political boundaries separating liberal from conservative (e.g., Billups and Sands, "Obama Term"; Blackwell, "Post-Racial Preference"; Hsu, "End of White America?"; McWhorter, "Racism").

7. This segment, which aired on MSNBC on January 27, 2010, was captured and heavily critiqued (e.g., Calderone, "Matthews").

8. Dyson is not, of course, directly referring to Matthews or this statement, but his analysis of the conservative appropriation of Martin Luther King Jr.'s "I Have a Dream" speech reflects the kind of position I am invoking here.

9. The Internet abounds with examples of such images (e.g., Apel, "Just Joking"; Silverman, "Racist Obama Email").

10. This argument—regarding Burke's influence on Ellison, and Ellison's scholarly study of Burke's work—is elaborated further in my book (Crable, *Ralph Ellison and Kenneth Burke*). My identification of Ellison's appropriation of Burkean concepts is based upon examination of unpublished letters, unpublished manuscripts, and other archival materials, including Ellison's personal library, housed in the Library of Congress. Given the nature of Ellison's markings in these volumes, and the date of their acquisition, there is substantial evidence to suggest that these were primary texts in the crafting of *Invisible Man*.

11. Examples of both types of stories abound in both mainstream and social media (e.g., Coates, "Is Obama Black Enough?"; Calderone, "Matthews"; CBS News, "Obama's Racial Identity Still An Issue."). Interestingly, there are also a host of stories asking if Obama is "too thin," "too fit," "too manly," "too cool," or "too young." I would argue that this fascination with his *excessiveness* may have its roots in anxiety over the instability of his racial identity.

12. Video of the ceremony was regularly interspersed with dramatic live shots of the crowd, typically focusing tightly on black faces or on moments of white-black camaraderie. Some news networks went further, adding live video from such places as the National Civil Rights Museum, where a predominantly black collection of spectators wept openly for the cameras; Kenya, where a room packed with black students cheered Obama; and Times Square, where blacks (sometimes paired with whites) embraced and gazed upward, even reverently, toward video screens showing the inaugural. For those watching the events on network television or the Internet, the story of the day was captured less in the key messages of Obama's speech than in these powerful images. By inserting these alternate visuals into the live feed, the coverage placed an interpretive frame on these events, erasing any ambiguity lurking in the audience's mind regarding Obama's racial identity. Complexity undermined by consistent visual definition, the man being sworn into office, Barack Hussein Obama, was declared the nation's first black or African American (not biracial or nonwhite) president. Casting the inauguration in these terms, however, meant that the coverage simultaneously confirmed an account òf Obama's identity that was consistent with, and not antithetical to, the American "racial divide."

13. One of the complicating factors involved in discussions of Obama's family heritage is the death of his mother. I would speculate that her absence from the political stage functions to make Obama's whiteness more abstract than it might otherwise be. Though Payne's presence at the Democratic National Convention was undoubtedly intended to make Obama's biracial identity concrete, their relationship—"his grandmother's brother," as NPR described him—was far too remote to overcome all that conspired to rhetorically divide them.

14. For Burke's explanations of the term, see *Attitudes toward History* (esp. 269). Ellison had heavily marked this specific page in his copy of Burke's text.

15. This, too, is a borrowed Burkean phrase—not surprisingly, since the comic vision presented in these pages might well be read as Ellison's riffing on *Attitudes toward History*.

PART TWO

THREE DAYS BEFORE THE SHOOTING . . .
Ellison's Ongoing Epic of America

RALPH ELLISON IN HIS LABYRINTH

ERIC J. SUNDQUIST

> "Something further may follow of this Masquerade."
> —HERMAN MELVILLE, *THE CONFIDENCE-MAN*

When he took shape in the mid-1950s, the character known first as Bliss and ultimately as Adam Sunraider was an offshoot of B. P. Rinehart—Bliss Proteus Rhinehart, as Ellison soon filled in his name with a variant spelling—the con man and trickster of *Invisible Man* whom Ellison considered "an American virtuoso of identity" (CERE 110). "He has lived so long with chaos that he knows how to manipulate it," Ellison remarked of the original Rinehart. "It is the old theme of *The Confidence Man*" (CERE 223). An apparent racial hybrid of unknown paternity, the Rinehart who occupied Ellison's years of transition between *Invisible Man* and the second novel that would remain unfinished at the time of his death in 1994 remained a figure of radical transformative capacities (Bradley 128–44). No less a virtuoso of identity, Bliss/Sunraider, as he appears in *Three Days before the Shooting...*, is a variation on the mythic Icarus, who perishes when he flies too close to the sun after escaping the Minoan labyrinth on waxen wings fashioned by his father, Daedalus. He is also, as his surrogate father, Alonzo "Daddy" Hickman, thinks of him, a "*mammy-made American Adam shaped out of this terrible confusion. Neither black nor white but as much a mystery as when some folks hear thick lips give voice to Shakespeare, Lincoln, or the Word*" (TD 741).[1] But Icarus and Adam are only two of his precursors—Oedipus,

Odysseus, Satan, Mephistopheles, and Prometheus, among others, are evident—and it is worth reminding ourselves that, even if Bliss/Sunraider is a flesh-and-blood character, Rinehart was *Invisible Man*'s true invisible man, a phantom, like Melville's Confidence-Man, known only in his masks. As a "man of parts," an operator "at home" in a "seething, hot world of fluidity" (IM 498), Rinehart was an appropriate prefiguration of the shape-shifting hero of Ellison's novel-in-progress, likewise conceived as a "trickster," a character with a "fluid core," even a kind of "shaman" (CERE 816; Library of Congress, Ralph Ellison Papers, ms. box I:140, folder 1, n.p. [hereafter box and folder information only]).[2]

Early on in his composition, Ellison went so far as to speculate that his novel's narrator, imagined at that time to be Rinehart's son, would have to stop his father before he "gets into the position of using the hydrogen bomb to destroy civilization," an apocalyptic scenario to which Rinehart would be driven because "he feels that life, or God, by making him a Negro has mocked him. Being a former boy preacher," Ellison reasoned, "he can think in such terms without seeming ludicrous." Although Sunraider as we know him in *Three Days* does not put civilization at risk, rudiments of this original plot remain in place. We are not allowed to know what Sunraider might have had in store beyond the grandiloquent speech he is making when his son, Severen, rises in the gallery of the United States Senate and brings him down in a hail of bullets, but the character we witness in *Three Days* accords with Ellison's original idea that the new Rinehart would be a "rootless American type" representative of those who become "actors and confidence men, demogogs [sic], swindlers, and spiteful destroyers of the nation" (ms. box I:141, folder 5). If Ellison's "mammy-made American Adam" was rootless, however, he was not without tradition.

Writing from Rome in 1956, Ellison advised his friend Albert Murray to check out "a book by R. W. B. Lewis, AMERICAN ADAM," which he thought "look[ed] interesting" (*Trading* 115). "Emancipated from history, happily bereft of ancestry, untouched and undefiled by the usual inheritances of family and race; an individual standing alone, self-reliant and self-propelling," Lewis said, the American Adam begins "under fresh initiative, in a divinely granted second chance for the human race." Where Lewis distinguished the American scene from the corrupted Old World, Ellison, having long since anticipated Lewis's caution that such a vision of innocence was perilously misleading, put his Adam, raised as a Negro despite his white skin, in a reverse minstrel mask. "What kind of change is possible for the solitary figure surrounded by space ... propelled by lonely, personal, and self-generated energy?," Ellison seemed to be asking himself in a passage he transcribed from Lewis's book. How might he conceive a new Adamic hero, to cite Lewis a few pages on, who "takes his start outside the world, remote or on its verges," its power, fashions, and history "precisely the forces he must learn, must master or be mastered by" (Lewis, *American Adam* 5, 86, 128; ms. box I:141, folder 6).

Lewis adduced the myth of an American Adam collectively, not from a single source such as the Roman myth of Aeneas, and the malleability of the roles in which his national hero appeared surely appealed to Ellison. Born to a white woman but almost certainly not fathered by the black man lynched for the crime, Ellison's Adam would be midwifed by Hickman, the dead man's brother and a onetime jazz trombonist turned preacher who christens the boy Bliss and trains him to rise from a small coffin on the cue "Lord, why hast Thou forsaken me?," a mock resurrection meant, as Ellison explained in an interview with John Hersey, to dramatize "the significance of being a Negro in America" in its relation to "the problem of our democratic faith as a whole" (CERE 791). Traumatized by the attempt of a demented white woman to claim him as her son, Bliss would nurse the delusion that the screen star Mary Pickford is his mother before eventually passing into the world of whiteness. Rocketing through a series of roles—minstrel, con man, hawker of wigs and bleaching creams, moviemaker, chauffer turned politician—until at last he becomes Senator Adam Sunraider, he would try, as Hickman imagines it, to "*turn back the clock so that he can be present at his own conception, observe the penetration, belly to belly, skin to skin.*" Attempting to undo the curse of race and cancel out the violence of his origins when his mother proved herself a white woman "*by letting hell yell rape from the pit between her thighs*," he would seek "*to be the total product of his own creation—Bliss immaculate*" (TD 463, 708).

As Bliss immaculate, he might solve the Oedipal riddle that haunts him, but at the cost of making himself "Mister Noname from Nowhere," as the character Janey thinks of him when she recounts to Hickman how Bliss sent his lawyer to make a deal governing Severen's future (TD 748). In a masking to which Ellison frequently returned in relating black vernacular sources to the classics—"I knew the trickster Ulysses as early as I knew the wily rabbit of Negro American folklore," he once observed (CERE 112)—his Bliss is kin to Odysseus escaping from the cave of Polyphemus: "Noman is my name; Noman is what mother and father call me and all my friends" (Homer, *Odyssey*, Rouse trans. 107).[3]

Yet Bliss's escape from the trap of race would by no means be complete. Hickman once thought that he could instill in this "*marvelous child of*

Ishmaelian origin and pariah's caste" the African American's "*stubborn vision and blues-tempered acceptance of this country's turbulent reality*" and turn him first into a spellbinding man of the gospel and then into a new Abraham Lincoln, through whom "*the combined promises of Scripture and this land's Constitution would be at last fulfilled and made manifest*" (TD 526–27). Instead, Bliss was destined to seduce a young woman who is part black, part white, and part American Indian and leave her pregnant with a child who will grow up hating the father he has never known and, at length, attempt to kill him as he is making an impassioned but enigmatic senatorial speech about the "sublime and cornucopian dream" to which "only a great and unified nation, a nation conditioned to riding out the chaos of history as the eagle rides out the whirlwind, can arise" (TD 240).

In "Brave Words for a Startling Occasion," Ellison's 1953 address upon accepting the National Book Award for *Invisible Man*, he quoted Eidothea's advice to Menelaus in *The Odyssey*. To discover what gods he has offended and so make his way home, she counsels, Menelaus must seize Proteus and hold him fast, though first "he will turn into all sorts of shapes to try you . . . into all the creatures that live and move upon the earth, into water, into blazing fire." In the Homeric account, Proteus does, indeed, change from a bearded lion to a serpent to a leopard to a great boar to running water to a tall tree in full leaf before succumbing (*Odyssey*, Rouse trans. 53). But Ellison's interest in the episode was metaphoric: "For the novelist, Proteus stands for both America and the inheritance of illusion through which all men must fight to achieve reality; the offended god stands for our sins against the principles we all hold sacred" (CERE 153–54). Here were themes that remained integral to Ellison's writing, fiction and essays alike, through the rest of his career. Yet nothing is more certain about the character who became Bliss and then Adam Sunraider than that, unlike Proteus, he cannot be grappled into submission. Having been made by his mentor, Mississippi "Sippy" Brown, into a "larcenous freebooter's conception of what an ideal American should be," Bliss/Sunraider turns out to be "so swindle-prone, fluent and shifty that absolutely *no one* [can] get him into focus." Composed of "so many ungraspable and shifting shapes," that is to say, he is the ideal citizen of Ellison's America—the nation he referred to as "a land of masking jokers" (TD 693, 699; CERE 109).

Bearing in mind Ellison's compositional note to himself that "Sunraider *is* a mythomaniac" (ms. box I:138, folder 3) we might find him anticipated in Joseph Campbell's figuring of Proteus as the archetypal "Shapeshifter," a "wily god" who stands for mythology itself and "never discloses even to the skillful questioner the whole content of his wisdom" (Campbell 381). Remembering Ellison's recurrent citation of William Butler Yeats's contention that assuming a "second self . . . the wearing of a mask" is "the condition of an arduous full life" (CERE 107; Yeats 317)—a way to press back against the flux and flow of time, and "modify that which is given," as Ellison put it at a Southern Historical Association roundtable in 1968 (CERE 146)—we might likewise find aspects of Ellison's hero in Elias Canetti's theory of masking, where Proteus is a shamanic performer in whom metamorphosis is carried to extremes. His uncontrolled, subversive transformation standing in opposition to the authority of king or state, this Proteus personifies the essence of the mask, which of necessity hides more than it expresses. "Charged with a menace which must not be precisely known," writes Canetti, the mask "comes close to the spectator" while at the same time it "threatens him with the secret dammed up behind it" (Canetti 344–45, 374–76, 381–82).

It will be apparent by now that we have begun to enter what John Callahan, detailing the role played in *Invisible Man* by antagonists such as Mr. Norton, Brother Jack, and Sybil, with whom the hero does battle in the place of a Minotaur, has called Ellison's "vernacular labyrinth" (Callahan, "Ellison's" 301–2). This labyrinth, it should be said, is also a briar patch—at once a tangle of vernacular threads and the natural habitat of "Mose," a wily black visionary forever bound for the Promised Land, of whom Ellison said in the wake of *Brown v. Board of Education* in 1954, "He's turned the Supreme Court into the forum of liberty it was intended to be, and the Constitution of the United States into a briarpatch in which the nimble people, the willing people, have a chance" (*Trading* 116–17). If we are to find Adam Sunraider, it is there we must seek him.

Delirious in his hospital bed after the assassination attempt, the mortally wounded Sunraider recalls—or should we say dreams or hallucinates?—meeting, at an unspecified Washington, DC, intersection, a "*bent little black-skinned woman*" who threatens him with "*an old-fashioned walking stick that she shook with awkward vigor.*" "*Oh, Ah knows you,*" she calls out. "*You old jacklegged, knock-kneed, bowlegged, box-ankled, pigeon-toed, slack-asted piece of peckerwood trash gone to doo-doo! Ah knows you, yas Ah do!*" Warning that she will "*put yo' nasty business in these white folks' street,*" she condemns him more precisely as "*simply nothing done gone to waste.*" But "*at least I am a walking personification of the negative,*" Sunraider imagines saying in reply. "*I know who I am*" (TD 408). His rejoinder activates a narrative chain of memory tying the senator to the core question of identity in *Invisible Man*. "When I discover who I am, I'll be free," dreams Invisible Man as he lies in his own hospital bed, threatened, so it seems, with lobotomy and castration. His self-diagnosis soon spins out in a sequence of unmaskings: "I yam what I am," he jokes with the sweet-potato man; "I am what I am," he asserts before embarking on his speech at the old folks' eviction; "I am what they want me to be," he muses about his role in the Brotherhood; "who actually was who," he asks as he takes the part of Rinehart; and, finally, "knowing now who I was," as he embraces invisibility (IM 243, 266, 269, 379, 493, 559).

In his characteristically allusive way, Ellison punned in his first novel on Yahweh's mystic, tautological revelation of Himself to Moses in Exodus (3:14): "And God said unto Moses, I AM THAT I AM." And he refers, at the same time, to the scene in *King Lear* where the broken king, challenged by the insolent Goneril and goaded by the Fool to recognize the deterioration of his authority and mental state, questions the meaning of his own identity: "Does any here know me? Who is it that can tell me who I am?" (1.4.226–30). Likewise more at home in the mythological landscape of gods and monarchs, Sunraider may or may not know who he is, though he, more than all others, must also know that, as a "walking personification of the negative," another role he inherits from Invisible Man (IM 94), and a figure of power whose canny manipulation of whites' racial fears makes him a "saint of negative permissiveness" (TD 25), as he is called by Welborn McIntyre, a white reporter speculating about the attempted assassination, he remains, by design, Mister Noname from Nowhere.

But let us return to the crossroads scene of the old black woman shaking her walking stick as she berates Adam Sunraider as "*jacklegged, knock-kneed, bowlegged, box-ankled, pigeon-toed, [and] slack-asted.*" Her rhetorical overkill finds a corollary in Hickman's own encounter, while searching for Sunraider so that he can warn him of the threat to his life, with the madly signifying walk-on character Leroy, whose "rocking gait" makes Hickman's mind reel with the names of cripples, white and black, he had known in the old days: *gambling cripples, pimping cripples, even con-man cripples as well as cripples who were hard-working men with families. And some who were musicians and dancers—like Peg Leg Bates, Chick Webb, and Big-time Crip. Then there were all those assorted neighborhood cripples. Characters like No-toes, Crip Wilson . . . yes, and Tippy-Lee Morton, who transformed walking with his mismatched legs into an act of graceful elegance. And there was Sugar-foot, and Crippled Charleston, Stilts Benford, String-halted Harry, Dog-trot Johnson, and Jake-leg Mac, who had to wear leg braces after drinking poisoned Jamaica Ginger. Oh, yes, and don't forget Funky-fingers Hagerson, that thin claw-handed pickpocket who worked small fairs, circuses, and tent meetings* (TD 550–51).

Hickman's mind-bending catalog of cripples is a reminder we may hardly need of Ellison's preoccupation with bowlegged and limping figures, outside his fiction no less than within it. "Somehow this little bandy-legged, hawk-nosed, brilliant, luminous man understood that the American covenant was not to be thrown away," he wrote of Oklahoma City newspaperman Roscoe Dunjee, by way of *Hamlet*—understood "that here [in the Constitution], with intelligence and passion, was the secret, the play within the play which would catch the conscience of kings" (CERE 454). The wildly clashing styles of the pimp-limping figure in "The Little Man at Chehaw Station," which sound "an integrative, vernacular note—an American compulsion to improvise upon the given," to take another example, are the signs of a joker addressing "the old, abiding American questions: Who am I? What about me?" (CERE 505–8). Nor should we be surprised to find, near the conclusion of a beautifully rendered catalog of things that infused Ellison's imagination as he came of age in Oklahoma City—the long passage includes, among other things, black idioms, polite manners and street manners, circuses and moving pictures, spring floods and blizzards, catalpa worms and jackrabbits, jazz musicians and fire-and-brimstone preachers, snapdragons, baked yams, and blue haw ice cream—"the limping walks affected by Negro hustlers, especially those who wore Stetson hats, [and] expensive shoes with well-starched overalls, usually with a diamond stickpin" (CERE 201). Indeed, after returning to his hometown to be feted following the success of *Invisible Man*, as he revealed in a 1953 letter to Albert Murray, Ellison composed a poem (*Trading* 54–55) in which he reflected on the vernacular wisdom he would like to have conveyed to his old friends and the young folks coming up:

I would with them make of us all heroes and fliers ...
And teach them the secret of that limping walk, that look of eye,
That tilt of chin, the world-passion behind that old back-alley song
Which sings through my speech more imperious than trumpets or
blue train sounds—

In *Three Days* such limping figures range from the incidental to the more consequential. McMillen, one of Hickman's informants in his search for Sunraider, affects a "pimp's limp," while McIntyre, who narrates the first book of *Three Days*, recalls a scene in a Salzburg restaurant when "*a little black bowlegged GI*" rebuked an American poet for mocking his nation's flag and thereby induced all their countrymen present to recite the Pledge of Allegiance (TD 611, 93). It is McIntyre, in fact, who encounters the first of the book's multiple limping trickster figures. In a coda to the story of his star-crossed relationship with Laura, a young black woman pregnant with his child whose mother cuts short their romance, McIntyre tells of his descent into a Harlem nightclub, there to be absorbed in the performance of Mother Smathers, a short, dark figure disguised as a nun and carrying a Bible and a tambourine in which she catches coins. No sooner have we identified Mother Smathers as a descendent of Black Guinea, Melville's Confidence-Man in his disguise as a "grotesque negro cripple" who shuffles about, making music with his tambourine and catching coins in his mouth (Melville, *Confidence-Man* 10), than her "strange, crablike steps" are taken up by Heapachange Hudson, who seizes the tambourine and launches into his own drunken, shape-shifting ritual. Establishing a prototype for the novel's many catalogs of protean action, Hudson appears as though he were a Spanish dancer, a prancing horse, a fish spinning on its tail, a circus bear, an aristocrat on roller skates holding his crotch, a trailer truck, a knock-kneed camel, a pecking rooster, a mating stallion, and at last "a transported supplicant in a frenzied rite, a twisted cripple with two dancing legs" (TD 120–23).

In another such scene that defies any paraphrase, McIntyre finds himself face to face with a trickster in his hallucinatory dream of "*the metaphysical nigra bastard*," the Jim Crow hitching-post groom blocking his doorway. An "iron monster" who gives the appearance of being able, like Anansi, the trickster spider of Afro-Caribbean tradition, to "*run straight up a vertical wall and walk across a ceiling with no show of exertion whatsoever*" but which McIntyre can move only with "short shuffling steps," the groom rides McIntyre like a horse; assaults him with a welter of allusions that are verbal testimony to his "*many, many metamorphoses*"; and, playing the dozens with "*a tongue that's as hot as the south end of a yellow jacket*," mocks McIntyre with a barrage of the aliases he has supposedly assumed as his mother's protean gigolo:

> And here's something else you didn't know, baby: She called me her "little man" . . . [and] sometimes her "darling darky darling." And again her "handsome African comodòro" and "Otello mio"—how do you like the swing of that? And in especially pensive moods it was in quick succession "Oh, my jigging Joy Boy, Master of my Solitude, Dark Secret Delight, Gypsy Lover, Cellmate, Joy Rocker, and Dirty Richard." And once in a moment of classical exuberance she called me her "Jockey Boy of Artemesion."

In this protracted improvisatory scene, McIntyre himself becomes the limping figure: he just keeps on "inching along," as advised in the spiritual to which Ellison alludes throughout the scene ("Keep A-Inchin' Along"), all the while trying to crack the thick code of the groom's "loquacious ventriloquist's voice" (TD 179–80, 184–85, 190–94).

Insofar as it is McIntyre's consciousness in which we first contemplate the mystery of Adam Sunraider, the several scenes in which he encounters or in fact becomes a limping trickster are the gates through which interpretation of Sunraider must pass. But it is Hickman's consciousness to which Ellison finally gave priority, and so must we. Let us therefore consider a sequence of three scenes that find Hickman on the streets of Washington, DC, in search of Adam Sunraider, and have a closer look at the character Leroy.

Emerging from the "JANUS BARNES HAIR SALON," its window featuring the image of "a double-headed black man," one figure with straight, gleaming hair and another with bushy, kinky hair, Leroy hoists Hickman off the ground while launching into a feverish monologue a hundredfold more riddling than anything Peter Wheatstraw, with his cartload of blueprints and his peppering riffs on Brer Rabbit and Brer Dog, could lay down for Invisible Man. Mistaking—or pretending to mistake—Hickman for a militant race nationalist, "none other than Chief SAM, the fucking *Liberator!*,"[4] Leroy attributes to him a host of aliases: Prince Marcus, Swami Joe, Clexo, Newfoundland Ike, Sweet-the-Monkey, Black John, Dennis the Inspirer, and Ras the Cleanser, the Hot Wind out of Africa. He delightedly retails having hit the numbers 4-11-44, a popular policy combination standing for enormous penis and the subject of familiar coon songs; he circles through a reenactment of Chief Sam's scalding courtroom harangue about black rape in the white mind, some "deep shit" seemingly concocted of LeRoi Jones and Eldridge Cleaver, with a side glance at William Styron's *Confessions of Nat Turner*; and he recalls Chief Sam's teaching by trial and interrogation that "there's brightness in blackness and whiteness in darkness," that "ye must think deep black thoughts like the whale" and go to "Constitution Avenue and peer into the many cracks that abound there, and watch out for the mirrors hidden within" (TD 547, 553–56).

Although Leroy recounts Chief Sam's ritual initiation of him, his tour de force testifying, a standout in a book of standout improvisations, is of course a ritual initiation of Hickman—and of the reader. The Constitution is "a script by which we seek to act out the drama of democracy, and the stage upon which we enact our roles," as Ellison argued in a variety of formulations (CERE 773). In Leroy's interrogation it is we who are to study the Constitution's cracks and mirrors; it is we, not just Leroy remembering the tutelage of Chief Sam, who are being offered the "blackness of truth" (TD 553).

Leroy springs upon Hickman immediately after his encounter with an old man who totes a large portable radio and rocks to the rhythms of Hickman's own old recording of "Jelly Roll Blues," all the while advancing "with a limp, and a pause, and a hand-on-hip strut ... smiling as though so entranced by the sound of his blues-spouting burden as to be totally unaware of the panic being stirred by the inchworm's pace of his progress." Jumped moments later by Leroy, Hickman wonders if Ole Uncle Bud, a tale-telling signifier of vernacular legend, has "run around the corner and come back to test him under a different disguise." Met at what Ellison calls the "*crossroads of time*"—and here Hickman digresses into a miniature riff on time in its many permutations: "*time on a cross*," "*colored people's time*," "*go seeking a man to find a boy who got lost in time-past like I'm doing*," and more—the Jelly Roll bluesman, identified in Ellison's computer file title as the "Messenger," has already hit Hickman with an onslaught of folkloric puzzles and spieled his own list of protean aliases: cat, invisible spook, Willie-the-poor-boy, the "old man of the mountains who ole Cab [Calloway] used to hi-de-ho so loud about," Wine-ball Bill, Daddy Step, Oddball Papa, and, most elaborately, "the unknown soldier who keeps the bowels of all of these congressmen and Supreme Cote judges roaring up a storm," the "nappy-headed judge of the court of last resort for this heah entire haunted house of a country." His "*crabbed way of walking*" is reiterated in the "rocking gait" of Leroy's stumbling "collapse-and-recover" flight from the barbershop, so why should Leroy not be the Jelly Roll messenger in a new mask? (TD 537, 539, 540–43, 547, 549–50). We are not aboard Melville's *Fidèle*, exactly, but we are surely in the world of *The Confidence-Man*.

Hoisted in the air as Leroy gets ready to unleash his verbal assault, Hickman finds himself face to face with "an incongruous battleground of conflicting colors" that "stared back with the fierce immutability of an African mask which bore grotesque scarification of mysterious design ... the white, red-ringed splotches of which appeared to dance above the blue-blackness of its surrounding flesh as though to challenge any quick assumptions as to its racial identity." When Hickman thinks, "*you've been grabbed by a red-white-and-blue black man*," he sends us in two directions at once (TD 549).

The masklike ambiguity of Leroy's face, what Hickman in a later flashback thinks of as "the translucence of [his] tricolored skin" (TD 561), is Ellison's creation, but standing in the background is Jim Crow Rice, the white blackface minstrel whose name came to designate the regime of racial exclusion set in motion by the end of Reconstruction and enshrined in law by *Plessy v. Ferguson* in 1896. In an analysis central to Ellison's aesthetic, Constance Rourke described the origins of T. D. Rice's act: "Rice had heard an old crippled Negro hostler singing in a stableyard as he rubbed down the horses, and had seen him dancing an odd limping dance as he worked—'rockin' de heel,'" and so learned his song:

> Wheel about, turn about,
>   Do jis so,
> An' ebery time I wheel about
>   I jump Jim Crow.

After using it in a backwoods play to great effect, Rice enlarged the piece to include other African American songs and dances in a single impersonation, most notably in the figure of a blackface Yankee dressed in red-and-white striped trousers and a long blue coat fitted with buttons made of five- and ten-dollar gold pieces—in essence, Uncle Sam in blackface. Although the figure of "long-tail'd blue" faded from the minstrel repertoire, says Rourke, "little limping Jim Crow" became firmly ingrained in the ritualistic design that underlay successive generations of what she called "white masquerade" in blackface—and, what is more, *black* masquerade in blackface (Rourke 72–73, 83–84, 87).

For Ellison, as we have long known, Rourke's interpretation of minstrelsy revealed it to be a "ritual of exorcism" wherein the mask of blackface, entangled in the red, white, and blue iconography of the national flag, created the conditions for a "comic catharsis." Subsuming the racial identity behind it, he recognized, the mask enacted a "willful stylization and modification of the natural face and hands," and functioned to "veil the humanity of Negroes thus reduced to a sign, and to repress the white audience's awareness of its moral identification with its own acts and with the human ambiguities pushed behind the mask" (CERE 103). To white minstrelsy's layer of blackface, however, blacks added their own signifying layers. When slave masters witnessed "the incongruity of tattered blacks dancing courtly steps" in comic imitation of plantation manners, as Ellison remarked in his homage to Duke Ellington, they misunderstood how a European cultural form was being Americanized, "undergoing a metamorphosis through the mocking activity" (CERE 681). Still, the mockery could also conceal a rueful undercurrent. It may have paid for "*Negroes to pretend to be blackfaced white folks pretending to be black,"* Hickman ruminates, but minstrelsy, including his own bandstand clowning, was also a form of *"guerrilla warfare"*—and yet, he continues, how is one to distinguish the sin *"against yourself and against all your people"* from *"sneering with contempt and exulting with pride"* in the *"mammy-made art"* of black Americans? (TD 858).

Ellison, it could be said, launched his novel from a scenario of signifying mimicry that turned back upon itself in a vicious but outrageously comic cycle. It may be that Bliss's passing is occasioned by deep dread of racial stigmatization. Witness, for example, his adolescent assault on the burnt-corked midget minstrel when Hickman takes him to the circus: "I hit him real quick and . . . could see the blackness smear away and the white coming through and then I hit him again . . . trying to make all the blackness go away" (TD 385). Even so, his decision may be less tragic than opportunistic. Caught in bed with the young wife of the Southern politician who employs him as a chauffeur, a scene whose prototype appears in the sexual education of Invisible Man when he is downtown speaking on the woman question, Bliss thinks fast: *"I'm a nigger; so you can forget about it, it don't count, I'm outside the game,"* to which the cuckold replies, *"I'm a busy man and no fool. Meanwhile I'll think about making you a politician"* (TD 248). In Ellison's conception, however, it was imperative that "Bliss's conversion into Sunraider [be a] source of mystery and power" (ms. box I:141, folder 1). Unlike the protagonist of *The Autobiography of an Ex-Coloured Man*, whose passing leads to despairing self-condemnation for having "sold [his] birthright for a mess of pottage" (J. W. Johnson 211), or Faulkner's Joe Christmas, who sleeps with white women and then tells them he is a Negro, courting his own eventual lynching and castration, or Dr. Junius Crookman, whose magic formula for "chromatic emancipation" in *Black No More* leads instead to a chaos of chromatic scapegoating (Schuyler 87), or Invisible Man himself, who feels the metaphysical sickness of conformity coming upon him "like that strange disease that affects those black men whom you see turning slowly from black to albino, their pigment disappearing as under the radiation of some cruel, invisible ray" (IM 575)—unlike these various exemplars in the literature of passing, Bliss's self-creation moves more emphatically in the direction of radical racial indeterminacy.

"One of the hidden jokes in the Tar Baby fable," Ellison wrote in his notes for the novel, "is the fact that he looks black but is really white" (ms. box I:57, folder 5). Bliss/Sunraider turns Tar Baby inside out. Although we will never know, nor will he, Sunraider may or may not be a white man masquerading as a black man masquerading as a white man. Here again, however, Ellison had in mind not only an American character but the character of America, whose democratic ideal was the protean fluidity Ellison accentuated when he told Robert Penn Warren that the great glory of being an American is that you "can be somebody else while still being yourself" (R. P. Warren 346). As though born of the Liberty Paints episode in *Invisible Man*, Bliss/Sunraider is "the whiteness hidden in blackness, or blackness concealed in the whiteness," a visual, cultural, and ontological paradox to which Ellison recurs throughout *Three Days*, as well as in numerous essays (TD 587).[5]

Not only are we presented with a set of protean American models for Bliss's transformation—his mentor Sippy Brown, writes Ellison, makes him an amalgam of Thomas Jefferson, Benjamin Franklin, P. T. Barnum, George Washington Carver, Groucho Marx, Billy Sunday, Yellow Kid Weil, William S. Hart, Teddy Roosevelt, Warren G. Harding, Gaston B. Means, and Lon Chaney, as well as "our own dam' Sam, John Henry, *and* Brer Rabbit" (TD 699)—but the two of them together, we are told, stand within a shape-shifting lineage of paired white and black figures who tell the story of race relations in American culture: Uncle Remus and the white boy who hears his stories, Uncle Tom and Little Eva, Ahab and Pip, Huck Finn and Jim, not to mention historic pairs such as George Washington and his slave valet William Lee or Matt Henson and Admiral Robert Perry or Shirley Temple and Bill "Bojangles" Robinson (TD 687–92). In Ellison's uncanny hero these cross color-line pairs melt into one—almost like the integrally hybrid nation everywhere "shaped in part by the Negro's presence," as Ellison argued in "What America Would Be Like without Blacks" (CERE 583)—Bliss/Sunraider is "a monster with two heads inhabiting a single body" (TD 685). He is the Janus-faced nation itself.

But the complexly layered masks of American minstrelsy, we should not be surprised to find, conceal further masks.

Set upon by a signifying trickster at the "crossroads of time" or accosted at an intersection by an old black woman wielding a walking stick, we are also in the world of Eshu-Elegba, the trickster deity of the Nigerian Yoruba who appears in black New World divination, that of Haiti in particular, as Legba, a crippled old man whose limp gives him the nickname of "Pied-cassé"—broken foot. Standing at the crossroads of youth and age, the human and the divine, life and death, body and soul, Legba is, in various accounts, the "Master of the Crossroads," "the God of the Cross-roads," and even "Sun-Lord of the Cross-roads," for it is there that he presides over the spells and incantations of sorcerers (Deren 97–99, 100; Métraux 101–2; Consentino 265). A sack over his shoulder, leaning on a crutch, Legba also conceals great strength and agility. In Paule Marshall's *Praisesong for the Widow*, for example, the seemingly crippled Legba manifests in Lebert Joseph, a diminutive figure of incalculable age in need of a walking stick when Avey Johnson first encounters him at the crossroads. In the nation dance, however, "his stooped and winnowed body" takes on the "illusion of height, femininity and power. Even his foreshortened left leg ... appeared to straighten itself out and grow longer as he danced" (Marshall 243). In his 1956 story "A Coupla Scalped Indians," in fact, Ellison himself attributed comparable shape-shifting erotic powers to the character Aunt Mackie.

As an archetypal figure "bearing the crossroads ... in messages that test our wisdom and compassion," as Robert Farris Thompson writes, Eshu-Elegba has often been associated with the devil by missionaries and other Christians. He is better understood, however, as "the ultimate master of potentiality" (Thompson 19), an "agent of metamorphosis" (Pelton 138) whose mutability subsumes mythological rivals, even those as commanding as Oedipus. Legba is "the destined answer to the Sphinx," says Maya Deren, in a characterization of Oedipus especially suggestive for Adam Sunraider, for "he was once the new-born infant sun, lived through the fertile prime of his noon, and is now the old sun, walking with a cane—the 'third leg'—in the afternoon of life" (Deren 98–99). On the American scene, Legba can be found down at the crossroads in the midnight meeting of a blues-singing guitar player with a limping old black man who will tune and play his instrument, then return it endowed with supernatural powers (Marvin 587). He might, like Peter (or Peetie) Wheatstraw, the stage name of William Bunch, style himself "the devil's son-in-law" and the "High Sheriff from Hell" (Sundquist *Cultural Contexts*, 123). Meeting this son of Legba as the blueprint-toting cartman full of "shit, grit, and mother-wit," Invisible Man wonders, upon hearing his rendition of Jimmy Rushing's "Boogie Woogie Blues"—"she's got feet like a monkeeee / Legs / Legs, Legs like a maaad / Bulldog"—what kind of creature he is singing about: "Was it a Sphinx?" (IM 176–77). Ellison's vernacular vocabulary was predominantly American, along with a mix of classical and European sources, but the fact that his private collection included a Janus-faced mask of Eshu reminds us that the African trickster was also an important part of his creative pantheon (Gates, *Signifying Monkey* 29, 32–34).

Leroy's emergence from the "JANUS BARNES" hair salon and his appearance as a *"red-white-and-blue black man"* (TD 549) also puts us in contact with another feature of Eshu-Elegba; namely, the legendary story of his multicolored cap. Variously described as black and white; red and black; red and white; red, white, and blue; or red, white, green, and black, the cap itself incorporates the crossroads (Thompson 19), and the story is told that, with a pipe in his mouth and a walking stick over his shoulder, Eshu-Elegba struts back and forth along a road in order to prompt a quarrel as to the color of his cap. Like Melville's Confidence-Man, who in his bewildering façade "spreads deception for its own sake" (Rogin 242), Eshu, when he is brought to court after friends come to blows over the question of his cap, confesses that "sowing dissension is my great delight" (Pelton 141). Life in their segregated nation having taught Hickman's congregation that "order and disorder are inseparable" (TD 526), Eshu is an appropriate archetype for the shape-shifters of *Three Days*—most of all for Bliss/Sunraider, whose gift for mimicry, baffling charm, rumored licentious behavior, and practical jokes style him a "holy fool manqué" (TD 33) and conform to the function of the trickster Ellison found in the anthropological analysis of Karl Kerényi: "to add disorder to order" and to render possible, "within the fixed bounds of what is permitted, an experience of what is not permitted" (CERE 106; Kerényi 185). Louis Armstrong, whose "clownish license and intoxicating powers" Ellison found to be "almost Elizabethan," was one such trickster (CERE 106; Kerényi 185). Ellison himself, not least as his second novel, year by year, grew more chaotic and distended, was perhaps another.

Before considering further the allegory of Eshu's cap, however, we should return once more to Hickman's progress through the streets of Washington, DC, in search of Adam Sunraider. Fresh from his interrogation by Leroy, Hickman comes upon a massive bronze door, "scarred as though battered by John Henry's hammer," and the plate-glass window of a subterranean storefront church that reveals a painting of "Christ marching to Calvary," an image that puts Hickman in mind of "the disappearing legs" of Icarus he has seen at his hotel on a tapestry based on Brueghel's *Landscape with the Fall of Icarus*, in which Icarus is depicted plunging into the sea, half-submerged.[6] That this Christ is black is no surprise, for he stands in a rich tradition of the black Christ, typically figured as a sacrificial lynching victim, in the writing of W. E. B. Du Bois, Countee Cullen, Langston Hughes, and others. But what initially stands out, as though the artist had been "improvising on his theme like a jazzman on a familiar tune," is that the "rough-hewn upright of the cross knif[ing] into the bruised flesh of Christ's straining shoulder" has attached to it "the travel-soiled bundle of a hobo." The further image brought immediately to mind, of course, is not a hobo but the archetypal advertisement offering a reward for a runaway slave, his sack tied to the stick slung over his shoulder. On closer inspection, however, Hickman finds that the bundle is, in fact, a "dishonored" American flag of "red-white-and-blue cotton" that has become "partially unrolled in the painful march" and now trails in the footprints of Christ (TD 562–64). What at first seems a "flaw in the painter's conception" in this "eye-assaulting scene-within-scene"—limping Jim Crow and "long-tail'd blue" united in a black Christ bearing the cross of slavery—is nothing less than the tragic "flaw" that Ellison located at the heart of American democracy. As he wrote elsewhere, it is "a flaw similar to the crack that appeared in the Liberty Bell," or, in a metaphor better suited to Sunraider—here Ellison's conception of America's original sin seems indebted to Frederick Douglass's "The Meaning of July Fourth for the Negro"[7]—the "serpentine malignancy that would tempt government and individual alike to a constantly recurring fall from democratic innocence" (CERE 775).

Why, though, does this black Christ with the slave's bundle in the form of an American flag bring to Hickman's mind the figure of Icarus disappearing into the sea? Coming upon the tapestry based on Brueghel's painting, Hickman feels compelled to "trace some hidden thread" and "identify the original melody on which the soloist was riffing," like a jazz musician or a preacher "blasting his listeners with freewheeling quotations." Seeking the "elusive clue [that] would lead to a parable or story" in the tapestry's own labyrinth, he pursues the "*hide-and-seek*" game of the weaver toward its "*invisible climax.*" When he finally sees "the lonely legs and grasping hand of someone who appeared to have plunged headfirst out of nowhere and into the wind-ruffled sea" unnoticed by the farmers and sailors in their everyday activities,[8] Hickman is led to make a vague association with Bliss and to wonder if the figure fell from some height or swam from shore to commit suicide the way "*the old folks tell us stories about Africans who took their children and walked into the sea until they drowned*" (TD 595–98).

In grafting the Ibo Landing story onto that of Icarus, Ellison chose the version congruent with Brueghel's landscape and Sunraider's tragedy. Rather than be slaves in America, in one telling, the Ibos chose death: "They linked themselves together with chains and they said a prayer. They said, 'Water brought us here, and water is going to carry us away.' Then they backed themselves out into Dunbar Creek and drowned themselves" (Barnes 139). A redemptive variation was equally prevalent, however, and Ellison would have encountered one version in "All God's Chillen Had Wings," included in *The Book of Negro Folklore*, compiled by Langston Hughes and Arna Bontemps, and another when he reviewed Bucklin Moon's *Primer for White Folks* in his 1945 piece "Beating That Boy." In "The Flying Africans," the example of the folktale Kenneth Porter provided for Moon's volume, the slaves walk into the water and can be heard singing as long as their heads are above the water. Although onlookers fear that the Africans have committed suicide, they soon see, "far out in midstream, a flock of great water birds take flight and wing their way into the rising sun, with exultant cries" (Porter 176).

The legend of flying Africans, among the most powerful to have evolved out of slavery into the modern era, was easily joined to Christian eschatology. In their traditional lyrics, spirituals such as "I'll Fly Away" pointed first of all to the afterlife—"Some glad morning when this life is over, / I'll fly away / To a home on God's celestial shore." Even if they did not reject Christianity—as did Malcolm X when, in comparing himself to Icarus, he vowed never to forget that "any wings I wore had been put on by the religion of Islam" (Malcolm X 287)—African American slaves and their descendants often found their heavenly reward overlaid with the kind of return home that appears in *Song of Solomon,* where Toni Morrison turned the mythic flight to Africa into an emboldening legend of redemption from exile, or what John Edgar Wideman heard promised in Bob Marley's adaptation of "I'll Fly Away" in "Rasta Man Chant": "*One bright morning when my work is over / I will fly away home*" (Wideman 86).

Icarus, as Hickman encounters him in Brueghel's rendering, has neither drowned himself nor flown away home. His flight cut short, he has plunged toward death—drowning but not yet drowned—where the painting freezes him. So, too, Sunraider lingers at the edge of death in his hospital bed colloquy with Hickman: "After flying so far and climbing so high and now here" (TD 459). But his tragic arc was implicit from the outset of Ellison's career. The motif of birds suddenly taking flight, an image of chaos resolving into order, recurs throughout Ellison's essays and fiction, and beginning with his earliest short stories such as "Mister Toussan" and "That I Had Wings," he was fascinated by the complex multicultural symbolism inherent in flying figures, especially those that are, in effect, limping flying figures. Joining the physical pain of segregation with the spiritual resources for delivery from it, "Flying Home," the most important of these stories, also played upon the African American folktale—"Colored Man in Heaven" and "A Flying Fool" are two of the titles given it[9]—about a black man who goes to heaven and raises hell by his acrobatic flying. In old man Jefferson's outlandish tall tale about his own heavenly flying, juxtaposed to the far less comic tale of Todd, the Tuskegee airman who has crashed after his plane gets tangled up with "jimcrows," he refuses the harness required of black angels and flies one-winged—so wild he "knocked the tips offa some stars" and caused "a coupla lynchings down here in Macon County" ("Flying Home" 155, 158).

Ellison returned to the embedded folktale in "An Extravagance of Laughter," an essay in which he recalled his own anxiety upon first arriving in New York. Whereas the visible signs of segregation in the South had provided a strange sense of security, he now felt that he was proceeding "in the manner of one learning to walk again upon a recently mended leg," a sensation that put him in mind of the tales of black folks in heaven required "to fly with one wing strapped to their sides" (CERE 616). Incorporating into his limping figures the common sociological argument that racism is crippling—an idea evident, for example, in Martin Luther King Jr.'s argument at the March on Washington that "the life of the Negro is still sadly crippled by the manacles of segregation and the chains of discrimination" ("I Have a Dream" 102) and made a pointed component of civil rights policy in President Lyndon Johnson's 1965 address at Howard University, of which Ellison remarked, "there was no hedging in it, no escape clauses" (CERE 740)[10]—Ellison also reminded us that the black American Adam was once and still a slave, bearing in his body the nation's original sin. "Canst thou not drive that old Adam away?" demands Ahab of the carpenter tasked with making him a new leg in *Moby-Dick* (471). Ellison's "mammy-made Ahab," as he calls him in *Three Days,* descends indirectly from *Invisible Man*'s Brother Tarp. Although doctors can find nothing wrong with Tarp's leg—"it's sound as a piece of steel," they say—he got his limp, we recall, from "dragging a chain." If Ellison's new Ahab is crippled, however, his shackle, like the one Brother Tarp gives Invisible Man, as we also recall, has "a heap of signifying wrapped up in it" (TD 685; IM 387–88).

In both "Flying Home" and "An Extravagance of Laughter," the black American Adam turned Icarus is also a potential phoenix,[11] for whose "vernacular, but transcendent, rising," as Ellison wrote in "The Little Man at Chehaw Station," we must always be on the lookout (CERE 519). But Adam Sunraider is no phoenix. Although, like the novelist, he plays "with the fires of chaos" so as to "rearrange reality to the patterns of his imagination" and embarks on his own Promethean theft of fire when he preaches a "fire sermon" with Hickman—"for man was beseeching the Lord for warmth when it was the *sun* itself he coveted"—his Icarian ascent is shadowed by his descent into hell (CERE 694; TD 302–10).[12] If he is supposed to be Satan, says Hickman's fellow minister, Wilhite, of Brueghel's Icarus, "I want to see his hooves and tail" (TD 595–99). But "the devil is never so black as he is painted," as we know from the man in gray, Melville's Confidence-Man in one of his many costumes (*Confidence-Man* 32). As much as Sunraider is a *"kite broken loose from its string," "whirling and tossing ... plunging earthward ... [like a] bird on its wing,"* he is also *"our fallen angel," "the devil"* coming into Jessie Rockmore's living room by television, and a "jack-legged highbinder," as Rockmore calls him after Sunraider bursts into his house and demands to know, "What are you doing in my coffin!" (TD 706, 636, 528, 165, 169–70). Ellison found a simple prototype for Sunraider as the devil when he reviewed Frank Goodwyn's 1944 novel *The Magic of Limping John,* whose title character, known by his "mule hoof" that was split when he got his foot caught "in the gate of Hell" (Goodwyn and Greenwood 14, 38), pretends to be El Diablo only to be taken over by the role and weighed down, as Ellison saw him, with the curses, as well as the gifts, of a god.[13]

But perhaps the most intriguing of Ellison's associations of Sunraider with the devil—more specifically, with Mephistopheles, who is also depicted, as in Goethe's *Faust*, as a limping figure[14]—occurs during the speech he is making when he is gunned down in the Senate. Elucidating the "riddles" and "national ambiguities" of a "covenant" requiring that we seek "ever the darkness in lightness and the lightness in darkness," all the while feeling himself taken over by "some mocking ventriloquistic orator of opposing views, a trickster of corny philosophical ambition," Sunraider presents us with a quotation set off orthographically in the text, as though for special notice: *"The land was ours before we were the land's"* (TD 237, 241–42).

Ellison alludes here to Robert Frost's poem "The Gift Outright," which Frost recited from memory at John F. Kennedy's inauguration after tempestuous conditions spoiled his attempt to read a poem composed for the occasion.[15] The poem may be interpreted as a tribute to manifest destiny, the land awaiting conquest and cultivation before the nation had yet achieved liberation from British rule ("She was our land more than a hundred years / Before we were her people"), and then submitting, as if in an act of love ("we found out that it was ourselves / We were withholding from our land of living, / And forthwith found salvation in surrender / ... / To the land vaguely realizing westward"). But Frost's cagey parenthetical line—"(The deed of gift was many deeds of war)"—reveals as well that dispossession, the necessary adjunct of possession, is the hidden secret of the national myth (Frost 348). Although "deed of gift" is a legal term meaning simply a gift given without expectation of return, Frost's source in all likelihood was Christopher Marlowe's *Doctor Faustus* (Von Frank 23), where Mephistopheles tells Faustus he must "bequeath [his soul] solemnly / And write a deed of gift with thine own blood." Once Faustus has signed in blood and uttered the blasphemous words "Consummatum est!," he believes he sees a Latin inscription on his arm commanding him to flee. But, he asks, "Whither should I fly? / If unto God, He'll throw me down to hell" (Marlowe 21, 23). Sunraider, we may surmise, is posing the same question to himself.

Ellison provided his own echo of Frost in the Juneteenth sermon that Sunraider retrieves in deathbed memory, where Hickman had instructed Bliss, "this land is ours because we came out of it, we bled in it, our tears watered it, we fertilized it with our dead" (TD 323). A vernacular rendition of Ezekiel's prophecy in the Valley of Dry Bones, the sermon is a rousing allegory of the black nation Israel raised up from captivity in the Babylon of America, but its baroque mixture of holiness and theatricality appears more foreboding—"*the celebration of a gaudy illusion*," as the delusional Sunraider thinks of it (TD 314)—when we consider that Ellison chose a Juneteenth holiday celebrated on the Fourth of July[16] as the occasion on which Bliss, when he shows up in Oklahoma as Mister Movie-Man, dresses the black townspeople appearing in his film in garish Halloween costumes and seduces the young mixed-race woman who will give birth to his parricidal assassin.

It is no coincidence, surely, that the story of this fateful Juneteenth encounter is rendered by Cliofus, the comedic storyteller and "word-drunk oracle" whose long tale, full of signifying digressions that are themselves protean elaborations, concludes the novel as we have it (TD 848, 860). Although Cliofus does not limp, he has to be brought on stage at the Cave of the Winds in a wheelchair, as if there is an inverse ratio between his crippling and the vital torrent of words that pours out of him, virtually unbidden. But perhaps like Legba, Cliofus's crippling is only an illusion. (As Donald Cosentino has said of Eshu-Elegba, "a paralytic trickster is a contradiction in terms" [Consentino 267].) Riffing on the inherent "*double-talk*" of words themselves, Cliofus quotes T. S. Eliot's "Gerontion"—"The word within a word, unable to speak a word" (TD 867)—but his allusion to Eliot's poem also points toward Ellison's comparable anxiety about creative impotence ("an old man in a dry month," "a dry brain in a dry season") and the labyrinthine dangers of signifying invention: "Think now / History has many cunning passages, contrived corridors / And issues, deceives with whispering ambitions, / Guides us by vanities" (Eliot 21–22). In a novel that ran the risk of giving way to protean tale-telling without end—in which the very idea of plot progression appears to have been set aside in favor of relentless improvisation—Cliofus, appropriately, has the last words.

In his notes for *Three Days* Ellison presented conflicting motives for Sunraider's racist demagoguery, speculating, on the one hand, that he sees himself as "putting pressure on Negroes to become more powerful through political action" and yet, on the other, that he feels humiliated by his own racial ambiguity and thus uses the "agency of racism to punish Negroes for being weak, and to achieve power of his own" (*Juneteenth* 360; TD 975). Hickman and his congregation had hoped that "*a little gifted child would speak for our condition from inside the only acceptable mask*," the mask of whiteness (TD 413). After Sippy Brown's "Pygmalion feat of transformation," however, Bliss is a man better suited to scams, costumes, and roles (TD 393), and thus a figure who, like Eshu-Elegba, wears a cap of many colors—black and white, or better, red, white, black, and blue—and sows dissension for its own sake. Although the novel's action disproves McIntyre's initial speculation that the assassination attempt itself is some kind of hoax, "yet another Sunraider plot to confound the public," the possibility remains that Sunraider, as Reverend Wilhite suggests, has been "doing something behind the scenes," working "another con game" meant to advance the interests of black people (TD 21, 428–29). As a more cunning invisible man, the new Lincoln in his trickster's disguise, Sunraider may even have been preparing to divulge his racial secret, a possibility Ellison entertained (Bradley 134), when he is cut down by his son the assassin. But we are probably closer to the truth in Ellison's notation that "Sunraider is a trickster who plays a serious role, and perhaps it is he who is behind what is happening" (TD 978).

And yet, behind what, exactly? Electing to "*extend myself and test my most far-fetched possibilities with only the agency of shadows*," as he thinks in discovering the illusory world of film, Bliss determines to live out the "*joke implicit in my being me*" while leaving others to pursue "*the mystery [that] went with me, entered with me . . . pursued me, shifting and changing faces*" (TD 393). As though "protean with changes of pace, location and identity," or like the parts of a "dismembered god" found "everywhere and anywhere at one and the same time" (CERE 101), the many trickster figures who populate the novel may best be understood as avatars of Bliss/Sunraider himself— "some white scoundrel, betwisted and painted up for a decoy," as Melville's man with a wooden leg says of Black Guinea and his sham performance (*Confidence-Man* 31). If so, they dramatize "the puzzle of the one-and-the-many," as Ellison called it in "Hidden Name and Complex Fate" (CERE 207), a "mystery as difficult as that of the Trinity," as he put it in a later note to himself (ms. box I:141, folder 1). "*E Pluribus Unum*," Sunraider shouts, as the Great Seal of the United States seems to hurtle at him during his speech, its eagle no American phoenix rising but a bird of prey descending with "sphinx-like eyes," bearing down in "an exploding chaos of red, white, blue, and gold." "Let us take wing with our emblem," Sunraider calls out in the face of this menacing hallucination, and "unite like the flexing feathers that lift it aloft. Let us forge ahead in faith and in confidence—E PLURIBUS UNUM!" (TD 242, 236).[17]

No doubt, Bliss/Sunraider may be seen as the one in the many, the many in the one. Truly a confidence man in whom we must have faith, a Whitmanian type "great enough to possess the greatness of the land" (CERE 83), he is likewise, as Ellison wrote of the pimp-limping Harlem joker in "The Little Man at Chehaw Station," "his own work of art"—but one in which "the man himself is hidden somewhere within, his complex identity concealed by his aesthetic gesturing" (CERE 507).

More than a decade later, near the end of his working life, as well as his mortal life, Ellison encountered on the streets of New York another such African American trickster. This young man, having likewise made "walking a form of art," displays the satiric vernacular step known variously as "Walking the Dog" and "Strutting with Some Barbeque." Rather than the madcap, mongrel mix of cultural styles sported by the joker in "Little Man," however, this black trickster features only a single, jarring ornament—a gray cap with Confederate Army insignia. "So you've joined the Confederacy," Ellison manages to sputter. Offering a grim "look of reply" before the two of them march on, the young man advances a short distance and waits for Ellison to look back before he, followed by Ellison, breaks out in "uncontrollable laughter" (CERE 839). Change the joke and slip the yoke.

We may never discover the mystery of Sunraider's identity—why, indeed, should we expect to discover it?—but Ellison offers what may be the most telling glimpse of him to Walker Millsap, a man hired by Hickman to track Bliss after he passes into the world of whiteness. Millsap records in the confidential report he prepares for Hickman that he has found Bliss playing the part of a Confederate officer in a film re-creation of the Battle of Bull Run, dressed "in Confederate gray, carrying a saber, and wearing a foot-long feather in his hat." Given the novel's immersion in the symbolic language of myth, we are entitled to wonder if the feather—an officer's ceremonial decoration appropriate to the treasonous part played by Ellison's own man in gray, his own Confidence-Man—is not the signature feature of Eshu-Elegba that appears when his divine powers come on (Thompson 28). Whether such an inference is warranted, Bliss, recognizing Millsap, gives him a sweeping salute that trails the feather in the dust, like the red, white, and blue flag trailed in the footprints of the black Christ, and then swaggers off "by doing a cute little hustler's limp" (TD 704–5). Something further, Ellison could have added, may come of this masquerade.

NOTES

1. The italics are Ellison's. Passages presented in italics represent one or another character's ruminations or recollections in the form of interior monologues, which at times take on a distinct authorial cast.

2. I would like to thank Adam Bradley and Grant Shreve for sharing with me notes from Ellison's papers at the Library of Congress that proved essential to my essay. I am also grateful to them for their incisive readings of an earlier draft, as well as to John Callahan, Marc Conner, Lucas Morel, and other participants in the 2012 "Symposium on the 60th Anniversary of *Invisible Man*" at Washington and Lee University for valuable comments on the essay in its first iteration.

3. Although Ellison seems to have relied principally on the translation of *The Odyssey* by W. H. D. Rouse, with Robert Fitzgerald's version in mind—"My name is Nohbdy: mother, father, and friends, / everyone calls me Nohbdy" (Homer, *Odyssey*, Fitzgerald trans. 156)— we may likewise imagine Sunraider assuming Bert Williams's famous stage persona of "Nobody," a role fit for Rinehart old or new. Although Williams's trademark song, written for the 1906 stage musical *Abyssinia*, is not specifically racial, its lyrics assumed racial meaning in association with his shambling, sad-sack character, whose pathos was underscored by his heavily corked blackface: "I ain't done nothin' to Nobody. / I ain't never got nothin' from Nobody, no time. / And, until I get somethin' from somebody sometime, / I don't intend to do nothin' for Nobody, no time" (Watkins 160–61, 175–76). It is this debilitating sense of "nobodiness" that for Martin Luther King Jr. marked the nadir of racial dehumanization (King, "Letter from Birmingham Jail" 93).

4. Ellison's Chief Sam is not an actual historical figure, but he was surely inspired in part by Alfred C. "Chief" Sam, who claimed to be an African chief and toured Oklahoma in 1913 (the year before Ellison was born) advocating emigration to Africa. Selling stock in Sam's Akim Trading Company, Chief Sam managed to raise enough money to lead a small group of followers to Liberia in 1914; see Bittle and Geis, *Longest Way Home*.

5. We may see Sunraider as an instance of that anxiety Ellison spoke of in outlining the dangerous temptations of minstrelsy: "When the white man steps behind the mask of the trickster his freedom is circumscribed by the fear that he is not simply miming a personification of his disorder and chaos, but that he will become in fact that which he intends only to symbolize; that he will be trapped somewhere in the mystery of hell (for there is a mystery in the whiteness of blackness, the innocence of evil and the evil of innocence, though, being initiates, Negroes express the joke of it in the blues), and thus lose that freedom which, in the fluid, 'traditionless,' 'classless,' and rapidly changing society, he would recognize as the white man's alone" (CERE 107).

6. When Hickman encounters the black Christ, it reminds him of the Icarus tapestry, but when he first sees the Icarus tapestry it puts him in mind of the black Christ. Although Ellison may have intended this temporal puzzle, it is more likely that he had not fully resolved the sequence of Hickman's movements in Washington, DC.

7. See Frederick Douglass's famous 1852 address "The Meaning of July Fourth for the Negro": "Oh! be warned! be warned! a horrible reptile is coiled up in your nation's bosom; the venomous creature is nursing at the tender breast of your youthful republic" (Douglass, "Meaning" 201).

8. Hickman's interpretation of Brueghel's scene bears comparison to those of William Carlos Williams in "Landscape with the Fall of Icarus" and W. H. Auden in "Musée des Beaux Arts."

9. For a suggestive reading of "Flying Home" in relation to "Colored Man in Heaven," see O'Meally, 70–74.

10. In his elaboration of the "race of life" argument, which dates to the nineteenth century and was used, for example, by Abraham Lincoln and W. E. B. Du Bois, Johnson said: "You do not take a person who, for years, has been hobbled by chains and liberate him, bring him up to the starting line of a race and then say, 'you are free to compete with all the others,' and still justly believe that you have been completely fair" (L. Johnson 636). Observing that neither Lincoln nor Franklin Roosevelt had "spelled out the meaning of full integration for Negroes" as Johnson did, Ellison concluded that he would be recognized "as the greatest American President for the poor and for Negroes . . . a very great honor indeed." Although Sunraider in no way resembles Johnson, it may be said that he, like the president, is someone "through whom the essential conflicts of democracy . . . are brought into the most intense and creative focus. He is the one who releases chaos as he creates order" even as he becomes "a prisoner of his role" (CERE 552, 562, 559–62).

11. The lesson of "An Extravagance of Laughter," which, like many of Ellison's long essays, unfolds as though it were a short story, lies in its dramatization of racial violence "transcended with cruel but homeopathic laughter." Thus, their tall-tale improvisation in the story of cops in Phenix City, Alabama, who beat a black man named Whyte who refuses to deny his name permits Ellison and his fellow Tuskegee students to pass through the town and emerge "like the mythical phoenix." Thus, too, Ellison's meditation on lynching, "a blood-rite" that propitiates the "insatiable god of whiteness," which is embedded in a lengthy exposition of the laughing barrel, in which Negroes concealed the mirth through which they became "master[s] of an outrageous and untenable situation" (CERE 635, 641, 653). Derived from the tradition among slaves of keeping their conversations and prayer meetings secret by using an iron pot or kettle turned upside down to catch the sounds, a practice with origins in West African religion (Dundes xv–xvi; Rawick 39), the laughing barrel is a most serious device—one through which a young black man fresh to New York from segregated Alabama might gingerly test his leg to be sure the irons of segregation had been removed.

12. Although Sunraider's name refers most immediately to Icarus and secondarily to Prometheus, Odysseus, Oedipus, and Eshu-Elegba, each of them a kind of "sun god," it may be worth noting that in Walter Farley's 1941 bestseller *The Black Stallion* one of the titular hero's archrivals is a horse named Sun Raider.

13. Goodwyn's southwestern novel drew on stock tales of El Diablo Cojo, the limping devil, but Ellison discovered beneath its simple story the basic pattern of religions, "from their birth in magic" and their manipulation of "the divine forces which control human destiny" to their institutionalization in orthodoxy, where they rule by "miracle, mystery, and authority" (Goodwyn and Greenwood, *Magic* 121). In P. S. McGeeney's 1936 novel *El Diablo Cojo (The Limping Devil)*, to take another example Ellison might have known, he is a notorious bandit with a shifting identity.

14. Mephistopheles's cloven hoof—the foot of a goat that betrays his disguises—is mentioned several times in Goethe's *Faust*. In a particularly bawdy passage in the Walpurgis Night scene, for example, Mephistopheles is addressed by the Old Witch as "Sir Cloven-Hoof" (Goethe 131). Sander Gilman notes that the limping devil and the limping Jew have been associated historically as figures of licentiousness and degeneracy, both of them marked by their disavowal of Christ's divinity (Gilman 107–9).

15. In a speculative note, Ellison found that the incident "foreshadowed both Kennedy's assassination and the stripping of [the] authority of Nixon... the moment of glory was attended by sings [*sic*; signs] that pointed to the burning of cities, the energy crises (that is the tendency of nature to get out of control, the wind's mocking of the poet and of the Camelot imagery that was to be appropriated by the Kennedy publicists[)]" (ms. box I:141, folder 6).

16. On the relationship between emancipation and the Fourth of July in Frederick Douglass, Martin Luther King Jr., and Ralph Ellison, see Sundquist, "'We Dreamed a Dream,'" 114–17.

17. In Sunraider's cadences one may hear echoes of Ellison's more staid, but perhaps also slyly ironic, remarks to the Harvard alumni, class of 1949, about the convulsive transformations in American law and custom in the twenty years since *Brown v. Board of Education*: "Let us not be dismayed, let us not lose faith, simply because the correctives which we have set in motion, and you have set in motion, took a long time.... What seems to be called for is an honest confrontation with our mistakes... and a willingness to confront the chaos, the *nemesis*, which is about us. After all, *nemesis* is only another word for peril" (CERE 425–26).

THE POLITICS OF FATHERHOOD IN *THREE DAYS BEFORE THE SHOOTING...*

LENA HILL

Some of the most perplexing characters in Ellison's long fiction are peculiar father figures. There is the power-hungry band comprised of the college founder who is described as the "cold, father symbol"; Bledsoe, the college president who calls Invisible Man "son" eleven times before emotionally lynching him; and Brother Jack, the Brotherhood leader accused of adopting the role of the "great white father." Then we have the sexually deviant tribe including Jim Trueblood, the incest-committing sharecropper, and Norton, the white Bostonian who *wishes* he could have committed incest. And then, too, there is the clan that sees beneath the surface, consisting of the Vet who commands Invisible Man to be his "own father" and Rinehart, the Harlem confidence man, who is alternately hailed as "daddy," "daddy-o," "pops," and "poppa-stopper." Indeed, Ellison's canonical tour de force is overrun by diversely dysfunctional daddies.

Given the general lack of resolution permeating the conclusion of *Invisible Man*, we should not be surprised to find a thorny father-son relationship at the center of *Three Days before the Shooting...* (2010). Reverend Hickman's extended reflection over his relationship to Bliss provides the frame for the undulating narrative, and like the fathers we meet in *Invisible Man*, Ellison gives us much to pause over in assessing Hickman through the lens of fatherhood. What kind of man—in the name of drawing sinners to God—forces his son to participate in a religious charade that both frightens his child and proves physically dangerous? The kind, Ellison suggests, who shares a good deal in common with the men who founded and led the United States of America. These men, regularly celebrated in visual art and afforded an almost religious respect, offer an unexpected means for examining Hickman. With their help, Ellison deftly connects fatherhood, and the attitude that individuals adopt toward this role, to a broader notion of US patriotism and independence.[1]

In the same way that Ellison muses over the contradictory natures of the founding fathers and individual presidents, he encourages readers to ponder Hickman, a father figure who, although flawed, dedicates himself to upholding the core principles of the country. As Ellison explains in a 1974 interview with John Hershey, Hickman captivated his imagination when he discovered that Reverend A. Z.'s "drama of recreating the Resurrection" relates to "the significance of being a Negro in America and ... with the problem of our democratic faith as a whole" (CRE 277). Ellison not only connects Hickman to the founders of the United States, but also to God the father who sacrifices his son for man's salvation, resurrecting him so sinners might be redeemed. In tracing this confluence of fathers through the visual objects that introduce them throughout the novel, the question I am interested in answering is what the celebration of this jazz-playing, charade-performing minister helps us clarify about the relationship between Ellison's fascination with fatherhood and interest in political ideology.

To answer this question, I examine Ellison's insistence that readers approach Hickman with admiration and forgiveness by presenting him within a carefully arranged exhibit of plastic art. In my work on Ellison, I have been interested in his creation of protagonists who must learn to become sophisticated readers of visual pieces.[2] Invisible Man confronts numerous objects of art, museum-like spaces, and visually rich sites that connote the importance of gaining visual literacy. Ellison highlights his protagonist's credulous nature by dramatizing his failure to discern the complexity of his identity as it is reflected by visual displays. *Three Days* shows Ellison building upon this technique to accentuate Hickman's sophisticated cultural sensibility and political understanding. As Anne Dvinge argues, with Hickman Ellison portrays the "searching and experimenting element of 'Americanism'" that insists "on a more complex vision, one that can hold past, present and future in one gaze."[3] By focusing on Ellison's curatorial impulse, I probe the ways his somewhat surprising selections of art signify his desire to link his protagonist's visual acuity with his political savvy.

By analyzing Hickman's interpretation of significant pieces of art, we discover the essence of what might be described as Ellison's independent political philosophy. After all, if the paintings, sculptures, tapestries, and other art objects populating the narrative consistently feature political father figures or direct our attention to classic father-son relationships, Hickman's contemplation of these images offers a possible key to unlock his political ideas. Ellison's dependence upon literature, and specifically his own creative writing, began with his work on *Invisible Man*. Reflecting on his first novel, he allowed, "I understand a bit more about myself as a Negro because literature has taught me something of my identity as a Western man, as a political being" (CERE 164). Thus, Ellison lays the foundation for Hickman's character and emotional relationship to the United States long before he began the forty-year journey of composition that led to the posthumous publication of *Three Days*. I turn to his early letters, interviews, essays, and first novel to construct the core pieces of Ellison's political views that form the heart of Hickman's personality.

ELLISON AND THE TRADITION OF THE SELF-MADE BLACK AMERICAN

Throughout the 1960s and '70s, African American artists and activists alike accused Ellison of failing to support the progressive political agenda of the left. From his optimistic yet ambivalent response to the 1954 *Brown v. Board* decision to his critiques of Black Arts movement writers whom he deemed excessively invested in politics to the detriment of their art, Ellison never sought to be designated an unconditional devotee to liberal ideology. Instead, his rejection of documents like Gunnar Myrdal's *An American Dilemma: The Negro Problem and Modern Democracy* (1944), which played an integral role in the landmark *Brown v. Board* decision, and his full-throated denunciation of the Moynihan Report (1965) came to define his view of the most dangerous elements of liberalism's posture toward African Americans. These documents exposed an attitude toward fatherhood—in a national and cultural sense—that provided a crucial element of contention for Ellison's evolving politics. He angrily noted, "Moynihan looked at a fatherless family and interpreted it not in the context of Negro cultural patterns, but in a white cultural pattern" (CRE 102). This misreading, Ellison intimates, disqualifies Moynihan from claiming any mantle of legitimacy or authority to discuss issues of race notwithstanding his liberal ideology.

Ellison's ire over such sociological pronouncements on black fatherhood merged seamlessly with his antipathy toward paternalistic political positions. As the product of a "fatherless home"—he lost his father at the age of three and his stepfather passed away when he was eleven—Ellison found no credence in popular notions alternately bemoaning the breakdown of the African American nuclear family and designating black citizens as perpetual children. While he passionately supported Lyndon B. Johnson's integrationist policies and chafed at Ronald Reagan's economic policies, Ellison's views on fatherhood endorsed ideas from liberals and conservatives alike. In fact, as he relentlessly turned to his writing to refine his notion of American democracy, Ellison bristled at what he deemed the many similarities between the two parties.[4]

The need to carve out an independent political philosophy led to his strong words for writers whose work bespoke an implicit subscription to sociologically derived beliefs about black culture. Referring to politically radical writers associated with the Black Arts movement, Ellison complained, "What bothers me about so many of these new, loud-mouthed guys is that they have no sense of what came before themselves. They have little sense of what their parents were like, and absolutely *no* sense of what their grandparents were like. Thus in their most militant assertions they turn out to have less respect for their Black forefathers than some of the whites who held their forefathers in slavery" (CRE 211). This absence of cultural knowledge, Ellison implies, results in their misunderstanding of black culture and American history; consequently, like Moynihan, they lack the authority to use their creative work to examine the African American dilemma concerning cultural and national fatherhood. Ellison, however, inserts father-son relationships in his fiction as a vehicle for exploring African Americans' position in US history as well as contemporary political affairs. Inevitably, characters who represent the most interesting father figures connect paternal proficiency to the attainment of emotional maturity rather than material success. Ellison, departing from the heart of the US myth of the self-made man in preference for a more Emersonian notion of self-reliance, locates the essence of black American self-determination in mental complexity as opposed to economic achievement.

My focus on fathers and sons in Ellison's fiction—and particularly their portrayal in visual art—highlights his broader discussion of the relationship between US citizens and their national forefathers. Ellison's repeated contemplation of flawed fathers linked to children by unlikely, sometimes even traumatic, circumstances metaphorically replicates the drama of black Americans' history in the United States. Time and time again, Ellison proclaims the dark past that initially brought black Africans to the United States as proof of their rightful claim to American citizenship as opposed to evidence of national illegitimacy based upon race. He insists upon the sophistication shown by slave "craftsmen and artists" and pointed to his own grandfather as proof of the cultural accomplishment and intellectual acuity of ex-slaves. In a 1976 interview he explained, "I did see my granddaddy and he was no beaten-down 'Sambo.' Rather he was a courageous, ingenious old guy who owned property, engaged in the Reconstruction politics of South Carolina, and who stood up to a mob after they had lynched his best friend" (CRE 338, 339). By spotlighting his grandfather's political agency, Ellison claims a paternal heritage of political power rather than victimization.

Almost ten years earlier, Ellison turned to Stanley M. Elkins's *Slavery: A Problem in American Institutional and Intellectual Life* (1959), a crucial source undergirding Moynihan's call for affirmative action. He rejected Elkins's "'Sambo' argument" and insisted that "despite the historical past and the injustices of the present," he had "to *affirm* [his] forefathers" just as he "*must* affirm [his] parents or be reduced in [his] own mind to a white man's inadequate—even if unprejudiced—conception of human complexity" (CRE 119). In other words, he alone reserved the right to assess and interpret the meaning of his history and its relationship to his present possibilities. If the positive conclusions he draws related to his forefathers deny him access to certain kinds of support from the social welfare state, that is a chance Ellison is willing to take. Like his grandfather, he vows to live in rebellious opposition to mobs that might attack his independence if the alternative leaves him caricatured and excluded from the national identity.

In looking toward *Three Days,* it is worth noting that Ellison's fierce declarations proclaiming his individual right to define himself actually emerged much earlier than his post–*Invisible Man* interviews and essays. The consistency with which he held these beliefs offers a revealing window into his conception of black American emotional self-sufficiency and political sensibility. Writing to Richard Wright in July 1945, Ellison muses about

> the most absurd paradox, in American history: that simply by striving consciously to become Negroes we are becoming and are destined to be Americans, and the first truly mature Americans at that. Just as the biggest joke I know on you, is that after all the struggle to become a responsible Communist writer and spokesman, you became instead something much more important: an artist and articulator of the most vital possibilities of American life.[5]

The unlooked-for result of US segregation, Ellison explains, is the emergence of an African American writer possessing a more authentic American character than his white peers and expressing the most honest, inspiring, yet uncompromising view of the nation's future. The maturity Ellison claims for black writers like himself and Wright relates directly to his notion of successful fatherhood, an ability to raise oneself and embrace independence through the force of mere conviction. Whereas many Americans accept their citizenship without thought, contemplative black citizens self-consciously shape their views of national character and individual responsibility, thereby representing models of self-reliance.

Ellison's passionate views on self-sufficiency soon translated to his rejection of Communism, a system that came to represent the antithesis of the freedom he discovered in writing. He averred to Wright,

> We *are*, we were *born* and became through our experience, the "conscience of the Negro people" although they dont [sic] fully recognize it yet. But I think our destiny is something more than that: it is to become the conscience of the United States. . . . A sense of responsibility based on a vision narrower than this is inadequate. There was a time when—and recently too—I hung back because of my poor education and clumsy writing; but no more. I'm stubborn enough to overcome some of this, and I find that when I have the broadest range for my passion it improves my writing, although that is still sadly lacking. We almost always feel more than we are able to express; the break with the c.p. has allowed me to come alive to many things of which I was becoming aware during my bitterly isolated college experience. I'm reclaiming that now—with the stimulation of B.B., I might add,— and forgotten passages of literature and repressed moods are becoming the wedges of insights. Some day I hope to do a surgical job on the repressive effect that c.p. sectarianism had upon my sensibilities along with the quickening effects of Marxism. I was never dead, but I was amorphous as hell, literally; and after my discovery of Marx too, too many questions, nebulous emotions and moods were left waiting breathelessly [sic] behind the doors of dogma.[6]

I quote this letter at length to establish Ellison's early recognition of the problems inherent in Communism and Marxist ideology.[7] At the very moment that Ellison wrestled with the potential political and intellectual power of creative writing, he rejected the restrictive nature of Communist Party doctrine. Linking his isolated college years to the confining nature of Marxist ideologues, Ellison steels himself to adopt a deep and abiding faith in his creative writing. His newfound confidence stems from his awareness of an ability to look upon the United States with rare honesty and sophistication, a skill he describes as becoming the "conscience of the United States." He attributes part of his awakening to the potency of Wright's *Black Boy* (1945), and he draws inspiration from the belief that he might pen literature with similar force. Indeed, as early as May 1940 Ellison shared his concerns regarding the danger of Communist ideology.[8] Furthermore, as soon as he committed to publishing creative writing that achieved similar authority as Wright's, Ellison again turned to the notion of fatherhood to describe the impact of his words. Remarking upon his discussions with Melvin Tolson, Ellison concludes that he and Wright have "become the fathers of our elders."[9]

Ellison's declaration of their precocious status stems directly from what he perceives to be their intellectual and emotional complexity, the most crucial attributes of a good father. Interestingly, the language he uses in his letters to Wright echoes key moments in Invisible Man's development. He clearly worked through certain issues with his first protagonist that he builds upon in *Three Days*. For instance, directly following Invisible Man's first speech for the Brotherhood, he ponders the meaning of his claim to have become "more human." He speculates, "Perhaps it was something that Woodridge had said in the literature class back at college. I could see him vividly ... before the blackboard chalked with quotations from Joyce," and "I could hear him: 'Stephen's problem, like ours, was not actually one of creating the uncreated conscience of his race, but of creating the *uncreated features of his face*. Our task is that of making ourselves individuals. The conscience of a race is the gift of its individuals who see, evaluate, record" (IM 354; italics in original). A letter to Wright shows Ellison anticipating Woodridge's mind-set. Ellison announces,

> I see it this way: they have no conscience, being Americans, and the only force capable of awakening a conscience within them, and the only force politically capable of keeping them in line until that happens, are the Negroes. It is our job as Joyce put it, "to create the uncreated conscience" of the Negroes.[10]

For Ellison, creating an "uncreated conscience" equaled accepting without apology the individual complexity that positions men to define their independence in distinctly American terms. A character's power to understand

and appreciate visual art becomes one of Ellison's standard artistic methods for establishing individual and social maturity.

In early drafts of *Invisible Man,* Ellison considered Woodridge at length, connecting the professor to the outrage of sociological findings that consigned African Americans to second-class citizenship and declared them incapable of masculine complexity and independence. In a manuscript version, Invisible Man seeks out Professor Woodridge in hopes of receiving something like fatherly advice following his fateful drive with Norton. He arrives only to find his teacher alone in his apartment wearing "the end of a woman's stocking ... to keep his hair in place." Woodridge greets his student's surprised stare with a challenge: "Well your sociology text teaches that we are part of what it describes the 'Lady of the races.' Do you remember that?" He proceeds, "Then even if the rumors about me were true, it shouldn't cause any surprise, should it? If you belong to the lady of the races isn't it all right to become a 'lady'?" Sinking deeper into his drunken stupor, Woodridge confides,

> I dream at night that all the students I've taught in these eight years are lined up before me, against the bare wall of a long hall, and I am moving along gripping a sharp carpenter's gouge and as I come to each student I stop and scoop out his eyes and drop them bleeding and gelatinous into a large white cotton sack that hangs chained to my neck. ... Its [sic] worse than that. Because none of the students seems to feel the pain. ... If only they could feel it and cry out in pain! Just one. Then I could stop: then I could teach them to see. ... This place is smoke in your eyes."[11]

In fascinating ways, this scene both returns to Ellison's early words to Wright and anticipates Ellison's extended investment in connecting complex, intellectually mature characters to visual art in *Three Days.* Woodridge embodies the conflicted man of thought who pushes against societal forces that discourage serious self-reflection. His ironic reference to sociological pronouncements that proclaim African American cultural weakness dramatizes the psychological damage he associates with such research when individuals uncritically accept it. The guilt he experiences from his participation in the brainwashing the college promotes leads to his nightmares of violently blinding black students. Instead of providing the intellectual tools to form an independent, mature conscience, he aids the work of men like Bledsoe, a malicious, scheming father figure. A different draft includes Woodridge admonishing Invisible Man, "Read, read all you can, and learn to read the meaning as well as the words," before the protagonist leaves the professor standing before a board with a Joyce quotation upon the board: "Welcome, O life! I go to encounter for the millionth time the reality of experience and to forge in the smithy of my soul the uncreated conscience of my race." Although he lacks the courage to follow his convictions, Woodridge remains convinced—just as Ellison discovers in reading Wright's *Black Boy*—that a rigorous engagement with literature represents the antidote for intellectual suppression and provides a foundation for maturing into the kind of man worthy of the title *father*.[12]

In apparent anticipation of *Three Days*, every version of the Woodridge scene portrays the professor's apartment as a space that validates the professor's sophisticated ideas on race and culture through the display of modern art. In one draft the protagonist observes "prints of modern painting which I could not understand hung from the walls," while in a different version he notes, "Prints of abstract paintings puzzled me from the walls."[13] But while most of these potential details in *Invisible Man* remain beyond the scope of the published text—or reworked in scenes related to the Vet or the woman in the red robe—Ellison places a character's appreciation of visual art at the center of his development of Hickman, a man who fully accepts the role of father as well as the task of serving as a moral guide for African Americans lacking a sophisticated political philosophy. In stark contrast to Woodridge, who eventually orders Invisible Man, "Now get OUT,"[14] or the Vet, who advises, "Be your own father, young man" (IM 156), Hickman accepts the fatherhood mantle, assuming the role of Bliss's daddy even as the child enters his life drenched in the kind of American chaos and absurdity that Invisible Man spends a good deal of his life attempting to escape. In crafting a character like Hickman, Ellison sketches the contours of a man uniquely prepared to accept responsibility for his actions and embrace the role of a cultural and national father. Moreover, Hickman's insightful interpretations of visual-art pieces that depict fatherhood in politically provocative terms signal his suitability for the task. He is a self-made black American prepared to offer new insight to the long discussion of moral leadership.

THE RESPONSIBILITY OF US CITIZENSHIP

The terms of Hickman's responsibility—tightly bound to his commitment to fatherhood—draw together the loose ends left by Ellison's early letters, *Invisible Man,* and the essays and interviews he continued to publish throughout his life. Indeed, the willing accountability that Ellison celebrates in Hickman traces its roots to the notion of self-reliance that animates Ellison's devotion to the craft of creative writing. With only his folk wisdom and self-understanding to guide him, Hickman not only accepts the role of "Daddy Hickman," but he also serves as a spiritual father to his black congregation and the many rural men and women who attend his revivals. His multiple father roles, in stark contrast to characters in *Invisible Man* who reject such responsibility, highlight his acceptance of the work society demands from its most mature citizens. The backdrop of visual art upon which Ellison continues to rely provides an unexpected means for assessing his insistence that we rigorously interpret the world in order to formulate a knowledgeable political ideology.

Ellison carefully inserts objects of art into his narrative to guide our assessment of Hickman's complicated relationship with Bliss, a relationship that symbolizes the intricate challenge facing proponents of racial reconciliation. Our analysis of these plastic art objects goes a long way toward unpacking Hickman and Bliss's father-son bond and understanding African Americas' contribution to the formation of a complex American identity. Although Ellison appeared dedicated to beginning the novel with Hickman's arrival in DC, the plot suggests that the "Hickman in Georgia & Oklahoma" sections precede the action in the nation's capital. With this in mind, I want to turn to one of the first exhibits Ellison gives us in the section that traces Hickman's sojourn in Georgia and Oklahoma and prepares him to travel to the US capital.

After reading a perplexing letter from Janey that ostensibly sets him on the road to reunion with Bliss, or Senator Adam Sunraider, Hickman pulls out a report from Walker Millsap. Millsap is an old acquaintance whom Hickman had asked to keep an eye out for the long-lost Bliss. The report details Millsap's discovery of a young man who fits Bliss's description and is currently connected to an African American trickster known as "Missippy Brown." In a somewhat bizarre digression, Millsap admits that the white-looking Bliss and brown-skinned "Sippy" remind him of two paintings featuring George Washington and his slave, William Lee. Millsap describes both paintings ekphrastically:

> In the first the General stands before a field tent holding a scroll of papers as he strikes a pose, à la Napoleon, with his left hand stuck in the breast of his jacket; while in the background, wearing a plumed turban, his round-cheeked, white-toothed young servant holds the bridle of his master's horse and grins as he looks knowingly at its docked, high-lifted tail. Incidentally, the portrait was done by a Frenchman....
>
> The second painting is actually a family scene in which, resplendent in dress uniform and boots with spurs, General Washington sits crossed-legged beside a table upon which his hat and the hilt of his sword rest upon a large military map. The map covers most of the table but the General appears to be staring far into the future as, to the right of the table, his young grandson stands close by with a hand resting on a globe of the world which sits on a convenient stand. And as the boy looks on, his willowy young lady of a sister (who sits across the table) is holding a furled end of the map in her delicate fingers so that Mrs. Washington (who sits beside her, richly bedecked in a ribboned bonnet, lacy scarf, and silken dress) may trace what appears to have been the course of one of the General's battles.... The General stares from the canvas as though contemplating the invisible viewers who would inherit it, and if so, he was right on target.
>
> Because across the table and in a corner behind the elegant ladies there hovers a shadow of the past—and that shadow is the point of all my bumbling attempt [sic] at description.
>
> Because the embodiment of that "shadow" is none other than the man who had been the young boy who appears in the first painting. Presented in semi-profile, he stands erect and attentive with his left hand thrust into the bosom of his vest and his eyes properly averted. His name was William Lee. (TD 687–88)

These lengthy passages capture the startling detail with which Ellison recreates the two visual images. Millsap's descriptions make clear that he refers to an engraving, *Le Général Washington* (figure 1) by Noël Le Mire, and a painting, *The Washington Family* (figure 2) by American portraitist Edward Savage. Ellison spotlights two eighteenth-century portraits featuring the ultimate father figure of US authority and mythic morality.

At first glance, the pictures of George Washington and William Lee that Millsap recalls appear to validate a narrative that African Americans uncritically accept national myths that insist upon absolute reverence for white inviolability. The image of Washington, the nation's first president and national

Noël Le Mire, *Le Général Washington*, engraving (1780). National Portrait Gallery, Smithsonian Institution, Washington, DC. Photo credit: National Portrait Gallery, Smithsonian Institution/Art Resource, New York.

father figure, conjures the US investment in moral rectitude embodied by the myth portraying Washington's relationship with his own father.

According to popular lore established by Parson Weems's widely read biography of the first US president, as a boy Washington responded to his father's inquiry about the death of his favorite cherry tree by admitting, "I cannot tell a lie, Pa; you know I can't tell a lie: I did cut it with my hatchet." To this admirable show of honesty, Mr. Washington purportedly exclaimed, "Run ... to my arms; glad am I, George, that you killed my tree; for you have paid me for it a thousand fold. Such an act of heroism in my son, is more worth than a thousand trees, though blossomed with silver, and their fruits purest gold."[15] With this mythologized incident, Washington's character was rooted firmly in the soil of American truth and virtue.

Ellison, however, reinterprets Washington's presence, revises his moral stature, and even redefines his relationship to his slave. In a direct challenge to the long-standing myth of Washington's heroic honesty, Ellison hints that his role as a national leader began shadowed by moral hypocrisy. Millsap, focusing on the engraving, translates William Lee's smile into a puckish

Edward Savage, *The Washington Family* (1789–96). Andrew W. Mellon Collection, National Gallery of Art, Washington, DC (1940.1.2).

recognition of the irony pervading the scene. The engraving shows Washington, holding the Declaration of Independence and the Treaty of Alliance with France, in the field during the American Revolutionary War. As the sole observer of Washington performing his virtuous commitment to liberty, Lee bears the responsibility of offering the first sign of approval for US principles, which suggests that he discerns the contradiction his black body parades: How can Washington magnanimously embody freedom pictured beside his African American slave? Implicitly noting this paradox, Millsap reminds Hickman, "Black William Lee was with George Washington for thirty-one years, during which time an undeclared independence of observation was, perhaps, his only self-defining area of freedom. But don't forget that although a slave he was still privy to many matters having to do with affairs of family, state, and politics. And if interested he might well have used his shadowy position as unsurveyed landscape for self-exploration" (TD 688–89).

Millsap converts William Lee from a powerless slave and symbolic contributor to the creation of mythic American character into a witness of US potential who refuses to overlook the hypocrisies separating American ideals from their realization. He also defines Lee's uninhibited vision as "freedom" leading to deeper self-understanding.

In other words, rather than illustrating his liminal status, Lee's position in the background attests to his special opportunity to ponder the true meaning of national moral character. Regarding the family portrait, Millsap speculates that in addition to keeping Washington grounded and humble, William Lee "deepen[ed] the painting's historical perspective" even as he "foreshadows other 'shadows' to come."[16] Unable to refrain from riffing, Millsap concludes,

> If I know anything about our people, old Bill has his eyes and ears wide open to what's going down, and *nobody*, not even the surveyor, slave-master, general and father of our country, knew what the hell he was *thinking*—much less the influence for good or evil that he might have been having on the first family's grandchildren. And here you might recall that the father of our country fathered no children of his own. (TD 688)

This passage captures the extreme nature of Ellison's commitment to African American self-determination and agency. He not only riffs on Lee's possible vision and thoughts, but he also claims for William Lee agency and culpability, unusual intimacy together with a peculiar opportunity to betray the first US president. Millsap appeals to the painting of the national family not so much to celebrate the importance of African American contributions to the early republic—in the vein, say, of Crispus Attucks, who is honored as the first man to spill blood in the fight for independence—as to hint at black Americans' power to influence their masters and master's children in self-serving ways. At the same moment that he reminds Hickman that Washington looked upon Lee as a son, he imagines the slave capable of transgression. Of course, the "influence" Lee most obviously wielded was the power of truth. Even as painters like Savage strove to codify the honor of the American family, the inclusion of Lee complicates the visual narrative. And Ellison seemed particularly invested in stressing the father-son relationship. Manuscript versions of the scene reveal that he added the final sentence noting that Washington "fathered no children of his own" only after drafting many versions of the scene.[17]

Ellison's selection of these visual pieces to initiate an argument about black complicity in US moral compromise is astounding. Millsap's interpretive musings suggest that African Americans have been evaluating and shaping the most powerful white men in politics since the country's inception. Ellison introduces the engraving and painting to declare a historically established role for black Americans: they are a consistent presence enjoying political agency often belied by their status. Such a legacy demands an acknowledgment of moral responsibility at a moment when many would argue that blacks lacked the political power for such an admission to be possible. Ellison begs to differ. In doing so, he advances his contention that African Americans have consistently contributed to the formation of US character as well as to its most revered institutions. If Lee fills the role that comes closest to that of a son to Washington, the slave cannot escape all accountability for the early republic. Then again, acknowledging Lee's influence from the inception of the country also makes it impossible to discount the impact of his vision of the nation and conception of US character. For Ellison, forthrightly accepting African American culpability for part of the country's failings guarantees blacks access to full, unfettered citizenship and inclusion in the national family.

While liberalism pointed to white America's many sins as the culprit for black psychosis, Ellison hints that African Americans have been part and parcel of the politics of manipulation, never losing sight of their surprising positions of authority and influence. The story of Sippy and Bliss also uncovers an unsettling facet of Hickman's role as a father. Sippy provides an undeniable double for Hickman. Millsap discovers that Sippy is dedicated to making Bliss "over into ... what an ideal American should be!" (TD 693), a goal that mirrors Hickman's original aspiration for Bliss, whom he hoped would grow into a man like Lincoln. By reenacting such a role, Hickman evokes the complicated legacy of US race relations, the construction of American identity, and the central role of fathers and sons.

INTERPRETING AFRICAN AMERICAN EXCEPTIONALISM

For Ellison, highlighting African American responsibility for part of the country's failings acknowledges the significance of blacks' contributions to the nation. While many black artists of the 1960s and '70s used their art to charge the nation with crimes of racial injustice, Ellison commits his second novel to initiating an extended rumination on shared guilt. For the most part, the agency he discovers in African Americans rests in their folk wisdom. In many ways, Hickman appears to descend from *Invisible Man*'s Mary Rambo. Ellison's implicit return to Mary can be read as his belated correction of the diminished role of the folk in his first novel. In a key scene from the unpublished drafts, Mary, whose boardinghouse sustains the black folk experience, receives a cubist portrait of Leroy, a young man who had lived at her house before Invisible Man arrives. When Treadwell, a white friend who had been a sailor with Leroy, delivers a portrait of the dead young man, Invisible Man stews over his inability to penetrate its modern-art technique. Mary, however, draws upon her mother wit to make short business of interpreting Leroy's cubist portrait and even goes so far as to compare the portrait to a previous painting that helps her assign messianic importance to Leroy.[18]

In the DC section of *Three Days,* Ellison develops a similar visual sophistication in Hickman. The preacher's perambulations around the capital foreground his interpretive dexterity and connect it directly to his folk sensibility. As Barry Shank has argued, Ellison's dependence upon black American folklore in his second novel might be understood as his insistence upon aestheticizing black folk experience so it might be used for "cultural evaluation" and "political as well as philosophical debate."[19] Hickman's scrutiny of the US capital as a series of visual displays exhibits the complexity of US history and national identity and proclaims Hickman's status as an exceptional reader of the fraught reality of US citizenship.

Depending upon repeated examples of ekphrasis, Ellison juxtaposes the preacher's interpretive ability with the disinclined or incapable powers of perception exposed by those around him. Senator Sunraider's white secretary provides a case in point. In response to Hickman and his black church members visiting the senator's Capitol office, she dramatizes the peril of refusing to view the world with fresh eyes and active engagement: "As she stood scanning their inscrutable faces she could not recall ever having encountered any of the group before," and "since she could not believe that such as they could ever associate anything having to do with the Senator with patriotic emotion their solemn appearance was simply illogical. . . . Therefore, their very presence was enough in itself to arouse suspicion . . . and suggested motives that were dark and devious" (TD 507–8).

In the earlier prologue published with Book I, Ellison underscores the museum-like quality of the senator's office to highlight the secretary's abdication of civic responsibility: "Suddenly they no longer seemed familiar, and a feeling of dream-like incongruity came over her. They were so many that she could no longer see the large abstract paintings which hung along the paneled wall. Nor the framed facsimiles of State Documents which hung above a bust of Vice President Calhoun" (TD 6). Both versions emphasize the secretary's need to account for Hickman and his followers according to her preconceived notions. In the latter account, her refusal to acknowledge the delegation beyond recognizable categories leaves her no option but to classify them as dangerous and radical, a conclusion also drawn by the naive guard that stops the group as they attempt to exit the Capitol. The secretary's inability to fit Hickman's party into the collection of objects constituting a visual display of national meaning on Sunraider's office walls solidifies her incapacity to read visually. The spectacular nature of her analytical failure offers a dramatic contrast to Hickman's discerning disposition. More significantly, the imminent threat to the senator's life highlights the serious consequences of abdicating personal responsibility.

Ellison presents the capital city as comprising a national gallery that challenges Hickman to reassess his understanding of African American citizenship. As he explores DC, the preacher confronts art objects that force him to consider his beliefs from a new point of view. When he stumbles upon what he takes to be a storefront church in a basement, he faces an arresting piece of art that forces him to reevaluate his notions regarding the relationship between sacrificial sons and patriotic responsibility:

> Then, in a flash, the confusion of brushstrokes and splashes sprang to form, becoming a large, unframed painting.
>
> Then came a chilling shock of surprise. For here, in the last place in the world he would have expected, he was staring at a depiction of Christ marching to Calvary....
>
> For now, through the clouded glass, he recognized the painting as a type of religious folk art familiar to Negro neighborhoods—an association of style and place immediately confirmed by the heavy symbolism of the scene's faded colors. For while the jeering, spear-wielding soldiers were unquestionably white, the skin of the thorn-crowned, cross-bearing Christ was unmistakably black....
>
> Then, drawn to the impression made in Christ's naked shoulder by the weight of the cross, he began to understand: For some two feet above the point where the rough-hewn upright of the cross knifed into the bruised flesh of Christ's straining shoulder, the artist, suddenly improvising on his theme like a jazzman on a familiar tune, had placed what on first sight had appeared to be the travel-soiled bundle of a hobo. There in the angle where the upright joined the sky-pointing arm of the cross it rested, a bundle consisting of red-white-and-blue cotton which was depicted as having become partially unrolled in the painful march and ended up trailing and distorting the footprints of Christ. And with eyes flying back to the point from which the striped cloth trailed he saw distorted white stars spring into

focus and exclaimed, "Good Lord!" And the cloth showed forth as a bundled-up flag. (TD 562–63)

Hickman's deliberate survey of the painting showcases his familiarity with the rendering of religious artistic themes for purposes related to contesting established power structures with unexpected representations of race. He notes that the painting falls into "a type of religious folk art familiar to Negro neighborhoods," reminding us of the crucial training he received from his folk experiences (TD 562). More impressive, however, is his estimation of the radical inclusion of the disfigured American flag. Hickman must extend his folk understanding to make sense of the pictorial portrayal of black civic martyrdom.

The painting initially strikes Hickman as symbolic beyond its most obvious deviations, and he instantly attempts to make sense of the threads that relate it to other schools of art. The hobo-bundle-American-flag emerges as evidence of Hickman's keen gaze, and he immediately comprehends the revolutionary effect of its inclusion. Ellison's insertion of a tattered Old Glory echoes African American artists of the Black Arts movement who repeatedly included the American flag in their radical accusations of the nation's broken trust. Although the painting Hickman confronts lacks the biting critique of works like Jeff Donaldson's *Aunt Jemima and the Pillsbury Doughboy* (1963), Faith Ringgold's *Flag for the Moon: Die Nigger* (1969), David Hammons's *Injustice Case* (1970), or Dana C. Chandler Jr.'s *American Penal System . . . Pan African Concentration Camps and Death Houses* (1971), it unquestionably participates in the critical conversation such works foreground. But whereas these Black Arts paintings distort the flag to denote the nation's abuse of African Americans, Ellison aligns the symbol of democracy with African Americans' patriotism—their willingness to die for US ideals.

In a 1965 interview with Robert Penn Warren, Ellison expounded upon the reality of black sacrifice as a necessary act in black Americans' struggle to achieve self-definition. By way of explaining the penetrating insight that colors African Americans' understanding of their white fellow citizens and US society, Ellison asserts that "part of the American Negro experience . . . lies in the idea, the *ideal* of sacrifice" (CRE 343; italics in original). Confronting this ideal, Hickman wastes no time in sizing up the painting and coming to terms with its representation of black Americans' painful historical and contemporary reality in the nation. What took Invisible Man the course of the entire novel to comprehend and accept, Hickman immediately begins to resolve as he channels his initial anger into positive action. In the space of a few hours, he is leading his church delegation toward the Lincoln Memorial, the sculptural reincarnation of a man of mythic meaning for African Americans. As Hickman gazes upon the sculpture—a plastic object conducive to prolonged contemplation—he focuses on Lincoln's great stone eyes and perceives the complexity of his character and his national meaning. During his extended moment of looking, Hickman discovers sympathy for the man who signed the Emancipation Proclamation. Ellison shows Hickman depending upon the sculptural monument to acquire new understanding:

> *Yes, with all I know about him and his contradictions—Yes! And with all I have learned about the ways of men, this country, and the world— YES! And with all I know about white men and politicians of all colors, backgrounds and guises—Yes! And with all I know about the things you had to do to be you and remain yourself—Yes! You are one of the few who ever earned the right to be called "Father.".... And though I'm against all of the unearned tribute which the weak and lowly are forced to pay to power based on force and false differences and false values— Yes! For you "Father" is all right with me.* (TD 576–77)

Hickman's ability to view Lincoln as a legitimate father figure even as he acknowledges the president's inconsistencies and contradictions illustrates his sophisticated measure of humanity. Ellison 'stills' his narrative to facilitate Hickman's probing reflection of Father Abraham. He need not enter the edifice of the National Gallery of Art, where art is organized to communicate an official narrative of US identity. Hickman performs the analytical work necessary to generate an accurate national narrative. The preacher's determination that Lincoln deserves the title *Father* suggests that his own experience with Bliss may provide a lens through which he evaluates the contradictory nature of the president credited with freeing blacks from slavery. Like Lincoln, Hickman has played a part riddled with inconsistencies. But the sum of his actions, echoing the man who brought slavery to an end, attests to his sincere ambition for greater good. Ellison hints that Hickman requires the sight of Lincoln, rendered in the silent solidity of stark white stone, to make sense of the many paradoxes that constitute US history. The ekphrastic moment enables his folk hero's resolution of the difficult relationships between fathers and sons, nations and men.

Hickman claims Lincoln as African American in tragic sensibility, and his rumination before the sculpture underscores their shared burden. His description of Lincoln sounds suspiciously like an account of the road that

Landscape with the Fall of Icarus (ca. 1525–69). Musée d'Art Ancien, Musées Royaux des Beaux-Arts, Brussels, Belgium. Photo credit: Scala/Art Resource, New York.

brings him to the nation's capital: "*Yes, it's you all right, just sitting and resting while you think out the mystery of how all of this mess could have come to be. Just puzzling out how all this could happen to a man's work after he had done all one could possibly do, and then take the consequences for giving the world his all*" (TD 577). Father Abraham, like Daddy Hickman, is not a perfect man. Nor was Father Abraham a perfect father to the nation in a time of trouble. But Ellison includes the sculpture to insist on the righteousness of those fathers willing to face the world with all their warts exposed. Just as Trueblood discovered that he was still a man and "nobody but himself" (IM 66), Hickman finds peace in his forgiveness of Father Abraham. Moreover, Hickman recognizes the possibility that imperfect men may best serve the nation as they honestly acknowledge their personal failings. Such unencumbered self-reflection defines Hickman's assessment of his own life, and Ellison suggests that the nation's most successful leaders reflect a similar sensibility. Good fathers, in a national and cultural sense, are first and foremost honest observers.

Hickman's accomplishment prepares him to grapple with a copy of *Landscape with the Fall of Icarus* (figure 3), traditionally thought to be by Pieter Brueghel the Elder. Ellison's introduction of the painting inserts Hickman's meditation upon the tapestry into the rich history of ekphrasis connected to the famously rendered landscape. The subject of both W. H. Auden's "Musée des Beaux Arts" (1938) and William Carlos Williams's "Landscape with the Fall of Icarus," the second poem in his Pulitzer Prize–winning *Pictures from Brueghel and Other Poems* (1962), the visual piece provides Hickman an unexpected occasion to extend his contemplation of the relationship between fathers and sons, Christ's sacrifice, and national identity. Auden's poem opens with a reflection on the visual history of suffering: "About suffering they were never wrong, / The Old Masters; how well, they understood / Its human position; how it takes place / While someone else is eating or opening a window or just walking dully along." By its end, the poet speaker presents the visual portrayal as exemplary in its depiction of a world too busy to pause over the tragedy before its eyes or the sound of "the forsaken cry." Harkening to Christ's despairing wail, "My God, My God, why hast Thou forsaken Me," from Matthew 27:45–46, Auden reads the painted masterpiece as part of the human tragedy against which even Christ, in the form of man, desperately fought: the pervasive feeling of desertion in a world too busy to care. Williams's verse, even more striking in its austerity, intensifies the fact of human obliviousness. His final stanza reports dispassionately, "a splash quite unnoticed / this was / Icarus drowning."

These modernist poets' engagement of *Landscape with the Fall of Icarus* gives voice to the confluence of Hickman's feelings. He has confronted the visualization of the nation's sacrifice of African American culture as depicted in the black Christ, God's son, laboring under the cross of racism; he has made peace with the father figure of Lincoln, a man who signed national freedom papers for African Americans without completely investing in the endeavor; and upon reaching DC, he must face the reality that even though his sense of impending tragedy matters little to the world—just as Christ's crucifixion and Lincoln's sacrifice appear as unremarkable to many throughout history—he must fulfill the role of a true father to Bliss, who has transformed himself into Senator Adam Sunraider. Remaining dedicated to Bliss allows him to perform his patriotic commitment to his country.

To make this point, Ellison's revised computer files devote untold pages to Hickman's perusal of the tapestry reprisal of *Landscape with the Fall of Icarus* in the Longview Hotel, and he grapples with the scene through numerous revisions. In each case, Ellison painstakingly re-creates Hickman's growing awareness of the details of the painted scene as he intersperses this discovery with Hickman's translation of the image into the black vernacular, the complexity of Hickman's Southern-black-Christian-jazzman experience. Hickman's natural sense of the need to read the Longview tapestry in relation to his fresh discovery of the painting of the black Christ's flag-laden march to Calvary announces his artistic sophistication.[20] After initially mistaking the tapestry for an "abstract painting, of which he was ignorant," Hickman contemplates the scene at length, clearly at ease with his ability to interpret its meaning (TD 592). It is only when he recalls the rules of art display established by museum exhibits, the necessity of relating one work to the next, that he becomes wary: "Then, recalling the shock at discovering a picture of Christ abandoned in a basement window he tensed, suddenly suspicious that what he had taken for a peaceful landscape might conceal similar details of shocking distaste" (TD 594). This incitement toward closer looking celebrates Hickman's reliance upon an African American artistic vocabulary. He muses that "the goal of both jazz musician and weaver was one of using their skills to arouse pleasure and wonder. And both did so by drawing upon that which was left carefully understated or concealed as a means for achieving a transcendent goal" (TD 595). Drawing from his own artistic experience, Hickman's patient analysis is rewarded by the discovery of the "lonely legs . . . of someone who appeared to have plunged headfirst out of nowhere and into the wind-ruffled sea." Moreover, he immediately recognizes a "vague sense of connection between the sprawling legs and the danger that had prompted his flight to Washington" (TD 597).

Hickman's interpretive skills permit him to personalize a scene that appears wholly unrelated to his life. We sense that although the tapestry portraying the iconic painting draws our focus to Icarus, Hickman remains subconsciously aware that the myth it depicts is as much about the son who loses sight of his father's directives as it is about the father's boundless ambition. Daedalus, Icarus's master-craftsman dad, looks upon life through grandiose eyes. And it is Daedalus alone who witnesses his son's death and must struggle with the guilt resulting from the tragedy of his own brilliance. We do not witness Hickman deciphering the meaning of the tapestry and his possible connection to Daedalus. Instead, he wonders whether the mystery of the lonely legs represents Jonah or Satan's fall from heaven. Ellison's multiple reconsiderations of the scene suggest that he intends for readers to identify with the majesty of Daedalus's ambition even as we, alongside Hickman, attend to the tragedy attending such genius. In light of US history, we seem prompted to recall Lincoln's famous words at Gettysburg. He reminded the nation that memories of sacrificed life must inspire a rededication "to the great task remaining" rather than sympathy alone.

This forward-looking approach corresponds with the foundation of what I identify as Ellison's political ideology. As a kind of final word on fathers and sons, we recall Ellison's contention that African Americans accepted the task of watching over the fate of US democracy. Black citizens consent to such a post not because they deem themselves perfect; rather, they recognize their cultural experience as arming them with an indispensable point of view with regard to national character. As Ellison's early letters to Wright reveal, he passionately believed that US destiny is fulfilled by men like Hickman who remain committed to realizing the nation's highest ideals even as they fall short in their individual lives. His flaws, like those of the country, do not disqualify him from serving its greatest causes. Ellison does not advocate perfection. He promotes a complex understanding of the world by men pursuing good for the nation as opposed to seeking personal advancement. Hickman is no Rinehart.

Indeed, Bliss's creative descent from Rinehart,[21] his racial indeterminacy, and his reprehensible conduct toward African Americans—including those who raised him—signal the extreme need for men like Hickman. He embodies a notion of fatherhood the country reveres. For Ellison, what his peers declared a politically conservative love of country proved difficult to escape. He vehemently rejected accusations that his investment in America's most fundamental ideals revealed a naive, elitist, or simply selfish sensibility. Ellison willingly pointed out US failings, but he counted his writing as contributing to the discovery of a solution. His penchant for placing characters before challenging visual art highlights the value he placed on encouraging individuals to do their part, to offer fiercely independent interpretations of the world as they explore their place in it.

As a jazzman turned preacher, Hickman does not emerge as the father of the year. He does, however, offer a needed revision of the myths around American fatherhood. His hope to have raised Bliss to be the American son that helped right the wrongs of the past connects him to men like Lincoln while highlighting the importance of his African American cultural heritage. Hickman's analytical acumen and insight places him in a radically different league from Ellison's first purveyor of visual art, Invisible Man, and captures his more mature political understanding. Fatherhood emerges as a metaphor for responsible citizenship and cultural maturity, the ability to act upon love. Reverend A. Z.'s appeal to a range of visual objects in an effort to make sense of the contradictory nature of American history and of African American experience demonstrates Ellison's belief in a democratic pluralism that affords individuals of all backgrounds legitimate access to interpreting US identity. The distinctness of Hickman's visual reading points to Ellison's faith in the agency and political potency of artistic knowledge. In the person of

Hickman, Ellison combines the common man with the critic and insists upon the exceptionalism of his blend as he unveils a new definition of American fatherhood.

NOTES

1. A number of critics have noted the importance of fatherhood in Ellison's work. Adam Bradley, for instance, specifically considers the role of fatherhood in *Three Days*: "The central drama of the novel in progress, the estrangement and reconciliation of fathers and sons, is also a signal drama of the American experience." See Bradley, *Ellison in Progress*, 114.

2. See Lena Hill, *Visualizing Blackness and the Creation of the African American Literary Tradition* (New York: Cambridge University Press, 2014), ch. 6 and coda 180–221.

3. Anne Dvinge, "Complex Fate—Complex Vision: The Vernacular and Identity in Ralph Ellison's 'Juneteenth,'" *Amerikastudien/American Studies* 51, no. 2 (2006): 203.

4. Michael Szalay examines Ellison's creative presentation of the similarities between political parties in *Three Days*. He claims that "Sunraider personifies the interrelation of Republicans and Democrats" and the entire novel functions as "an elaborate account of the dialectical relationship . . . between Kennedy and Abraham Lincoln." See Szalay, "Unfinished Second Skin," 820.

5. Ellison to Wright, 22 July 1945, box 97, Richard Wright Papers, Beinecke Library, Yale University (hereafter RWP).

6. Ellison to Wright, 18 August 1945, box 97, RWP.

7 Barbara Foley draws a different conclusion in her superbly researched *Wrestling with the Left: The Making of Ralph Ellison's "Invisible Man."* Nevertheless, a straightforward assessment of many of Ellison's early letters to Wright challenges her central claim that he retained his affinity with Marxism well into his compositional work on his first novel. She addresses these letters from a very different point of view. For instance, in chapter 1, "Forming a Politics," she nods toward them without quoting them at length to note that they represent a man who "remains committed to some of the long-range goals of Communism" and retains many of his "leftist commitments" (66). Ultimately, this claim is hard to support in the face of the remarkable clarity of the letters.

8. Ellison wrote to Wright after returning from the National Negro Congress in 1940. He shared his hope that African Americans will soon "be awakened from their 'Marxist' fog" to discover their "pent-up folk consciousness." He then admits, "I guess what I am trying to say in the article I am enclosing, is that the 'river' is harnessing itself! You told me I would begin to write when I matured emotionally, when I began to feel what I understood. I am beginning to understand what you meant." Ellison's investment in connecting his personal, artistic maturation process to a broader cultural development emerges clearly in *Invisible Man*. His naive protagonist's painful evolution echoes the journey he travels in his letters to Wright. See Ellison to Wright, 11 May 1940, box 97, RWP.

9. Ellison to Wright, 22 July 1945, box 97, RWP.

10. Ellison to Wright, 18 August 1945, box 97, RWP.

11. "Woodridge," box 146, Ralph Ellison Papers, Manuscript Division, Library of Congress, Washington, DC (hereafter REP).

12. At other points in the drafts, Woodridge vehemently denounces the power of books. He even goes so far as to proclaim, "I wipe my ass with this literature, this condom to abort reality!" See "Woodridge," box 146, REP.

13. "Chapel" folder (first draft and notes), box 144, REP.

14. "Woodridge," box 146, REP.

15. See Mason L. Weems, *The Life of Washington*, ed. Marcus Cunliffe (Cambridge, MA: Belknap, 2001), 12.

16. Ellison's laborious description of Lee in the "shadows" suggests his familiarity with a long tradition of US art that positions African Americans in shadowy spaces. Ivy Wilson uncovers the striking nature of this practice and argues that "the compositional logic of American genre painting strategically organized zones in terms of centers and margins in various settings, such as parlors . . . as a means to illustrate the forms of democratic belonging in the United States." See Wilson, *Specters of Democracy: Blackness and the Aesthetics of Politics in the Antebellum U.S.* (New York: Oxford University Press, 2011), 105.

17. See box 127, folder 4, REP.

18. "At Mary's" folder, box 142, REP.

19. Barry Shank, "Bliss, or Blackface Sentiment," *boundary 2* 30, no. 2 (Summer 2003): 55.

20. Conflicting details in *Three Days* make it somewhat unclear as to whether Ellison intended Hickman to visit the Christ painting before he studies the tapestry or afterward, but considering the numerous drafts, it seems more likely that he favored the sequence I note.

21. See Bradley, *Ellison in Progress*, 125.

FATHER ABRAHAM
Ellison's Agon with the Fathers in *Three Days before the Shooting . . .*

MARC C. CONNER

"But what quality of love sustains us in our orphan's loneliness; and how much is thus required of fatherly love to give us strength for all our life thereafter?"
—RALPH ELLISON, "TELL IT LIKE IT IS, BABY" (CERE 35)

In one of his most moving and poignant essays, "Tell It Like It Is, Baby," Ralph Ellison bravely confronts his great childhood trauma: the death of his father when Ellison was a mere three years old. An enormously complex essay, "Tell It" begins with Ellison trying to come to terms with the tremendous activity of the nascent civil rights movement as he observes from afar in Rome, and concludes with his efforts to render in his ongoing second novel the "pattern of classical tragedy" that defines American culture. In between, Ellison devotes the bulk of the essay to relating a dream sequence that conflates the death of his father with the death of Abraham Lincoln, and his efforts to plumb the meanings both for himself and for America of these losses of the father figures—what he terms "the tortuous and extended dream that was my childhood with my father gone." Ellison began the essay in 1956, but found its scope and implications were beyond his powers; he then returned to it in 1965 and published it that year.[1] The near-decade of this essay's effort reveals much of Ellison's creative process and points us to the roots of his second novel,

which finally saw publication in 2010 as *Three Days before the Shooting*....
Like the "Tell It" essay, *Three Days* presented Ellison with an array of father figures and challenged him to confront and become reconciled with his many absent fathers—biographical, historical, and literary—in its very writing.

By viewing *Three Days* through the lens of Ellison's struggle with the defining influence of fathers, we see why Alonzo Hickman, the great father figure within the novel, fails in rearing the child Bliss as a savior of his people; and we see why Bliss's own flight from his community and home is doomed to fail, resulting in his fragmentation of identity and tragic loss of coherent self. Furthermore, the father-struggle brings into relief Ellison's highly self-conscious efforts to position himself in relation to both American literary traditions and modernist world literature—in many ways, this is his primary contest as a writer, one that defines his work from the 1930s until his death sixty years later. Consequently, in *Three Days* Ellison grapples with paternal influence in three dimensions: *literary* fathers, and of principal importance are two very different high modernist writers, F. Scott Fitzgerald and James Joyce; *biblical* fathers—*Three Days* is one of the most profound engagements with the inheritance of the Bible in modern Western literature; and finally *biographical* fathers, in both the real and imagined figure of Lewis Ellison. Through these confrontations with patriarchy, Ellison explores his most fundamental, and personal, concerns. Approaching the novel with these elements in mind reveals the full meanings of what "our orphan's loneliness" came to be for Ralph Ellison during the forty years in which he wrote his ongoing epic of America.

ELLISON'S LITERARY FATHERS: MISREADING WRIGHT AND FAULKNER

Literary influence upon Ralph Ellison has been both overdetermined and woefully underexamined.[2] The two dominant influences on Ellison's work, according to the scholarly consensus, are Richard Wright (upon *Invisible Man*) and William Faulkner (upon *Three Days*). Joseph Skerrett expresses the strong reading of Wright's effect upon Ellison: "For Ellison, Richard Wright was more than a mere contemporary. Although Wright was only ten years older than Ellison, he was a presence, an image as well as a person, a reality that had to be dealt with both in the imagination and in the marketplace. Whatever place a young black writer might make for himself in the critical public attention would be a place won, to some degree and in some fashion, from Richard Wright" (Skerrett 219). Although most Ellison scholars concur that Ellison moves beyond Wright's influence in and through the writing of *Invisible Man*, Timothy Parrish has recently argued that Ellison "wrote because Richard Wright had written," and goes on to argue that we misread Ellison if we underestimate the extent of his own "seething" "'black' anger" that he inherited from and shared with Wright. "Wright inspired Ellison to write," Parrish summarizes, "and when Ellison did write it was to add to the story Wright had told. Without Wright, there would be no *Invisible Man*, and in that sense no Ralph Ellison either." Nevertheless, although Parrish makes a strong case for Wright's near-determining influence on Ellison, he also maintains that Faulkner remained the more daunting literary father: "I do not think that Wright was the authorial father figure Ellison had to replace," he concludes; "that role was more properly Faulkner's" (*Genius* 85, 97–99).

Parrish does not pursue the Faulkner relationship further, but the strong proponents of the Faulkner influence, such as Norman Podhoretz and Arnold Rampersad, maintain that in his efforts to overcome this strong precursor, Ellison was either paralyzed or inadequate. They argue that a major reason that the second novel fails is because Faulkner was too strong a precursor figure for Ellison to overcome, and therefore Ellison devolved into mere imitation. Rampersad, in his 2007 biography, claims Faulkner as the dominant and ruining influence on the second novel, stating that in his work on *Three Days* Ellison "was in thrall to Faulkner" and that his "obvious indebtedness to . . . Faulkner is both effective and defective" (359, 457). Podhoretz makes the most strident claim to Faulkner's overinfluence in his essay "What Happened to Ralph Ellison?," where he claims that Faulkner is "the ghost haunting the prose" of the second novel: "The hands may be the hands of Ellison," he writes, but "the voice is the voice of William Faulkner." This Faulknerian overinfluence, Podhoretz claims, explains Ellison's inability to finish the *Three Days* project: "My speculation is that Ellison—a man of great intelligence and literary education—knew that Faulkner had invaded and taken him over and that this was why he could never finish the book. I can imagine him struggling for 40 years to get Faulkner's sound out of his head" (56).

Certainly, we know that Ellison viewed Faulkner as a major voice in American fiction—Ellison himself tells us this early and often in his writings. In 1955, right when Ellison was doing serious writing on the *Three Days* project, he expressed his long-standing admiration and even envy for Faulkner's work: "I can remember reading things by Faulkner long before he was generally acclaimed, and just wishing that I could have written those things. I mean they are powerful and they are still good, and I think they'll be here forever" (CRE 60). But the easy argument that Ellison was unable to get past the figure of Faulkner merely simplifies and reduces the issue of literary influence—indeed, it really just allows a critic to dismiss Ellison's post–*Invisible Man* writing without making the hard effort of entering into and truly grappling with that work.[3] For within the material of the second novel one sees that Ellison is moving both beyond and around the concerns, styles, ideas, and voices of Faulkner. Indeed, in his writings Ellison emerges as one of the most skillful *readers* of William Faulkner; he puts before us a Faulkner who actually looks a lot like Ralph Ellison (which is much different than the other way around).

For Ellison, Faulkner's crucial achievement consisted of conceiving of and expressing the black American as a fully formed, complex human figure in fiction. Ellison famously decried the inability of twentieth-century American novelists to "conceive Negro characters possessing the full, complex ambiguity of the human," to portray the black character "as that sensitively focused process of opposites, of good and evil, of instinct and intellect, of passion and spirituality, which great literary art has projected as the image of man." But, he argued, Faulkner, like Twain, could move beyond stereotype and category and create black figures who were all too human in the most complex sense: "Indeed, through his many novels and short stories Faulkner fights out the moral problem which was repressed after the nineteenth century.... Faulkner was actually seeking out the nature of man. Thus we must turn to him for that continuity of moral purpose which made for the greatness of our classics.... Perhaps his is the example for our writers to follow, for in his work technique has been put once more to the task of creating value" (CERE 82, 98). This is precisely what the African American novelist Charles Johnson has praised in Ellison's own work: "He envisioned a black American personality as complex, multisided, and synthetic as the American society that produced it" ("Acceptance Speech" 208).[4]

Hence, the figure to whom Ellison is most drawn in Faulkner's writing is Lucas Beauchamp in *Go Down, Moses,* the mixed-race man who embodies Faulkner's growth into fully human expressions of the black character: "When Lucas Beauchamp first appears in Faulkner's work he appears as a stereotype," Ellison comments, "but as he was developed throughout successive novels, he became one of Faulkner's highest representatives of human quality" (CRE 117). Ultimately Lucas shows Faulkner's effort "to redefine evil," and in this Lucas becomes "one of the great heroes of Faulkner's work" and "one of the great examples of humanity" (CRE 227). This, Ellison claims, was decisive to Ellison's own work: "The beginning (and he made the beginning because he was willing to identify), and one of the best, most successful, meaningful and rich projections of a Negro in fiction was made by William Faulkner. He made it possible for me to look at certain aspects of Negro life" (CRE 137). Ellison ultimately insists that Faulkner was a precursor to, even a fellow traveler with, the civil rights movement itself, in ways that even most black American writers were not: "If you would find the imaginative equivalents of certain Civil Rights figures in American writing, Rosa Parks and James Meredith say, you don't go to most fiction by Negroes, but to Faulkner" (CRE 131). This parallels Parrish's claim that Ellison himself is the key imaginative figure of the civil rights movement that followed upon the publication of *Invisible Man* in 1952, and that his extraordinary essays of the 1960s and 1970s articulated the civil rights message. Parrish writes, "Ellison, perhaps more than any other American writer, was the essential visionary of post–Civil War America," and further, "Ellison . . . was the black intellectual who could envision an America that would, within a generation of Martin Luther King, Jr.'s death, elect . . . a black president" (*Genius* 6).

In short, Ellison's Faulkner is a version of Ralph Ellison himself, or, put differently, Ellison pushes further and perhaps even completes what Faulkner had begun. Hardly a simple example of ruinous overinfluence, the Ellison-Faulkner relation seems precisely an example of Harold Bloom's theory of *Clinamen,* in which one poet misreads another poet by implying "that the precursor poem went accurately up to a certain point, but then should have swerved, precisely in the direction that the new poem moves"; or even *Tessera,* which implies "a token of recognition" by the later poet that "read[s] the parent-poem as to retain its terms but to mean them in another sense, as though the precursor had failed to go far enough" (*Anxiety* 14). Ellison's *Three Days* has a resemblance to Faulkner that is critical and revising, confirming Ellison's *power over,* rather than enthrallment to, his precursor. As Bloom describes this process, "the uncanny effect is that the new poem's achievement makes it seem to us, not as though the precursor were writing it, but *as though the later poet himself had written the precursor's characteristic work*" (16; emphasis added)—a sort of fulfillment of Ellison's early wish to have himself written the words of Faulkner.[5]

My purpose in lingering here on these issues of influence is less to make a claim about these controversial theories, nor even ultimately about Ellison and Faulkner (though to some extent I have done both); but rather, I seek to clear a bit of space in the Ellison discourse in which we can talk about Ellison and other writers without having to devote more space to Wright (about whom, I think, enough has been said) or to Faulkner (about whom, as I have indicated, too much has been said).[6] Interpretation of *Three Days before the Shooting . . .* has been particularly retarded by an overemphasis on Faulkner's influence, and it is to this book, and the ways in which Ellison critically engages other writers within it, that I now would like to turn.

ELLISON AND FITZGERALD: THE AMERICAN TRAGIC SUBLIME

One of the defining narratives in *Three Days* is Bliss's rejection of his earthly father and his desperate attempt to father himself, in the long-standing mode of the archetypal American Adam quest figure. This narrative constitutes the novel's tragic impulse, and the tragedy lurking within the American conscience, in Ellison's view: the hero's self-damning determination to transcend human definition and limitation—to rival the creative power of God. This narrative reveals Ellison's fraternal kinship with another high American modernist who lurks behind and within Ellison's imagination. Ellison's fascination with and indebtedness to F. Scott Fitzgerald remains one of many insufficiently explored vistas in Ellison studies. Although, as John Callahan has stated in the only detailed essay comparing Ellison and Fitzgerald, "at first glance the two make an unlikely pair of literary bedfellows," nevertheless "there are more than a few fascinating connections between their lives, their work, and their respective and very American, provincial great expectations." Callahan argues that each writer is consumed with the mysteries and betrayals of the American Dream, and in particular with "the boomerang of nemesis, which follows in the wake of overweening, overreaching hubris" ("Ellison, Fitzgerald, and 'Dark Fields'" 128). He notes that both authors locate America's fundamental meaning in unexplored geographic spaces, what he terms "the provinces"—"Fitzgerald's 'dark fields of the republic' and Ellison's 'Territory' mark the provinces as the metaphorical center as well as the geographical heart of the nation" (122). To these overarching, national parallels between Fitzgerald and Ellison, I would add that both writers felt keenly the very personal loss of the father figure. Whereas Ellison lost his father at the age of three, Fitzgerald at the age of eleven saw his father lose his job, his confidence, and his sense of purpose in a manner that marked his son forever. Fitzgerald recalled near the end of his own life his father's decline after losing his position, becoming "an old man, a completely broken man. He had lost his essential drive, his immaculateness of purpose. He was a failure the rest of his days" (Bruccoli 23). Fitzgerald expressed this idea of the lost father through Dick Diver in *Tender Is the Night*: Dick's anguished recognition of the loss of his earthly father, and indeed of all fathers—"Goodbye, my father—goodbye, all my fathers" (205)—voices Fitzgerald's own sense of having at a young age lost his father as any sort of reliable guide; and this is precisely a version of Ellison's inconsolable "orphan's loneliness."

Fitzgerald's own description of his father makes Edward Fitzgerald into a virtual anti-Gatsby—no "drive," no "immaculateness of purpose"—for what is Gatsby but a being driven by an immaculate purpose, at least in his own mind? We may speculate that Gatsby is precisely a replacement or compensation for the failed father figure of Fitzgerald's own life, and Gatsby's own earthly father, Henry C. Gatz—described as "a solemn old man, very helpless and dismayed" (175)—represents to some degree Fitzgerald's own failed father. For Gatsby, in rejecting his father and having no discernible mother, makes of himself his own creation—as Nick says of him, he "sprang from his Platonic conception of himself" (104). And it is exactly here that we see the striking parallel between Jay Gatsby and Ellison's Bliss of *Three Days before the Shooting . . .* : Bliss never knows his father or his mother, and in rejecting his foster father, Daddy Hickman, he attempts to father himself and become, like Gatsby, a self-creation. In each of these figures we can glimpse the fantasy of their respective authors: to compensate for the loss of the father figure by creating an imaginary character who rejects the very need for earthly parents.

This fundamental parallel between Bliss and Gatsby is reinforced at other points in the novel. When Bliss, in his incarnation as "Mister Movie-Man," is wooing Lavatrice (who will become the mother to Severn, the son who will ultimately shoot down his father, Sunraider), he muses on his choices: to stay with her and share love, or to abandon her and continue pursuing his increasingly extreme ambitions. This is precisely the Gatsby conundrum: to stay with Daisy and share a merely human love, or to climb the "ladder" that "mounted to a secret place above the trees," there to "suck on the pap of life, gulp down the incomparable milk of wonder." Gatsby determines to unite the earthly and the transcendent, to kiss Daisy and thereby "wed his unutterable visions to her perishable breath" (117). When Bliss faces this same choice, he states the fundamental question not just for himself, but for Ellison throughout this sprawling, majestic epic of America—how does one join love and history?

> *Oh, if only I could have controlled me my she I and the search and have accepted you as the dark daddy of flesh and Word. . . . I should have faced them down—faced me down and said, Look, this is where*

I'll make my standing place and with her in all her grace and sweet wonder. But how make a rhyme of a mystery? If I had only known then what I came to know about the shape of honor and the smell of pride—I say, HOW THE HELL DO YOU GET LOVE INTO POLITICS OR COMPASSION INTO HISTORY? (TD 391–92)

For Bliss, the challenge is not just to combine his love of woman with his desire to master American history, but also to reconcile himself with his Daddy Hickman and by extension the mystery of family, which includes for him the ultimate mystery of the mother-love that is denied him and is forever unknown to him. Just as Fitzgerald's Gatsby is fatherless and motherless—indeed, his unmentioned mother is a complete blank in his history—so too Bliss lacks and longs for both father and mother. Each is an emblem of Ellison's orphan's loneliness.

Bliss's inability to reconcile these multiple challenges of love leads him into the movie houses, which throughout *Three Days* stand for confusion, chaos, and the illusion of the image. There he beholds the woman or women whom he mistakenly identifies as his mother, and he thinks to himself that he can find her, and thereby find the peace he desires, but not if he maintains his love relations with another woman or with Hickman: "Yet when I came out of all that intensified time into the sun the world had grown larger for my having entered that forbidden place and yet smaller for now I knew that I could enter in if I entered there alone I ran—Bliss ran" (TD 392). In order to attain this idealized—and tragically, illusory—female figure, Bliss must isolate himself from the human world. In rejecting Lavatrice and the human love she offers, Bliss flees the realities of familial love, the love also offered him by Hickman and his community, for the fantasy of being able to return to maternal bliss, the hoped-for oneness of creator and created.

In this fantasy of sublime transcendence of human boundary, Ellison consciously echoes and signifies upon the decisive moment of *The Great Gatsby*. When Gatsby recalls his decision to pursue Daisy and all she represents—a transcendent love, a fairy call, a rejection of human limitation—he renders this choice in precisely the same rhythmic language that Ellison employs: "Gatsby saw that the blocks of the sidewalk really formed a ladder and mounted to a secret place above the trees—he could climb to it, *if he climbed alone,* and once there he could suck on the pap of life, gulp down the incomparable milk of wonder" (117; emphasis added). The parallel phrasing is striking: Ellison—"I could enter in if I entered there alone"—and Fitzgerald—"he could climb to it, if he climbed alone." In both cases, the questing hero must forsake the love of an idealized woman if he is to attain the sublime heights he desires. This most fundamental of American hero patterns, what R. W. B. Lewis termed "the American Adam," is the strongest of parallels between Gatsby and Bliss, and hence between Fitzgerald and Ellison.[7]

The figure of Gatsby obsessed Ellison throughout his life. Late in his career, in the 1985 essay "An Extravagance of Laughter," Ellison continued to ponder Gatsby and his peculiarly American "act of immaculate self-conception" (CERE 634) and the doom that such self-creation ultimately implies. Again, this dynamic was exactly what he was writing into the figure of Bliss, which is why in the "Hickman in Washington, D.C." sections—which Ellison was composing in the mid-1980s, at exactly the same time as the "Extravagance" essay—Hickman meditates with such obsessive curiosity on the reproduction of Bruegel's *Landscape with the Fall of Icarus*. Here Hickman beholds the defining fate of Bliss, who will become the Raider of the Sun, which is also the doom of Gatsby. As Hickman says sadly to Wilhite as they interrogate the painting—in a phrase that clearly applies to Bliss but that also could be said by Nick Carraway of Gatsby—he is "liable to wake up in the middle of the night still worrying about who that man was and how he could have reached so high to fall so low" (TD 599). The Fitzgerald influence on Ellison consists especially of this presentation of the Luciferian hero, the son of the morning—for what is Bliss but the holy community's embodiment of hope?—whose fall, to quote Isaiah, "didst weaken the nations" (Isa. 14:12).

Ellison believed that the spectacular flights and falls of these remarkable questing figures constituted the entire tragic arc of all great American literature. Speaking in a 1972 interview of Ahab in *Moby-Dick*, and comparing him to Jay Gatsby, Ellison articulates this theory of the constant dynamic of exceeding, and then reasserting, limit and boundary: "Tragedy always involves making the ideal manifest in the real world. . . . Americans are called upon to regulate themselves. God is not going to stop us and no foreign enemy is going to stop us. We have to stop ourselves. We have to define what is human and see that we live within it without creating a stultifying atmosphere, and see that within it a human ingenuity will not be discouraged" (CRE 224–25). In the inevitable defeat of these questing figures, Ellison argues, we do see alienation and death—yet through the telling of their story, we see "a promise of redemption": "Oedipus is defeated and Christ is defeated; they're both defeated in one sense, and yet they live. . . . Gatsby ends up dead but the narrator does not; he gives us the account. So you don't have absolute defeat or absolute victory. You have these ambiguous defeats and survivals which constitute the pattern of all literature" (CRE 225–26). This same pattern defines the story of Bliss in *Three Days*.

Ellison greatly admired the way Fitzgerald sought to integrate the totality of modern American experience into his novels. In his comments on *The Great Gatsby*, he emphasizes the importance of the "Negro" man who witnessed the "death car" in that novel, and the way this connects with what he calls "the broader context of the novel that is revealed in the understated themes of race, class, and social mobility," including Tom Buchanan's concern about racial mixing and other prominent instances of race and ethnicity that pervade the novel on, we might say, its lower frequencies. Ellison prized the way Fitzgerald could, "across the division of race," "absorb and project some of the cultural complexity of the total American scene" (CRE 334–35). This sounds a lot like the way Ellison talks of Faulkner, too, and is in many ways even more praising of Fitzgerald's ability to get at the fundamental elements of American character and culture.

It is no accident that in his final, unfinished novel, *The Last Tycoon*, Fitzgerald evokes the figure of Lincoln, who, as we have already seen in "Tell It Like It Is, Baby," becomes a fixation for Ellison. Callahan sees this mutual interest as further evidence of both authors' keen understanding of the nature of American tragedy: "In each posthumous narrative," he writes, "the evolving character and posthumous fate of Abraham Lincoln are evoked with an elegiac, tragicomic sensibility expressive of that 'willingness of the heart' and 'conscience and consciousness achieved,' which Fitzgerald and Ellison, respectively, identified with the tragic dimensions of the true American hero" (Callahan, "Ellison, Fitzgerald, and 'Dark Side'" 127).

Thus, the parallels with Fitzgerald's work, and particularly between Gatsby and Bliss, reveal Ellison's shared vision of the sublime destructiveness written into the American Adam—the Adamic hero's status as "the ideal of newborn innocence" and also "the hero of a new kind of tragedy" (Lewis, *American Adam* 6). For what is Bliss but the immense promise of innocence, and at the same time the tragic embodiment of that loss of innocence in America's tragedy of race and history? As Hickman says in the wake of Bliss's birth, "It was like the Lord had said, 'Hickman, I'm starting you out right here—with the flesh and with Eden and Christmas squeezed together . . . because this is a beginning" (TD 471). The tragedy of the novel is that Bliss—like Gatsby—rejects his past. As Ellison sketched in one of his many notes about the project, "Sunraider is not killed because he abandoned Severen's mother, nor because of his overt political acts, but because he betrayed his past" (TD 976). This is the despairing impulse of *Three Days*, and it is a powerful impulse, as the book sounds the grim depths of America's failures far more profoundly than does *Invisible Man* (and more profoundly, in my view, than any of Faulkner's works with the exceptions of *Absalom, Absalom!* and *Go Down, Moses*). Yet this is only one part of the tenor of *Three Days,* as Ellison balances this tragic story with a more affirming, even redemptive story. Here he invokes, and grapples with, another influence, that of James Joyce. For Ellison understood that Joyce's writings offer the regenerative model that he sought, the affirmative "yes" to the past, to human relations, and ultimately to American history itself. This affirming urge pushes against and balances the tragic impulse of *Three Days* and ultimately defines Ellison's own tragicomic vision—the vision that pervades and defines the *Three Days* project.

ELLISON AND JOYCE
The Language of Affirmation

Ellison's involvement with Joyce was lifelong. Ellison frequently referred to Joyce as one of the formative influences on his work, first encountered during his days in Dayton after his mother's death, when he was trying to master the writer's craft (CRE 8). He later acknowledged the importance of *A Portrait of the Artist as a Young Man* for *Invisible Man*: "Sure, I had read Joyce. I had read Portrait any number of times before I thought that I would write a novel" (CRE 231). But he goes on to point out that this was only part of the influence on him: "But I was also concerned with the problem of heroism and with the mythology of the hero. I had read Rank's *The Myth of the Birth of the Hero.* I wasn't using these things consciously, but they are just a part of my sense of how myth structures certain human activities" (CRE 231). So Ellison was always careful both to acknowledge Joyce's influence, and to suggest that Ellison's own writing evaded an excess of that influence. We see this in the midpoint of *Invisible Man,* when Ellison overtly brings Joyce into the novel. Invisible Man has just delivered his first formal public speech that marks his emergence into the artistry of the orator. At this moment the narrator recalls his English teacher, Mr. Woodbridge, and his argument that "'Stephen [Dedalus]'s problem, like ours, was not actually one of creating the uncreated conscience of his race, but of creating the *uncreated features of his face*'" (IM 354; italics in original). The timing of the reference is intriguing—Ellison wants us to connect his narrator's emergence as an artist figure with the model Joyce defined in his modernist classic *A Portrait of the Artist as a Young Man,* not merely to parallel the Invisible Man's development to that of Stephen Dedalus, but also to offer his own critique and rereading of Stephen's, and Joyce's, model of the young artist.

Ellison suggests that Joyce does not quite fully address the need for the disempowered subject—whether an Irish Catholic in Protestant- and England-ruled Dublin, or an African American in white-supremacist America—to insist upon his own face, his embodied identity in his own self-expression; in short, to assert the visibility of these invisible men. If Joyce suggests that the heroic artist can fly past the nets of history, Ellison revises this model to suggest that such transcendence is both more difficult and more ennobling for the black American. As Morris Dickstein has argued about this passage, "Ellison's emphasis is always on *imaginative* freedom within political and social *un*freedom, within limits that can only be partly transcended" (144). In his re-vision of Joyce's work, Ellison emphasizes the extent to which the artist is embedded in the social and historical world, thereby applauding Joyce's model of the heroic individual artist, but also insisting upon the ineluctable limits of the larger cultural realm in which that artist lives. In the "*Portrait*" passage, consequently, Ellison again offers a paradigm of Bloom's theory of creative misreading as "a critical act, a misreading or misprision, that one poet performs upon another," through which the poet "wishes to find his own original relation to truth ... but also *wishes to open received texts to his own sufferings*" (Bloom, Map of Misreading 3–4; emphasis added). That last suggestion has so much purchase on Ellison's writings and their relation to Joyce's influence: Ellison wants to subject Joyce's Künstlerroman to the same pressures of race, history, and power that his own anonymous hero faces. By so doing, Ellison announces his own project, a correction or expansion or revision of Joyce's project, a *portrait-of-the-artist-as-a-young-black-American-man*. This thereby accomplishes what Bloom designates as the strong poets' task: "to mis[read] one another, so as to clear imaginative space for themselves" (*Map of Misreading* 5).[8]

If *Invisible Man* is a creative misreading of Joyce's *Portrait*, then *Three Days* is a space-clearing revisionist response to both *Ulysses* and *Finnegans Wake*. Indeed, Ellison's supreme literary effort following the success of *Invisible Man* became to mirror, rival, and perhaps surpass Joyce's great modern epics. This is precisely what Ellison aims for in *Three Days*, which means that his forty-year masterwork is also a struggle with Joyce, the strongest figure in the tradition of modernist narrative.[9] In a compelling reading of Joyce's dominance of modernity, Morton Levitt has argued that Joyce can "stand for all Modernist art," that "the Modernist Age might as tellingly be labeled the Age of Joyce." He enumerates the defining elements of Joyce's work, elements that Ellison himself admired and adapted: "In Joyce we find that marriage of sensibility and technique which is characteristic of the period as a whole; he provides in his life the model of the Modernistic artistic endeavor.... In Joyce we find in detail the most significant Modernist innovations and concerns [including] the diminished yet central vision of man surviving, of man persisting, a revised yet still powerful humanist vision." Levitt's elaboration of Joyce's importance to subsequent novelists seems to me a strikingly accurate statement of how Ellison himself viewed Joyce:

> It is the aura of Joyce that attracts me, just as I believe it compels all those novelists who follow him. For admirers and detractors alike, it is this presence (that is, the continuing Modernist presence which Joyce represents) that may prove to be the central fact in their lives as novelists: a metaphor of the novel's potential as innovative form and humanist vision. (Levitt 9–11)

My contention is that in *Three Days* Ellison grapples with modernity itself. It is as if Joyce, Joyce's works, and the age that Joyce defined all assume the place of the father Ellison is simultaneously trying to reconcile with and to overcome.[10]

This constant engagement with Joyce in *Three Days* is apparent in the recurring, and defining, scene of Hickman and his congregation at the Lincoln Memorial, a tableau Ellison treats several times in the narrative. Here Hickman experiences what we can rightly call an epiphany as he stands with his congregation before the statue of Lincoln, seeing in Lincoln's face a powerful resemblance to the black American, "*not in the features but in what that look, those eyes, have to say about what it means to be a man who tries to live and struggle against all the troubles of the world with but the naked heart and mind. . . . Yes, that look and what put it there made him one of us*" (419). As he reflects on the meaning of Lincoln within the full context of American history, as the embodiment of what Ellison describes as "the conflicts within the human heart" between America's principles and its reality (CERE 153), Hickman silently creates a litany of affirmation:

> *And too full to speak, he smiled; and in silent confirmation he was nodding his head, thinking, Yes, with all I know about him and his contradictions, yes. And with all I know about men and the world, yes. And with all I know about white men and politicians of all colors and guises, yes. And with all I know about the things you had to do to be you and stay yourself—yes! . . . You're one of the few who ever earned*

> *the right to be called "Father." . . . So yes, it's all right with me, yes Yes, and though I'm a man who despises all foolish pomp and circumstance and all the bending of the knee that some still try to force us to do before false values, Yes, and Yes again. And though I'm against all the unearned tribute which the weak and lowly are forced to yield up based on force and false differences and false values, yes, for you "Father" is all right with me, Yes. . . .* (419–20)

Twelve *yeses* in this single paragraph, a dozens indeed.[11] Beyond doubt, here Ellison gestures toward the conclusion of Joyce's *Ulysses,* in which Molly Bloom offers a series of yeses in response to her memories of her first love with Leopold Bloom. Molly affirms their human love, the preservation of that love in memory, and the uncanny ability of human beings to forgive and continue to cherish another person. As Joyce scholar Zack Bowen states, "The end of the book is one of the most moving in literature. The affirming soul of the great Gea-Tellus figure takes all of human strife, suffering, and triumph to her bosom and provides eternal affirmation to those who seek it"; in this affirmation, "one is struck by her vitality, her sense of life and freedom" (Bowen 549). For Joyce, this is not merely a personal affirmation, but is ultimately a rejection of the nihilistic impulses in modernity, and an affirmation of the counter-impulse of regeneration and love. As described by Maria DiBattista, Molly's concluding affirmation announces "the sacramental infusions of procreative grace . . . on the epochal and cosmological cycles that shape the course of human history." Joyce constructs a response to the "nightmare of history" envisioned by Stephen Dedalus in which Molly's maternal and erotic "yes" "confers identity, integrity, and direction to the 'lost' and dissociated soul of modernity" (DiBattista, 169, 191).

How does Joyce's "yes" compare to Hickman's affirmations before the statue of Lincoln? Here at the heart of *Three Days* Ellison points to that same spirit of affirmation and reunion that Joyce invokes, but with the signifying or revisionist difference that Joyce himself describes in *Ulysses* as "history repeating itself with a difference" (*Ulysses* 535) This emphasis on procreative grace is precisely what Ellison seeks to invoke in relation to Lincoln, but on a national, not a personal, level. Ellison proffers the "yes" to a father figure (*"You're one of the few who ever earned the right to be called 'Father'"*) who would gather up the lost and wandering orphans of American history and restore to them direction, belonging, and identity. And unlike Molly's affirmation, Ellison's "yes" comes not in response to a private memory, but rather to Hickman's meditation on a very public symbol, the grand statue of the man whose example and whose sacrifice has the potential to unify and regenerate American history itself. This is the Lincoln whom Ellison describes—not without a touch of irony—as "the personification of democratic grandeur and political sainthood" (CERE 562). This is the Lincoln as both personal and national father who so haunts Ellison's dream in "Tell It Like It Is, Baby"—whom Ellison there describes as "a kind of father of twentieth-century America" (CERE 46).

The figure of Lincoln, real and ideal, is a sustained concern throughout Ellison's life and work. We have noted already the intimate dream in "Tell It" in which the death of Lincoln is conflated with the death of Ellison's father. We see this concern also, as Lucas Morel points out, in the great funeral scene for Tod Clifton in *Invisible Man*, in which the narrator's aim, and eloquence, are meant to parallel "the dead commemorated by Abraham Lincoln in his Gettysburg Address" (Morel, "Ellison's Democratic Individualism" 63). Ellison cites Lincoln among the key writers that "have shaped American literature" in a way that goes beyond "racial categories": "the framers of the Declaration, the Constitution and Lincoln" are Ellison's touchstones for a prophetic and value-laden American writing (CERE 732). Indeed, Lincoln is inextricably tied to Ellison's effort to understand twentieth-century African American life and culture—what in many ways is the guiding quest of *Three Days*—as Ellison himself expressed in a 1959 letter to Albert Murray: "When you start lifting up that enormous stone, the Civil War, that's kept so much of the meaning of life in the North hidden, you begin to see that Mose is in the center of a junk pile as well as in the center of the cotton boll. All the boys who try to escape this are simply running from the problem of value—Which is why those old Negroes whom I'm trying to make Hickman represent are so confounding, they never left the old original briar patch. *You can't understand Lincoln or Jefferson without confronting them*" (*Trading* 206; emphasis added). As Thomas Engeman argues about the importance of Lincoln to Hickman:

> Hickman admires and emulates the great president. Lincoln was the political messiah, the president who first realized for Blacks the equality promised in the Declaration of Independence, while going beyond the principles of the Declaration. In his "Second Inaugural Address," Lincoln argued for a Christian magnanimity toward the suffering of those "who had borne the battle, their widows, and orphans" in the North *and* South. Hickman believes the end of racial war, like the end of the Civil War, could be accomplished through the spirit of Christian reconciliation. (99)

Furthermore, Hickman sees Bliss as having the potential to be another Lincoln, and Bliss's failure to achieve that potential is precisely a statement of Bliss's downfall:

> Bliss, since you *had* to go the way you did, why didn't you pattern after Abraham Lincoln?
> That time is dead, he's dead and they whipped him in the end.
> But they had to kill him in order to stop him, Bliss. He had heart, boy. *That* was the man for you to follow. He was a big man, who had the mud between his toes. He knew pain and how to hold it and ride it out. He wasn't simple, Bliss. He was one of the most complicated of all the great men. He had been baptized in many streams.[12]

In effect, Hickman's hope, which is the hope of *Three Days* and the hope of the nation, is given form in the body of Lincoln. Lincoln becomes for Ellison a metaphor for America's rare ability to fulfill its promise, and also its tragic insistence on slaying the very figures who would reach toward that dream of fulfillment. As Hickman says, "*Sometimes the good Lord accepts His own perfection and closes His eyes and goes ahead and takes His own good time and He makes Himself a* man" (TD 420).[13] And all of this tribute and attribution of value is expressed through Ellison's allusion to the conclusion of Joyce's *Ulysses*.

We see, then, that the heart of Ellison's novel is intimately bound up with Ellison's response to Joyce's work. The influence extends further: Ellison's agon with Joyce in *Three Days* goes beyond *Ulysses* to engage ultimately with the dream world of *Finnegans Wake*. Though some scholars have noted the Joyce-Ellison correspondences within *Invisible Man*,[14] very little has been written about the ways in which Joyce's own decades-in-the-making epic, *Finnegans Wake*, influenced Ellison's thought—but that influence is in fact profound.[15] List notes how Ellison's work mirrors Joyce's effort in *Finnegans Wake*: "Joyce undertook a Homeric task in the Wake, a task which Ellison would pursue through far less experimental prose but with similar purpose" (51). In *Three Days* in particular we see the influence of the *Wake*. Ellison stated that one of his favorite books that he owned was the 1928 edition of Joyce's *Anna Livia Plurabelle*, which forms the eighth chapter of *Finnegans Wake*.[16] That chapter begins with the washerwomen at the Liffey gossiping, "O tell me all about Anna Livia!," and a few lines later, "O, tell me all I want to hear," "Tell me. Tell me." This is precisely the voice we hear on the very last page of the Book II typescript of *Three Days*, as Hickman listens in horror and fascination to the voice of Sister Maud cry her outrageous stories about her lost little babies, with the repeated exclamation "Tell me, tell me!" This construction appears sixteen times in the final fifteen lines of this page—climaxing in her concluding exclamation, "Aaah, tell me, tell me!" (455). Sister Maud's voice (like Joyce's Anna Livia Plurabelle (ALP), she is the archetypal female: her name is an obsolete English word, meaning "an old woman, a hag" ["maud"]) repeats its wild accusations, fantasies, and confessions until Hickman is moved to acknowledge the heart of her wisdom: "'I believe that in all your confusion and pain you have seen the promise and the responsibility unafraid and it seems to me that you're reminding us of some things that we can't afford to forget'" (454). Remarkably, in a book suffused with male voices, here a female voice emerges that is able to offer an alternative wisdom and to point for the questing hero his direction. With both Ellison and Joyce, the voice of gossip takes over the narrator's control and becomes pure story, depicting the eternally recurring and renewing qualities of language. As William York Tindall describes the Joycean device (in words that also apply to Ellison's version), the gossiping voices become "the river of life" created by "those two washerwomen on the banks": "'Tell me. Tell me,' gossip's refrain, proceeds through the dialogue of the washerwomen, who, wringing out old clothes and the old year, ring in the new," thereby constructing "a triumph of sequence, rhythm, and sound" (Tindall 140).

Joyce viewed the ALP section as the heart of *Finnegans Wake*, on which he said he was "prepared to stake everything" (Joyce, *Letters* 3:163). Ellison recognized the importance of this work: he pays homage to it, and signifies upon it, at the end of Book II of *Three Days*. Realizing Joyce's insights of language, Ellison channels those insights into a particularly American vernacular history and context. List argues that both Ellison and Wright "were intrigued by the skill of both Joyce and Eliot to employ a 'double vision,' to intuit ancient universal archetypes in the pedestrian events of modern life. And Ellison, more so than Wright, *was fascinated in their musical, syncopated uses of language*" (16; emphasis added). Ellison emphasizes in particular the influence of music and language in the *Wake* upon his own creative process:

> Joyce and Eliot, for instance, made me aware of the playful possibilities of language. You look at a page of *Finnegans Wake* and see references to all sorts of American popular music, yet the context gives it an extension from the popular back to the classical and beyond. This

is just something that Joyce teaches you that you can do, and you can abstract the process and apply it to a frame of reference which is American and historical, and it can refer to class, it can refer to the fractions and frictions of color, to popular and folk culture—it can do many things. (CERE 286–87; also qtd. in List 16)

This is a crucial statement by Ellison of not only the Joycean influence on his work, but also his overall theory of *literary* influence, every bit as powerful as his oft-cited comment that a writer has both "relatives" and "ancestors," the former of which he cannot choose and the latter of which he must choose.[17] Ellison rejected any simplistic theory of the relation between writers as a father-versus-son conflict. His own relation to Wright was often depicted in this way, and Ellison resisted this, saying that "writers as artists are sons of many fathers, or at least the sons of many writers' *styles*." He then elaborates his own sense of influence as being closer to a woman in childbirth: "It seems to me that instead of seeking for a father principle, the writer, as *writer*, is seeking ways to give birth to books." Ultimately Ellison insists that the writer must practice a rigorous Emersonian self-reliance when it comes to influence, must depend upon his own natural (and national) resources, and must—in one of his own most pithy expressions—"take the best and leave the rest" as he works toward his own original expressions:

A writer learns (and quite early, if he's lucky) to depend upon the authority of his own experience and intuition. He must learn to dominate them, but these are his capital and his guide, his compass and crud-detector, his sword and his cross; and *he defers to the authority of others at the peril of his artistic individuality*. His drive is to achieve his own artistic possibilities by whatever artistic means necessary. (CERE 319–20; emphasis added)

This captures Ellison's uses of the ALP section of *Finnegans Wake*. As noted previously, ALP's voice of affirmation and linguistic power is "the principle of regeneration," "for ALP gives birth and washes away sins ... she is the regenerative agent ... [the] 'water of life'" (McCarthy 566–67). These same principles underlie Ellison's own epic, an epic that treats America much the way Joyce treats Ireland, as a microcosm of universal principles. And at the heart of both epics is the experience of disintegration and reintegration: "Like the *Odyssey*, the *Wake* is an epic of dispersal, but a dispersal that goes beyond Homer's ruined fleet of ships, a dispersal effecting most insistently the construction of identity itself, the attempt to formulate the self as a coherent whole" (Devlin 67). We might well describe this aim—"to formulate the self as a coherent whole"—as Ellison's most persistent effort in his writings, from such early stories as "Boy on a Train" and "A Party down at the Square" through the central question of *Invisible Man* all the way to the near-final words he wrote in *Three Days,* when McIntyre pursues his investigations into the identity of Bliss/Sunraider and asks the lingering question of the entire book: "'Tell me . . . did you recognize the white man?'" (TD 967). And of course this search for the self is precisely what Ellison depicts in Hickman's relentless quest to reestablish Bliss's identity and selfhood.

By pointing us toward the opening of the ALP section ("Tell me, tell me") Ellison is thereby able to incorporate its famous conclusion—the only part of *Finnegans Wake* that Joyce chose to record himself reading. In the final pages of the ALP chapter, the meaning expands, creating what Tindall terms "a greater poem, a hymn to renewal, the fall of night, death, and the living river" (146). This is the promise of renewal and redemption, the unrelenting life force of language itself, that Ellison depicts in Sister Maud's voice and in other uncanny speakings in *Three Days,* particularly the astonishing stream of words that emerges from Cliofus in the final part of the computer typescript, "Hickman in Georgia & Oklahoma." In a sixty-one-page section, Cliofus essentially talks and talks, with hardly an interruption by other characters or by the narrator. Ellison titled the first file of this section "WORDS," suggesting that language itself is its very subject as well as its form. As Hickman watches the performance in fascination, he realizes that Cliofus embodies the vernacular impulse itself: "'But who knows? Maybe he's not only a man who's plagued by his words, but a man of the Word transcendent . . .'" (892). In the computer sequences in particular, Ellison's fascination with how the African American vernacular accomplishes this transcendent flow of river-like language becomes an overt concern of the narrative—not just in the spectacular example of the Cliofus section, but also such sections as Leroy's rant upon seeing Hickman in Washington, DC (546–61), which prompts Hickman to recall the glory days of African American vernacular culture in the "fine barbershop" of "the old days," with its "discussions of politics, sports, and automobiles, and . . . tall tales, jokes, and improbable lies . . . endless bull sessions in which the topics included anything from the ways of white folks, to the contrast between history as written in books, heard from grandparents who had lived it, or simply described in terms of the truth as they knew it" (547). Ellison adapts Joyce's deep mythic archetype of language and tale-telling and puts it into the context of the African American vernacular—in Bloom's phrase, Ellison opens Joyce's text to his own suffering, and thereby reveals a far more complex understanding of authorial influence than has heretofore been described in the writings about Ellison.

PATRIARCHS, SACRIFICES, AND COVENANTS
Ellison's Orphan's Loneliness

What is it that unites all of these concerns in Ellison's work—his efforts to evade and reconceive literary influence among the great modern novelists; his complex revisionary relationships with Fitzgerald and Joyce; and especially his responses to and adaptations of Joyce's late epics throughout the *Three Days* project—and how do these concerns speak to Ellison's almost primal trauma of the loss of his father when he was only three years old? The crucial link is the obsession with paternity, which ultimately lies behind Ellison's entire contest with modernity itself. The great modern authors were the founding fathers to Ellison's creative impulse—the ancestors that he chose were Hemingway, Eliot, Malraux, Dostoevsky, Faulkner (CERE 185), high moderns all. Ellison retold many times his formative experience of encountering Eliot's *The Waste Land* at Tuskegee—a poem that "seized my mind" (CERE 203)—and making the poem an object of deep study that revealed to him the intersections of modernity and African American vernacular culture. As Larry Jackson notes, "Importantly for Ellison, the poem combined qualities of jazz and the classics.... Though marked by a sophisticated tone and furiously intellectual references, the poem also beckoned toward the raucous and jagged vernacular" (*Emergence of Genius* 151). Jackson goes on to argue that it was Ellison's encounter with Eliot's poem that initiated his vocation as a writer: "The poem by Eliot reoriented [Ellison's] perspective away from the world of music and toward literary composition.... Within weeks of reading it, Ellison began to write his own free verse" (151).[18] In effect, Ellison set up modernity itself as the precursor with which he would grapple in his effort to enter the lists of the giants of world literature.

This unyielding effort to overcome the father parallels, and surely finds its cause in, Ellison's personal odyssey to recover the father whose death impelled Ellison into an early manhood. Consequently, Hickman in *Three Days* is more than just the father that Bliss both seeks and evades; he is simultaneously the embodiment of fatherhood that Ellison restlessly seeks and knows he can never ultimately attain. Indeed, if Ellison were as anxious about having a child, and as frustrated by his and Fanny's inability to do so, as Rampersad reports, it is not unlikely that this frustration would further fuel his sense of anxiety about fatherhood and his own block at becoming a father figure in life as well as in literature.[19]

Yet it is crucial to note Hickman's identification and affirmation of Lincoln as "father." For if the act of poetic misreading is also an attempt to kill off the overwhelming father, what does it mean if Ellison's affirmation of "Daddy Hickman" reaffirms the father and indeed sets him on high as the voice of authority and command? To understand this, we must return to the moment when Bliss echoes Gatsby in his desire to enter the forbidden place alone. For immediately after this, Hickman thinks of "all the old scriptural stories of Isaac and Joseph and upon our slave forefathers who killed their babes rather than have them lost in bondage" (TD 393). This comparison with biblical figures recurs when, in the "Bliss's Birth" section, Hickman muses, "But for what Jehovah could I even play Abraham to that little Isaac?" (TD 470). In his agonizing effort to make sense of what has gone wrong between him and his adopted son, Hickman turns to the patriarchal tales of the Old Testament, and the patriarchal name of Abraham pervades this book. The patriarchal mythos of the Old Testament saturates Hickman's consciousness, and the defining story that Hickman and Bliss enact is precisely the story of Abraham and Isaac—the archetypal father-son trauma that inaugurates the foundation of the nation.

Bliss's very name is a version of Isaac, which means literally "he who laughs," and Bliss is Hickman's son of his old age, as Isaac was for Abraham and Sarah. Hickman is the original patriarch, since Bliss has no other earthly father; through his oath to care for the son, Hickman initiates a new covenant with God that emerges from his conversion experience that is inseparable from Bliss's birth. If, therefore, Hickman stands for Abraham as the founder of the covenant, this puts Bliss in the tremendously demanding position of Isaac, the inheritor, the indebted one. As Genesis commentator Leon Kass states, "Isaac, like every son that comes after him, stands *within* a tradition. In this respect, Abraham, is unique, Isaac is not" (352). Like Isaac, Bliss inherits the tremendous burden of a patriarchal covenant to which he has not even given assent, and so, like Isaac, he cannot help but doubt the burden placed upon him: "And what is this desire to identify with others," Bliss asks himself in the middle of his hospital-bed confessions with Hickman, "this need to extend myself and test my most far-fetched possibilities with only the agency of shadows? Merely shadows. All shadowy they promised me my mother and denied me solid life" (TD 393). Yet unlike Isaac, who submits to this inheritance and becomes the silent, shadowy figure among the patriarchs, Bliss will reject the inheritance, as he rejects the black community that rears him in love, but that also puts upon him the demand to save the nation, to free both black and white America from the original sin that threatens the nation's destruction: "*And to think*," Hickman muses after his meditation on Lincoln, "*we had hoped to raise ourselves that kind of man*" (TD 421). Like Abraham, who prepares to kill his child as a sacrifice to his obedience to the covenant, Hickman, for all his love and care devoted to Bliss, similarly places too great a burden upon the child and threatens his destruction. Bliss flees to avoid this sacrifice, yet thereby fails to accomplish the liberation from the father that Isaac attains. As Kass explains, in the sacrifice of Isaac,

> what is destroyed ... is Abraham's claim to paternal possession of his son. . . . Isaac is no longer simply the son of his father. Whether he knows it or not, he is now also the son of the covenant, a link in the chain that carries the new way. Abraham's near sacrifice of Isaac in effect becomes, for Isaac, the sacrifice of his father, or, to speak more carefully, the rite of passage in which Isaac is forced to say good-bye to his primary identity as the son of his father. . . . For Abraham the test is over; for Isaac it is just beginning. Isaac is on his own. (359)

This description reveals Ellison's vision of the Hickman-Bliss relationship, which is a remarkably symmetrical inversion of the biblical Abraham-Isaac relation. By refusing his sacrificial role, Bliss fails to successfully move from childhood to adulthood, fails to reconcile himself to his social world and is therefore unable to enter into that world as a unified, coherent self. Instead he flees and fractures that self into Mister Movie-Man, Senator Sunraider, and multiple other fragmented identities. Daddy Hickman comes at the moment of Bliss's dying to try to call Bliss back to that childhood self, to reconcile Bliss to father and community in order to save Bliss himself. We can only wonder if Ellison thought the effort a success or a failure, if, as Callahan provides a possible ending in *Juneteenth*, "the sound of Hickman's consoling voice, calling from somewhere above" can bring Sunraider back to his childhood self, or if Hickman has indeed come too late, and the "dark hand" reaching for Sunraider at the end will pull him down to hell.[20]

And here we see Ellison's own ongoing, never-resolved agon with his own father. In a letter to Stanley Edgar Hyman in 1955, just as the *Three Days* project was taking its initial shape and weighing heavily on his mind,

Ellison writes: "Oh where is the foundling's father hidden?" (Rampersad 311). We can understand this cri de coeur as Ellison's animating principle—the foundling's search for the father is for Ellison's writing both his efficient and his final cause; that is, it propels the writing and is the goal or telos of the writing itself. For ultimately Ellison himself is the foundling, always searching for the father taken from him at the age of three. As he explains in "Tell It Like It Is, Baby," he is haunted by a dream in which he sees an older man, causing him to feel "as though I had lost something precious ... what had I done—what had I failed to do?" The man transforms into a sheet-covered corpse, and finally into the image of his father, as he had been in Ellison's last glimpse of him. And here Ellison utters the poignant cry that dominates his fiction, and especially *Three Days before the Shooting* ... : "*But what quality of love sustains us in our orphan's loneliness, and how much is thus required of fatherly love to give us strength for all our life hereafter?*" *Three Days* is Ellison's effort to answer precisely these questions through the voice and figure of Hickman. As Ellison wrote about Hickman to Murray, "All I can do is ask him hard questions and write down his acts and his answers" (*Trading* 204). Through Hickman and Bliss, Ellison sounds the depths of his orphan's loneliness and thereby, perhaps, becomes the father he seeks. Thus, he may be able to subdue the chaos bequeathed to him when Lewis Ellison died in 1916, and perhaps, through his writing, he is able to reconcile the displaced son with the distant father.

NOTES

1. Ellison was invited in January 1965 to contribute an essay for the centennial issue of the *Nation*, perhaps a "postscript ... of the polemic about the Negro artist in which you have been engaged," or "some other aspect of the civil rights business" or "some other area of American life and culture." Ellison returned to the 1956 essay draft, which included the dream description and meditation on his father and on Abraham Lincoln, and added the prefatory comments (an excerpt from a letter from his old Oklahoma friend Virgil Branam and two paragraphs) and the concluding sentence about his novel-in-progress to the original draft; he also made a number of revisions to the early draft. (Ralph Waldo Ellison Papers, Manuscript Division, Library of Congress, boxes I:107 and I:223.)

2. As I have argued elsewhere, scholars tend to note important parallels between Ellison and other writers—especially Eliot, Malraux, Melville, Joyce, and others—but rarely explore these parallels in any sort of detail (see Conner, "Litany of Things"]). Notable exceptions include the following: Butler, "Dante's *Inferno* and Ellison's *Invisible Man*" (comparing Ellison and Dante); Dietze, "Ralph Ellison and the Literary Tradition" (Ellison and Malraux); Ealy, "A Friendship That Has Meant So Much" (Ellison and Warren); Frank, "Ralph Ellison and

a Literary 'Ancestor'" (Ellison and Dostoevsky); O'Meally, "Rules of Magic" (Ellison and Hemingway); and Rovit, "Ralph Ellison and the American Comic Tradition" (Ellison, Melville, and Whitman). For a superb overview of the history of Ellison criticism, see Butler, "Probing the Lower Frequencies."

3. Podhoretz, long an intellectual opponent of Ellison (see his negative responses to *Shadow and Act* in 1965 and 1966 [Rampersad 409, 435]), based his claims only on his immediate reading of *Juneteenth*, prior to the publication of the bulk of the *Three Days* manuscript in 2010; Rampersad shows no evidence of having worked on either the *Juneteenth* book or the wealth of material on *Three Days* that was readily available in the Library of Congress archives to which he had unlimited access. The biography never discusses *Juneteenth* nor does it engage the forty-two boxes of manuscript material on *Three Days*, treating only briefly the published excerpts from the second-novel project.

4. Johnson delivered these remarks during his National Book Award acceptance speech, with Ralph Ellison in the audience, at the ceremony in 1990.

5. Interestingly, Bloom himself, in his brief writings about Ellison, acknowledges Ellison's debt to Faulkner but insists that the true American precursor for Ellison was his namesake, Ralph Waldo Emerson. "The Invisible Man," Bloom argues, "is a black Emersonian [who] has more in common with Emerson, than with T.S. Eliot or with Faulkner." Ellison is able to "transumptively triumph by making Emerson black," and can thereby become "more Emersonian than Emerson himself had been" ("Introduction," *Modern Critical Views* 3). His Invisible Man—and, I would argue, Ellison himself—"is finally the only authentic American, black or white, because he follows the American Religion, which is Emersonian self-reliance. He insists upon himself, refuses to go on imitating his false fathers, and evades both Rinehart and Ras. True, he is the Emersonian driven underground, but he will emerge more Emersonian than ever, insisting he has become Representative Man" ("Introduction," *Ellison's "Invisible Man"* 5).

6. Of course, there are other fissures in the Faulkner-Ellison influence. Obviously, Ellison does not suffer as Faulkner did in articulating the black voice and experience; whereas in, for example, *The Sound and the Fury* Faulkner resists rendering Dilsey's voice in the first person, Ellison has no such block with rendering black voice and experience, and indeed *Three Days* is a veritable encyclopedia of black speech and experience. Furthermore, the great Faulknerian concern is the American South, which he renders with incomparable depth and eloquence—but of course Ellison's concern is with the Oklahoma Territory, and the impetus that gives life to *Three Days* is, as he famously wrote to Al Murray in 1952, "to get real mad again, *and* talk with the old folks a bit. I've got *one* Okla. book in me I do believe" (*Trading* 44). Ellison's landscape is the Western Territory, "'where lies my destructive element, that substance I'm told the artist must dunk himself in'" (Rampersad 267). And finally, the religious vision that animates *Three Days* sets it apart from much American literature, including Faulkner's work on the whole: Faulkner never could have told the story of Hickman and his congregation, nor could he have rendered the spiritual consciousness of young Bliss with the detail and intimacy that Ellison achieves.

7. R. W. B. Lewis famous describes this self-reliant, Adamic figure: "A radically new personality, the hero of the new adventure: an individual emancipated from history, happily bereft of ancestry, untouched and undefiled by the usual inheritances of family and race;

an individual standing alone, self-reliant and self-propelling, ready to confront whatever awaited him with the aid of his own unique and inherent resources" (*American Adam* 5). Lewis's study in its final pages points to both Gatsby and the Invisible Man as more contemporary examples of the American Adam hero; the Invisible Man in particular "is willing, with marvelously inadequate equipment, to take on as much of the world as is available to him, without ever fully submitting to any of the world's determining categories." He possesses "that odd aura of moral priority over the waiting world which was a central ingredient in the Adamic fictional tradition" (198). Ralph and Fanny Ellison first met Lewis in 1949 and, as Rampersad reports, Lewis "would become one of their closest friends" (Ralph became godfather to Lewis's son Nathanial in 1962). When Lewis met Ellison, he was working on *The American Adam* and had already read the "Battle Royal" excerpt from *Invisible Man* published in 1947. Lewis recalled being impressed with the fact that Ralph "knew a great deal about nineteenth-century American literature" and that "he believed in its greatness, its moral power but also its complexity" (Rampersad 238–39, 391). Lewis reviewed *Invisible Man* in the *Hudson Review* when it appeared, describing its hero as "the Negro heir of all the rootless, searching, self-deceiving American innocents," bringing into relief its roots in the nineteenth-century American novel, and emphasizing the hero's passages through trials to "achieved identity" ("Eccentrics' Pilgrimage" 145, 148–49). It seems an obvious conclusion to surmise that Lewis's *American Adam*, appearing just three years after the publication of *Invisible Man*, was influenced by Ellison's work.

8. Kathryn Stelmach Artuso, in her comparative study of Irish literature and the literature of the American South, makes a similar point about Ellison's critical response to Joyce. Citing another Joycean allusion in *Invisible Man*, Artuso argues that "the unnamed narrator both upholds and undermines the Black/Irish connection, often foregrounding his distance as an outsider from events such as the Joycean epiphany, which should ideally merge the spiritual and the sensual into an aesthetic vision, a vision of freedom. The narrator's epiphany is instead figured in ironic and wholly eroticized terms, while the imagery connotes not freedom but the threat of other levels of bondage behind the Veil" (115).

9. Patrice Rankine, in his study of classicism in African American literature, perceives the ways in which Ellison's late writings parallel Joyce's longer works, arguing that "an exploration of . . . Ellison's essays, *Invisible Man*, and *Juneteenth* reveals a skillful deployment comparable to James Joyce's uses of the Ulysses theme in his novel" (150).

10. For a reading of how Ellison's unpublished memoir, "Leaving the Territory," refers to and draws upon Joyce's *Finnegans Wake*—especially in its engagement with the elusive father figure—see my "'Leaving the Territory': Ralph Ellison's Backward Glance" (Conner).

11. In the longer version of this scene that Ellison constructed later, in the "computer sequences" that serve to elaborate upon the material of the earlier drafts, Ellison omitted one yes and added several additional words, but overall the passage is not significantly different.

12. Quoted in the "Notes" by Ellison that conclude the *Juneteenth* volume (362).

13. There are two files of material collected by Ellison on Lincoln in the Library of Congress files (boxes I:191 and II:73), indicating his fascination with Lincoln. It is noteworthy that the Civil War historian (and three-time Lincoln Award–winner) Allen Guelzo concludes his magisterial study of the Emancipation Proclamation by quoting Hickman's paean to Lincoln from *Juneteenth* (Guelzo 285). Guelzo's concluding pages focus on the

legacy of Lincoln in particular for African America. He notes the shift from viewing Lincoln as the "Great Emancipator" and "a lifelong enemy of slavery" (and emphasizing the Juneteenth holiday as the emblematic "Emancipation Day") to, in the wake of Black Nationalism and the post–civil rights era, viewing Lincoln as, in Lerone Bennet's words, "'a reactionary white supremacist'" (qtd. in Guelzo 274–80). Guelzo invokes Ellison, one suspects, as a useful counter to "the slow, almost unnoticed withdrawal of African-Americans from what was once the great consensus of blacks' admiration for Abraham Lincoln" and a reminder of the "time when Lincoln and his proclamation enjoyed a far more golden importance in the minds of black and white Americans alike" (280–81). Similarly, Lucas Morel has written about Ellison's invocation of Lincoln in this same passage of *Juneteenth,* and noted the "kindred spirit" of Ellison and Frederick Douglass in their complex, historically informed, and on the whole positive (even reverential) views of Lincoln (Morel, "America's First Black President?" 151–52).

14. Robert List (*Dedalus in Harlem*) and Patrice Rankine (*Ulysses in Black*) are the most prominent to have explored the Joyce-Ellison connections; see also Conner, "'Leaving the Territory.'" List's book, though it suffers from being out of print and rather dated, is an excellent and thoughtful comparison of the two writers. But surprisingly few others have followed this lead—indeed, an MLA search in June 2013 on "Joyce" and "Ellison" yields a mere eight hits, half of them unpublished dissertations and two of them general anthologies or handbooks. This is yet another surprisingly unexplored area in Ellison studies.

15. In the 1965 interview "A Very Stern Discipline," Ellison cites *Finnegans Wake* and *The Sound and the Fury* as representative examples of "the perspective of folklore" that Ellison reads with such "fullness of attention ... because I'm eager to discover what it has to say to me personally" (CERE 742–43).

16. In a 1988 letter to Mr. Roger Cameron he recounts his delight "back in the Thirties when a friendly book dealer allowed me to buy the 347th signed copy of Anna Livia Plurabelle for the even then unbelievable sum of $1.25! This transaction took place on Harlem's 125th Street, and since the dealer was well aware of its market value I suspect that he allowed me to have a signed copy of Joyce at such a ridiculous price for the sheer pleasure of watching the expression on my face" (Ellison to Roger Cameron, 18 August 1988, Ralph Waldo Ellison Papers, Manuscript Division, Library of Congress, box 56:1).

17. In his magnificent essay written partly in response to Irving Howe's misreading of Ellison's work, Ellison insists that writers such as Hemingway were more influential on him than fellow African American writers such as Wright: "But perhaps you will understand when I say he did not influence me if I point out that while one can do nothing about choosing one's relatives, one can, as artist, choose one's 'ancestors.' Wright was, in this sense, a 'relative,' Hemingway an 'ancestor.' Langston Hughes, whose work I knew in grade school and whom I knew before I knew Wright, was a 'relative'; Eliot, whom I was to meet only many years later, and Malraux and Dostoevsky and Faulkner, were 'ancestors'—if you please or don't please!" (CERE 185). Certainly Joyce would be listed among Ellison's most prominent "ancestors"—and indeed the fact that Ellison readily lists Faulkner, but omits Joyce, in this list suggests to me that while he had grown quite confident in his relation to Faulkner, Ellison was still in the process of comprehending his relation to Joyce. This essay,

composed in the winter of 1963–64, is contemporaneous with Ellison's first decade of work on *Three Days*.

18. Although Rampersad offers a muted challenge to Ellison's own argument that Eliot transformed him as a writer, and questions why Ellison gave less credit to Morteza Sprague (Rampersad 77), his Tuskegee English teacher who was pivotal to Ellison's entry into literature, nevertheless Jackson notes that Sprague admitted to Ellison that "he hadn't read [Eliot's] mystifying poem" (151) and hence Ellison was left to his own devices to come to grips with this complex work. Ellison later dedicated *Shadow and Act* to Sprague, a gesture of significant gratitude and respect.

19. See Rampersad, *Biography*, 228, 338–39. It is noteworthy that Rampersad depends upon an anonymous (and biased) source for this condemnatory view of Ellison.

20. Callahan chose to end *Juneteenth* with that marvelously ambiguous image: "*And as a dark hand reached down, he seemed to hear* the sound of Hickman's consoling voice, calling from somewhere above" (Ellison, *Juneteenth* 348; italics in original). This captures the uncertain judgment of Bliss, and leaves us wondering if Hickman is able to reclaim the wandering son or if Bliss is now irretrievably lost on his passage to hell. Of course Ellison did not indicate how the book would end; the passage Callahan chose occurs near the end of the Book II typescript (TD 412), but is immediately followed there by Hickman's profound reflections on Bliss's fate and his comparisons between Bliss and Lincoln. Callahan moved this material to chapter 14 in *Juneteenth*, to be followed by the "Bliss's Birth" section as the penultimate chapter (Ellison never clearly determined where "Bliss's Birth" would be located, but his notes indicate its position somewhere in Book II [editor's note, TD 457]), and then the concluding "coon cage" section as the final chapter. The placement of "Bliss's Birth" seems to me exactly right—this is the true climax of not just Book II, but also of the entire second-novel project, and it ranks among the finest prose fiction ever written by an American. Placing it near the end of the entire *Juneteenth*/Book II narrative, in the full context of the Bliss-Hickman relationship, brings that section into its full significance. Callahan's decision then to end with the surreal section that begins with Hickman asking Bliss, "'Son, are you there?'" and ends with Bliss's Dantesque descent toward the inferno (TD 394–412) is a strong interpretive choice, one that certainly brings into relief the major questions that cluster about the entire narrative.

RALPH ELLISON'S *THREE DAYS*
The Aesthetics of Political Change

TIMOTHY PARRISH

> Part of what's taken so long is that so many things have changed so fast in our culture that as soon as I thought I had a draft that brought all of these things together, there would be another shift and I'd have to go back and revise all over again.
> —RALPH ELLISON, 1982 (CRE 385–86)

Ralph Ellison is arguably American literature's most self-consciously national writer and there is the sense that regardless of the form in which he was writing—essays, short fiction, or novels—he was always telling a version of the same story. I make this claim at the outset because it is important to understand that the fact that Ellison did not "finish" his second novel should be no bar to readers reading the book and recognizing it for the important work that it is. Recent trends in academic criticism have questioned the logic of national narratives, but Ellison always understood himself to be writing a version of an American story, one that goes back through the Declaration of Independence to the days when Africans arrived in North America as slaves, and then back up through the Civil War, Abraham Lincoln, Martin Luther King Jr., and the whole complicated era of Ellison's time as a writer. Moreover, Ellison, like Marcel Proust or William Faulkner, understood the present through its ongoing engagement with the past. Consequently, Ellison's work, no matter its varied form or shifting plot, conveys a sense of ongoing continuity. With an aesthetic orientation that conceives of experience in terms of its capacity to carry the past forward through one's continual engagement with the present, an Ellison novel will inevitably resist endings that provide closure. However, because Ellison imagined that his novels were both taking their form from American history and *giving form to American history* (analogous, say, to Homer giving form to the Trojan War), they cannot be read only as narrative experiments in modernist consciousness.

"The great men of letters," remarks the narrator of *Remembrance of Things Past* (1913–27), "have never created more than a single work" (Proust 3:382). Ellison's work confirms this thesis and his second novel achieves a remarkable continuity and formal consistency when it is read according to this Proustian logic. If everything Ellison wrote reflects on everything else he wrote, then he described the plot of all of his writing when he described the plot of the second novel: "In my mind all of this is tied up with the significance of being a Negro in America and at the same time with the problem of our democratic faith as a whole" (CRE 275). Speaking again of the second novel, he said that "it is that aura of summing up, that pause for the contemplation of the moral significance of the history we've been through, that I have been reaching for, in my work on this new book" (301). From this perspective, Ellison was not just a novelist, but a kind of epic poet writing in a prose form that took on the contours of fiction, history, and myth simultaneously. The second novel brings together these ways of thinking and forms what we might call Ellison's "Book of America," an evolving canon unto itself.

Consider the previous two paragraphs an introduction to an essential American writer who in many ways we have still yet to meet on his own terms. I say this because Ellison's second novel is a major work of American literature and judging by early responses, or perhaps I should say nonresponses, readers are uncertain what to make of it. This is in part understandable because for about fifty years we have thought of Ellison as a novelist who wrote only one novel. Yet now we have on our hands a second novel so vast and protean that it is in fact multiple and could be said to constitute more than one novel. More than that, despite 1,136 pages that make up *Three Days before the Shooting . . .* , alternative versions of the novel still rest unpublished in the Library of Congress, along with many other Ellison writings, including a memoir. Some time will have to pass and much work will have to be done in order to grasp what Ellison has left us. The only barriers between us and what Ellison has achieved are, inevitably, our own misperceptions about the kind of writer Ellison was; indeed, it is not simply that Ellison's novels differ from the expectations we bring to them, but that his work attempted to radically reorient our understanding of what a novelist is and what a novel can do. It may be that, ultimately, *Three Days* will be considered the summit of Ellison's achievement. The modest goal of this essay is to establish a context for understanding what Ellison's second novel does (and does not do) and to suggest an outline for possible readings of the book. The less modest goal of the essay is to suggest how in many ways we still do not understand Ellison at all and to offer a corrective to some of our received opinions concerning his body of work.

The terrain for discussing Ellison usually is drawn according to the following lines. He was an African American writer who mastered the form of the novel in the work known as *Invisible Man*. In so doing, Ellison brought a distinctively African American vision and aesthetic to the American canon. Indeed, as the epigraphs from Melville and Eliot attest, *Invisible Man* was a self-conscious revision of the American literary tradition cast through the eyes of a black narrator who was, implicitly and explicitly, excluded from that tradition. Thus, the act of writing the book constituted a paradox. If a literary tradition assumes that some people exist beyond or outside that tradition's logic, then how can someone who exists outside of that logic write a book that encapsulates and transforms the very tradition that excludes him and his people? If such a person were to write such a book, then wouldn't the assumptions governing the existing tradition be so transformed as to render that tradition extinct? Conversely, if the story of the "outside" group joins the tradition which had excluded it, doesn't that mean that the outside group has been rendered extinct as well? Ellison posed and answered such questions through *Invisible Man* but because his novel exposes a paradox that few if any were able to identify and confront, his achievement was rendered anomalous. The paradox is this: to accept *Invisible Man* on the terms that it demands, you have to quit seeing others through the prism of race. Who has been able to do that? Once you do that, it is no longer anomalous to recognize that the work of a black author is the climax to the American literary tradition, nor is it anomalous to recognize that the American literary tradition can be recognized as the embodiment of African American literary expression. The history of *Invisible Man* criticism is largely an argument wherein the disputants fight to preserve the assumptions regarding race that the book itself destroys not as a matter of subjective fantasy but as a cool assertion of reality. The second novel does not do away with any of these concerns; in fact, it deepens them.

That said, the fact that Ralph Ellison was a novelist may not be the most important fact about him, though I think we are still a long way from understanding what a radically transformative novelist he was. W. E. B. Du Bois famously said that "the problem of the Twentieth Century is the problem of the color-line" (*Souls* vii). The most important fact about Ellison is that he employed the form of the novel as his mechanism for investigating how the American experiment of democracy became a laboratory for exploring whether the fact of the color line could be erased, if not forever then at least for a time. *Invisible Man* remains the century's definitive exploration of Du Bois's assertion, and a decade into the next century we are no closer to solving the problem Du Bois identified. Ellison's second novel takes up the same questions that animated *Invisible Man* but, as we shall see, casts them along different lines and toward different conclusions. Ellison might have chosen to have "only" been a philosophical essayist like his namesake, Ralph Waldo Emerson. However, inspired by the great modernist works of James Joyce, T. S. Eliot, and Louis Armstrong, Ellison committed himself, as a writer, to articulating his vision of American history and its relationship to race while at the same time expanding our understanding of the form of the novel. With *Invisible Man* and his second novel, he accomplished these aims.

To understand what Ellison did as a writer generally and with the second novel specifically, we will have to reorient our understanding of what the Ellisonian novel is and what it tries to do. It is commonplace, for instance, to say that Ellison wrote like a blues or a jazz artist. But what does such a claim mean? At the outset of his story, the narrator of *Invisible Man* points us to Louis Armstrong as the muse of his tale, but he also suggests that his role is to give form to Armstrong's "music of invisibility." In other words, without the intervention of the narrator, Armstrong's song may not last so that others can know it. To put it more bluntly, a jazz performance, as marvelous as it may be, is not and cannot be a novel. Yet, if Ellison was a modernist jazz novelist, then Armstrong was a modernist jazz musician. The two roles are not the same and require different talents and methods of execution. As a reader of Joyce and Eliot, Ellison was positioned to see how the aesthetic theories and practices of the literary modernists were consistent with the performance aesthetic of the jazz artists he knew and admired. Where literary modernism and jazz modernism intersected was in their shared sense that improvisation and contingency could be the crucial components of any aesthetic production. In other words, "stories" may be told and retold, but they are never complete. Furthermore, the manner of telling, its style and pizzazz, is at least as important as what is being told. This is why collectors want every version of a Louis Armstrong version of a particular song. No performance is the same and each one comments on and transforms previous versions.

By a similar logic, modernist works such as *Ulysses*, *In Pursuit of Lost Time*, *The Trial*, and *The Man without Qualities* also seem unfinished and subject to endless possible interpretation. Ellison knew the tradition of Armstrong and he knew the tradition of Joyce and that he knew both traditions made him similar to possibly no other person on the planet. Understanding this fact about Ellison is crucial to understanding his achievement as a writer and why his second novel deserves to be read as carefully and for as long as *Invisible Man* is and will be read.

To explore the question of the color line in the wake of modernity (and American history), Ellison combined in his works the jazz tradition embodied by Armstrong and manifold others with the high modernist and mostly European literary tradition of Joyce, Proust, and Thomas Mann. Although most readers recognize that these two aesthetic traditions intersect at the point of Ralph Ellison, it is not clear they have been able to assimilate this fact and thus the meaning of this intersection. Ironically, to speak of Ellison as a jazz novelist likely segregates him further from the achievement of the European modernists, just as to speak of Ellison as the inheritor of Joyce or Proust seems to segregate him from the jazz tradition. Why? For the same reason that *Invisible Man* remains such an anomalous work: the achievement challenges the fundamentally, if unwittingly, racist assumptions readers of all stripes bring to Ellison's work and to the genres embodied in that work. Challenging assumptions about race so embedded in our consciousness that we cannot see them even when they are brought to light has been more than enough to make Ellison arguably the least appreciated great American novelist. However, that problem is compounded to the extent that Ellison's novels are subjected to expectations that have still not fully grasped the implications of his jazz-modernist aesthetic. Readers of Ellison must confront their own confusions about race at the same time they must wrestle with their assumptions about what a novel is supposed to be. Of course, these very challenges are why Ellison chose the novel as the delivery mechanism for expressing his vision. He hoped that the novel's very formal fluidity would create possibilities in which his readers could reinvent themselves as something other than what they are.

Here we may turn more directly to the obvious "problem" the second novel raises for most: *what is this strange, long, possibly unfinished book and how do I read it?* First, you have to surrender the notion that the book you read can have an ending beyond the one you give it. Like *Invisible Man*, the second novel identifies and explores the paradoxes and contradictions that inhere in thinking that is predicated on ideas of "race." Like *Invisible Man*, the second novel adopts a fluid, improvisational form that explicitly denies as a premise of its form that aesthetic closure is either desirable or possible. Thus, the second novel makes explicit the formal and interpretative challenges that Ellison's work have always raised. However, unlike *Invisible Man*, which was able to mask itself as a traditional (premodernist) novel simply because it appears to have a beginning, middle, and end (but really does not since the reader has to complete the book's concluding gesture), the second novel cannot be read effectively until the reader fundamentally reorients his or her assumptions about what a novel is and how Ellison is using this form to explore his aesthetic and philosophical questions about race and identity in the context of American history. The primary reason Ellison did not finish the second novel is the same reason Armstrong recorded multiple versions of "St. James Infirmary Blues" or "(What Did I Do to Be So) Black and Blue?" Each performance registered the artist's perspective, itself evolving, of a particular work that was being transformed under the continual pressure of time and changing history. As an artist who was writing about the relationship between race and American ideals during a time in which the assumptions about race and American society were changing, Ellison made that sense of contingency an ongoing part of his novel-in-progress. To reinforce the point, he made one of its central characters, Hickman, a former jazz trombonist. Moreover, by suggesting that Bliss, one of the main characters of the second novel, was also Rinehart, a key character in *Invisible Man*, Ellison was undoing whatever seemed to be finished about his first novel. We are back to Proust's insight: the great artist never creates more than one work.

If we truly accept that Ellison is a jazz novelist, the notion of an unfinished novel should not be that disorienting. However, as Ellison knew, most of his readers' tastes will not have been formed by the jazz tradition and even if they have been, they may decide, as his narrator does, that a novel requires different assumptions from its readers than a jazz performance requires from its listeners. Here the model for understanding Ellison's work is largely European and one that has not been altogether absorbed by American intellectuals. In works such as *In Pursuit of Lost Time* or Robert Musil's *The Man without Qualities* no conclusion is possible, yet both works are generally regarded as the pinnacle achievements of the novel form in their language. Proust's book can only end when the narrator's consciousness ends because the narrative is, on every page, the confrontation and expression of that consciousness's perpetual engagement with the meaning it makes as a perceiver. In the same way, Ellison's work refuses to separate Ellison's historical vision from his aesthetic vision since Ellison's understanding of the American past is fundamentally an engagement with how the past is always being transformed into a conception of the present. With its multiple drafts and different versions of the same incidents, often from alternative narrative perspectives, the second novel ceaselessly portrays whether the novelist's art can transform the past, or history, to create a present different from the past. The version that has been published as *Three Days before the Shooting . . .* (2010) cannot be said to constitute its definitive form simply because there is no definitive form it can take. To read it in its full complexity, one will have to engage a book that has multiple versions, changing narrative perspectives, and no conclusion.[1] Such a book demands that the reader who engages its premises must try to create his or her own book from what is read. The second novel is Ellison's—but it is the reader's too.

A book that has multiple versions, changing narrative perspectives, and no conclusion. A book that demands that the reader who engages its premises must try to create his or her own book from what is read. Purely as an experiment in literary form, the novel that Ellison's work most recalls is one whose formal inventiveness no one questions: Robert Musil's massive, unfinished *The Man without Qualities*. Begun in 1921, partly published but left unfinished and in multiple variants at Musil's death in 1942, this thousand-page novel, centered on a character who identifies himself as being "without qualities" beyond those imposed upon him by the external world, presents its readers with almost all of the same difficulties that readers will find in *Three Days*. The first volume, parts 1 and 2, concludes with no resolution to the action imminent. The second volume suspends the action from the first and begins a different narrative line.[2] Affinities of structure aside, though, the key reason that these two books bear comparison is their shared aesthetic: each author was enacting an aesthetic vision that assumed that what they were writing could not be finished. Both authors were committed to key tenets of modernism, but they also both develop those sensibilities in ways that involve an almost uncannily similar understanding of how art can be used to re-create history. Their novels explore their intuition that through fiction they could re-create history, or find a truer history, than the one that had become all too real. Their novels are deeply political and visionary at the same time and it is a catastrophic misreading of their works to suggest that either author was in flight from history or from his time.

Their "unfinished" novels take place on the edge of a historical precipice and identify that precipice as the point on which their stories are told. *The Man without Qualities*, begun in the 1920s, portrays the shocking unexpectedness of World War I at the same time that it cryptically alludes to the building terror of Hitler. The plot of part 1 centers on what is ironically called the "Parallel Action" being undertaken by a committee that has been established in response to news that the Germans are planning a celebration of Kaiser Wilhelm's thirtieth year in power. Not to be outdone by their German-speaking counterparts and their fatuous celebration of empire, the Austrians come up with a plan to celebrate their own empire, which Musil dubs "Kakania," that will instead celebrate the seventieth year of Emperor Franz Joseph's rule. The "Parallel Action" is established in 1913, and for hundreds of pages its members argue over how Austria's cultural and military heritage should best be celebrated. No suggestion, however, conveys the slightest cognizance that by 1918 the Austro-Hungarian Empire will be kaput, or that the start of war in 1914 will resolve the committee's arguments. The need for a new vision of culture and society is as urgent as it is unrecognized in Musil's depiction of a ruling elite sitting on top of a historical powder keg on the verge of blowing them and their assumptions to kingdom come.

In *The Man without Qualities* Musil created a new form—a modernist historical novel that depicts the past from within the past's continuous unfolding even as the narrator often seems to stand somewhere beyond the past being portrayed. The reader of the novel understands that his or her present reality derives from the same world that the characters know and is in many ways an extension of that world, yet the reader also knows that the reality the characters assume to be true is about to be shattered by the war. However, this knowledge does not put the reader in a superior relationship to the characters but rather emphasizes the contingency of their own understanding and the fragility of their assumptions about their society. Ellison's novel occupies a similar doubled or perhaps tripled conception of the past. Each novel often seems in the process of being swallowed by a present that it is also struggling to understand. For Musil that present was Hitler. For Ellison that present was the uncertainty brought on by the civil rights movement. Most readers are used to reading in a stable present, but that certitude is denied in Ellison's second novel since it implies a past that is being transformed every passing second by a shifting contemporary reality, and also a recovered past that is potentially transforming the present. The reader cannot decide, and Ellison will not let the reader know, what Bliss/Sunraider's fate will be. He could be a martyr for a new era in which racial lines are no longer divisive or his death could be just another violent episode in a war that never ends.

Proust also portrayed the ways in which the present is forever being made from the past, or, in Faulkner's phrase, how the past is not even past. Proust, though, gave his multivolume narrative a sense of a coherence by making one of the book's characters its narrator. Thus, his novel could attribute an aesthetic consummation of vision to its narrative that results in the book the reader is reading. Past and present are continually transformed within the narrator's consciousness, but there, in the narrator's mind, the narrative creates a coherence that Musil and Ellison evade. Moreover, because the narrator's consciousness "ends" with the conclusion of the book, the reader may feel that the otherwise endless book has a true formal ending.

While *Invisible Man* arguably follows this pattern since it presents itself as the drama of a single individual coming to artistic consciousness, neither *The Man without Qualities* nor *Three Days* employs this Proustian tactic because each book refuses the premise that its narratives can be contained by a single vision, no matter how capacious. Both make the reader's sense of history a part of the structure of their novels. Yet each work estranges its readers from the history they think they know by situating itself in the moment before a cataclysmic historical event, and then seeking to create a utopic space within that "known" history in order to reimagine a way of seeing that differs from the one that history has seemingly committed us to. Both Musil and Ellison are obviously "modernist" writers, but in this aesthetic they fundamentally reject the either/or between "reality" and "art" often attributed to modernist works. More Bergsonian than Proustian, these two novels assume a universe that is in the process of being made, or remade, in every moment.

Although Musil wrote to interrogate his present moment, an implied fantasy of the book was that as long as the book continued, World War I could not happen. In this respect only, the book can be said to constitute the familiar modernist world apart. Likewise, one can choose to read Proust's work as merely the exploration of a single consciousness. Ellison, however, explicitly connects the aesthetic of his novels to a view of history. Moreover, he conceives of history always as a force that impinges upon the aesthetic possibilities of his works. On the Ellisonian view of American history, for instance, as long as Americans share the idea that their country and its history is an experiment to discover what kind of society might be created from a shared commitment to equality for each of its citizens, then American history should be understood as a process working to reveal this Edenic end implicit in its beginning. On the other hand, no faithful representation of American reality or history could truly portray this Eden except as either an ideal or a form of delusion.

Emphasizing Ellison's aesthetic preoccupation with the representation of history, the historian Leon Litwack has suggested that *Invisible Man* can be read as a history of black experience during the period between the end of the Civil War and *Brown*: "For thousands and thousands of Southern black men and women, the 'odyssey' of Ellison's hero summed up the entirety of their lives" (xii). Litwack's point was that *Invisible Man* gave an account of the humiliation suffered by black Americans between the Civil War and the civil rights movement that was more powerful than any work of history could convey. On the other hand, Ellison was not just projecting a historical situation into fiction but also trying to imagine through fiction a reality different than the one history seemed to name. "I believe that fiction does help create value," Ellison often insisted, "and I regard this as a very serious—I almost said 'sacred'—function of the writer" (CERE 300). For Ellison, his "sacred" task was to impress upon his readers an understanding of American history that recognized how the past functions as a boomerang, one that when it hits you opens your mind to the recognition that in America the end is always in the beginning. In *Invisible Man*, this meant constructing a novel in which the black protagonist's story could be recognized as one that spoke to and for all of its readers.

As broad as such a claim may seem, it must be understood as partial since it obscures the racial paradox that Ellison's work exposes. To be sure, as a work of literature, *Invisible Man* like any other work of literature invites anyone who reads it to identify with the narrator's story. Yet, there is a level on which the novel articulated a depth of experience known only to the black Americans who had lived it. A major portion of the book's achievement was putting into literary form the communal rituals, practices, and languages that African Americans had created between and among themselves to create a home in a strange and hostile land. When Ellison identified James Joyce and T. S. Eliot as his literary ancestors, he spoke of their ability to transform folk forms into literature. Ellison is often accused of being arrogant or elitist, but his gesture arguably was one of humility. These other writers gave him a form to tell a story that was not his alone but that of a people into which he was born. In this sense, Ellison invented neither the form nor the story of *Invisible Man*—it was the work, as it were, of the great modernist redactor of African American experience.

In the second novel Ellison broadened his narrative conception so that it confronted more explicitly than *Invisible Man* did the contested and confused relationship between "white" Americans and Americans "of color." Where *Invisible Man* allowed the reader to think that the story ends with the narrator's comprehension of his invisibility, the second novel, by its very unfinishedness, obligates the reader to situate his or her reading of the characters' plight within his or her understanding of the history they share with the characters. As with *Invisible Man,* readers cannot give an interpretation without assessing how that reading is influenced by their own assumptions about race. The focus of the novel is Bliss, who passes for white and may be white, but his ancestry is uncertain. Bliss is raised by Alonzo Hickman, his adoptive father, and grows up among blacks. His son, Severn, is also raised among blacks. Where Bliss eventually becomes a race-baiting senator, Severn finally refuses to identify as white and tries to kill his father. Acknowledging the challenges of integration after nearly a century of Jim Crow, Ellison was exploring the transformation that was taking place as Americans, white and black, were learning to confront in ways they had never been allowed to before, the fact that each group had become a part of the other's story.

Bliss challenges the either/or logic of race thinking, just as the novel's narrative perspective also resists racial typecasting. Thus, parts are written by a white narrator, McIntyre, who is trying to understand his own relationship to black Americans. As he is made to confront his own misperceptions about American reality, he also struggles to get to the bottom of the mystery of Senator Sunraider's assassination. In Book I, he observes that the senator allows an old Negro, Hickman, to keep him company as he lies (presumably) dying in his hospital bed. The mysterious relationship between Hickman and Bliss that McIntyre happens upon is the heart of the novel; arguably, these two characters are coprotagonists, depending on which section of the novel one is reading. Through them, Ellison unveils and then probes the complicated past and present that white and black Americans share. The novel tries to imagine whether a space might exist, or be created, in which the often-murderous American past can be transformed into a present in which all Americans can see each other without being overwhelmed by guilt, rage, and an overwhelming urge to deny the humanity of the other. Such a peaceful present could only occur if Americans were able to collectively transform their conflicted past into something everyone could acknowledge as true.

Despite its comic elements, the novel often seems to cast a cold eye on such a possibility. It is not clear that McIntyre will get to the bottom of the Bliss mystery. Moreover, the novel is often uneasy about how a changing American society will affect the traditions of African Americans. When Ellison toyed with dedicating his second novel to "the Negro or that vanished tribe into which I was born," he was presumably acknowledging that the endless transformation of American experience was going to change what it meant and had meant to be African American, just as the novel explores the ways in which white Americans cling to their "white" identity at the cost of their American identity. As the eloquent spokesperson for the "invisible" tradition of African Americans, Ellison understood very well that not all blacks would want to have their story shared with Americans from outside their tradition. Ellison told John Hersey in 1974 that American "society has structured itself to be unaware of what it owes in both the positive and negative sense to the condition of inhumanity it has imposed on the great mass of its citizens. The fact that many whites refuse to recognize this is responsible for much of the anger erupting from young blacks today" (CERE 808). On the other hand, Ellison, like Du Bois, believed that the story of black Americans was essential to the American story since their struggle from slavery to become free American citizens is what made the American commitment to equality something more than a cynical fantasy.

Ellison's work in general but the second novel in particular constitutes a dialectic—or a dance if you will—between the American past that blacks knew (but whites often denied) and the American present in which arguably a future different from the past might be imagined. Defining his "ideal reader," Ellison said that he wrote to those who were aware of and committed to "the systems of values, beliefs, customs, sense of the past, and that hope for the future which have evolved through the history of the Republic" (CERE 800). This reader would understand Ellison's claim in "Society, Morality, and the Novel" that Americans "are fated to live up to our sacred commitments or die, and the Civil War was the form of this fateful knowledge" (CERE 710). Standing alongside the essays he was writing in this period, the second novel is the fictional realm Ellison created to explore the possibilities of this fateful knowledge when after *Invisible Man* it suddenly seemed that American society was willing to confront the deepest meaning of the Civil War. Addressing in one sustained narrative act Americans past, present, and future (living in a present that was hopefully better than the one Ellison addressed in his lifetime), Ellison wanted to leave a book in which all Americans could know themselves and thus fulfill his "sacred" task as an American writer.

As an engagement with American history and in particular the relationship of black experience to American experience, Ellison's second novel will only enhance our understanding of his vision. As an American writer confronting how the past shapes the present and how the present is reformed through an engagement with the past, Ellison's most difficult problem was how to confront the American tendency to forget the past in such a way that amnesiac Americans could acknowledge what it was they were otherwise forgetting or denying. Speaking of (and for) Americans, Ellison remarked that "we don't remember enough; we don't allow ourselves to remember events, and I suppose this helps us to continue our belief in progress. But the undercurrents are always there" (CRE 297). Once one accepts that Ellison's novel is an attempt to sum up a situation that was constantly changing and that this situation included the perspective of the novelist as he was writing (especially evident in the Hickman sections in part 2), then its unfinished state reveals itself as an aesthetic necessity rather than as evidence of artistic uncertainty.

Thus, readers are misguided to think that the novel was not or could not be published because Ellison did not finish it. In ways that Ellison himself could not recognize, he did not finish it because *he was writing a book that could not be finished.* Ellison himself gave us a clue for understanding his book when he admitted that "part of what's taken so long is that so many things have changed so fast in our culture that as soon as I thought I had a draft that brought all of these things together, there would be another shift and I'd have to go back and revise all over again" (CRE 385–86). Or, as he said in 1974, "one of the things that really chilled me" was "the eruption of assassinations" since his novel centered on the attempted assassination of a senator in a context of political upheaval. Although Ellison was attempting to sum up an ongoing historical situation, he was nonetheless arrested when life beyond the page started to emulate the pages he was writing: "For me suddenly life was stepping in and imposing itself on my fiction" (CERE 796). Rather than being exhilarated that his historical vision was being confirmed by contemporary reality, Ellison felt that his task was Sisyphean. "I managed to keep going with it," he added, "I guess because there was nothing else to do" (796).

Ellison began his novel just as the civil rights movement was transforming American society in ways that were unimaginable before they happened and fifty years later seem utterly inevitable even though it is hard to say they ever were. When Ellison wrote *Invisible Man,* by contrast, he had no idea that two years after that book's publication the "invisibility" created by legalized segregation would be changed by *Brown* and the leadership of Martin Luther King Jr. This sudden change in American reality was what caused him to say he had failed of eloquence because "many of the immediate issues" that inspired the book were "rapidly falling away" (CERE 217). Ellison spoke too soon, though, or perhaps he understood the future implications of *Brown* better than his contemporaries. As the civil rights movement gained momentum and inspired violent resistance, Ellison found himself living in a time where the historic violence directed toward blacks became a matter of national concern. At times the 1960s seemed to be restaging the battles of the Civil War nearly a hundred years after it had supposedly ended.

Ellison said the second novel was supposed to be comic but at the heart of its structure was an act of violence that reflected both the bloodshed of the American past and the blood being spilled in Ellison's American present. The trigger of Ellison's drama is Severn's attempt to assassinate Senator Sunraider as he is giving a speech on the Senate floor. The would-be assassin is the senator's son and he wants to murder his father for denying him his patrimony. Severn and Senator Sunraider, who is also known as Bliss, share a complicated (racial) heritage that neither of them can define. Sunraider was born of a white mother but does not know who his father is. He was raised by Alonzo Hickman among blacks and in effect passed for black as a child. Severn is the child of an Indian mother and he grows up among some of the same people who raised his father. Eventually, Sunraider leaves those who raised him to resurface as a senator whose power derives in part from his ability to manipulate racial fears for his own political benefit. Although he supports Severn financially, he never acknowledges him as his son. Thus, Bliss/Sunraider represents at once how American history and identity is necessarily a mixture of peoples and traditions and in addition how Americans have worked to deny both the facts and the implications of what might be called its mulatto past.

Severn's act of violence is the perhaps inevitable gesture of frustration directed against a historical orientation that refuses to acknowledge the costs of denying the reality of so many Americans it presumes to speak for. Where Hickman will forgive his adopted son for his transgressions against the black Americans who raised him, Severn cannot forgive his father his transgressions against his own son. Yet, Hickman and Severn carry the same burden. They know that "in a racially rigged society," the success of most white Americans has depended on the denial of the humanity of African Americans. As Ellison told John Hersey, "We [blacks] know that as the nation's unwilling scapegoat we paid for much of it" (CERE 805). Ellison was often criticized by other black intellectuals for being too optimistic in his view of American society, but the second novel reveals an Ellison who was vividly portraying the source of black anger toward hypocritical white Americans. The question for Ellison, as for Hickman, was how to transform that violent anger into something that could redeem American society rather than destroy it.

Shortly before he is shot, the senator proclaims, "We are a nation born in blood, fire, and sacrifice, thus we are judged, questioned, weighed—by the revolutionary ideals and events which marked the founding of our great country" (TD 237). In a sense, Severn's assassination attempt proves the truth of his father's words. Every page of the book reflects on the contradiction between the senator's eloquent words and the acts of his life that belie those words. He asks: "How can the many be as one? How can the future deny the past? And how can the light deny the dark?" (241). To Hickman, these questions cannot be answered without the senator acknowledging his wrongs and then trying to address them. To Severn, the wrongs can never be sufficiently acknowledged and thus the senator must be killed. To Millsap, another Bliss watcher, the questions are endless and unanswerable because with Bliss one never knows "where illusion ended and reality began, and what would happen if he ever stopped acting and decided to limit himself to a single role" (TD 705).

That Bliss/Sunraider's attempted assassination occurs while he is giving a speech that sounds eerily like one of Ellison's own essays underscores the author's ambivalence about his project. On one interpretation of the novel, the senator's insistence that "where we have been is where we shall go" and that "in the going and in the arriving our task is to tirelessly transform the past and create and re-create the future" reads like a perfectly Ellisonian, and perfectly optimistic, interpretation of the American drama. However, here these words are part of a fiction and they are spoken by a character who is "a creation" within the fiction "so swindle-prone, fluent and shifty that absolutely *no one* could get him into focus" (TD 699). In other words, it may be that Bliss's eloquent words are only a lie, a con. Even in fiction, there may be no American reality that can transcend the divisions brought on by the too-real illusions of race.

It is worth noting that Ellison understood Bliss to be a version of *Invisible Man*'s Rinehart—a character never actually present in *Invisible Man* since the narrator is only mistaken for him. In *Invisible Man* Jack-the-Bear finds himself mistaken for Rinehart. He quickly discovers that whoever Rinehart is, "Rinehart" occupies a number of different identities, from preacher to pimp. Rinehart's permeability inspires the narrator to realize that he need not be fixed to any particular identity. Although he chooses to embrace "invisibility" as a form of empowerment, he does so with the assumption that he is risking being seen by the reader. When Rinehart appears as Bliss in the second novel (and thus puts the two novels in necessary relation to each other), his status as a character is no more fixed than it was in *Invisible Man*.

His identity is continuous, but this principally means that he can absorb any lie (or contradiction) into the truth of his reality. He is never who he seems. There may be no end to Bliss, and his incarnations assume no fixed truth. The implications of this insight for understanding American history are as promising as they are terrifying.

An episode from the "Hickman in Georgia" section brilliantly illustrates the essential ambivalence that is the root of Bliss's character. Writing to Hickman, Millsap describes encountering Bliss (long after he has run away from Hickman) on the set of a movie being made about the Civil War. Millsap is covered in "black-face, filthy as could be," when he sees Bliss dressed up in "Confederate gray, carrying a saber, and wearing a foot-long feather in his cap!" (704–5). In that moment, Millsap says, Bliss "recognized me!" but "to make sure I would know who he was, he swaggered off after the Jeb Stuart character by doing a cute little hustler's limp!" (705). In almost the same gesture, Bliss dons the guise of Johnny Reb and a streetwise urban black character, as if to say that in the comic-tragedy that is America one is but a version of the other.

For Millsap, who for years has been spying on Bliss and reporting back to Hickman, the comedy of the moment is as disturbing as it is bottomless. Whatever roles they take on, he and Bliss are merely pretending to be movie characters and thus their costumes should not reflect their "true" identities. Still, Millsap wonders if American history is in fact a type of movie in which the actors change roles but the roles never change. Can only some American actors change roles and are the others doomed to perform in a "nonwinnable 'non-role'?" Who is Bliss? Who is Millsap? Playing the role of a slave in this movie, Millsap thinks, "I 'was,' but was not; the war 'was,' but not truly, only 'reely'!" (704). If the Civil War was only a charade, a rehearsal for D. W. Griffith's *Birth of a Nation* (1915), then perhaps the Edenic promises of American history are ever only illusions for black (and ultimately all) Americans. When Bliss bows and tips his cap to Millsap, he gallantly acknowledges the absurdity of the game they are each fated to play and his own dexterity in changing roles at will.

Determining the meaning of Bliss is the question the book continually raises but cannot answer. He is a trickster figure whose slipperiness is essential to the novel's fluid form. In 1988 Ellison said if the "*genus americanus*" were to exist, then "he would be ingenious. He would certainly have a strong sense of the comic. He would be one who hides himself as he reveals himself—a bit of a trickster ... who would understand the past but who'd be determined not to be hampered by the past" (CRE 391). In the second novel

Bliss is that figure, one who evolves from Bliss Proteus Rinehart, the trickster figure in *Invisible Man*. In 1955, Ellison said that "Rinehart is my name for the personification of chaos. He is also intended to represent America and change. He has lived for so long with chaos that he knows how to manipulate it.... He is a figure of chaos in a country with no solid past or stable lines; therefore he is able to move about easily from one to the other" (CERE 223).

Where Rinehart is arguably a positive character in *Invisible Man* insofar as he provides the Aristotelian "recognition and reversal" that leads to the hero's self-illumination, Bliss Proteus in the second novel is a comic-tragic one whose tragedy threatens to overshadow his comedy. In his notes, Ellison says that "Bliss Proteus Rinehart returned to his part very much as a man to his mother or a dog to his vomit" (TD 976). The "past" that should not "hamper" the ideal American is both something that Bliss struggles to escape and that Ellison's novel struggles to remake. Bliss runs from his childhood with Hickman but only to embody a prior form of being American that Hickman wishes were gone. The fluidity of American culture celebrated in *Invisible Man*'s epilogue becomes a cover for Bliss's casual exploitation of society's racism, just as Bliss's protean self reveals the deep, unchanging historical pattern that Jack-the-Bear rejected. If at one point Bliss is seen playing a dashing Confederate soldier, elsewhere he appears as a film director convincing blacks in Oklahoma to reenact their history as a filmed farce. In these sections Bliss is both a confidence man and a proto–D. W. Griffith living out his own version of *Birth of a Nation*: the force that structures and casts the cyclic drama of American reality.

Opposed to the cynical reading of Bliss is the one that insists that his story can be rewritten, or reenacted, so that its logic is transformed into a different one with different roles for its players. When Bliss's own son rises up to kill him, this act suggests that Bliss's story must change or end. This attempted assassination intentionally echoes the story of Lincoln who, in Ellison's terms, was the martyr for the knowledge that Americans "are fated to live up to our sacred commitments or die, and the Civil War was the form of this fateful knowledge" (CERE 710). Bliss's story cannot escape Lincoln's shadow, which covers the novel. Like Ellison's 1965 essay, "Tell It Like It Is, Baby," *Three Days* insists on the enduring, even foundational, meaning of Lincoln's tragedy. It is no coincidence that drafts of the novel begin with Hickman and his congregation "praying quietly within the Lincoln Memorial" (TD 9). Through Hickman's consciousness the novel imagines Lincoln as living presence whose tragedy gives structure to the American present. Moreover, Hickman sees in Bliss's life and impending death a version of

Lincoln's story. If Bliss can be brought home to the people who raised him, if Bliss can acknowledge the wrongs he has done to those whom he betrayed, then the end of his life might signal the beginning of a new American story. Bliss's deathbed resurrection would continue the story that Lincoln's death left incomplete and the American past would at last yield a new and better present.

In an especially powerful passage, Hickman faces Lincoln's statue and thinks of what "those sorrowful eyes reveal about what it means to be a man who struggles to reconcile all of the contending forces of his country out of a belief in simple justice.... Yes, that look in those eyes and the struggles which placed it there—those are what made him one of us" (TD 575). The struggle that Hickman identifies in Lincoln's eyes is the same one that he has enacted through his life with Bliss. Yet even as he chooses Lincoln as "one of us," as he did with Bliss, Hickman's vision of "the sculpture's mysterious power" is dimmed by the fact that "he stared up into eyes that seemed to gaze beneath their shadowed lids toward some vista of perpetual dawn that lay far beyond infinity" (575). In this passage, Lincoln, with his forever-seeing eyes that are now contained within Hickman's vision, is placed in a constantly evolving present. The "vista of perpetual dawn that lay far beyond infinity" evokes Ellison's own sense of confronting in his novel a moment that is ever receding and ever shifting. As Hickman's present reshapes the past, Ellison points to a distant moment when equality between blacks and whites is reality.

Lincoln may not have imagined his story to make him one with the slaves his actions freed, but subsequent events have transformed the meaning of Lincoln's life so that he has become "one of us." "Yes, he was one of us," Hickman affirms, because "he became the one man who pointed the way for all who are willing to pay the price of true freedom" (576). Hickman's reformulation of Lincoln's meaning is generous because it overlooks Lincoln's equivocations concerning the future of the freed slaves as equal American citizens. Likewise, Hickman is willing to forgive Bliss his transgressions if only he will acknowledge that he too is "one of us" and not merely the cynical manipulator of such an aspiration. To be "one of us" need not mean that Bliss is black any more than Hickman thinks that Lincoln is black; what matters is that they acknowledge each other as Americans.

In this scene, Hickman sees through Lincoln's eyes, or perhaps we should say Lincoln's eyes are seeing though Hickman. Whether the American present being envisioned is destiny or simply Hickman's futile hope is open to question. It may be that the friendship between Bliss and Hickman can exist only in an idyllic past because the dream of an Edenic equality cannot withstand American reality. At stake in the second novel is not—as was the case in *Invisible Man*—the assertion of a vibrant and ongoing African American culture and way of seeing, though that is everywhere present, but the question of whether the civil rights movement will enact a new era in American history where blacks and whites collectively know each other through a mutual understanding brought on by love, and not hatred or fear. This Edenic vision forms the still point toward which the novel's many narratives approach and from which they fall away, while the violence of Bliss's fate, the bitterness of Jessie Rockmore's burial, and the rage of LeeWillie Minifees's immolated Cadillac say Eden cannot be regained because it never was.

Asked about the time span of his novel, Ellison told John Hersey "roughly from 1954 to 1956 or 1957," before explaining that the year in which the novel takes place cannot be precisely defined. "It's just a matter of the past being active in the present—or of the characters becoming aware of the manner in which the past operates on their present lives" (CRE 300). In this respect, Ellison's second novel recalls the work of William Faulkner, but with a crucial difference. In Ellison's novel the present is not simply defined by the past. The novel instead understands the past to be part of an evolving present that may change the past's meaning. In *Absalom, Absalom!* (1936), for example, once Quentin Compson has relived his past through its telling, there is nothing left for him to do but die. He has no future he can imagine except as a kind of living death. Indeed, he understands his life to have ended well before he was born and there is no post–Civil War reality in which he wants to live. If history moves past the Civil War, the novel does not want to know or imagine this possibility.

In *Three Days*, however, the recounting of the past that happens between Hickman and Bliss, at its most hopeful, stages the potential resurrection of the American present into a reality unlike what has defined American history to that point. Where Faulkner wrote an elegy for the Old South and its confused notions concerning the dignity of slavery, Ellison was trying to recount in a fictional form a version of America that could move beyond such confused notions. Ellison's work insists that the American present could never be as it was (and is) without the collective experience of slavery. Moreover, the ever-evolving present contains as well the collective sense of betrayal experienced by black Americans when the gains promised by the Civil War were surrendered during the Reconstruction era. Thus, Ellison's novel sought a way to balance the bitter reality of slavery and its ongoing aftermath with a possible present in which equal rights were finally (or possibly) safeguarded for everyone. The uncertainty of achieving this balance obligates the narrative to be provisional, contingent, and uncertain.

Ellison's work therefore probes whether it is possible for Americans to break the Faulknerian logic whereby the present is merely the repetition of the past. In Book II the novel moves toward a past that is not traumatizing and a present that is not merely an iteration of what has come before. As Daddy Hickman keeps company with Bliss in the hospital where Bliss is almost certainly dying, he tries to inspire his adopted son to accept the past they have shared and a present that remains theirs to invent. In a sense, Bliss must acknowledge Hickman as his true father, just as white Americans during the civil rights movement had to acknowledge that the meaning of American democracy had been carried forward by the slaves and their descendants as surely as its ideals were associated with Thomas Jefferson or Lincoln.

In Ellison's "Book of America," the Civil War and the death of Lincoln mark the point where black Americans become the heroes of the American story. Bliss represents the protean nature of American experience, but Hickman is the book's moral conscience. Without Hickman's guidance, the fluid sense of American experience that Bliss enacts is always and only a cynical manipulation of power with no goal other than the preservation of power. Hickman exists within a tradition that has sustained itself despite efforts to deny him or his parishioners their humanity. Bliss, on the other hand, is wounded, dying, at risk precisely because he has had nothing to sustain him except an empty individualism.

The novel contrasts Bliss's trickster gift for individual self-invention with the communal harmony of Hickman's congregation. In Book II, Ellison explores this harmony through an investigation into what Hickman calls "our kind of time" (323). This multidimensional "time" evokes the ongoing communal identity created by African Americans since slavery at the same time that it enacts the elastic sense of time the novel seeks to embody. Just as in *Invisible Man* where time is understood to move like a boomerang, "time" in the second novel looks back to Hickman's history and identity as a black American among other black Americans while looking forward to the possibility of an American present in which Bliss and Hickman can look at each other as equals. In such a time, they would no longer be divided by a past into which each was born. Rather, they would hope to transform that past and each other through the creation of a moment in which they know one another through their shared commitment to each other as Americans. The past would not be lost or denied but regained through an improved commitment to a transformed present. Likewise, because this work is fiction and not mere history, Ellison's novel aspires to create through its engagement with its reader the time in which Americans, or his readers, can re-create their country and themselves as something consistent with its Edenic aspirations.

As Bliss lies dying, he and Hickman experience the pastness of the past as a living memory through which they may change their present relationship. If Bliss, and the history he embodies, is to be saved from the history he has come to embody, it can happen only through the healing power of the communal spirit that Hickman shares with him. In this scene, Bliss's memories literally surface through spilled blood. Severn's shooting of his father initiates a ritual—one that could conceivably provoke further violence or prompt the acknowledgment of wounds unacknowledged. With Hickman there to prompt his memories and to help him re-create "our kind of time," Bliss may potentially be healed. "How do we know who we are, Daddy Hickman?," the senator recalls asking Hickman long ago, and, as his life may be ebbing way, he is asking it again. Having achieved his power as senator by denying his identification with black Americans, he now rediscovers his communal relationship with Hickman.

> We know who we are by the way we walk. We know who we are by the way we talk. We know who we are by the way we sing. We know who we are by the way we praise the Lord on high. We know where we are because we hear a different tune in our minds and in our hearts. We know who we are because when we make the beat of our rhythm to shape our day the whole land says amen! (323)

Nothing—not race, not history—divides Bliss from Hickman here. Hickman and Bliss carry out a sense of shared identity that recalls that of Twain's Jim and Huck, but with a crucial difference. Whereas Jim and Huck had to escape society to find each other, Hickman and Bliss love one another through the practice of a shared communal ritual. Through their union, the novel acknowledges that even where American stories seem separate, as memories of black and white Americans often seem, they are in fact joined. The rhythm Bliss and Hickman create through this ritual comes from the "sense of time" they have known and made together—and may continue to make together.

Through this call and response, Ellison portrays a fleeting vision of an American utopia. In those moments he and Hickman are carried "back to a bunch of old-fashioned Negroes celebrating an illusion of emancipation, and getting it mixed up with the Resurrection" (314). Here Bliss is no longer the racist "white" Senator Sunraider but the boy preacher of indeterminate race that Hickman raised. Their interaction is grounded in something more than speech as they find themselves "moving beyond words back to the undifferentiated cry," to a time when the pain of being divided and marked according to one's race was either unknown or forgotten: a world of living possibility. I say this is an American utopia and not an African American utopia (which it clearly is as well) because Ellison, with his aspirations to be a national writer, is evoking a world in which one's race is not a bar to individual or communal self-expression. Bliss and Hickman are re-creating the past but the novel casts it as a version of the receding future that Hickman thinks he sees in Lincoln's eyes.

The reader of *Three Days* cannot know either who Bliss is or what he may still become. Bliss's racial indeterminacy suggests an American present untainted by exclusionary race pride. At the same time, the novel asks how the past comes into the present as something other than a dangerous nostalgia. Confronting the appeal of this nostalgia, which must taste like lotus flowers, is a necessary consequence of confronting racism in its many guises. In "Hickman in Georgia & Oklahoma," Love New argues that Americans black and white must learn to surrender what is finally a shared legacy of racism. New further suggests that whites and blacks have been equally the victims of a "State history" that has always defined people by race. Speaking of Lincoln's "sacrifice," New says that "when he's killed the land gets sick, and to cure the sickness proper things must be done to redeem the sacrifice and appease his spirit." Thus "not only did they fail to do the proper things to appease his spirit, they lied about it! And that's what made for this deep sickness that's in the land and in all the State people—Yao!" (815). In the second novel Ellison confronted how this "sickness" had infected "all the State people." Bliss's lingering death, which is the sickness of the State, precedes the birth of a new nation that the novel cannot yet depict. What exists instead comes from Love New: "If you accept the fact that you are neither black nor white, Gentile nor Jew, Rebel-bred nor Yankee-born, you have the freedom to be *truly* free" (850).

Love New's perspective suggests that Bliss's suspended death, his unfinished story, is vital to the novel's aesthetic. To be sure, killing Bliss would have completed the novel, just as the onset of World War I would have ended Musil's novel. In a sense, the novel's sense of suspense depends on making the reader ask, what will Bliss think the moment he dies?—as if in a Tolstoyan moment of recognition the "truth" of the novel will be spoken. The novel's more complex truth, though, is that there is no ending to American history that can yet be written. The "real" Bliss Proteus Rinehart remains unrealized. By leaving Bliss's fate open, Ellison's novel perpetually exists as if in an unending American present, one that is reinforced by the unsettled state of the text. Since Bliss is an extension of *Invisible Man*'s Rinehart and a descendant of Homer's god Proteus, it is possible that he cannot die, except perhaps as an American. Ellison's struggles with the manuscript suggest not a failure to finish but the recognition that Bliss Proteus *cannot be killed*. He is more than a single character and his story is ever changing. He was Lincoln and he was King and he was Stonewall Jackson too. For this reason, one can read the book to always be addressing the totality of American history—from Washington through Lincoln up to Obama and beyond. From this perspective—one that works with *Invisible Man* as well—the novel cannot end until the story of America and its struggle to realize its Edenic promises ends too.

With his second novel Ellison had hoped to give to the evolving American present an aesthetic form in which Americans might recognize the drama of their continuing story through his art. If Ellison never finished his novel, then the form he left it in may turn out to be the perfect one for his aesthetic aspirations. Doubtless different editions of the book including the alternative sections currently not published will eventually surface. Such rival versions need not compromise the integrity of the work. Think of it as an early hypertext that might be better read through the technological possibilities a digital edition would allow.[3] Imagine interactive versions where the readers themselves were allowed to finish, or perhaps further, the ongoing story of Bliss. Such an ending, put in the hands and under the responsibilities of would-be readers, replicates the one Ellison left for *Invisible Man*. Indeed, since Bliss is an extension of the earlier novel's Rinehart, Ellison invites the reader to see both novels as stories that can be finished only in the realm beyond the novels. In either case, Ellison portrays the American story as one being made by all Americans, a story that will continue to be made and remade until a vision of Eden gives way to a present in which the American promise of equality for all has been surrendered and forgotten.

NOTES

1. The editors of *Three Days before the Shooting . . .* privilege part 1, or that which is labeled Books I and II, because they seem to be the sections Ellison was closest to publishing. In contrast, my reading of the book assumes that all drafts are equal. Thus, I understand the sections in part 2, especially the three Hickman sections, to be just as important as part 1.

2. Not until 1978 was an edition of Musil's collected works finally available in German. It included conflicting sketches of how the novel might be ended, alternative drafts to the published chapters, as well as critical essays that were not known until that time.

3. In 1995 German scholarship succeeded in transferring Musil's oeuvre to CD-ROM, enabling readers to encounter in one place the conflicting sketches of how his great novel might have ended and alternative drafts to the published chapters, as well as Musil's many critical essays and notes about his work.

RALPH ELLISON'S *THREE DAYS BEFORE THE SHOOTING...* AND THE IMPLICIT MORALITY OF FORM

GRANT SHREVE

> Equally is it true, however, that a world that is finished, ended, would have no traits of suspense and crisis, and would offer no opportunity for resolution.
> —JOHN DEWEY, ART AS EXPERIENCE

Early in the composition of his second novel Ralph Ellison typed the following note to himself: "Find the myth in which the hero descends into hell by following cord and is thus able to escape. This seems like a basic form to give this thing organization. Because, god knows, it seems to run all over the world" (Ralph Waldo Ellison Papers, Manuscript Division, Library of Congress, ms. box I:140, folder 1). In this note Ellison momentarily evokes and conflates the myth of Theseus and the Minotaur with Christ's descent into hell in an attempt to organize what was quickly becoming a sprawling epic. Textual evidence further down the same page, however, suggests he only intended to recall the Theseus myth. In the most recognized version of the story of Theseus and the Minotaur, King Minos, having conquered the Athenians, declares that seven Athenian boys and seven girls are to be sacrificed to the Minotaur every nine years. On the third iteration of this gruesome ritual, Theseus, the founder of Athens, vows to enter the labyrinth as a substitute for one of the boys and slay the monster. Before he enters, Ariadne gives him a thread to record his path. Armed with the thread and a sword he had smuggled in, Theseus tracks and kills the Minotaur, effectively ending the practice of the ritual sacrifice of Athenian youth.

Ellison recalls this myth in an effort to lay hold of a symbol or story that might lend his chaotic novel-in-progress a formal structure. Yet by referring to the story of Theseus, he invokes a myth explicitly concerned with a state-endorsed practice of ritually sacrificing members of an oppressed people instituted both to ensure the psychic health of the state and also to reaffirm that population's debased status within a social hierarchy. In an American context this aspect of the myth immediately calls to mind the horrors of Jim Crow and the ritual lynching of African Americans in the nineteenth and twentieth centuries. Whether Ellison had considered these dimensions of the myth is unclear. It is, however, highly suggestive that in a rare moment of written reflection on his second novel as a whole he arrives at a mythic model for the work whose content pertains directly to the abolition of ritualized, sacrificial violence. Implicit in this early, short note is an underlying tension between sacrificial violence and literary form that would become the central problem of Ellison's second novel over the next several decades.

Ellison believed that novels were the literary-aesthetic form most conducive to a democratic society and, as such, had an important civic function to perform. At the end of his essay "The World and the Jug," Ellison half-comically reports to the critic Irving Howe that the demands made on him by the Negro Freedom Movement are "that I publish more novels" (CERE 188). This phrase attests to Ellison's conscious alignment of his novelistic project with the political project of integration. The Supreme Court's decision in *Brown v. Board of Education* marked a momentous occasion in Ellison's life and career. Ellison aligned himself with *Brown*'s promise of racial integration politically, ethically, and aesthetically. Integration shapes and energizes the work and significantly raised the civic stakes of his aesthetic project. As Lucas Morel has aptly put it, "Ellison deliberately used the word 'integration' to illustrate how profoundly he saw the connection between what he was doing in his stories and what others were doing in the streets for the Civil Rights Movement" ("Recovering" 2). In the 1969 Haverford Statement, Ellison asserts, "I am stuck with integration, because the very process of the imagination ... is nothing if not integrative" (CERE 433–34). However, despite his clear alignment with the ideal of integration, Ellison's enthusiasm for the historic significance of the Supreme Court's decision in *Brown* was tempered by his sense that legal measures alone would not be sufficient to enable what he called in a letter to Morteza Sprague "the only integration that matters—that of the personality" (Ellison, Letter to Morteza Sprague 39), a phrase that Eric Sundquist has argued represents "the burden" of the second novel ("We Dreamed" 112). Ellison's guarded support of political integration did not preclude his recognition of the need for a concomitant and sufficiently complex psychological integration as well. For him, literature, and especially the novel, was uniquely situated to promote this dimension of integration.

Ellison believed that the novel was a privileged form capable of having a transformative effect on an individual's perception of reality and her or his relation to it. He argued throughout his career that the novel was inherently democratic and that its purpose was to serve democratic ends. By its own peculiar alchemy, fiction could reshape society and social relations, for "whenever fictional technique makes conjunction with an image of reality, each is mutually transformed" (CERE 699). The novel became in Ellison's mind a *necessary* component of *Brown*'s promise. *Brown* merely opened the door to a kind of transformation of both personal and national identity, and the novel could carry Americans through it.

In order to fulfill these psychological and civic ends through fiction, Ellison immersed himself in theories of classical tragedy (the most compelling example from antiquity of an art form directed to the improvement of a social order) and constructed a tragic plot that compressed the moral essence of American history into the biography of a single character. Yet tragedy, because it relies upon the ritualized death of the hero, ultimately reproduces precisely the kind of sacrificial violence Ellison most abhorred and most vehemently sought to expel from society. Ellison's formal means of participating in the project of integration through literature are undermined, as we shall see, by their recourse to sacrificial mechanisms that reinforce hierarchical distinctions.

This essay is divided into two parts. The first analyzes Books I and II of *Three Days before the Shooting . . .* (which comprise the typescripts Ellison composed in 1972, nearly complete drafts that represent the second novel in as nearly publishable a form as it would ever be) alongside published and unpublished material relating to Ellison's understanding and utilization of tragedy, tragic plots, and tragic catharsis. Ellison, I argue, situates his hero Bliss/Sunraider at the center of a tragic plot, the culmination of which we witness from two different perspectives at the beginning of Books I and II. Both tragic hero and scapegoat, Bliss functions as the unlikely bearer and most extravagant expression of the collective hubris of America. He is the figural embodiment of the nation's continual "moral evasion" and Ellison actively seeks to engineer a readerly identification with Bliss's moral failings, an intimacy with his character, and a cathartic release at his death and funeral. Yet the novel never arrives at that crucial moment of resolution and release. The narrative ends precisely at the moment when Bliss's plot might have concluded and thus offered a resolution to the sweeping, multi-decade narrative.

It is for this reason catharsis becomes a critical term necessary for effectively tracing the fractures in Ellison's second novel. The absence of a cathartic moment in the tragic narrative signals a moral dilemma generated by an element of plot that Ellison was unable to resolve. The second part of this essay examines the work Ellison produced in the wake of his inability to complete his second novel during the first major phase of composition. In the 1980s and '90s Ellison composed several long narrative sequences on his computer in which he returned to earlier segments of his narrative, expanding them at length through the perspective of the Negro preacher and ex-bluesman Hickman. Although these episodes take place in the same fictional America as the earlier parts of the narrative, they represent a radical formal departure from the 1972 typescripts. In their introduction to *Three Days*, the editors highlight the ongoing thematic concerns that animate the various fragments. Similarly, Adam Bradley and Michael Szalay have attempted in their respective accounts of the text to establish thematic continuity between the various fragments of the novel. When the computer sequences are read in the light of Ellison's failure to resolve Bliss's tragic narrative, however, their formal discontinuity from the earlier material emerges. By subordinating thematic concerns to formal concerns we may better trace the causes of Ellison's abandonment of plot and his substantive changes to the very form of the novel over the *longue durée* of its composition.

As Ellison's novel progressed, the demands of his formal commitments precipitated a moral quandary that subsequently required a radical reevaluation of the morality implicit in the form of his novel. In place of a tragic plot that enables psychic transformation and integration through dramatic catharsis, Ellison develops in the wake of the 1972 typescripts a fictional form that proceeds by a logic approximate to what Kenneth Burke—the American philosopher whose influence on Ellison's thinking and critical vocabulary can be felt across his entire career—calls "dialectical transcendence," a type of formal development that enables the transformation of an audience but does not rely exclusively on victimage ("I, Eye, Ay" 875). The stylistic and formal differences evident in the computer manuscripts are therefore less representative, as some have suggested, of psychological strain, old age, recalcitrance, or technological psychosis than of a profound and substantive reorientation to the form of the novel itself and its moral capacities. What had heretofore been the underground history of Ellison's career as a novelist reveals itself in *Three Days before the Shooting* . . . neither as simple failure nor as an untroubled commitment to improvisation and incompletion, but as a deep, critical, anxious, and abiding commitment to exploring the moral foundations of a literary aesthetic.[1]

I. BLISS'S TRAGEDY AND ELLISON'S FAILURE OF RESOLUTION (1956–72)

Books I and II of *Three Days before the Shooting* . . . comprise the longest continuous movement of the second novel and represent the work as near to completion as it ever got. Book I begins on the floor of the Senate chamber in the minutes before a mysterious gunman emerges out of the nebulous crowd to shoot the charismatic, polarizing, and racist Senator Adam Sunraider at the conclusion of a speech. Welborn McIntyre, a white, liberal journalist from the Northeast who is present at the shooting and who finds himself compelled to investigate the inscrutable assassination attempt, narrates the book. For most of this section he is seated directly outside the dying senator's private hospital room facing the elderly Negro preacher Alonzo Hickman, who occupies the narrow hall with him, waiting for news of the senator's condition and desperately seeking to account for the preacher's presence. The assassination, McIntyre's investigation of it, and his confrontations with Hickman generate the complex movements of McIntyre's consciousness that constitute much of the action and drama of the book. As McIntyre delves ever deeper into the racial mystery that lies at the center of the assassination, he finds himself confronting a series of troubling memories from his childhood and early adulthood, all having to do with repressed racial and sexual encounters. Because of the fact that it triggers the return of so much repressed material, McIntyre's investigation of the racist senator and the Negro preacher is also a dramatic enactment of the psychological integration of a Northern white liberal who, until this event, had believed himself unburdened by stereotypes and racialist assumptions. The assassination forces McIntyre to wrestle with the complexity of race in America through dreams, memories, and even a physical confrontation with Hickman. Ultimately, the book does double duty as both an excavation and revision of the liberal imagination and a stage upon which to represent the antics of the trickster figure (Senator Sunraider) in the guise of a national political actor.

Despite its bravura prose and memorable scenes, Book I is in many ways an explicitly (though oddly) didactic text. McIntyre dramatically models the integration of the personality Ellison had endorsed in his letter to Morteza Sprague. This portion of the novel puts on display the deep psychological work that true integration requires in order to produce a character fully conscious of the complexities of American identity. What propels this psychic work for McIntyre is his investigation into the attempt on Sunraider's life and his urgent desire to uncover this tragedy, which he senses is extremely personal. Ellison had always intended McIntyre's narrative to lead into Book II, wherein the story of Sunraider/Bliss is reconstructed through a complex, antiphonal exchange. Ellison means, therefore, for Sunraider's tragic narrative to function similarly for his readers as it does for McIntyre.[2]

Like Book I, Book II begins in the Senate, but this time from Sunraider's perspective as he hallucinates the Great Seal of the United States made animate and interrogative and improvises a chaotic, patriotic, and eloquent speech. The shooting, Hickman's spontaneous jeremiad, and his transportation to the hospital room all occur within Sunraider's fractured consciousness, which is interrupted by fragments of memories. Over the course of the book we learn that his given name is Bliss, that Hickman raised him as a Negro, and that he had trained to be a preacher. After a crazed white woman accosts him during a Juneteenth sermon mistaking him for a child she says she's lost, Bliss flees Hickman and Hickman's congregation to search for his mother and to discover his racial and genealogical origins. During this phase of his life he begins assuming progressively more complex masks. The two most important masks he wears are those of an amateur filmmaker in Oklahoma and, of course, that of the race-baiting Northern senator. The majority of the book is set in Sunraider's hospital room as Hickman and Bliss/Sunraider alternately speak to one another and think to themselves. In this way the two re-create Bliss's narrative and trace its tragic line.

As a result of his study of Burke and others, theories about classical tragedy deeply inform Ellison's construction of the second novel and its civic and psychological ends. In "Tell It Like It Is, Baby," a 1965 essay that Ellison intended as a kind of conceptual frame for his second novel, he includes two explicit references to Gilbert Murray's *The Classical Tradition in Poetry* (1927), a clear nod to the influence of classical forms and the *theory* of classical forms on his work. Ellison's notes confirm and extend this relationship.

In one unpublished note from the 1960s, Ellison meditates on the novelist as tragedian:

> If tragedy thrives on pollution in the private-civic area, a tragic novelist must of necessity deal with (not protest) but conditions which should be protested—but in his own terms, in the terms of art and not according to some politician's analysis of civic illness. Fiction—when it grapples with life and the human condition in its own terms—needs no apology. Its struggle lies in its willingness to confront the complexity of life without bowing to any special interest other than that of the novelist—and in this he is guided by *the implicit morality of the form*. This morality arises (historically) from its concern with mobility, with the democratic challenge of hierarchy in the interest of equality, and from its dedication to charting the humanization of reality. (ms. box I:141, folder 1; emphasis mine)

This passage displays Ellison's attempt to square categories of classical tragedy with the situation of the democratic novelist. Civic pollution is refigured as a set of conditions that are the content of direct political protest. Such conditions impede the "democratic challenge of hierarchy" and reinforce the hierarchical psychosis (the term is Burke's) that plagues American democracy and that is most visible in the ongoing racial crisis. The novelist, through his art, must therefore be committed to expelling this pollution from both the social body and the mind of the individual. And this finally constitutes the "implicit morality of the form."

Tragic catharsis is the formal means of expelling this pollution from an individual's psyche and thereby heeds the "implicit morality" of novelistic form by rattling the columns of hierarchy and reaffirming democratic equality. For this reason Ellison took great interest in the transformative potential of tragic catharsis. Throughout his notes he repeatedly copies a phrase of Burke's: "Pollution is the subject of catharsis, and catharsis is the subject of poetry." On the page following the long note quoted previously, Ellison has copied out by hand a quotation on tragic catharsis from William Rueckert's study of Burke, *Kenneth Burke and the Drama of Human Relations* (1963):

> An act of great pride, the specifically human action which initiates the tragic rhythm, and the whole of the tragic rhythm itself, seems naturally to arouse what Burke calls the specifically "personal emotions as such": pity, fear, anger, and the like. That is, the tragic act, the

tragic rhythm, and tragedy are "ideal cathartics"; by means of them the poet can effect the most thorough purgation; the more thorough the purge, Burke says, the healing or regenerating effect for the audience individually and collectively; the greater the regenerative effect, the better able is literature to fulfill one of its primary functions, which is to fight individual and social "illness" by means of symbolic purges. (Rueckert 222, qtd. in ms. box I:141, folder 1)

If the novelist's aim is to "fight individual and social 'illness,'" or "civic illness," as Ellison has it, then to organize the movement of his plot toward a catharsis that would pave the way toward an eventual redemption could induce in his audience a profound moral transformation. Although skeptical of attempts at "national catharsis" achieved through naive social policy, Ellison maintained a deep conviction in the possibilities of a catharsis produced through art during the major phase of composition of his second novel.[3]

Below the Rueckert quote on the previously cited note, Ellison has appended a handwritten nota bene about Richard Wright's failure to appreciate the utility of catharsis: "Richard Wright attempted to depict pollution but shied away from catharsis because he saw it as allowing 'white' people off the hook. His motive was to punish. But tragedy is directed to a broader audience and that audience is united, as well as divided, by the general pollution" (ms. box I:141, folder 5). Catharsis, rather than merely excusing racist attitudes and maintaining hierarchical divisions, unites a community through the "general pollution." It is also the formal means of expelling it. This particular note resembles and anticipates the central critique Ellison makes of Wright in his essay "Remembering Richard Wright." In that essay he writes, "In *my* terms, Wright failed to grasp the function of artistically induced catharsis ... or its power to cleanse the mind and redeem and rededicate the individual to forms of ideal action" (CERE 675). Ellison maintained a conviction that the kind of catharsis available through art had a redemptive and purifying power.[4]

Because catharsis is an effect of form, Ellison needed a tragic plot and a tragic hero. By the 1960s, Bliss—the racially ambiguous orphaned child of a white woman who accuses Hickman's brother of raping her—had become Ellison's tragic hero, and his biography, fragmented as it is, constitutes the novel's tragic plot. It is a story that, because of its formal incoherence, we as readers help bring into being through our own participation in its imaginative reconstruction in the hospital room. Hickman intended to raise Bliss as a savior for American Negroes because Bliss's ambiguous racial identity would enable him to communicate the cause and values of Negroes to white America. Because of his child's need for the comfort of a mother and a sense of origin, Bliss abandons the lofty, abstract ideals Hickman had raised him to fulfill and flees into a world of shadows, illusions, and masks represented by the sudden advent of cinema and his fascination with the medium. Bliss functions as the living embodiment of both American innocence and a peculiarly American fascination with social hierarchy that undercuts a commitment to equality and haunts both American history and American identity. Severen, Bliss's son and eventual assassin, is the nemesis produced by that hubris.[5] The nation's continual evasion of the moral problem posed by its treatment of its Afro-American population, according to Ellison, both defines and stains American history and defers the possibility of the full articulation of American identity. Bliss bears the full weight of this historical problem on his shoulders as he enacts a compressed repetition of it. His tragic narrative is *our* tragic history and his death is calculated to produce a cathartic reaction that would ideally force a reader into a confrontation with these fundamental problems of American identity.

Tragic catharsis requires the death of a hero and functions as a mostly benign form of scapegoating. By marshaling the resources of his art, the tragedian promotes an audience's identification with the hero and then proceeds to stage his death. The complex emotional purge that this moment produces has, as Ellison fully believed, the potential to awaken an audience to its own personal and social sins and expel them from the collective psyche. We weep and tremble and emerge cleansed. Bliss acts as Ellison's American hero and his American scapegoat. On Bliss's overburdened back Ellison would be able to proffer a vision of an integrated society and a redeemed America.

The dilemma occasioned by this aesthetic vision is the highly problematic fact that in order to produce catharsis, an individual (even a symbolic substitute) must be ritually sacrificed for the psychological purification of the reader or larger social body. Ellison's own confrontations with the realities of racial scapegoating in America attuned him to the ways in which sacrifice was utilized to reinforce hierarchical distinctions by dehumanizing victims and reaffirming an illusory ontological distance between spectator and scapegoat. Ellison attempts to circumvent this problem by promoting a deep readerly intimacy with Bliss, which would thereby collapse that distance and prevent the occurrence of what George Thomson refers to as the "conservative" version of catharsis, where catharsis is induced not to transform but to maintain the status quo (384). This intimacy is encouraged most explicitly by the formal techniques evident in Book II. The cramped quarters of the hospital room, for instance, which only Hickman, a nurse, and the reader are allowed to enter (not even the federal agents who guard the door tread across the threshold), encourage a sense of sustained closeness and private participation in the unfolding of the tragic plot. Similarly, the nonlinearity of Bliss's biography, the antiphonal structure of the section, and frequent lapses of consciousness and dialogue in the book (all techniques inherited from high modernism) demand the engagement of the private reader (and not a public audience) in the reconstruction of the tragic narrative. Aesthetic form implicates the reader and destroys the distance between the persecutory witness and the tragic scapegoat. By inviting the reader into an intimate engagement with the tragic hero, Ellison attempts to compel a deep recognition of the relationship between Bliss's history, national history, and the American reader's personal history.

But despite this array of literary devices, which Ellison utilizes in part to enable tragic catharsis without reproducing the sacrificial logic of lynching, he nevertheless failed to write Bliss's death. Ellison's refusal to kill his tragic hero signals that the sacrificial mechanism necessary to produce a cathartic resolution remained persistently untenable. From early on, Ellison envisioned his novel progressing through the stages of the ideal tragic plot with the addition that his plot would conclude in comic redemption, as it does in the gospel narrative. In one note he instructs himself to "[u]nfold it [the novel] narratively, from purpose, through passion, from pollution through guilt to scapegoating to catharsis, to redemption to perception" (ms. box I:140, folder 5). But the chronological plot of the novel as we currently have it ends at the moment where Bliss should die and provide the ideal reader the experience of cathartic release. The tragic plot ceases before its hero has exhausted his breath.[6]

Ellison had sketched out variations on an ending to Bliss's narrative. The following notes date from the 1950s to the 1970s:

> Then body is surrendered, since whites dont want to have anything todo with it, and it is packed in dry ice and flown back South or to Southwest. Where funeral is held. And it is here that his young preacher days are described in tribute not so much to Bliss but to the groups hopes and ideals. They get up and describe his early life. (Use short exclamation by women which is somewhere in the pile of m.s.). (ms. box I:141, folder 4; evidence elsewhere on the note suggests that this is from the early 1950s)

> What if they [Hickman and congregation] decide, having little money left after paying Hickman's fine etc, that they will return Bliss home in Jessie Rockmore's old coffin. . . . And tht leaving for the railroad station the hearse catches fire in sight of the Lincoln Memorial? (ms. box I:140, folder 7)

> Open with his [Sunraider's] body rejected by his political collegues in response to the scandal centering around his death and his identity. In the dark of night his body is removed from the hospital, placed in a meat locker, covered with a plastic shower curtin and covered with dry ice and flown south with the Negroes (ms. box I:141, folder 4)

> What if they decide, having little money left after paying thier bills, a fine and McMillen's fare home, to return Bliss home for burial in Mr. Jessie's old coffin, after which it will be transfered to something more ground-worthy. And that on their way from the airport the hearse catches fire on the road (ms. box I:141, folder 5)

> this ceremony [Ellison refers here to the phantom car sequence] might well fit in with original idea of having them return the Senator south in dry ice for resurrection (as Bliss) and burial (ms. box I:141, folder 4)

Although the particularities shift and change, the central event depicted in each of these notes is the same: Sunraider dies, has his history exposed, is scapegoated and expelled by his fellow politicians, and is at last sent home with Hickman to either Georgia or Oklahoma. No available materials suggest Ellison wrote anything more than these scattered notes elaborating this final movement of Bliss's narrative. On the basis of these, however, we can clearly see what the novel's shape was to have been. By identifying with Sunraider's narrative as it is told antiphonally in the intimacy of a private hospital room and recognizing in that narrative a version of our own personal and national moral evasions, we would ideally be compelled to weep over the senator's body as Hickman did on the Senate floor and be ritually prepared for a psychological resurrection.[7] This resurrection and redemption would be made explicit at Bliss's funeral. But Ellison's composition seizes at the very moment that catharsis should occur. The authorial hand, which here resembles Abraham's, seems to stay itself and to retract from the sacrificial act.

The chronological plot of the novel actually ends on page 422 of *Three Days*, poised on the narratological and moral precipice of Sunraider's death. Although Ellison continued to write within the world of the novel for decades, he never advanced the plot beyond this point. In this moment, the dying Sunraider has fallen asleep and Hickman is left alone to meditate on the entire tragic movement of the senator's life. As he considers the madness of the events that have transpired, he recognizes that soon the authorities will investigate the circumstances of the shooting and discover Sunraider's past. He concludes that they will not seek after the truth about Sunraider's and Severen's respective identities and the circumstances that led to the attack at the Senate chambers but instead invent "some lie that will protect them from the truth" (421). To acknowledge the truth would amount to a recognition that "they slipped up in places where they'd rather die than be caught slipping. A tint of skin—ha!" (421). For figures of authority and power to recognize the racial and cultural complexity embodied in Bliss and Severen, as well as the freedom each was able to practice beneath and within oppressive social forces, would necessitate a simultaneous acknowledgment of their own failure to effectively legislate race and to maintain rigid hierarchical distinctions.

Hickman's meditations then move into a broader consideration of racial violence and scapegoating practices:

> Why can't they face the simple fact that you simply can't give one bunch of men the license to kill another bunch without punishment, without opening themselves up to being victims? The high as well as the low? Why can't they realize that when they dull their senses to the killing of one group of men they dull themselves to the preciousness of all human life? Yes, and why can't they realize that when they allow one group of men the freedom to kill us as evidence of their own superiority they're only setting the stage so that these killers will have to widen the game, since if anyone can kill niggers the only way left to prove themselves superior is by killing some white man high in the public eye? Attack the head since the feet are too easy a target? (421–22)

In this series of rhetorical questions, Hickman plays out the logic of sacrificial violence to its limit point. Because scapegoating dehumanizes its victim, he reasons, there will come a time when victims will have to be chosen from further and further up the hierarchical ladder. The target will eventually land on "some white man high in the public eye." Violence, Hickman observes, will never be contained. The final question he asks himself further confirms the eschatological tenor of the passage: "How can you resist praying for the day when they shall turn upon one another as they did once before and purge this land with blood? How can you resist praying for the day when the sacrificer will be the sacrificed, when the many-headed beast will rend itself, tooth, nail, and fiery tail and die?" (422). In his invocation of the ten-headed beast of Revelation 13, Hickman imagines, however briefly, an apocalyptic future in which the white population turns against itself in a second Civil War fueled entirely by the fever of retributive violence.

Hickman quickly rejects this apocalyptic nightmare in favor of a more characteristically Ellisonian vision of democratic progress, which he arrives at through his religious faith, a faith deeply wedded to a tragicomic democratic sensibility. Instead of an apocalyptic version of what the character Jessie Rockmore calls "metaphysical progression," Hickman imagines a chaotic dance floor: "So you're in it Hickman, and have been in it and there's no turning back. Besides, there's no single living man calling the tune to this crazy dance. Talking about playing it by ear, this is one time when everybody is playing it by ear because everybody in the band and all those out on the dance floor is as blind as a mole in the hole" (422). The nonviolent, improvisatory ethic Hickman arrives at in this crucial moment, the very moment that should precede the death of the tragic hero, contradicts the ethic of sacrificial violence (Ellison killing Sunraider for the sake of catharsis) implicit in the scene of his utterance. While Ellison's formal scheme during this phase of composition demands the symbolic sacrifice of a victim in order to produce a catharsis in his reader, Hickman suddenly and powerfully rejects sacrificial violence altogether. The preacher's thoughts are an interrogation of the logic underlying Ellison's entire formal apparatus. Hickman, at this instant, is Samson brought to Ellison's temple. And once there, he rises up to shake its columns.

Long before he composed this scene, Ellison had related to Albert Murray experiences of a kind of dissonance between character and author. In a 1959 letter to Murray, Ellison, detailing what it was like to write Hickman's sermons and speeches, exclaims, "That old bastard [Hickman] knows how to get under even so initiated and tough a skin as mine" (*Trading* 204). Hickman's meditations, read alongside the fact that Ellison's novel suddenly stops advancing chronologically, suggest that the old preacher did indeed get under Ellison's initiated skin. But Hickman's thoughts also constitute a considered response to the historical moment in which Ellison is writing and this history bears on the sudden fracturing of the text.

The ethical quandary of enacting sacrificial violence at the level of form in the interests of civic improvement has a clear historical dimension as well. Kenneth Warren has argued persuasively for how fundamental occasion is to Ellison's critical writings. Ellison's essays, argues Warren, work by "turning a single instance into an X ray of the social organism infected by race at that historical moment" (*So Black* 22). Although not occasional per se, Ellison's fiction is highly sensitive to even the subtlest historical vicissitudes. From one perspective, the first major phase of the civil rights movement charts the progressive failure of sacrificial violence to produce solidarity and positive social change. Emmett Till's violent death in 1955, which exposed the realities of ritualized racial violence in the South to a national audience, was a national disgrace that became a spiritual imperative.[8] But the chaos that erupted in the wakes of the assassinations of the 1960s along with increasing calls to violence from the burgeoning Black Power movement marked what Ellison would have perceived as a reentrenchment of the logic of sacrificial and retributive violence. If one of Ellison's central aims in his novel was the integration of the personality through aesthetic form, then the formal demand that he perform an act of sacrifice must have finally repulsed his efforts as both a historically and morally untenable path; he had failed to be "guided by the implicit morality of the form." As a result, Ellison was compelled through his sheer commitment to this morality of form to radically reengineer the shape his second novel would take and to abolish sacrificial violence as the engine for dramatic movement. The computer sequences that Ellison labored over in the 1980s and the 1990s are the fruits of this revisionary enterprise.

II. DIALECTICAL TRANSCENDENCE IN THE COMPUTER SEQUENCES (1982–94)

Ellison's tragic plot reached a crisis point at some point in the early 1970s. As we have seen, tragic catharsis had ceased to be a morally sustainable form for imagining and promoting psychological and civic transformation (specifically, through psychological *integration*).[9] Because of this crisis (undoubtedly alongside other factors), Ellison made little progress on his second novel in the 1970s. However, he renewed his efforts with vigor in the early '80s.

The two long computer sequences he wrote during this period, which together consume more than 600 manuscripts pages, abound with energy and interest. The action in both occurs prior to the assassination in the Senate. The first, "Hickman in Washington, D.C." reimagines the three-page prologue to Books I and II as a three-hundred-page picaresque in which Hickman meanders through a quasi-mythical Washington, DC, and the second, "Hickman in Georgia & Oklahoma," which takes place even earlier, describes Hickman's journey from Georgia to Oklahoma to uncover Severen's assassination plot and to discover missing pieces of Bliss's personal history. Despite their verve and breadth, the computer sequences noticeably fail to *resolve* the plot of Ellison's novel, an omission bewildering even to the novel's editors. While Ellison's notes show that he continued to diagram and trouble over his plot well into the 1990s, the computer sequences themselves reveal that he was simultaneously developing a formal approach to the American novel that no longer relied on plot as the mechanism of transformation.

In a 1965 essay on Emerson's "Nature," Kenneth Burke describes and differentiates two kinds of symbolic operations that "involve *formal development*" and "give us kinds of *transformation*" ("I, Eye, Ay" 880; italics in original); these are dramatic catharsis and dialectical transcendence. In the former, Burke tells us, "transformation comes to a focus in *victimage*" (880; italics in original). The latter, however, achieves transformation by "seeing things in terms of some 'higher' dimension, with the spirit of which all becomes infused" (880–81). Or, as he states it later in the essay, transcendence "involves dialectical processes whereby something HERE is interpreted *in terms of* something THERE, something *beyond* itself" (894). In "Hickman in Washington, D.C." Hickman echoes this phrase when he reflects on the purpose of sermons specifically and art more generally. He claims that sermons move their audiences with "tonal and rhythmical excitement from the known to the unknown, and from the old and familiar into that which was new and still unfamiliar" (TD 596). He goes on to propose that all artists further engage their audiences by "drawing upon that which was left carefully understated or concealed as a means for achieving a *transcendent* goal" (595; emphasis added). As with a sermonic performance, communion of the group is only possible once it has been "raise[d] above the sheer sound and fury of that which is so faintly heard and so dimly seen" (595). The repeated emphasis on transcendence as the aim of art marks a subtle but important shift in Ellison's sense of literature's function. Further confirming Ellison's investment in an ideal of transcendence through competitive cooperation, Burke, interestingly, argues that the social office of transcendence (what he calls *pontificating*) was typically reserved for priests. It is not surprising, then, that the central figure of Ellison's computer sequences is a preacher.[10]

Burke's version of "dialectical transcendence" does not entirely account for the nuances of the computer sequences, but it provides an initial useful gloss on the formal techniques that Ellison marshals in his late fiction, which float above and defer from the tragic plot. Contrary to Lawrence Jackson's claim that "the frustrating irony of Ellison's career ... was that he concluded it as a critic, at a time when he seemed most to doubt the value of shaping the artist's reality" ("Ellison's Politics" 200), Ellison had not abandoned the transformative potential of the novel as a particular and powerful democratic symbolic action, but had radically altered the method of achieving this transformation. Throughout the computer sequences Ellison has characters announce that they are deferring the advancement of plot by producing or extending a dialogue. The deferral of resolution, therefore, opens a narrative space in which Ellison develops a new formal approach to the novel where plot ceases to be—as it was for Aristotle—the central element of fiction.

Early in "Hickman in Georgia & Oklahoma," the second and longest of the two computer sequences, Hickman opens a letter concerning a burial ceremony a former congregant wishes him to conduct: "Of course I will, he thought, and *the plot's no problem*, because just last week I was out there and noticed that somebody ... had looked ahead and given it their attention" (665; emphasis added). In this short aside Ellison, via Hickman, slyly comments on the status of his own *literary* plot. The tragic plot becomes figuratively linked to a burial plot, and because "somebody" has already attended to it, Hickman, like Ellison, need not bother with it, but only speak over it. This line, comically and quietly, announces a dramatic shift in Ellison's relationship to his novel and its plot. In marginalizing the tragic plot, Ellison subordinates the animating formal concerns of Books I and II (ritual, myth, tragic catharsis) to thematic ones, and the plot diffuses into a picaresque punctuated by contemplation, interpretation, dialogue, and improvisation. When sacrificial violence and tragic action do appear, they typically do so at one remove from the novel's time-present, as in the case of Millsap's letter, Love New's stories, and Cliofus's verbal re-creation of Bliss's cinematic enterprise. Throughout the computer sequences dialogue becomes the form through which characters transcend their immediate conditions and aspire toward a vision of national character—moving from the Many to the One. In these final writings, tragic movements are subordinated to dialogic ones.[11]

The device Ellison most consistently utilizes to these ends is Hickman's dialogic consciousness. Near the beginning of "Hickman in Georgia & Oklahoma," Hickman flies to see Janey in Oklahoma and upon arriving has a flashback to his youth as a jazz musician. The narrator pauses to describe the operation of Hickman's consciousness: "Increasingly such flashbacks were accompanied by interior dialogues in which a voice from his life as an irreverent young bluesman mocked his present role of spiritual leader and reminded him of his lingering worldliness. Marked by a conflict between his past and his present it was an ongoing dialogue in which the younger self badgered and teased while his older self stubbornly asserted its spiritual authority" (715). The two selves inhabiting Hickman's mind frequently argue with one another as Hickman struggles to arrive at tentative interpretations of the various phenomena he encounters. Although the two voices are most explicit in "Hickman in Georgia & Oklahoma," the dialogic tension between the tragicomic bluesman (the aesthete) and the preacher (the moralist) is evident as well in "Hickman in Washington, D.C." Elsewhere, Ellison relies on long dialogues between characters to generate a series of prolonged reflections on American history, folktales, national identity, and even on the plot of the novel itself. These include Hickman's novella-length dialogue with the omni-racial shaman Love New, his frequent colloquies with Wilhite, and his quasi-telepathic interactions with the gargantuan American jazz muse Cliofus. Most important to this new organizing principle is that it does not explicitly rely upon the exercise of authorial violence in order to achieve resolution. Instead, the episodes in the computer sequences utilize these techniques in an effort to ascend toward a transcendent understanding of the nation through language before regrounding themselves in the chaotic world of experience and practice.

During his errant wanderings in Washington, DC, Hickman stumbles upon an old barbershop called the Janus Barnes Hair Salon. Underneath the shop's name is a painting "the surprising subject of which was a double-headed black man whose faces were staring in opposite directions. And noting that the hair on one of the heads was straight and gleaming and that of the other bushy and dull, he [Hickman] smiled" (547). The mythological heritage of the business, as well as the emblematic painting on its door, points to the kind of world in which Hickman now walks. The barbershop, long a mythic site of African American conversation and signifying, is here linked symbolically to the dialectical image of Janus, the god of transitions and motion. Ellison subtly collapses dialogic exchange with the transformation achieved through dialectical transcendence.

The demands made on Ellison's novel by what he termed the "implicit morality of the form" led him to the strange and intricate expanse of the two long computer sequences. These late efforts represent an attempt to compose a transformative and integrative American novel without the stain of sacrificial violence. But although Ellison seems to develop this formal scheme to the novel as an alternative to the sacrificial logic undergirding tragic action, he well knew, as Burke did, that even dialogue and dialectic could contain what Burke called "traces of victimage": "In the Platonic dialogue, there are traces of victimage, insofar as some speakers are sacrificed for the good of the dialogue as a whole" ("I, Eye, Ay" 876). Ellison, in a 1972 interview conducted by John O'Brien, takes a stance on scapegoating that is similar to Burke's, but far less circumscribed:

> In order to have a human society you are going to have to have some form of victimization. . . . You're scapegoating right now; I'm scapegoating right now. That's the way language works; it's built in. The moment you begin structuring values, some are going to be ideal and some are going to be less ideal. . . . And in a political system you are going to end up with some form of inequality. . . . The human challenge is to moderate this and you can only do this by consciously keeping the ideal alive, by not treating it as a folly, but by treating it as Thoreau and Emerson were treating it, as a conscious discipline which imposed upon you a conscientiousness which made you aware, every hour and every day. To impose a human vision upon the world . . . but it's so easy to drift. (O'Brien 228–30)

Novelistic form becomes both the site at which this inescapable feature of language and society can be most fully interrogated and also the site where an ideal can be constructed and realized. Certain characters and dialogues in the computer sequences, however, trouble over the scapegoating practices latent even in such unassuming moments. As both Burke's and Ellison's statements attest, in any dialogue with transcendence as its aim, some terms and some speakers are going to be elevated at the expense of others. For Ellison, particularly, this concern emerges from the anxiety over unintentionally reinscribing what Hickman, in speaking about the folk hero Stackalee, calls "*outskirts* history" (604), a term that names the complex and strange events that enable history but cannot be contained within history's neat, circumscribed boundaries. Hickman worries about the storyteller who, "whether he be judge, historian or politician—steps in and pretends that he's the voice of God, which is their nickname for history. Then he sets out to re-create the world by word of mouth, and all that doesn't fit into the tale he wants to tell he leaves out. And that makes room for a whole world of complications that go unnoticed" (603). The problem of consciously excluding something from a tale, of scapegoating the outskirts to fortify the inskirts, is a problem not only of history but also of literary fiction. Ellison takes pains to represent the figures of the outskirts, but they also have a tendency to introduce cracks into the novel's form.

The most potent example of this kind of figure is Leroy, the crazed disciple of "Chief SAM, the fucking *Liberator*" (556), who bursts forth from the Janus Barnes barbershop as Hickman ponders its dialectical sign. Leroy's bizarre interaction with Hickman is less a dialogue than the reconstructed memory of a catechistical vision and, as such, leaves Hickman utterly mystified. Additionally, where Hickman ponders, Leroy acts. Before Hickman even knows his name, Leroy has lifted the old preacher up by his thighs to survey the capital. Leroy recalls his vision of Chief Sam instructing him to "remember that when such as ye steps into a scene the action changes, for it has been structured to exclude thee" (553). Leroy's face, which repulses Hickman with its ugliness, resembles an American flag. Because of a "drastic loss of pigment" the "skin-sick stranger" is, Hickman notices, a "*red-white-and-blue black man*" (549). Scarred and masked by an "appall[ing]" (549) gradient of color, Leroy, too, Ellison indicates, *is* America. Leroy's presence disrupts not only mainstream American culture, but also Hickman's and Ellison's formal method of transformation. Characters like Leroy challenge the formal model of dialectic transcendence by being both its victims and its competitors.

The persistence of victimization and scapegoating in even the most benign symbolic action begs for a solution. Ellison offers one in Hickman's long ekphrastic encounter with a woven rendition of Brueghel's painting *Landscape with the Fall of Icarus*. While waiting for Wilhite in a hotel lounge in Washington, DC, Hickman chances upon a tapestry depicting the Brueghel painting. Because he knows neither the original painting nor its title, he approaches the work in perfect innocence of its mythic and historic context. The long sequence chronicles his experience of the painting and his attempt to discover through an analysis of its parts a meaning he is certain it conceals. The structure of the episode is not dialectical in a strict sense and the two competing voices in Hickman's consciousness are less prominent here than in other scenes. However, the progress Hickman makes on the painting is decidedly progressive and reaches toward a world beyond the merely experiential one evident in the painting.

As Hickman's reflections progress they become indistinguishable from those of the third-person narrative voice (thus affirming the homology between Ellison's and Hickman's aesthetic sensibilities) and lead him into a long meditation on the forms and aims of art. Hickman contemplates the figures of the jazz musician, the weaver, the sermonizer, and the storyteller, all of whom mutually inform one another, and all of whom have transcendence as their shared end. These aesthetic reflections then become a digressive riff of their own, which reveals much about how Ellison intended posterity to receive his unfinished masterpiece. Hickman pauses to consider the practice of those storytellers who pretend not to know what their stories mean as a "way of flattering [their] listeners' intelligence while persuading them to a willing participation in [their] spinning of tales" (596). This dumbshow serves as a narratological version of the call and response of sermonic performance: "Like a preacher, [the storyteller] mimed and 'called' and his listeners responded" (596). In Book II we saw how Ellison exploited the ritual device of the antiphonal sermon in order to invite the reader into an intimacy with his characters and to encourage identification. Here that formal device is decoupled from a dramatic mode and reconfigured for a reflective one. Hickman's thought makes another turn in the next sentence when he casually wonders if "in a deeper sense ... playing dumb was also a self-sacrificial act through which good storytellers prepared their audiences to receive and enjoy such hard-earned wisdom as might underlie the surface of his tale's comedy" (596–97). By "pretending to be too stupid to recognize its underlying message, the storyteller assumed the burden of its underlying pain and embarrassment" (597). In the midst of this ekphrastic scene, Ellison unfolds his tentative solution to the haunting problem of victimage. In a striking moment of authorial reflection, Ellison substitutes himself as a comic scapegoat for Bliss's tragic scapegoat.

Instead of striving to further evacuate the novel's form of sacrificial gestures, Ellison assumes the burden of victimage. Ellison, as distinct from the characters he gives voice to, remains eerily silent and "dumb" in the computer sequences (597). Because he finally refuses to assume the role of the author who, like the historian or the politician, "steps in and pretends that he's the voice of God" (603), Ellison is unable to assert a final vision through either the designs of plot or the ascending rungs of dialogue. As a result, he remains the most uncertain presence in the text and his face the one most thoroughly masked. His silence, however, enables all his characters to retain a voice without being unceremoniously swept aside by the necessities of tragic action or the machinery of dialectic. The various intrusions of Leroy, Love New, Cliofus, and a host of others constitute interruptions in the time of the novel, obstructions against the formulation of a final word. Unable to extricate himself from a sacrificial economy, Ellison suspends his fictional world by a continual extension of composition and a subsequent failure to resolve the novel into a fully coherent, publishable work. In so doing he marks himself as the text's victim, the figure at whose expense other figures are given voice.

By identifying his late storytelling as a sacrificial act, Ellison also displaces the burden of transformation through transcendence onto the reader. Dialogue remains formally significant for the narrative not only at the level of character but also at that of reader and text. In the first phase of composition Ellison had sought to transform his audience through the enactment of a cathartic resolution to a tragic plot. When the consequences of that act of symbolic scapegoating were fully revealed, he began composing episodes animated by dialogic exchange rather than tragic progression. But even this mode, once it was assumed as a formal mechanism for completing the novel, required that some actors (some number of the Many) would have to be subtly sacrificed for the sake of transcendence (the One). The progress of the second novel confirms what is latent in the note about Theseus with which this essay began: that literary form and sacrificial violence are deeply intertwined. Completion and resolution, even as mere narratological categories, are touched with the sacrificial motive. As an ultimate ideal and the animating social vision of the second novel, *integration,* whether imaginative or political, could not be fully achieved so long as scapegoating remained the formal means of fulfillment. The various forms that Ellison's second novel takes progressively radicalize this central notion. And it is this commitment, finally, that proves to be the guiding moral principle of the second novel.

Ellison's notes reveal that he struggled until the end of his life to render his second novel complete, but he undoubtedly recognized the possibility that he might not live to see it finished. As Hickman's reflections about storytelling suggest, Ellison theorized to himself at length about the aesthetic value of an unfinished and unresolved work. The value, he suggests, is not merely in aesthetically reproducing a particular social and political vision of play, improvisation, and revisionary possibility, as Muyumba and others have maintained. Instead, Ellison manages at the end of his life only to hold a sacrificial economy in suspense, to weave a portrait in time. Resolution cannot be achieved within the bounds of the text, but the novel's abiding faith in reading and dialogue encourages us to transfer the urge for completion outside these bounds. That is, instead of blithely following in the author's path and accepting the sacrificial mechanisms that ensure resolution and completion (whether catharsis or transcendence), the novel, unfinished, compels us both to engage the multitude of issues it raises, the interruptions it stages, and the complex, protean vision of America it embraces, and also to assume the mantle of responsibility for our own participation in subtle rituals of scapegoating and sacrifice, whether in the seminar room, the courtroom, or on the street corner. As Ellison's late essay "The Little Man at Chehaw Station" proves, Ellison had great faith in an American audience, and *Three Days* puts that faith to the test. Ellison's prose, dense with literary and historical allusion and rife with vernacular acrobatics, demands a store of patience, care, and attention and, as such, advocates a fiercely engaged reading practice that does not balk at difficulty. The language itself requires the active cultivation of consciousness and conscientiousness, a competitive cooperation, and a symbolic contest for transcendence. It dances before us and calls us to respond.

NOTES

1. In the past two decades there has been a critical tendency to locate Ellison in the mainstream of American pragmatism and to read him as a philosophical heir to Emerson, James, and Burke. Gregg Crane, for instance, makes a compelling case for what he calls Ellison's "constitutional faith": "In its embrace of change, improvisation, and revision, Ellison's conception of aesthetic and ethical judgment closely parallels a pragmatist strain of American jurisprudence" (110). This welcome advance in our understanding of Ellison's political philosophy, however, is not so easily applied to his aesthetic project as a whole. Typically, treatments that too readily interpret Ellison's primary aesthetic mode through jazz improvisation viewed under the lens of philosophical pragmatism obscure Ellison's deep commitment to formal completeness. Critics who extol Ellison's pragmatism often fall into the trap of considering the unfinished quality of Ellison's second novel a natural and therefore intended consequence of pragmatist thinking. Walter Muyumba, for instance, speculates that in *Juneteenth* "Ellison eschewed traditional linearity . . . in favor of an exploded form that conveyed the contingency of narrative forms and a holistic literary attitude" (85). Granted, Muyumba did not have access to *Three Days before the Shooting . . .* , but his assessment still attributes an unwarranted amount of intentionality to the incompleteness of the text. Whatever their flaws, pragmatist approaches to the incompleteness of the second novel are at least charitable in their attempts to understand it. On the other side of this question we find Arnold Rampersad (Ellison's biographer), Toni Morrison (qtd. in Bradley 210), and Lawrence Jackson, all of whom consider the second novel a decided failure and thus evidence either of Ellison's hubris or his belated recognition that both his politics and his aesthetics were regrettable anachronisms. Adam Bradley, who coedited *Three Days*, has offered the most well-reasoned and judicious attempt at accounting for the second novel's incompleteness to date. Bradley locates Ellison's inability to finish the second novel in a set of intractable compositional obstacles, which importantly acknowledges Ellison's anxiety over his second novel without dismissing it as a simple failure or eliding the *progress* Ellison made. Although my own argument differs from Bradley's, I am indebted to him for clearing so much difficult and important analytic ground.

2. This argument takes the position that Ellison, who had been widely embraced by white, liberal intellectuals after the publication of *Invisible Man*, was targeting the complacency and self-satisfaction of this inbuilt audience in Book I, well aware that white liberals would be among the first to champion and promote his second novel. This first section of the second novel therefore allows Ellison both to critique this audience and to articulate his intellectual distance from them. One especially potent instance of this occurs when McIntyre falls asleep in the hospital room and has a long dream vision where he is harassed, interrogated, and signified upon by an iron hitching-post boy. The figure, an embodied half-living racial stereotype, minces McIntyre's comfortable liberal conscience. In a particularly telling moment, the iron statue says, "*I know you too well, baby. You're one of those who love humanity real good, like a proper Christian should. You help the poor and the needy and you contribute to the care and feeding of the unknown heathen hordes abroad. You love everybody and anybody until you see their faces, or hear their voices raised in passionate description of the truth of their own condition. But then, baby, your love goes limp. Your sterling 'integration of personality' tarnishes and cankers, and then Uncle Sugar grabs the scatological imperative and hides himself like foxes in holes*" (187). The phrase *integration of personality*, which Ellison earlier used in his letter to Morteza Sprague to articulate an ideal, is deployed here to demonstrate the inadequacy of a *merely* Jungian, therapeutic version of integration. The Jungian "integration of personality," which is synonymous with individuation, or the process by which an individual confronts and *integrates* the conscious self with the unconscious (or shadow) self, requires an individual to confront the *archetypes* occupying her or his unconscious. The hitching-post boy's harangue exposes the distance between the abstract *archetype* and the *living human face*. Ellison's own version of the "integration of the personality," which McIntyre's vision energetically dramatizes, demands an encounter not with an archetype/scapegoat but with a living, breathing human.

3. For an example of Ellison's critique of naive catharsis, see his *Time* essay "What America Would Be Like without Blacks." In this essay Ellison savages contemporary arguments advocating the purgation of blacks from American society. This "fantasy of benign amputation that would rid the country of black men" is, like "the illusion of secession," an attempt to "use the black man as a scapegoat to achieve a national catharsis" (CERE 583). Such acts would "by way of curing the patient, destroy him" (583). This view is naive because it attempts to induce catharsis through a gesture of amputation rather than integration. Ellison goes on to demonstrate that Afro-American culture is so deeply entangled with mainstream American culture that no amount of colonization could extricate and realize the "fantastic vision of a lily-white America" (582). Catharsis, for Ellison, must be achieved via integrative, not divisive, means.

4. In her study of Burke and Ellison, Beth Eddy argues that Ellison was deeply suspicious of tragic catharsis throughout his career. Although she is correct in claiming that by the mid- to late 1970s Ellison felt that "something too close to scapegoating seems still to be going on in [catharsis]—something that leaves [him], if not Burke, uncomfortable" (127), Eddy fails to acknowledge Ellison's complex and changing relationship with catharsis. Her evidence for this claim comes from Ellison's 1977–78 essay "The Little Man at Chehaw Station" where Ellison writes that "at his best he [a reader] does not ask for scapegoats but

for the hero as witness" (CERE 503). Eddy is right to hear Ellison's *late* disillusionment with tragic catharsis but neglects his early commitment to its psychological and civic possibilities when effected through a sufficiently complex piece of art.

5. Severen, who had been Ellison's tragic hero in the very early phases of composition, ceases by the 1960s to be a character at all and instead becomes a functional element in a tragic scheme. Severen is conceived during a profound instance of the American evasion of identity—Bliss's seduction of Lavatrice. In this episode, Bliss, having fled Hickman's congregation and remade himself as a film director, is fully embodying the Adamic mode. Severen is the progeny of Bliss's façade of innocence. He haunts the novel in the same way that Ellison believed America was haunted in the post–civil rights era by our own assumed innocence, which is our hubris. Ellison develops this argument in his 1974 lecture, "Address to the Harvard College Alumni, Class of 1949" (CERE 419–30).

6. This conflict is not merely evident at the level of form, either. Questions about the efficacy and justice of sacrificial and retributive violence are thematically active throughout the typescripts and evidence the fact that Ellison was using his characters to think through these difficult issues at the same time that they were being debated publicly during the civil rights years. They are evident, for instance, in Hickman's figural representation of Bliss as the boy who led Samson to the Philistine temple and in Hickman's rejection of sacrificial violence in the episode "Bliss's Birth," and are central to the obfuscated justifications for Bliss's transformation into Sunraider.

7. In a note to himself, Ellison wrote, "Tragedy, which took its plots, its contents and heroes, ended in death, because in this world the human individual knows no resurrection. (Except psychologically: R.E.)" (ms. box I:141, folder 6). This note, until the parenthetical, is a direct quotation from Jane Harrison's seminal *Epilogemena to the Study of Greek Religion* (25). Ellison's small but substantive addition to Harrison's claim confirms his abiding sense in the possibility of a kind of psychological transformation that can occur in the wake of artistically induced catharsis.

8. In *Eyes on the Prize: America's Civil Rights Years 1954–1965*, Juan Williams, to cite one prominent, mainstream example, begins his history of the civil rights era with Emmett Till's murder.

9. Although Ellison abandoned tragic catharsis as an effective mode of transformation, his late essays (especially "An Extravagance of Laughter") evidence a continued exploration of the therapeutic and transformative potential of comic catharsis.

10. Bryan Crable persuasively delineates the ebbs and flows of Ellison's relationship to Burke in his recent book *Ralph Ellison and Kenneth Burke: At the Roots of the Racial Divide*. Crable shows that despite Ellison's deep engagement with Burke's writings, his relationship with Burke was strained from the outset by the disparity in their approach to America's racial divide. This strain came to a head in the 1950s and '60s. By the 1970s Ellison had significantly distanced himself from Burke personally, although he still continued to engage intellectually with Burke's work (Crable 211). The two, however, resumed correspondence in the early 1980s after Burke admitted to his "lurking Nortonism." The renewed friendship may have encouraged Ellison's reinvestment in the Burkean project. Echoing my sense of the transcendental project animating the computer sequences, Crable argues that in his

essays Ellison "attempted to transcend the antithesis between the generically human and the racial" and, as such, "began to sketch a more Burkean position on race than Burke himself was able to achieve" (135).

11. See Puchner (2010) for a brilliant discussion of the genre of the Socrates play and a complex genealogy of the form that includes Kenneth Burke. Ellison's commitment to dialogue as a dramatic form of philosophizing and a philosophical form of narrativizing places him in this tradition.

PART THREE

RALPH ELLISON AND AMERICAN CULTURE

Ellison Past, Present, and Future

"IN A STRANGE COUNTRY"
The Challenge of American Inclusion

LUCAS E. MOREL

Eight years before the publication of his landmark novel, *Invisible Man*, Ralph Ellison explored the theme of civic belonging—what it means to be included as a citizen of the United States. His 1944 short story, "In a Strange Country," considers the challenge of inclusion in a country where historically race, in its association with American slavery, complicated the nation's attempt to secure the rights and privileges of all of its citizens. The black American protagonist, through his encounter overseas with a few hospitable Welshmen, learns to appreciate his own country despite the evident racial hostility he has experienced living in mid-twentieth-century America.

This short story covers an evening in the life of a black American merchant marine on shore leave in Wales as he recovers from an assault by white American servicemen.[1] "In a Strange Country" was the original title of Ellison's pre–*Invisible Man* novel, and its plot dealt with a black air force pilot captured by Nazis only to find he is the highest-ranking officer amid white American POWs at a German concentration camp (IM xi). To readers of *Invisible Man*, it is no surprise to find Ellison already operating in an ironic mode, a fitting way to address the gap between American principle and practice.

Starting with the title, his short story invites the reader to consider what he means by a "*strange* country." Is the "strange country" Wales, the setting for the story, or the United States of America, the protagonist's native—but antagonistic—land?[2] What is strange about Wales, and conversely, what is strange or estranging about America? The reader soon learns that the protagonist is in some ways alienated from his native land by virtue of his race.[3] How is Wales different from the United States? This difference or strangeness is ironic because the "strange country" that is Wales is alluring in its foreignness to the protagonist: "Coming ashore from the ship he had felt the excited expectancy of entering a strange land" (Ellison, "Strange Country" 138). It is not a threatening unfamiliarity for the main character because the assumed familiarity of his own country, given its white-supremacist history and current laws and practices, is presumed to be troubling and threatening for the black protagonist.

This stranger to Wales, whom Ellison calls "Mr. Parker" (suggestive of the jazz saxophonist Charlie Parker[4]), likes the Welsh ale, demonstrating a very practical multiculturalism or integration at work. But he has not left his Southern black roots behind: "He looked guardedly at the pretty, blue-aproned barmaid." This reflected Mr. Parker's male virility as well as his keen awareness that in the American South a black man has long been taught—in word and terrifying deed, as the tragic murder of Emmett Till would show to a nationwide and international audience in 1955—not to look a certain way at a white woman. But in this foreign land, the American stranger gives himself permission to sneak a peek at a pretty, presumably white barmaid, apparently not fearing the kind of outcry and backlash that would ensue if he was caught doing so back in the states.

The assault by white American soldiers initially led him to feel "blind rage" ("Strange Country" 139) even toward the Welshmen of the pub, despite the fact that they had rescued him from his own countrymen. But inwardly he reflects that their sincere politeness "disarmed" him. Wryly he tells himself: "*He* had been the one so glad to hear an American voice" (139). Upon reflection, this stranger in Wales observes not only the *diversity* of whiteness between Americans and Welshmen, but between the Welsh and the English: he calls the Welsh "a different breed" (139). In a 1989 essay, Ellison would note, "Discrimination teaches one to discriminate between discriminators"—or at least those who looked the part (CERE 829). The pub owner, Mr. Catti, calls it a disgrace to his own country that a visitor could be mugged as Mr. Parker was, but of course the true disgrace was that the American's own fellow citizens would assault him solely because of his race. Mr. Parker waves off Mr. Catti's indignation by calling the incident "a sort of family quarrel" ("Strange Country" 139). This charitable description of the mugging reflects his decision that, despite the assault, and the long American history of racial bigotry reflected in it, he would rise above their wrongdoing. As a black American, he had learned to take this thuggery in stride by making a joke of the incident. Humor, Ellison recounted, was among "those human qualities which the American Negro has developed despite, and in rejection of, the obstacles and meannesses imposed upon us" (CERE 79); it was part of "an American Negro tradition which teaches one to deflect racial provocation and to master and contain pain" (CERE 159). Outmanned, Mr. Parker found a way, rhetorically, to be the bigger man in his nonchalant dismissal of getting jumped by men who not only were fellow Americans, but also fellow servicemen who should have been fighting with him, not against him.

Mr. Parker is surprised to hear Mr. Catti call black Americans "Yanks," given that the white Yanks in Wales have so far given little evidence of their likeness to black Yanks. Nevertheless, the pub owner's remark that in Wales there are "Yanks all over the place. Black Yanks and white" (139) reflects a foreigner's recognition that something unites Americans across the color line, even if the conduct of one racial group toward another does not always reflect this unity. Foreigners like Mr. Catti recognize the Americanness of blacks in ways that blacks themselves may miss or take for granted.

Mr. Catti then invites the American to his club to hear him and other locals sing. Mr. Parker is initially reluctant, which prompts Mr. Catti to assure him, "It's a private club" (139), suggesting the unlikelihood of another altercation in a public place. This "private club" serves as an analogy to a political community, which is also a private club of sorts. The suggestion of inclusivity and exclusivity is apparent by the mere invitation to the private club. The question becomes, why has the black man not been included in the land of his birth? Why have black Americans not felt welcome in—members of—a country they have, as a people, spent many years building, both voluntarily and under coercion? Should not their citizenship, according to the Constitution, entitle them to all the benefits afforded white members of the American club?

Upon hearing that the club was showcasing some local singing talent, Mr. Parker's "interest was aroused," as "all music was a passion to him" (139). Music, for Ellison, becomes an important means of integrating society. Mr. Parker is later told that the singers represent a variety of occupations, from mine owner to miner to union official. The Marxist class conflict of owner and worker, bourgeoisie and proletariat, is transcended by the harmony of music. At first dubious of this resolution of class conflict, he is told by Mr. Catti, "When we sing, we are Welshmen" (143). Faced with a Welsh nationality forged in the crucible of their conflict with the English, Mr. Parker remembers the camaraderie of "mixed jam sessions" back in America,[5] leading him to reflect inwardly, "When we jam, sir, we're Jamocrats!" (143). Here is recognition of the integrating function of music. With music he finds the only worthy partisanship one that unites the players according to their devotion to their craft. Mr. Parker describes the political unity of his shipmates and himself as "a unity of economics," a joint effort in the war to defend an economic way of life. But when it comes to music, this he calls a "'gut language,' and, alluding to Shakespeare, the "'food of love'" (143), something common to all nations and cultures.[6] Whether it is the patriotic folk songs of the Welsh, whose singers comprise a diversity of backgrounds and occupations, or the harmonious compositions and jam sessions of American jazz troupes, the reader learns that music can help diverse individuals transcend their differences by making distinctive but complementary contributions to produce art.[7] If music can do this, why not politics?

"Welcome to our club, sir" (141). This hospitality and respect extended by the club manager, Mr. Triffit, is pregnant with meaning for the American stranger or guest, given the inhospitality rendered him less than an hour before by fellow Americans. The Welsh welcome to an American stranger contrasts strikingly with his being mobbed by his own countrymen. The reader is given to understand that not only is he *not* welcome back home by the majority-white society, but they also refuse to permit him a peaceful and pleasant sojourn on shore leave. The club manager follows his hearty welcome by saying, "We're happy to have you, sir." Again, have black people ever been so warmly and respectfully accepted in the land of their birth? Has American society ever, in word or deed, told blacks how happy they were to have them as fellow citizens?

After the American offers a toast to Wales and to his hosts, Mr. Triffit helps Mr. Parker gain some appreciation for the United States in his toast "to America, God bless her." He responds, "Yes, and to America" (141). America should be toasted, if only for the promise of human equality and liberty it represents and for the fulfillment black Americans have fought and secured by fits and starts from a reluctant white America. As the scene plays out, with various songs sung with verve and meaning, Mr. Parker perceives the national pride conveyed therein, much to Mr. Catti's delight. He informs Mr. Parker that one of the songs was about "a battle in which we defeated the English" (142).[8] It appears music, like all human art forms, is never too far from politics. The Welsh, like black Americans, have suffered oppression as a people. What's more, as Mr. Parker learns through the songs of the Welsh, they are not simply the victims of English bigotry but have been able to forge an identity, a culture, out of this experience. This may prove to be a source of hope for Mr. Parker about the situation of blacks in America.

What is clear is that the hospitality he experiences in the foreign land of Wales, by men—white men—with a kindred devotion to music, moves him to think anew about what any men are capable of, and hence what hope he might have for white fellow citizens upon returning to the familiar soil of America. As Mr. Parker reveals in an inward interrogation of himself: "But what do *you* believe in? *Oh, shut—I believe in music!* Well! *And in what's happening here tonight. I believe . . . I want to believe in this people*" (144). The Welsh have truly gotten under his skin, and "he felt with vague terror, all evening he had been exposed, blinded by the brilliant light of their deeper humanity, and they had seen him for what he was and for what he should have been" (144).

With "a growing poverty of spirit" (142), Parker compares the robust songs of Welsh patriotism with the lack thereof among black Americans. He salutes the Welsh as a "warrior nation," complimenting them on their ability to forge nationhood out of struggle, and wonders why it did not happen for blacks in the same way.[9] Black Americans were oppressed as well, yet remained in the land of their oppressors, but with "no song of ours that's of love of the soil or of country. Nor any song of battle other than those of biblical times" (142). This reference to the Old Testament, given the context of an American abroad who "felt now, among these men, hearing their voices, a surge of deep longing to know the anguish and exultation of such love" (142–43), reminds one of that great lamentation in Psalm 137, verse 4: "How shall we sing the LORD's song in a strange land?"[10] This allusion to the story's title also foreshadows the poignant conclusion to the story, when Mr. Parker surprises himself by singing along with the Welshmen as they honor him by closing with a rendition of "The Star-Spangled Banner."

Ellison has Mr. Parker hear himself singing (145–46), and includes a short excerpt from the American national anthem: "Gave proof through the night / That our flag was still there."[11] This sentence suggests the hope that black Americans have had that despite the long "night" of domestic oppression (namely, slavery, followed by black codes, Jim Crow, and segregation), there was "proof" that majority-white America still believed its profession about human equality. The American flag truly was "our flag," the flag of all Americans regardless of color, and hence really could represent a common country and thus a common protection of the rights of all her citizens. As Frederick Douglass once put it: "Our hearts believed while they ached and bled" ("Oration in Memory" 313).

With American readers familiar with the words to their national anthem, Ellison leaves it to them to supply the preceding phrase, "And the rockets' red glare, the bombs bursting in air." The irony of being able to see the American flag still waving because of the explosions of bombs intended to destroy that flag and the nation it represents was certainly not lost on Ellison. Setting his story during a time of war, Ellison uses the imagery of violent national conflict perhaps to imply that progress at home could follow from progress abroad as Americans, black and white, defended their homeland from foreign threats, providing all the more imperative to combat domestic threats to the freedom of all American citizens. In Ellison's mind, American wars have historically proven a propitious time for black Americans to gain greater security of their rights. As he wrote in an introduction to the thirtieth-anniversary edition of *Invisible Man*, "Historically most of this nation's conflicts of arms have been—at least for Afro-Americans—wars-within-wars.... And in order for the Negro to fulfill his duty as a citizen it was often necessary that he fight for his self-affirmed right to fight" (IM xii).[12]

As the song ends, Mr. Parker is a jumble of emotions: "A wave of guilt shook him, followed by a burst of relief. He stood in confusion as the song ended, staring into the men's Welsh faces, not knowing whether to curse them or to return their good-natured smiles" (146). The guilt followed by relief indicates a shift of attitude: he moves from his habitual disdain upon hearing words that do not comport entirely with practice to a newfound rest in the knowledge that he had a country, a country worthy of his service and one of which he could be proud and with which he could be identified (even as a "Black Yank"). Mr. Parker is a changed man. He sings the American national anthem with a feeling unbeknownst to him. The fact that he tears up during his singing of it indicates it got to him in a way that is new. If not wholly reconciled to the land of his birth, Mr. Parker comes to new terms with it. He is willing to accept it more, call it his own, even be proud of it, despite the ways it has hurt him. He has learned something new about its contradictions. After all, he did sign up for the merchant marine—just as Ellison did, "as a more democratic mode of service" than the segregated army (IM xiii)—which suggests there was enough about America he believed worth defending even if it did not afford him the full complement of his rights.[13]

Contrast this with the cynicism reflected in Mr. Parker's thought to himself earlier in the story, before the singing began: "Do the State some service. They won't know it. And if these men [his Welsh hosts] should, it doesn't matter" (144). With this gloss on *Othello*, Ellison puts a spin on the original, where Othello says, "I have done the state some service, and they know't. /

No more of that" (act 5, sc. 2, ll. 344–45). By the end of the story, Mr. Parker has shed at least some of his pessimism regarding America, as he sings the national anthem with sincerity: "For the first time in your whole life, he thought with dreamlike wonder, the words are not ironic" (146).

Mr. Parker has found something about America he is willing to defend against its enemies. Somehow he has learned he cannot defend only its good points. Not that he justifies or endorses the evil done by white Americans, but that in an imperfect world, where deeds always fall short of words, words still matter and give birth to deeds, even if not entirely consistent with the words. This is a theme Ellison will return to in *Invisible Man,* especially in the epilogue when Invisible Man mulls over his grandfather's advice and what he calls "the principle" (IM 574–75).

The story closes with the conductor and Mr. Catti commenting on how well Mr. Parker sang. "Why, if he'd stay in Wales, I wouldn't rest until he joined the club," Mr. Morcan said. "What about it, Mr. Parker?"

"But Mr. Parker could not reply. He held Mr. Catti's flashlight like a club and hoped his black eye would hold back the tears" ("Strange Country" 146). The "pressure toward self-scrutiny," as Ellison described it many years later, was almost too much for him to bear (IM xiv). But as Robert Butler observes, what only looks like the result of a physical assault—a blackened eye—at the story's end becomes a symbol of greater vision as a result of Mr. Parker's clarifying interaction with the white Welshmen: "His black eye (146) mentioned in the story's final sentence, therefore, is no longer a sign of pain and blindness; rather, it is an eye that can clearly see the off-beat ironies and complexities of his American identity, endowing his life with 'a vast new meaning' (146)" (Butler, "Ellison's 'Black Eye'" 144). Mr. Parker's heroic self-scrutiny points the way to a national self-scrutiny whereby America would align its political and social practices more closely with its democratic principles, resulting in the acceptance of blacks and other nonwhites into the mainstream of American social and political life.

What would it take for Mr. Parker to join the American club? What would an invitation look like in "the land of the free and the home of the brave"? This is where Ellison's use of the word *inclusion* becomes instructive. He mentioned this in a 1970 *Time* magazine essay entitled "What America Would Be Like without Blacks." There he wrote, "The most obvious test and clue to that perfection [of American democracy] is the inclusion, *not* assimilation, of the black man" (CERE 586). He found the term *assimilation* much too constricting, for it suggests that blacks in America, despite their many years—many generations—in America, made no contribution to its creation, development, or progress. Inclusion also implies that blacks exercised no discernment in what they experienced in the New World. Ellison thought blacks noticed not only those American things (religion, politics, mores, music—that is, culture) worth accepting, holding onto, and incorporating into their individual and communal lives, but also those things in America they had no use for—ways of thinking and acting that should not constitute an American way of life. Taking music as just one example, Ellison maintained that "from the days of their introduction into the colonies, Negroes have taken, with the ruthlessness of those without articulate investments in cultural styles, whatever they could of European music, making of it that which would, when blended with the cultural tendencies inherited from Africa, express their own sense of life, while rejecting the rest" (CERE 285).

Reflecting on the role that blacks have played in the American drama, Ellison observes of the black American that "he sees his own condition as an inseparable part of a larger truth in which the high and the lowly, the known and the unrecognized, the comic and the tragic are woven into the same American skein" (CERE 503). So, to be included, and not merely assimilated, presumed an agency and initiative, thereby according a greater respect for the capacity of "the included" to observe, weigh, sift, and determine for themselves what it means to live in America—which is to say, what it means to live as Americans.

This is a twofold challenge, as far as the American color line is concerned. The challenge posed implicitly by the founding ideals was for the white majority to use its numerical—and hence political—might on behalf of right, the protection of the rights of each individual regardless of race. The challenge for the numerical minority, the racial minority, was to insist that they were included, and therefore deserved the equal protection of their rights and opportunities as full members of the American club. For Ralph Ellison, the "land of the free" reposed a duty upon each member of that land to be "brave" in their understanding and effort to be at home in America. Thus, on various occasions, Ellison referred to black Americans as "an assertive people." Unlike his invisible man (for most of the novel, at least), who refused "to run the risk of his own humanity," black Americans recognized that in the United States, "the obligation of making yourself seen and heard was an imperative of American democratic individualism" (CERE 672, 221, 355).

Bravery for black folks in the United States is precisely what drives the novel *Invisible Man,* in various and sundry guises, not to mention Ellison's unpublished novel *Three Days before the Shooting....* During the writing of *Invisible Man,* Ellison had also written of "the Negro's perpetual alienation in the land of his birth" (CERE 321), a tragic consequence of living in a land where the protection of individual freedom too often meant the freedom of the majority to preserve the color line.

"A people must define itself," Ellison noted, "and minorities have the responsibility of having their ideals and images recognized as part of the composite image which is that of the still-forming American people." He also talks about how art, especially music, was the vehicle for black American "assertion of our own sense of life." No mere acceptance of what the great wide world around them had to offer, especially when that world included oppressive and inhumane ideas and forces. It meant taking it all in, and then weighing, sifting, discerning what was worth keeping, holding onto, what to discard, and then "assert[ing] our hopes and dreams against the complications of living in the South—or for that matter of living in America ... and then determining to go beyond it." Simply put, "It was an assertion of our own sense of life" (CERE 99, 439).

This appreciation of what blacks made of their experience in America belies those critics of Ellison who claim that he denied or ignored the oppressive forces in America that limited the freedoms and opportunities for blacks—as if there was ever a single day that he woke up and forgot what color skin he had. In fact, it was precisely his awareness of these vicious aspects of American history that made him appreciate all the more what blacks were capable of producing when confronted with "definitions of our humanity which we could not accept" (CERE 439). The virtues borne of living in the American crucible where race was invested with mystical significance were qualities Ellison saw and wished more Americans, black and white, noticed, appreciated, perhaps adopted for themselves, but at least recognized for the sustaining forces that they were—sustaining for any individual who was the "target of discrimination," not to mention the nation that benefited from their efforts not only to resist but also to find a way to thrive and build a culture from what they found about them (CERE 823).

This is why Ellison, on several occasions, observed, "Civil rights are only the beginning" (*Living with Music* 248). As he saw it, important as it was to get a level playing field legally, what remained to be seen was what blacks would do with what he called elsewhere "a fair field of testing" (CERE 830). What would blacks do then? What would they reveal by way of their distinctive contribution to American society and culture?

Ellison worried about the next generation of blacks, especially as they headed to college. At Bard, where he taught in 1959, he complained about black students simply imitating the white students, whom he found impoverished in terms "not only of literature, but of life." He was disappointed that none of the black students enrolled in his course or even sought him out to strike up a conversation. He remarked, "Maybe I'll make some contact with the Negroes and try to give them some sense of those things from their backgrounds which they must not lose" (*Trading* 204, 205).

On this point, allow me to quote a passage from *Invisible Man*. The protagonist is daydreaming and he pictures a scene from a Southern black church, a call-and-response sermon:

> "Brothers and sisters, my text this morning is the 'Blackness of Blackness.'"
> And a congregation of voices answered: "That blackness is most black, brother, most black..."
> "In the beginning..."
> "At the very start," they cried.
> "...there was blackness..."
> "Preach it..."
> "...and the sun..."
> "The sun, Lawd..."
> "...was bloody red..."
> "Red..."
> "Now black is..." the preacher shouted.
> "Bloody..."
> "I said black is..."
> "Preach it, brother..."
> "...an' black ain't..."
> "Red, Lawd, red: He said it's red!"
> "Amen, brother..."
> "Black will git you..."
> "Yes, it will..."
> "Yes, it will..."
> "...an' black won't..."
> "Naw, it won't..."
> "It do..."
> "It do, Lawd..."
> "...an' it don't."
> "Halleluiah..."
> "It'll put you, glory, glory, Oh my Lawd, in the WHALE'S BELLY."
> "Preach it, dear brother..."

"... an' make you tempt..."
"Good God a-mighty!"
"Old Aunt Nelly!"
"Black will make you..."
"Black..."
"... or black will un-make you."
"Ain't it the truth, Lawd?" *(IM 9–10)*

Given America's history of racial slavery and segregation, one might title this sermon "The *Bleakness* of Blackness," for there was a lot that was bleak for blacks in America. But this sermon suggests that this would tell only half the story: the "*Blackness* of Blackness" is also meant to suggest those virtues of the black American experience that were forged in the crucible of America's development, by fits and starts, as a free nation. "The history of the American Negro," Ellison insisted, "is a most intimate part of American history" (CERE 214).

Now, bravery for the majority white population in America requires that they wrestle with the "complicated truths" of applying the nation's founding ideals to all members of the American citizenry. As stated by the Reverend A. Z. Hickman, a lead character from *Three Days*: "In this country men can be born and live well and die without ever having to feel much of what makes their ease possible" (TD 415–16). This can be seen, for example, when people discuss the pros and cons of affirmative action. When white opponents of the policy argue that neither they nor their parents or any relations ever owned slaves or discriminated against racial minorities, Ellison would alert them to the fact that their way was paved, nonetheless, by not having to compete against a portion of the population:

> This society has structured itself to be unaware of what it owes in both the positive and negative sense to the condition of inhumanity that it has imposed upon a great mass of its citizens. The fact that many whites refuse to recognize this is responsible for much of the anger erupting among young blacks today. It makes them furious when whites respond to their complaints with, "Yes, but *I* had nothing to do with any of that," or reply to their demands for equal opportunity in a racially rigged society, "We're against a quota system because *we* made it on our individual merits"—because this not only sidesteps a pressing reality, but is only partially true. Perhaps they

did make it on their own, but if that's true the way was made easier because their parents did not have to contend with *my* parents, who were ruled out of the competition. (CERE 808–9)

Ellison acknowledges that there were also plenty of troubles to go around; both whites and blacks had obstacles to overcome. But he adds that "the relative benevolence of democracy shared by their parents, and now by them, was paid for by *somebody* other than themselves, and was being paid long before many of them arrived on these shores.... The point is one of moral perception, the perception of the wholeness of American life and the cost of its successes and failures." So bravery would entail having the courage to construct a more comprehensive account of the development of American progress and prosperity, and this as a basis for ensuring that all Americans get a fair shot at achieving the American dream. Of course, not all white Americans are up to this task. As Hickman notes elsewhere in *Three Days*, they are "caught between what they profess to believe and what they feel they can't do without" (TD 1011).

The challenge of American inclusion is one that reposes upon both whites and blacks, in distinctive ways, given the legacy of black slavery in America. For whites, as the majority of the citizenry, the challenge is managing the freedom inherent in majority rule—exercising their political might in a manner consistent with individual rights. While they committed themselves on paper, as Ellison repeatedly points out, to "sacred principles" that we know as "democracy, equality, individual freedom and universal justice," being human, they are "given to the fears and temptations of the flesh." Thus, America's history as the chronicle of a diverse people comprises an attempt to interpret and apply "abstract, ideal, spiritual" principles that "insist upon being made flesh." As Ellison puts it, "They interrogate us endlessly as to who and what we are; they demand that we keep the democratic faith" (CERE 505, 506).

And so, the closing line of the American national anthem, "The land of the free and the home of the brave"—which Ellison does not write into his story, but which we presume Mr. Parker sings in the final scene ("Strange Country" 146)—provides a hint of what the natural liberty of human beings entails in a republican form of government: namely, whenever people are free to exercise their liberty, they will be required to exercise bravery to make good on that freedom—bravery not only in defense of that freedom but also in its very exercise.

NOTES

1. Ellison wrote this story before the beating and blinding of Isaac Woodard, a black US Army sergeant, became national news in 1946. After his honorable discharge in February 1946, having served in the Pacific on labor detail, Woodard was traveling home by bus from Georgia to North Carolina when he was taken off the bus by South Carolina chief of police Linwood Shull, who with his deputies proceeded to beat and eventually blind Woodward, who was still wearing his army uniform. See Andrew H. Myers, "Resonant Ripples in a Global Pond." For this incident and similar outrages committed during World War II against black veterans, as well as the political aftermath, see Lynda G. Dodd, "Presidential Leadership and Civil Rights Lawyering," and John Egerton, *Speak Now against the Day*.

2. For commentary on this and Ellison's other stories about Wales, see Daniel Williams, "Invisible Man's Welsh Routes," in *Black Skin, Blue Books,* and Daniel Williams, "Emlyn Williams and Ralph Ellison," in *Beyond the Difference*.

3. A few years after he published "In a Strange Country," Ellison wrote "Harlem Is Nowhere," which described "the Negro's perpetual alienation in the land of his birth" (CERE 321).

4. Ellison's interest in music, especially jazz and the blues, can be readily seen in the many essays he wrote about these and other musical genres. See Ellison, *Living with Music*. On Charlie Parker, see Ellison's 1962 *Saturday Review* essay, "On Bird, Bird-Watching, and Jazz" (CERE 256–65).

5. For Ellison's account of the jam session as "the jazzman's true academy," see CERE, 244–46. This same 1959 *Esquire* essay also speaks of mixed jam sessions (CERE 237, 238, 248) where "passing a test of musicianship, sincerity and temperament," and not the American color line, was the criteria of inclusion (CERE 249).

6. Thanks to Daniel Lowenstein for catching this allusion to the first line of the bard's *Twelfth Night*. In this passage, Mr. Parker also dialogues with himself by assuming the persona of Othello. Shakespeare's ambivalent character, something of a persona non grata, suits Mr. Parker's status as a black American serving his country at a time when blacks were not allowed to fight in an integrated army, let alone enjoy the benefits of full citizenship in a segregated America before the 1954 *Brown* decision and the 1964 Civil Rights Act.

7. See the 1976 interview of Ralph Ellison by Ron Welburn (originally published in *The Grackle: Improvised Music in Transition* [1977–78]); Ellison, "Ralph Ellison's Territorial Vantage" in *Living with Music*, 24–25, 28–30.

8. The lyrics of "Land of My Fathers," the national anthem of Wales (1856), read as follows:

This land of my fathers is dear to me,
Land of poets and singers, and people of stature;
Her brave warriors, fine patriots,
Shed their blood for freedom.

Chorus

Land! Land! I am true to my land!
As long as the sea serves as a wall for this pure, dear land
May the language endure forever.

Old land of the mountains, paradise of the poets,
Every valley, every cliff a beauty guards;
Through love of my country, enchanting voices will be
Her streams and rivers to me.

Chorus

Though the enemy have trampled my country underfoot,
The old language of the Welsh knows no retreat,
The spirit is not hindered by the treacherous hand
Nor silenced the sweet harp of my land.

Chorus

"Hen Wlad Fy Nhadau"

Mae hen wlad fy nhadau yn annwyl i mi,
Gwlad beirdd a chantorion, enwogion o fri;
Ei gwrol ryfelwyr, gwladgarwyr tra mâd,
Tros ryddid gollasant eu gwaed.

Chorus

Gwlad, Gwlad, pleidiol wyf i'm gwlad,
Tra môr yn fur i'r bur hoff bau,
O bydded i'r heniaith barhau.

Hen Gymru fynyddig, paradwys y bardd;
Pob dyffryn, pob clogwyn, i'm golwg sydd hardd
Trwy deimlad gwladgarol, mor swynol yw si
Ei nentydd, afonydd, i fi.

Chorus

Os treisiodd y gelyn fy ngwlad dan ei droed,
Mae hen iaith y Cymry mor fyw ag erioed,
Ni luddiwyd yr awen gan erchyll law brad,
Na thelyn berseiniol fy ngwlad.

Chorus

Source: http://www.wales.com/en/content/cms/English/About_Wales/Wales_Fact_File/WelshNationalAnthem/WelshNationalAnthem.aspx (accessed 16 June 2015).

9. Although he laments that black Americans have not produced songs lauding any military successes as the Welsh have (cf. *Three Days* and other writings where Ellison shows a greater appreciation for what blacks have achieved in the midst of white-supremacist oppression, especially through the black church), he realizes the uniqueness of the black experience in America. This uniqueness, which has much to do with the fact that they never developed a wholly separate existence in the face of slavery and segregation (cf. the American Indian on this issue and note Tocqueville's observations), helps explain both why the Welsh achieved in ways black Americans did not and why the American Negro *has* achieved in ways the Welsh have not. In short, where the Welsh exalt their separate identity from the British, the Negro has become more than merely a black man in an ostensibly white America. America's founding creed makes no reference to race, and its culture, especially its religion (Christianity), offered a way of life that did not expressly bar the African from its claims. While America's practice certainly did not live up to her principles, this was not uniformly the case. Moreover, given the nature of mankind, the capacity of individual minds to learn and adapt as well as adopt human ideals, black Americans were able to become Americans despite the efforts of a significant majority who strove to prevent it.

10. "By the rivers of Babylon, there we sat down, yea, we wept, when we remembered Zion. We hanged our harps upon the willows in the midst thereof. For there they that carried us away captive required of us a song; and they that wasted us required of us mirth, saying, Sing us one of the songs of Zion" (Ps. 167:1–3).

11. For a recent account of the origin of the American national anthem and a chronicle of its use and abuse through American history, see Marc Ferris, *Star-Spangled Banner.*

12. On this topic in general, and especially the "Double-V" campaign ("victory over our enemies from without" and "victory over our enemies from within"), see Rawn James Jr., *Double V,* and Jonathan Rosenberg, *How Far the Promised Land?*

13. For a less sympathetic interpretation of the story's patriotism, see Barbara Foley, *Wrestling with the Left,* 124–27. Foley emphasizes earlier drafts that "reveal Ellison's win-the-war patriotism to be laced with ambivalence," and cites an alternative draft that presents Mr. Parker as unrelenting in his desire for revenge against the white servicemen who assaulted him at the story's outset; to wit, "the published versions of his wartime stories repress the decidedly unpatriotic speculation that violence is needed to abolish not just international fascism, but its Jim Crow equivalent" (127). Cf. the 1981 introduction to *Invisible Man,* where Ellison observes that "historically most of this nation's conflicts of arms have been—at least for Afro-Americans—wars-within-wars." Acknowledging that "for the Negro to fulfill his duty as a citizen, it was often necessary that he fight for his self-affirmed right to fight." Ellison goes on to explain that his chief aim was to portray the "conscious struggle for self-definition" (IM xii, xiv). See also William J. Maxwell, "Creative and Cultural Lag," in *Historical Guide to Ralph Ellison,* 59–83, esp. 65, which describes "In a Strange Country" as comprising "elaborate negotiations between American nationalisms and leftist cosmopolitanism." For Ellison's decision to join the merchant marines, see Arnold Rampersad, *Biography,* 167–71, and Lawrence Jackson, *Ralph Ellison: Emergence of Genius,* 282–83, 297–98.

INVISIBLE MAN'S GRANDFATHER AND THE AMERICAN DREAM

STEVEN D. EALY

In "Chiefly about War Matters," an essay published anonymously in the *Atlantic* in July 1862, Nathaniel Hawthorne wrote,

> There is an historical circumstance, known to few, that connects the children of the Puritans with these Africans of Virginia in a very singular way. They are our brethren, as being lineal descendants from the Mayflower, the fated womb of which, in her first voyage, sent forth a brood of Pilgrims on Plymouth Rock, and, in a subsequent one, spawned slaves upon the Southern soil,--a monstrous birth, but with which we have an instinctive sense of kindred, and so are stirred by an irresistible impulse to attempt their rescue, even at the cost of blood and ruin. The character of our sacred ship, I fear, may suffer a little by this revelation; but we must let her white progeny offset her dark one,--and two such portents never sprang from an identical source before.[1]

While it turns out that this is not literally true—the same ship that carried the Pilgrims did not then carry a hold full of slaves to their fate—it could have been true, for there were many "Mayflowers" and some of them carried slaves as cargo. But whether *the Mayflower*, which held out the promise of freedom for the Pilgrims, held out the promise of slavery and death on other journeys, this possibility points to a deep truth about our national history:

the Ship of State carried within it both passengers destined for freedom and passengers destined for slavery,[2] and the races somehow have to make their fates—and that of the nation—together.

This intertwining of freedom and slavery unfolds in many ways in Ralph Ellison's *Invisible Man*, but I will examine it by focusing on a character that bedeviled the novel's narrator from beginning to end. Before we turn to the narrator's grandfather, however, I want to say a word about the unnamed narrator himself.

Traditionally, the character telling this biographical story is identified either as "the narrator" or IM, initials for Invisible Man. This is understandable, both because of the title of the novel and its opening line: "I am an invisible man" (IM 3). While I am following this convention, it should be noted that the novel's narrator gave himself another name. He perhaps anticipated his future readers' inattention to this point by complaining in the epilogue, "I have also been called one thing and then another while no one really wished to hear what I called myself" (IM 573). In the novel's prologue he gave himself a name and an explanation for it: "Call me Jack-the-Bear, for I am in a state of hibernation" (IM 6).

It is worth pausing to consider the implications of the name Invisible Man bestows on himself. First, "Jack-the-Bear" resonates within black folklore and offers a nod toward the Duke Ellington composition of the same name recorded in 1940.[3] Second, thinking of the narrator as Jack-the-Bear or "JB" points to links between *Invisible Man* and other literature. Archibald MacLeish's later Pulitzer Prize–winning drama *JB* also deals with an antagonist who suffers unexpected misfortunes. *JB* is MacLeish's reworking of the biblical story of Job in a contemporary setting, and *Invisible Man* itself contains subtle allusions to the Book of Job.[4] Thus, with Jack-the-Bear, and *Invisible Man* more generally, waves radiate in all directions, with ripples into the future and allusions to the past and present.

Finally, Jack-the-Bear is a trickster, and may be a shape changer. Certainly as the narrator moves through the novel, his appearance seems to change. He points to this possibility when he says, "I am what they think I am" (IM 379).[5] If nothing else, thinking of the narrator as a potential trickster links him closely to other characters in the novel. It ties him even more closely to his grandfather, who has hidden his secret identity for most of his life, and offers proof that he is indeed his grandfather's grandson. Thinking of the narrator as the trickster Jack-the-Bear also suggests that he may have more in common with Rinehart, the character of many guises or disguises, who appears near the conclusion of the novel (IM 483–500, 504, 575–76).

As Invisible Man's story unfolds, he silently changes shape to fit his new situation. Just as the narrator discovers the many sides of Rinehart while walking through Harlem, so too readers see the many faces and voices of Invisible Man as they watch him as high school valedictorian, as an aspiring leader of his race while in college, as a factory worker, as a spokesman for the Brotherhood, and finally as the Underground Man. All of this is simply to suggest that Ellison provides a multitextured narrative, most of which I will ignore in this paper in order to follow one of the many threads that make up this complex novel.

I

As Invisible Man recounted at the beginning of chapter 1, "It goes a long way back, some twenty years" (IM 15). According to Invisible Man, "My grandfather is the one. He was an odd old guy, my grandfather, and I am told I take after him. It was he who caused the trouble" (IM 16). What exactly was this trouble caused by his grandfather? The impetus behind the entire novel is provided by his grandfather's deathbed words. The legacy that Invisible Man's grandfather leaves him is an oracular speech to puzzle over, but we learn through the course of *Invisible Man* that his grandfather also provided him with materials to help him unravel the meaning of his final scandalous words. Invisible Man himself offered a succinct account of the incident.

> On his deathbed he called my father to him and said, "Son after I'm gone I want you to keep up the good fight. I never told you, but our life is a war and I have been a traitor all my born days, a spy in the enemy's country ever since I give up my gun back in the Reconstruction. Live with your head in the lion's mouth. I want you to overcome 'em with yeses, undermine 'em with grins, agree 'em to death and destruction, let 'em swoller you till they vomit or bust wide open." (IM 16)

At this the youngest children holding vigil were whisked out of the room and the grandfather uttered his final order, "Learn it to the younguns." I called the grandfather's words *scandalous* because Invisible Man's parents were scandalized by them; according to Invisible Man, they "were more alarmed over his last words than over his dying" (IM 16). Rather than heeding Grandfather's final command, however, Invisible Man's parents attempted to forget about it and cover over this final indiscretion and embarrassment. Invisible

Man himself "was warned emphatically to forget what he had said," but no doubt in part because of his parent's reaction and in part because the words themselves seemed incongruous, coming as they did from "the meekest of men," Grandfather's final words were indelibly etched on his mind.

Before we turn to the task that occupied Invisible Man throughout his life, understanding just what Grandfather meant by that final speech, I want to examine the things that Grandfather taught Invisible Man during their time together. Grandfather's very last words are those of a lifelong teacher—"Learn it to the younguns."

As a prelude to Grandfather's lessons, let me emphasize a most important fact about his grandfather's life. As presented in Invisible Man's narration, the first thing we learn about Grandfather was that he was born into slavery (IM 15). We also learn Grandfather gave up his gun during Reconstruction and that he heard of and believed Booker T. Washington's "Atlanta Exposition Speech" of 1895:

> About eighty-five years ago they were told that they were free, united with others of our country in everything pertaining to the common good, and, in everything social, separate like the fingers of the hand. And they believed it. They exulted in it. They stayed in their place, worked hard, and brought up my father to do the same. (IM 15–16)[6]

Invisible Man's depiction of his grandparents, incidentally, helps explain the consternation created by the apparently out-of-character outburst of Grandfather on his deathbed.[7] Grandfather himself cautioned that his deathbed speech was uncharacteristically blunt by admitting to Invisible Man's father that he had never before told him that he had been at war his entire life.

I will delineate what Grandfather "learned" Invisible Man, keeping in mind that many of the lessons Grandfather passed on were originally learned while a slave and that everything he learned later was lessons learned by an ex-slave. Grandfather's experiences had taught him to practice what the Reverend Homer A. Barbee, in his address on the Founder, called "the black art of escape" (IM 122). In the Founder's case this art involved first hiding from and evading potential captors, but at a deeper level escape involved learning to hide in plain sight. This is the lesson Grandfather had passed along on his deathbed—"overcome 'em with yeses, undermine 'em with grins, agree 'em to death and destruction" (IM 16).

The black art of escape is grounded in psychology—understanding exactly what whites want (even better than they themselves do) and, at least apparently, giving them exactly that. While talking with the young Mr. Emerson during his first attempt to land a job interview, Invisible Man remembers something that Grandfather told him long ago: "Don't let no white man tell you his business, 'cause after he tells you he's liable to git shame he tole it to you and then he'll hate you" (IM 186). Almost as an afterthought, Grandfather added, "Fact is, he was hating you all the time." The fact that "he was hating you all the time" is a truth that the white man hides from others (at least in polite company), and at the deepest level may be hiding from himself also. If he is particularly good at hiding this truth from himself, he perhaps approximates what Socrates calls the "true lie—the lie in the soul."[8]

Grandfather's lesson was reinforced by Dr. Bledsoe in his meeting with Invisible Man after he had chauffeured Mr. Norton, one of the founding trustees of the college, first to the incestuous Trueblood's shack, and then to the disreputable Golden Day roadhouse for a drink of whiskey. While at the Golden Day, a fight broke out and Mr. Norton fainted. Invisible Man explained to Bledsoe that Norton understood how the incident at the Golden Day occurred, but Bledsoe responded, "Listen to me, boy, . . . Norton is one man and I'm another, and while he might think he's satisfied, *I* know that he isn't!" (IM 140).

Whether Bledsoe is a representative of Grandfather's approach to life or is the antithesis of Grandfather, of course, is a question worth pursuing in some other venue. But it is clear from Invisible Man's conversation with Bledsoe that he had failed to grasp the basics that his grandfather had expounded in his deathbed speech, for Invisible Man apparently cannot imagine the possibility of dissimulation on his own part:

> "But I was only driving him, sir. I only stopped there after he ordered me to . . ."
> "Ordered you?" he said. "He *ordered* you. Dammit, white folk are always giving orders, it's a habit with them. Why didn't you make an excuse? Couldn't you say they had sickness—smallpox—or picked another cabin? Why that Trueblood shack? My God, boy! You're black and living in the South—did you forget how to lie?"
> "Lie, sir? Lie to him, lie to a trustee, sir? Me?"
> He shook his head with a kind of anguish. "And me thinking I'd picked a boy with a brain," he said. (IM 138–39)

Some of Grandfather's lessons were matters of instruction to be learned through investigation, study, or careful thought, and others were matters of practice to be picked up through socialization. Until articulated on his deathbed, Grandfather's approach to dealing with whites remained in the arena of practice and tacit knowledge, so subterranean that it was a shock to consider that this outwardly content and docile man had been duplicitous his entire life.

Another example of Invisible Man's working out of Grandfather's practical lessons surfaced during his fight at the paint factory with his supervisor, Lucius Brockway. "He blanched at being called old, and I repeated it, adding insults I'd heard my grandfather use. 'Why, you old-fashioned, slavery-time, mammy-made, handkerchief-headed bastard, you should know better!'" (IM 227).

When we turn to Grandfather's articulated lessons we discover that he provided coverage of a good deal of the liberal arts curriculum, to include history, psychology (already touched on earlier), political philosophy, and religion and theology. Much of the history that Grandfather taught Invisible Man was his own lived history—the world of slavery, of Reconstruction, and of Jim Crow. Perhaps the prime example of just how much Grandfather knew and the reality of life even for educated blacks in the world of Jim Crow was illustrated by Grandfather's literacy test and its aftermath:

> The thing to do was to be prepared—as my grandfather had been when it was demanded that he quote the entire United States Constitution as a test of his fitness to vote. He confounded them all by passing the test, although they still refused him the ballot. (IM 315)

Questions from the practice of politics to questions of political philosophy were all part of Grandfather's curriculum for Invisible Man. His grandparents "exulted in" Booker T. Washington's vision of one hand and separate fingers, as already noted, and Invisible Man did take to heart what grandfather had to say about Washington. While in high school Invisible Man "visualized [him]self as a potential Booker T. Washington" (IM 18), and he opened his graduation oration with a quotation from Washington's "Atlanta Exposition Address" (IM 29–30). Invisible Man was admittedly confused in his understanding, because the humility championed by Washington and articulated in his oration seemed to be undermined by Grandfather's words of treason and deception. So Invisible Man "delivered an oration in which [he] showed that humility was the secret, indeed, the very essence of progress" while acknowledging (initially only to himself, for he—perhaps unknowingly—had already started to practice that "black art of escape") that he did not believe in the truth of what he was saying but believed "only ... that it worked" (IM 17).

Booker T. Washington was not the only political thinker to whom Grandfather introduced Invisible Man. He tells Brother Tarp, one of the old stalwarts in the Brotherhood's Harlem district office who befriends him, that his grandfather used to tell him about Frederick Douglass. Tarp hangs a picture of Douglass in Invisible Man's office, and we discover again the deep impact Grandfather had on Invisible Man and his resistance to whatever it was that Grandfather was teaching: "I sat now facing the portrait of Frederick Douglass, feeling a sudden piety, remembering and refusing to hear the echoes of my grandfather's voice" (IM 378–79).

Finally, Invisible Man learned something about religion at his grandfather's knee. Grandfather introduced him to Christianity's first theologian, the apostle Paul, through an epigram capturing the crucial moment in Paul's life: "You start Saul, and end up Paul" (IM 381). Grandfather then makes what in a homily would be called the practical application of the biblical story—"When you're a youngun, you Saul, but let life whup your head a bit and you starts to trying to be Paul—though you still Sauls around on the side."

As with many of Grandfather's lessons, this pronouncement takes on an oracular dimension that suggests there are eddies just below the surface that the less observant listener will miss, and that make the application more problematic than first appears. Young Saul was a committed and pious persecutor of Christians,[9] while the apostle Paul was a committed and pious evangelist for Christ. So what Grandfather perhaps seems to be saying—that Saul/Paul is the old story of the normal movement from youthful fervor to seasoned patience and openness—does not really gibe with the biblical story of Saul's conversion. Saul's change of heart, in the biblical account, is not due to lessons learned in the school of hard knocks ("let life whup your head a bit") but to a divine intervention as potent and as mysterious as that encountered by Moses at the burning bush. The original "road to Damascus experience" that changed the course of Paul's fervor but did not dampen it was a vision of Christ talking directly to him—a vision so powerful that it knocked him to the ground and left him temporarily blind.[10] Grandfather's depiction of Saul/Paul concluded by pointing to the complexity of the conversion experience that does capture an essential part of Saint Paul—"you starts to trying to be Paul—though you still Sauls around on the side." Paul himself, through a number of images in his letters, depicts this inner dynamic of a man confronted and saved by God who is still but a man. Paul writes that he was given "a thorn in the flesh"[11] to keep him from becoming conceited.

In Romans he acknowledges the struggle of the will: "For the good that I would, I do not: but the evil which I would not, that I do."[12]

Grandfather also taught Invisible Man something about the ancient concept of fate, even though Invisible Man did not understand it clearly. As Invisible Man was driving Mr. Norton, Norton reflected on his relationship with the Founder and his own role as one of the "original founders" of the school, characterizing his connection with the school as "a pleasant fate" (IM 39, 40). Invisible Man found this expression curious, one that did not fit either with what he had learned in Woodridge's literature class or from his grandfather, "the first person who'd mentioned anything like fate in my presence," for "there had been nothing pleasant" about Grandfather's view and he had unsuccessfully tried to forget about it (IM 40).[13]

Invisible Man's telling of his tale is proof of the success of his grandfather as teacher, because all of these examples of things he learned from him are recounted during the course of the novel. Students can perhaps relate to Invisible Man's attitude toward Grandfather—he had nightmares about him, he felt persecuted by him, he tried to forget what his grandfather had said but could not, and while he could not forget he also could not figure out what the heck it meant. I now will attempt to think along with Invisible Man as he struggled with the meaning and significance of Grandfather's deathbed speech.

II

Invisible Man opened his narrative by telling us that "it goes a long way back, some twenty years" (IM 15) and that it was his grandfather "who caused the trouble" (IM 16). The "trouble," I have shown, was contained in Grandfather's last words. By the time Invisible Man had spun his tale out and settled back to reflect on what he has learned, he admitted that he was "still plagued by his deathbed advice" (IM 574). He tried one more time to sort out what Grandfather meant, musing (to himself, as well as to us) that "perhaps he hid his meaning deeper than I thought, perhaps his anger threw me off—I can't decide" (IM 574).

So Invisible Man began to enumerate the possibilities. "Could he have meant—hell, he *must* have meant the principle, that we were to affirm the principle on which the country was built and not the men" (IM 574). But a careful rereading of the deathbed scene does not yield any obvious discussion of principles; rather, it offered instructions on being a secret traitor behind enemy lines. In his inimitably sardonic way, Invisible Man pointed obliquely to equality as a principle at play in the American experience early in his account: "I am no freak of nature, nor of history. I was in the cards, other things having been equal (or unequal) eighty-five years ago" (IM 15). Is equality perhaps "the principle"?

In the chronology established within the novel, eighty-five years ago was also about the time Booker T. Washington delivered his famous address in Atlanta (IM 15). This roughly coincided with the 1896 Supreme Court decision in *Plessy v. Ferguson,* which established as constitutional law the doctrine of "separate but equal," the legal foundation of Jim Crow. To get at the deeper meaning Invisible Man is searching for, we have to remember the lessons Grandfather taught, especially his knowledge of the Constitution and the two political thinkers he told Invisible Man about: Booker T. Washington and Frederick Douglass.

It is not surprising that Invisible Man's grandfather should have an interest in these two thinkers and activists, because they too were born into slavery: Douglass in Maryland in 1818, and Washington in Virginia in 1856. At a young age Douglass became a house servant in Baltimore, and the matron of the house began to teach him to read and write, in defiance of state law, an education that he continued secretly when the formal lessons ended. At the age of twenty or so, Douglass escaped and made his way to Massachusetts, where he became a well-known antislavery speaker. Born on the cusp of the Civil War, after emancipation the young Washington migrated with his family to West Virginia. Washington worked as a janitor to pay his way through Hampton Normal and Agricultural Institute and is best known for his role in leading Tuskegee Institute from its beginning in 1881 until his death in 1915.

At one level both Douglass and Washington serve as exemplars, models of successful former slaves worthy of emulation. A brief consideration of a representative speech of each might help in determining whether they also inform the intellectual and cultural world of Invisible Man and his grandfather.

Frederick Douglass's "What to the Slave Is the Fourth of July?" was delivered on July 5, 1852, at the invitation of the Ladies Antislavery Society of Rochester, New York. In this Fourth of July oration, Frederick Douglass simultaneously celebrated the courage and honor of the signers of the Declaration of Independence and those who fought and won the American Revolution, and deplored their and the nation's hypocrisy in refusing to extend its principles to all. He began by distancing himself from the signing of the Declaration. "It is the birthday of *your* National Independence, and of *your* political freedom."[14] He rehearsed the colonial struggle with Great Britain in a way that lent itself to a reflection on the contemporary American national scene. Britain, according to Douglass, acted with "that blindness which seems to be the unvarying characteristic of tyrants, since Pharaoh and his hosts were drowned in the Red Sea."[15] British indifference to the colonial cry for liberty set into motion the course of events that eventually lead to American independence, for "oppression makes a wise man mad," and "with brave men there is always a remedy for oppression."[16] Here is Douglass's summary characterization of "the fathers of this republic":

> They were peace men; but they preferred revolution to peaceful submission to bondage. They were quiet men; but they did not shrink from agitating against oppression. They showed forbearance; but that they knew its limits. They believed in order; but not in the order of tyranny. With them, nothing was "settled" that was not right. With them, justice, liberty and humanity were "final"; not slavery and oppression.[17]

Douglas then asked the central question of his address: "What have I, or those I represent, to do with *your* national independence?"[18] He offered an initial response to his question: "I am not included within the pale of this glorious anniversary!"[19] Looking at America "from the slave's point of view," he began his critique:

> Standing, there, identified with the American bondman, making his wrongs mine, I do not hesitate to declare, with all my soul, that the character and conduct of this nation never looked blacker to me than on this 4th of July! Whether we turn to the declarations of the past, or to the professions of the present, the conduct of the nation seems equally hideous and revolting. America is false to the past, false to the present, and solemnly binds herself to be false to the future. Standing with God and the crushed and bleeding slave on this occasion, I will, in the name of humanity which is outraged, in the name of liberty which is fettered, in the name of the constitution and the Bible, which are disregarded and trampled upon, dare to call in question and to denounce, with all the emphasis I can command, everything that serves to perpetuate slavery—the great sin and shame of America![20]

Douglass then provided a sweeping analysis of the internal slave trade, the operation of the Fugitive Slave Law, and the failure of the church to condemn the enslavement of millions.

Douglass concluded by holding out the possibility of the ultimate triumph of liberty for all by rallying to the Constitution rather than the Declaration of Independence. Douglass argued that the Constitution contained "neither warrant, license, nor sanction of" slavery, and that, when "interpreted as it ought to be interpreted, the Constitution is a glorious liberty document." He continued,

> Read its preamble, consider its purposes. Is slavery among them? Is it at the gateway? Or is it in the temple? It is neither. While I do not intend to argue this question on the present occasion, let me ask, if it be not somewhat singular that, if the Constitution were intended to be, by its framers and adopters, a slave-holding instrument, why neither slavery, slaveholding, nor slave can anywhere be found in it.[21]

In Douglass's reckoning, the "plain reading" of the Constitution shows it "to contain principles and purposes, entirely hostile to the existence of slavery."[22] He concluded with a stirring call to action in the hope that the blight of slavery soon would be eradicated.

While Douglass looked ahead to the day in which the promise of liberty would be enjoyed by all, Washington's "Atlanta Exposition Address" was delivered in 1895, three decades after the constitutional abolition of slavery. Washington first addressed fellow Negroes, and then offered some advice to "the white race." He told his black audience that "our greatest danger is that in the great leap from slavery to freedom we may overlook the fact that the masses of us are to live by the productions of our hands, and fail to keep in mind that we shall prosper in proportion as we learn to dignify and glorify common labor." He concluded this portion of his lecture with two cautions: "It is at the bottom of life we must begin, and not at the top. Nor should we permit our grievances to overshadow our opportunities."[23]

To his white audience, Washington warned against employing foreign labor and invited them to look to the "Negroes whose habits you know, whose fidelity and love you have tested ... who have, without strikes and labor wars, tilled your fields, cleared your forests, built your railroads and cities, brought forth treasures from the bowels of the earth."[24] He characterized these black laborers as "the most patient, faithful, law-abiding, and unresentful people that the world has seen,"[25] and then concluded this portion of his address with the image that so captured Invisible Man's grandparents.

> As we have proved our loyalty to you in the past, in nursing your children, watching by the sick bed of your mothers and fathers, and often following them with tear-dimmed eyes to their graves, so in the future, in our humble way, we shall stand by you with a devotion that no foreigner can approach, ready to lay down our lives if need be, in defense of yours, interlacing our industrial, commercial, civil, and religious life with yours in a way that shall make the interests of both races one. In all things that are purely social we can be as separate as the fingers, yet one as the hand in all things essential to mutual progress.[26]

Washington then addressed his entire audience: "There is no defense or security for any of us except in the highest intelligence and development of all."[27] He concluded with a warning. Washington stated that "the agitation of questions of social equality is the extremest folly," and assured his white listeners that "the wisest among my race understand" this and that progress in this area "must be the result of severe and constant struggle rather than of artificial forcing."[28] Finally, Washington offered two hopes, or rather, stated the two things that must prove to be true if his plan for mutual progress and cooperation is to succeed. First, "no race that has anything to contribute to the markets of the world is long, in any degree, ostracized." Second, the leadership and population of the South must unite "in a determination to administer absolute justice, in a willing obedience among all classes to the mandates of law."[29]

The impact of Washington's address on Invisible Man's grandparents was electric: "They believed it. They exulted in it. They stayed in their place, worked hard, and brought up my father to do the same" (IM 15–16). Invisible Man's grandparents lived their lives under the aegis of Booker T. Washington up until Grandfather's final moments. Thus the stage was set for the already documented consternation and puzzlement at Grandfather's deathbed injunction.

These two addresses are separated by more than just a chronological span of four decades. They are separated by the Civil War, the amendment of the Constitution to outlaw slavery and to grant citizenship and voting rights to former slaves and their descendants, the period of Reconstruction, and the move toward Jim Crow. These differences in context in which the addresses were delivered help to explain their difference in tone. One of the puzzles that Invisible Man may have reflected on during his long years of pondering his grandfather's legacy oration was the relationship between Douglass's and Washington's views. Do they offer a complementary perspective on the American system, or do they offer fundamentally different models for black engagement in American politics?

As Invisible Man pondered his grandfather's final words, he developed three possible explanations of what they might mean: first, embrace the moral foundation of the country but reject the immoral men involved with the founding; second, accept the men as well as the principle; or third, accept the principle and realize that we are somehow united with the men by an unbreakable bond. Whether these alternatives move in some sort of progression or whether they are mutually exclusive are questions worth noting. My conclusion, based on the analysis that follows, is that each step taken by Invisible Man offers a deeper and more comprehensive understanding of political morality.

Invisible Man's first interpretation of Grandfather's deathbed speech was that "we were to affirm the principle on which the country was built and not the men, or at least not the men who did the violence" (IM 574). This sounds like the famous claim that we are a "government of laws and not of men," which is often understood to be the foundation of the rule of law. Does this mean Grandfather "knew that the principle was greater than the men, greater than the numbers and the vicious power and all the methods used to corrupt its name?" (IM 574). How does this reading affect our understanding of the people who built the country? Can we distinguish between the vicious and the nonvicious in the nation's founding? What exactly is "the principle" to be affirmed? Where exactly did the principle come from? Is it possible the nation's foundational principle is something "they themselves had dreamed into being out of the chaos and darkness of the feudal past"? (IM 574). Is it possible that the same men who dreamed the founding principle into existence also "violated and compromised [that very principle] to the point of absurdity even in their own corrupt minds"? (IM 574). Were the founders of a pure or a mixed nature? Were all of those involved in the early building of the country complicit and implicated in our foundational violence, or only some?

Invisible Man never clearly articulated what "the principle" was.[30] Was "eighty-five years ago" an impressionistic nod toward Lincoln's "four score and seven," and thus an invitation to look to the Declaration of Independence for "the principle"? The Declaration itself speaks of "these truths"—plural, not singular—that "we hold . . . to be self evident," not of a "principle." Lincoln in the Gettysburg Address made "the proposition that all men are created equal" the cornerstone of the Union. Is a proposition the same as a principle? What are the implications of reducing "these truths" to "the principle"? The Declaration was never specifically mentioned by Invisible Man, but the Constitution was, so perhaps we should look to that document for "the principle." The preamble provides a listing of purposes to be achieved through the Constitution, but again they are multiple rather than one. Is "the principle" to be found there?[31]

Invisible Man's second interpretation of his grandfather's oration is perhaps more confounding than the first. "Or did he mean that we had to take the responsibility for all of it, for the men as well as the principle, because we were the heirs who must use the principle because no other fitted our needs?" (IM 574). What are the implications of this view? Does "taking responsibility for all of it" somehow entail an affirmation of "all of it, . . . the men as well as the principle"? He suggested that "we of all, we, most of all"—meaning the progeny of slaves and ex-slaves, the sons and daughters of Jim Crow, the very targets of discrimination—"had to affirm the principle, the plan in whose name we had been brutalized and sacrificed." Is it possible that in some way even the vicious men of the founding were unwitting benefactors to the descendants of slavery? Invisible Man hinted, but only hinted, at this possibility when he claimed that "we are older than they, in the sense of what it took to live in the world with others." Was the persecution that Invisible Man's "we" had undergone an unanticipated boon, a refining fire that "had exhausted in us, some—not much, but some—of the human greed and smallness, yes, and the fear and superstition"? Was this what Invisible Man meant when he said, "Because we, with the given circumstance of our origin, could only thus find transcendence"?[32]

Invisible Man did not stop here, however, for he considered yet a third possibility: "Did he mean that we should affirm the principle because we, through no fault of our own, were linked to all the others in the loud, clamoring semi-visible world," linked to all others, including the Brother Jacks and the Mr. Nortons? Invisible Man mused, "Had he seen that for these too [that is, the Jacks and the Nortons] we had to say 'yes' to the principle, lest they turn upon us to destroy both it and us?" (IM 575). This possibility, that we are all linked together, suggests that if we cannot all survive together, we will surely fall or fail together.

In *A Man for All Seasons* Thomas More shocks his son-in-law when he says that he would give even the devil the protection of the law.[33] This seems to be the sense of Invisible Man's third alternative, and in a 1956 letter to Albert Murray, Ellison captured the basic point in down-home language that Jack-the-Bear would appreciate:

> Mose is fighting and he's still got his briarpatch cunning; he's just been waiting for a law, man, something solid under his feet; a little scent of possibility. In fact, he's turned the Supreme Court into the forum of liberty it was intended to be, and the Constitution of the United States into a briarpatch in which the nimble people, the willing people, have a chance. And that's what *it* was intend[ed] to be.[34]

But even beyond this there may be another implication contained in this third interpretation: the crucial step in breaking the cycle of violence that we often find in social and political life must be taken by the victims of violence who offer reconciliation rather than retribution when they gain power. This possibility may seem an unfair burdening of people already burdened by repression or violence. Given the experiences documented throughout history, ancient or modern, even raising the possibility that newly empowered peoples might intentionally forgo the use of their power to wreak justice on their former tormentors may be written off as wild utopian daydreaming. Yet something along these lines appears to have taken place when Nelson Mandela assumed the presidency of South Africa.[35] This possibility was a cornerstone in establishing the Truth and Reconciliation Commission, which was charged with investigating crimes during the period of apartheid and considering requests for amnesty on the part of perpetrators of this violence.[36] Concerning the work of this commission, Chairman Desmond Tutu wrote, "Thus, we have trodden the path urged on our people by the preamble to our founding Act, which called on 'the need for understanding but not for vengeance, a need for reparation but not retaliation, a need for *ubuntu* but not for victimisation.'"[37]

In a 2004 interview, Archbishop Tutu explained the meaning of the word *ubuntu*: "*Ubuntu* is a concept that we have in our Bantu languages at home. *Ubuntu* is the essence of being a person. It means that we are people through other people. We cannot be fully human alone. We are made for interdependence, we are made for family. When you have *ubuntu*, you embrace others. You are generous, compassionate."[38] Is this understanding of human interconnectedness and the implications Tutu draws from it an essential component of Invisible Man's interpretation that "we should affirm the principle because we, through no fault of our own, were linked to all the others"?

There is evidence within the novel that a radical commitment to *ubuntu*—to embracing the connectedness of humanity—is indeed implied in Invisible Man's third alternative. In the prologue Invisible Man had asserted that "the invisible victim is responsible for the fate of all" (IM 14). There is even evidence to suggest that Invisible Man himself had begun to practice something along these lines while working for the Brotherhood. While looking down at the crowd that had gathered in Mount Morris Park for Brother Tod Clifton's funeral, Invisible Man wondered what drew all of these people—did they show up because they knew and loved Brother Tod or because this was an opportunity to protest or perhaps to find some common ground or purpose? Then Invisible Man asked himself, "Was either explanation adequate in itself? Did it signify love or politicized hate? And could politics ever be an expression of love?" (IM 452).[39]

These then are the possible interpretations of his grandfather's oration that Invisible Man was turning over in his mind as the novel comes to an end: (1) we can affirm the principle, but reject the men who perpetrated violence, or (2) we can affirm both the principle and the men, or (3) we can affirm the principle and attempt to enter a social dimension of grace through a recognition of our common humanity that links us even to our persecutors.

Invisible Man had not resolved the puzzle left him by his grandfather by the end of the novel, but since his mind would not let him rest (IM 573), he kept at it. And Invisible Man's puzzlement, even after 581 pages, is not the end of the story but is an invitation to his readers and listeners to try to resolve the puzzle also. In saying this, I mean not just the puzzle of his grandfather's closing statement, but also the question of the relationship between Douglass and Washington and the puzzle of the principles of the nation and the status of its founders.[40]

III

Although Invisible Man had not finally unraveled the mystery of his grandfather's last words, there were a few important lessons that he had learned in the course of his narration. As Invisible Man said on more than one occasion, "The end was in the beginning" (IM 571, 6). Perhaps the most important lesson that Invisible Man would ever learn—more important even than unraveling Grandfather's oracle—he revealed to us early on. At the beginning he said, "All my life I had been looking for something, and everywhere I turned someone tried to tell me what it was. I accepted their answers too, though they were often in contradiction and even self-contradictory. I was naïve" (IM 15). In a very basic way, this admission summarizes the entire tale, and near the end Invisible Man confirmed this view of himself by stating, "My problem was that I always tried to go in everyone's way but my own" (IM 573). So what was the lesson Invisible Man learned through his study of his own life? "I was looking for myself and asking everyone except myself questions which I, and only I, could answer. It took me a long time . . . to achieve a realization everyone else appears to have been born with: That I am nobody but myself" (IM 15). The most important thing Invisible Man learned is that there are some questions that he had to ask of and answer for himself.

Invisible Man learned something else of importance in the course of his narrative. After attempting to flee from him for almost the entire novel, Invisible Man discovered that his grandfather was human: "Once I thought my grandfather incapable of thoughts about humanity, but I was wrong" (IM 580). Speaking of Grandfather, Invisible Man said, "He accepted his humanity just as he accepted the principle. It was his, and the principle lives on in all its human and absurd diversity." In some way, Invisible Man's discovery of the importance of love grew out of his acceptance of his grandfather's humanity.[41] Just before he admitted that he was wrong about his grandfather, he reflected on the importance of love: "Too much of your life will be lost, its meaning lost, unless you approach it as much through love as through hate" (580). Invisible Man had become a man of many skills—"I denounce and I defend and I hate and I love"—and he drew as a conclusion from this that "perhaps that makes me a little bit as human as my grandfather" (580). Invisible Man's dawning understanding of his grandfather provides a key link between the personal and the political, and his appreciation of the importance of love relates to Desmond Tutu's emphasis on the importance of *ubuntu*.

In "Why Do We Read Fiction?" Ralph Ellison's friend Robert Penn Warren[42] argues that we are attracted to fiction because we have an ambivalent attitude toward conflict: "We, at the same time we yearn for peace, yearn for the problematic."[43] When we enter into a story,

> we are in suspense to learn how things will come out. We are in suspense, not only about what will happen, but even more about what the event will mean. We are in suspense about the story in fiction because we are in suspense about another story far closer and more

important to us—the story of our own life as we live it. We do not know how that story of our own life is going to come out. We do not know what it will mean. So, in that deepest suspense of life, which will be shadowed in the suspense we feel about the story in fiction, we turn to fiction for some slight hint about the story of the life we live. The relation of our life to the fictional life is what, in a fundamental sense, takes us to fiction.[44]

Since "life more abundantly lived is what we seek,"[45] reading fiction allows us to expand our experience through participation in a "publically available daydream" on one condition—"you have to accept the fact that the name of the hero will never be your own."[46] So, however much we may identify with Invisible Man, I must recognize that I am not Invisible Man and you must recognize that you are not Invisible Man. This does not mean that we cannot learn something about life—even something about our own life—from reflecting on Invisible Man's experience. Perhaps what we can learn about ourselves through reading Invisible Man's story should be designated as structural knowledge—a deeper understanding of the phenomenology of human life—as distinguished from the particular or local knowledge of Invisible Man's own search for understanding and, ultimately, for self-understanding.

The narrator's basic insight learned through the course of this novel—"I was looking for myself and asking everyone except myself questions which I, and only I, could answer"—is one such structural truth. There are some questions we each face that only we ourselves can answer. In the words of the old spiritual,

> You got to walk that lonesome valley
> Well, you got to walk it by yourself
> Ain't nobody else gonna walk it for you
> You got to walk it for yourself.[47]

Invisible Man's answer (or, more accurately, answers, because he had identified a number of possibilities but had not yet decided between them) to the puzzle that bedeviled him throughout the novel, on the other hand, is one that I would characterize as particular knowledge, an understanding of Invisible Man's grandfather. We may be interested in that puzzle also, and we may want to expand our interest from what Grandfather meant to what the United States means, but for an answer to that puzzle we cannot escape doing our own thinking, even as we compare notes with Invisible

Man. Perhaps the Vet's advice to Invisible Man is the novel's lesson for us all: "Be your own father, young man. And remember, the world is possibility if only you'll discover it" (IM 156).

In Invisible Man's meditation on Grandfather's deathbed oration, perhaps we find a melding of Invisible Man's concerns with those that his author was also struggling with. Invisible Man had discovered, in the words of Ralph Ellison, "the clash between the American dream and everyday American reality" (CERE 31). This clash, Ellison believes, can be traced back at least to Thomas Jefferson's draft of the Declaration of Independence, which contained "a flaw similar to the crack that appeared in the Liberty Bell" (CERE 779). So, much in the spirit of his protagonist Invisible Man, Ellison writes, "It ain't the theory which bothers me, it's the practice: My problem is to affirm while resisting."[48]

Finally, I must note Invisible Man's last word to us. His final word was a question: "Who knows but that, on the lower frequencies, I speak for you?" (IM 581). If this sentence is indeed a real question, and not merely a thinly disguised assertion of a "self-evident truth," the answer to the question is not obvious. I would hazard the view that Invisible Man probably does speak for some of us and not for others. Whether he speaks for us individually, however, he certainly attempted to speak to us, and it is in his speaking to us at the deepest levels that the power of this novel resides.

Invisible Man then, and his creator Ralph Ellison, have done us the same good turn that Grandfather did for Invisible Man: they have left us with a riddle to puzzle over, a riddle that may bedevil us and that will enrich us as we turn it over and over in our mind looking for its ever-elusive solution. The end may indeed be in the beginning, as Invisible Man said, but the path to understanding is often a long and winding trail that at times seems to give out right in the middle of a dark wood.

NOTES

1. Nathaniel Hawthorne, "Chiefly about War Matters," by "A Peaceable Man," *Atlantic Monthly* 10, no. 57 (July 1862): 50. Found in *The Centenary Edition of the Works of Nathaniel Hawthorne, Volume XXIII: Miscellaneous Prose and Verse*, edited by Thomas Woodson, Claude M. Simpson, and L. Neal Smith (Columbus: Ohio State University Press, 1994), 420. For the history of the *Mayflower*, see R. G. Marsden, "The 'Mayflower,'" *English Historical Review* 19, no. 76 (October 1904): 669–80.

2. Nathaniel Philbrick adds an interesting twist to these considerations. In 1676, fifty-six years after the Pilgrims' journey to North America, the *Seaflower* departed Plymouth

Colony for the Caribbean with a cargo of 180 Native American slaves. See *Mayflower: A Story of Courage, Community, and War* (New York: Viking, 2006), xiv.

3. Ralph Ellison, "A Special Message to Subscribers," in CERE, 349; Delores V. Sisco, "*Invisible* Man," in *Icons of African American Literature: The Black Literary World*, ed. Yolanda Williams Page (Santa Barbara, CA: Greenwood Icons Series, ABC-CLIO, 2011), 187-210, at 190; Steven C. Tracy, "A Delicate Ear, a Retentive Memory, and the Power to Weld the Fragments," in *A Historical Guide to Ralph Ellison*, ed. Steven C. Tracy (New York: Oxford University Press, 2004), 85–114, at 89. In addition to Jack-the-Bear's place in black folklore, it also relates to tales of Native Americans; see James Teit, "European Tales from the Upper Thompson Indians," *Journal of American Folklore* 29, no. 113 (1916): 301–29, where sec. 4 is "story of bear-boy; or Jack the Bear," at 308–12. Also see Barbara Foley, *Wrestling with the Left*, 411–12.

4. "And I tore myself away, hearing the old singer of spirituals moaning, 'Go curse your God, boy, and die'" (IM 10). This is what Job's wife tells him at Job 2:9. "Sure I had heard of it, but this was *real*" (IM 159). Compare Job's response to God at Job 42:5: "My ears had heard of you but now my eyes have seen you" (New International Version [NIV]). Reflecting upon women giving birth, Invisible Man thinks, "What a hell of a time to be born" (IM 287); compare Job's cursing of the day of his birth in Job, ch. 3.

Both the Book of Job and *Invisible Man* share the same structure: a prologue and epilogue, in a very different style than the bulk of the book, brackets the book's action. There is a long tradition in biblical studies trying to relate the prose prologue and epilogue to the poetic dialogue that makes up the bulk of the text, and some critics argue that the conventional prose brackets are designed to tame or make safe for conventional belief the radical encounter between Job and his friends, and Job and God. See Moshe Greenburg, "Job," *The Literary Guide to the Bible*, ed. Robert Alter and Frank Kermode (Cambridge, MA: Harvard University Press, 1987), 283–304, esp. 283–85 and 299–301. One might ask whether the prologue and epilogue of *Invisible Man* might serve the same function for the novel.

5. This comment points to another passage in which Invisible Man offered a more audacious name for himself by identifying himself with Yahweh. During his encounter with a street vendor, he quipped, "I yam what I am!" (IM 266). When Moses asked God who he should say had sent him to the Israelites to deliver them, God replied, "I AM WHO I AM" (Exod. 3:14). A few pages later Invisible Man said exactly that: "Never mind, I am who I am" (IM 269). In a letter to Ellison dated February 9, 1952, Albert Murray wrote, "By the way, *Invisible Man* equals IM equals I'M equals I AM"; see Ellison and Murray, *Trading Twelves*, 32.

6. Booker T. Washington said, "In all things that are purely social we can be as separate as the fingers, yet one as the hand in all things essential to mutual progress." See "Atlanta Exposition Address (September 18, 1895)," *African-American Social and Political Thought 1850–1920*, ed. Howard Brotz (New Brunswick, NJ: Transaction, 1992), 358.

7. For a similarly jarring scene, see the apparent deathbed renunciation of her faith by the Prioress in Francis Poulenc, *Dialogues of the Carmelites* (Milan: Ricordi, 1998), 90–100 (act 1, sc. 4). The libretto is based on Georges Bernanos, "The Dialogues of the Carmelites," *The Heroic Face of Innocence* (Grand Rapids, MI: Eerdmans, 1999), 75–77.

8. Plato, *Republic*, Book II, 382a–382d.

9. Acts of the Apostles 7:58–8:3.

10. Acts of the Apostles 9:1–30.

11. 2 Corinthians 12:7 (Authorized [King James] Version [AV]).

12. Romans 7:19 (AV). See the entire passage, Romans 7:14–25. Paul also writes some important things on the question of slavery in Galatians 3:28 and the short letter to Philemon. The letter to Philemon deals with a slave, Onesimus, whom Paul is returning to his master Philemon. This letter was used by proslavery advocates in the antebellum debate to prove that slavery was justified by the Bible. In my judgment, a careful reading of the letter shows that Onesimus is being returned so that Philemon may act as his Christian brother and free him voluntarily rather than being instructed or ordered to do so by Paul.

13. Paul Tillich offers a penetrating perspective on fate in his discussion of the polarities of human existence—"individuality and universality, dynamics and form, freedom and destiny"—in volume 1 of his *Systematic Theology* (Chicago: University of Chicago Press, 1951), 165. For Tillich our destiny involves where we begin, not where we end up. In relation to this understanding of fate or destiny, cf. Invisible Man's late encounter with Mr. Norton (IM 578) and consider Invisible Man's comment in the prologue: "But that's getting too far ahead of the story, almost to the end, although the end is in the beginning and lies far ahead" (IM 6; cf. 571).

14. Douglass, "Meaning," 182.

15. Ibid., 184.

16. Ibid.

17. Ibid., 186.

18. Ibid., 188 (emphasis added).

19. Ibid., 189.

20. Ibid., 190.

21. Ibid., 202. Cf. Ellison: "The Constitution marked the gloriously optimistic assertion and legitimization of a new form of authority and the proclaiming of a new set of purposes and promises" (CERE 778).

22. Douglass, "Meaning," 202.

23. Washington, "Atlanta Exposition Address," 357.

24. Ibid.

25. Ibid., 358.

26. Ibid.

27. Ibid.

28. Ibid., 359.

29. Ibid.

30. See James Seaton, "Affirming the Principle," *Ralph Ellison and the Raft of Hope: A Political Companion to "Invisible Man,"* ed. Lucas E. Morel (Lexington: University Press of Kentucky, 2004), 22–36, esp. 25–33.

31. Ellison referred to the Declaration of Independence, the Constitution, and the Bill of Rights as "the 'sacred documents' of this nation" (CERE 412). He frequently discussed these documents, either together or separately (see CERE, 299–300, 412–16, 458–62, 777–79, 781–83, 844).

32. This reading is reminiscent of a comment made by Jack Burden, the narrator of Robert Penn Warren's *All the King's Men* (New York: Harcourt Brace, 1982 [1946]): "I tried to

tell her how if you could not accept the past and its burden there was no future, for without one there cannot be the other, and how if you could accept the past you might hope for the future, for only out of the past can you make the future" (435).

33. MORE: And go he should, if he was the Devil himself, until he broke the law!
ROPER: So now you'd give the Devil benefit of law!
MORE: Yes. What would you do? Cut a great road through the law to get after the Devil?
ROPER: I'd cut down every law in England to do that!
MORE: Oh? And when the last law was down, and the Devil turned round on you—where would you hide, Roper, the laws all being flat? This country's planted thick with laws from coast to coast—man's laws, not God's—and if you cut them down—and you're just the man to do it—d'you really think you could stand upright in the winds that would blow then? Yes, I'd give the Devil benefit of law, for my own safety's sake."

Robert Bolt, *A Man for All Seasons* (New York: Vintage International, 1990 [1960]), 66.

34. Letter from Ralph Ellison to Albert Murray (16 March 1956), *Trading Twelves*, 116–17.

35. See the chapter entitled "Forgiving" in Anthony Sampson, *Mandela: The Authorized Biography* (New York: Alfred A. Knopf, 1999), 512–25. Consider this exchange from an interview:

Richard Stengel: Sometimes people do criticize you for not being a more rousing speaker.
Mandela: Well, in a climate of this nature, when we are trying to reach a settlement through negotiations you don't want rabble-rousing speeches. You want to discuss problems with people soberly, because the people would like to know *how* you behave or how you express yourself, and then they can have an idea of how you are handling important issues in the course of these negotiations. The masses like to see somebody who is responsible and who speaks in a responsible manner. They *like* that, and so I avoid rabble-rousing speech. I don't want to incite the crowd. I want the crowd to understand what we are doing and I want to *infuse* a spirit of reconciliation to them.
Stengel: Would you say your speaking style is different now than in the old days before you went to prison?
Mandela: Well, I have mellowed, very definitely, and as a young man, you know, I was very *radical* and using high-flown language, and fighting everybody. But now, you know, one has to lead and . . . a rabble-rousing speech therefore is not appropriate.

Nelson Mandela, *Conversations with Myself* (New York: Farrar, Straus and Giroux, 2010), 325–26. John Carlin offers an astute journalistic account of the social and political dynamics of Mandela's effort to make South Africa one nation in *Playing the Enemy: Nelson Mandela and the Game That Made a Nation* (New York: Penguin Press, 2008).

36. "Perpetrator and victim are not always fixed labels." Desmond Tutu and Mpho Tutu, *Made for Goodness* (New York: HarperCollins, 2010), 145; also see the discussion of "being heard into healing" on 146–56. During the hearings of the Truth and Reconciliation Commission, Tutu said that "yesterday's oppressed can quite easily become today's oppressors.... We've seen it happen all over the world and we shouldn't be surprised if it happens here" (Anthony Sampson, *Mandela: Authorized Biography*, 523).

37. Desmond Tutu, "Foreword by Chairperson," *Truth and Reconciliation Commission of South Africa Report*, 5 vols. (29 October 1998), 1:8, para. 32, http://www.justice.gov.za/trc/report/finalreport/Volume%201.pdf (accessed 3 April 2015). For an assessment of the work of the Truth and Reconciliation Commission, see Donald Woods, *Rainbow Nation Revisited: South Africa's Decade of Democracy* (London: André Deutsch, 2003), 192–201. Here is a summary statement from Woods that offers a balanced evaluation:

> So the Truth Commission succeeded not only in educating many South Africans about their country's past but also in educating them about the real nature of their compatriots on both sides of the divide. Many of the families of victims said they were finally at peace after hearing what had really happened to their loved ones, and many said that being able to locate and bury their bodies meant more to them than revenge against the killers. As to whether the process achieved reconciliation, the answer had to be a mixed one, a yes and no. No, in the sense of replacing all resentment and bitterness with forgiveness and love.... But yes, in the sense that there were striking examples of perpetrators and victims reconciling and even embracing. (193–94)

A similar assessment is offered in Allister Sparks and Mpho Tutu, *Tutu: Authorized* (New York: HarperCollins, 2010), 229–30. Archbishop Tutu offers his own detailed account of the purpose and activities of the Truth and Reconciliation Commission in *No Future without Forgiveness* (New York: Doubleday, 1999). Ellison reflects on this same dynamic in terms of catharsis. Consider this note to himself in his working papers: "n.b. Richard Wright attempted to depict pollution but shied away from catharsis because he saw it as allowing 'white' people off the hook. His motive was to punish" (Ralph Ellison Papers, Library of Congress, ms. box I:141, folder 1, n.p.).

38. "Desmond Tutu's Recipe for Peace," http://www.beliefnet.com/Inspiration/2004/04/Desmond-Tutus-Recipe-For-Peace.aspx?p=1 (accessed 3 April 2015). Also see Tutu and Tutu, *Made for Goodness*: "*Ubuntu* is the Xhosa word used to describe the 'end and befriend' survival behavior. *Ubuntu* recognizes that human beings need each other for survival and well-being. A person is a person only through other persons, we say. We must care for one another in order to thrive" (15); "As I described earlier, in our own South African lexicon godly perfection is described by the multifaceted concept of '*ubuntu*.' *Ubuntu* recognizes the interconnectedness of life. My humanity, we say, is bound up with your humanity. One consequence of *ubuntu* is that we recognize that we all need to live our lives in ways that ensure that others may live well. Our flourishing should enhance the lives of others, not detract from them.... God's invitation to wholeness always includes more than ourselves. God's invitation to wholeness is *ubuntu*" (47); "The logic of Christian faith—indeed, the logic of

ubuntu—is that our lives are not all about us" (75); "Compassion teaches us to sit with the father of the prodigal knowing that the story might not end as we hoped. *Ubuntu* theology is an understanding of life that values community. *Ubuntu* affords us the ability to endure knowing that our suffering in this moment may not be redeemed in our lifetime. *Ubuntu* allows us to affirm Dame Julian of Norwich when she observes that, in the fullness of time, 'all shall be well. . . . And all manner of things shall be well.' Even when suffering holds no gifts for its victims, in the spirit of *ubuntu*, it can yield gifts for the wider community" (108).

In *No Future without Forgiveness* Tutu offers an important discussion of justice:

> One might go on to say that perhaps justice fails to be done only if the concept we entertain of justice is retributive justice, whose chief goal is to be punitive, so that the wronged party is really the state, something impersonal, which has little consideration for the real victims and almost none for the perpetrator. We contend that there is another kind of justice, restorative justice, which was characteristic of traditional African jurisprudence. Here the central concern is not retribution or punishment. In the spirit of *ubuntu*, the central concern is the healing of breaches, the redressing of imbalances, the restoration of broken relationships, a seeking to rehabilitate both the victim and the perpetrator, who should be given the opportunity to be given the opportunity to be reintegrated into the community he has injured by his offense. This is a far more personal approach, regarding the offense as something that has happened to persons and whose consequence is a rupture of relationships. Thus we would claim that justice, restorative justice, is being served when efforts are being made to work for healing, for forgiving, and for reconciliation. (54–55)

39. For a subtle explication, John F. Callahan, "The Lingering Question of Personality and Nation in *Invisible Man*: 'And could politics ever be an expression of love?,'" *Ralph Ellison and the Raft of Hope: A Political Companion to "Invisible Man,"* ed. Lucas E. Morel (Lexington: University Press of Kentucky, 2004), 218–29.

40. I deal with some of the puzzles surrounding the Constitution in "Publius on 'Liquidation' and the Meaning of the Constitution," *History, on Proper Principles: Essays in Honor of Forrest McDonald*, ed. Stephen M. Klugewicz and Lenore T. Ealy (Wilmington, DE: ISI Books, 2010), 49–64. If I had to identify one principle as "the principle" foundational to America, I would say "self-government" (see ibid., 63–64). For a discussion of the differing American and British understanding of "self-government," see Hans Eicholz, "Self-Government and the Distinctive Character of American Civil Society," *Ideas on Liberty* 51, no. 7 (July 2001), 8–12.

41. Cf. Warren, *All the King's Men*: "And that meant that my mother gave me back the past. I could now accept the past which I had before felt was tainted and horrible. I could accept the past now because I could accept her and be at peace with her and with myself" (432).

42. Steven D. Ealy, "'A Friendship That Has Meant So Much': Robert Penn Warren and Ralph W. Ellison," *Ralph Ellison's "Invisible Man": New Edition*, ed. Harold Bloom (New York: Infobase, 2009), 127–40.

43. Robert Penn Warren, "Why Do We Read Fiction?," *New and Selected Essays* (New York: Random House, 1989), 56.

44. Ibid. See Tutu and Tutu, *Made for Goodness*: "The grace of unanswered prayers is the knowledge that we are subjects in the story of our own lives. We all have some creative authority in the course of history" (104–5).

45. Warren, "Why Do We Read Fiction?," 56.

46. Ibid., 58.

47. This traditional American gospel song, recorded by many artists over the years, is available at many websites with slight variations. Among the artists with renditions available online are Mississippi John Hurt, George Jones, Bruce Springsteen, Woody Guthrie, and the group Alabama. Most of these links feature both a performance and written copy of the lyrics. The version here is based on memory.

48. Callahan, "Lingering Question of Personality and Nation," 225.

MOURNING AND MELANCHOLY
Explaining the Ellison Animus

ROSS POSNOCK

> "Be your own father"
> —THE VET, *INVISIBLE MAN*, 156

We all know that Ralph Ellison, both the work and the man, have incited controversy, but that it remains unabated is worth remarking, as one veteran scholar did at the March 2012 Ellison conference, noting the intensity with which scholars and critics have gone after Ellison. Perhaps he had in mind the scorn of Houston Baker, the first black president of the Modern Language Association, who in 1999 wrote that as the civil rights and Black Power movements got underway in the sixties and seventies, "Ellison reclined in butter-soft seats at exclusive Manhattan clubs. . . . America's industrial, democratic, lobotomizing machine—like the sleep of reason—had produced a clubbable monster in Ellison" (Rampersad 548). Yet the animus began decades before, with the publication of *Invisible Man* in 1952, and Ellison, at least at first, put it to excellent use—his most famous and influential essay is a response to the criticism of Irving Howe, whose early '60s lament from the left regarding the absence of "clenched fist militancy" in the novel sparked Ellison's epochal statement of intellectual freedom, "The World and the Jug." It is fair to say that Howe summed up at the time and predicted the basic terms of the "case" against Ellison, a judgment that offered a seemingly stark choice: between the artistic freedom of the modernist artist or the responsibilities of political engagement, grounded in racial representativeness. Even though the brilliant rebuttal of "The World and the Jug" complicated these terms, refusing the simplistic opposition between politics and art, the binary leftist case has been repeated in various inflections throughout the decades.

But with the 2007 publication of Arnold Rampersad's biography a new element in the critique entered, one less political, more personal, and yet collective, as if Rampersad's stress on Ellison's human foibles and failings gave voice to a generational sense of grievance. It is this affect—of grievance mixed with melancholy, stemming from a disappointed idealized sense of Ellison—that the following pages selectively document, describe, and attempt to explain. My examples are Rampersad's biography and Barbara Foley's 2010 critical study, *Wrestling with the Left: The Making of Ralph Ellison's "Invisible Man."* The latter is perhaps a less likely source of personal disappointment given the seemingly impersonal, staunchly Marxist critique she levels at the novel. Foley undertakes an exhaustive reading of the novel's ur-text and Ellison's apprentice short fiction of the thirties and forties. Yet I argue that both critics, in their different ways, enact the unresolved mourning that is melancholy, to borrow and adapt Freud's terms in "Mourning and Melancholia."

Ellison once told this little anecdote, his response to a young white professor who remarked to him: "'Mr. E., how does it feel to be able to go to places where most black men can't go?' Said I to him, 'What you mean is, how does it feel to be able to go places where most white men can't go'" (Rampersad 468). Where Ellison went, where most people, black or white, "can't go," made him a pioneer—the first "Negro" (his preferred term) to publish a novel that entered the canon of masterpieces of world literature and the first black author to be accorded all the honors and celebrity and prestige that the United States could bestow on a writer—White House dinners (President Johnson became a friend); six-figure endowed university chairs (NYU's Schweitzer Professor); ubiquity in a host of media, including magazines, television, and the college lecture circuit; trustee/member/adviser on the loftiest boards and social clubs and honorary societies. About all that was missing, alas, was that fabled call to Stockholm; the one that Toni Morrison received in 1993 and that Barack Obama would get in the following decade. It is to the president—who also, of course and even more spectacularly, has gone where most men or women, black or white, "can't go"—that I eventually want to compare Ellison, particularly to compare the dynamic of idealism and hostility that they both incite as unprecedented icons and targets. Have the burdens of being an exemplar ever been more onerous?

What follows attempts to make psychological sense of the animus against Ellison. Yet the very familiarity of this topic is enough to warn one away or to foreclose the matter by classifying Rampersad and Foley as simply recent inflections of Irving Howe. I think Rampersad and Foley are related to Howe but express something new: a certain affect of disappointment. For them, Ellison, for all his lavish gifts—indeed precisely because of them—induces a sense of frustration. An "if only" and a wistful "what might have been" hovers, threatening to define his legacy for these critics—which is to say that Ellison stimulates a fantasy of possibility that expresses his critics' neediness. "What might have been" presides over Rampersad's biography, which often all but says: if only Ellison had been a generous, encouraging father/mentor/colleague to more and younger and female black artists, spending less time drinking martinis at the Century Club with patrician white folk and more time nurturing his people. And when he did help younger writers he admired—Stanley Crouch or James Alan Macpherson, for instance—why did he have to be so candid and critical in recommending them? Why so parsimonious both emotionally and financially? Why so hungry for and relishing of friendship with whites of power? What made him display a surface impeccability in dress and manners but without "real serenity," as Cornel West said of Ellison, whom West admired while regretting his exorbitant (to West) "American nationalism" (Rampersad 549). Perhaps serenity's alleged absence was one manifestation of what Rampersad correctly calls the "high psychological price he had paid for his success"—the price of "distance" from his only living sibling, Herbert, and the lifelong "challenge of appeasing or evading" the parental ghosts, the father, who died early when Ellison was three, whom he revered in memory; and the mother whom he loved, ignored, and was ashamed of in her poverty (Rampersad 266). Ellison once told Richard Wright: "We are not the numbed, but the seething. God! It makes you want to write and write and write, or murder" (145). And James Baldwin, in an oft-quoted remark, said that Ellison was the angriest man he knew.

While it is worth remarking the uniquely personal sources of Ellison's pain, his numbness and his seething, it is equally important to step back and understand that his affect is not simply nor solely personal but inescapably registers collective trauma: a representative man, a race pioneer, enduring the humiliation, entangled with enjoying the privileges, of white-supremacist paternalism. About the psychic disfigurement inflicted by white America no one was more candid than the prodigiously gifted and accomplished W. E. B. Du Bois, another chilly elitist father. In *Dusk of Dawn* (1940) he wrote of the "group imprisonment" of caste segregation that made him a "group man" rather than "an individual." Of the "spiritual provincialism" into which he had been born, Du Bois writes: "This fact has guided, embittered, illuminated and enshrouded my life" (*Writings* 651, 656). In short, given that white supremacy emptied or attenuated the very notion of the free individual even for the most creative black Americans, psychological speculation needs to maintain a double register that acknowledges the primacy of "group imprisonment" that makes individual and collective difficult to separate. And perhaps this double perspective is most needed when the person under discussion seems a proud exception, an indomitable individualist who had "made a decision early on that he wasn't going to let racism consume him," as an old friend said of Ellison (Rampersad 503).

Rampersad's relation to Ellison displays both deep disappointment and idealization. The latter impulse is harder to detect but produces his sense of injury evident in his biography's pervasive frustration and sadness at what he emphasizes as Ellison's moral and human limitations. The frustration is inevitably Oedipal and all but confessed; Rampersad remarks that to many of the best younger writers Ellison was "perhaps the cold, fearsome father, or the absent but haunting father." And when he quotes David Remnick's long list of black writers whose "integrationist vision" clearly derives from Ellison, Rampersad cannot help but add: "In fact, Remnick might also have named almost every black American artist, male or female, of any consequence and complexity, including many who, viscerally offended or simply turned off by what they saw as Ralph's elitism, did not wish to be identified with him" (548, 563). Love him or hate him, this difficult, unsentimental man, schooled in pain by a father who deserted him in death, was the Father whose love, or at least notice, one craved. Given the cathexis, the rage of his progeny was inevitable. This is the psychological ground of the grievance against Ellison that Rampersad unconsciously but unmistakably sets before us as the basic lens through which he writes his biography. The emotional color the lens projects is "melancholy," which is the word Rampersad quotes Toni Morrison using to describe Ellison's attenuated career, based, for her, on the contrast between "the largeness of *Invisible Man*" and the "narrowness of his public encounters with blacks." She adds: "For him, in essence, the eye, the gaze of the beholder, remained white" (549).

But another current in Rampersad's book portrays Ellison as the chilly father, and as the sacrificial victim of his own near inhuman rigor. Here is Rampersad dilating on Ellison's possible thoughts upon hearing the news of his old friend, the sociologist Horace Cayton's lonely death in a Paris hotel:

"He may well have reflected on the fact that of the promising young black writers and intellectuals on the scene around 1940, he was one of the few ... still visible. And he had surpassed them all. Only his failure to finish his second novel, as well as the pain caused by his refusal to kneel before anti-intellectualism, separatism, and cynicism, still challenged him. He could do little about them except to soldier on. He would not resign his vocation as an artist, and he could not give in to what he saw as the lunacy of the age" (465). In the background of this portrait of self-justification, we can practically hear Sinatra's "My Way"—the bootstrap anthem to indomitable individualism. Later Rampersad reprises this note, as he speaks of the "inevitable" "pain" of holding tenaciously to beliefs and ideals (the promise of American democracy) that are "constantly violated": "pain was inevitable. The duty of the writer is to speak truth to power," but also, quoting Ellison, "to accept the punishment that goes with telling the truth" (561). Punishment was not in short supply, indeed was right at hand given Ellison's inability to finish his decades-long writing of his second novel. "The longer the book remained unfinished," said his friend Stanley Crouch, "the more excruciating the pain. And for a long time, sadly, he lived with a constant sense of having failed" (Rampersad 551).

Ellison's self-sacrifice, his embrace of the punishment and pain that come with truth-telling, is itself impressive but as a legacy it seems more bruising than inspiring, for it operates by inflicting its own painful judgments. His chilliness to a Toni Morrison, a Nicki Giovanni, an Arnold Rampersad (for the biographer narrates his own, now infamous, encounter with Ellison's stingy hospitality) understandably rankled. But because the personal sense of injury still lingers, it obstructs the achievement of a necessary intellectual distance that might breed historical empathy founded on the attempt to inhabit both Ellison's perspective and the larger political and psychic trauma in which his generation, like Du Bois's, was embedded. This double perspective might permit us to see Ellison's public behavior apart from our purely personal disappointment, and even consider the strengths of his civic life. Yes, the great man could be arrogant and cold, too self-consciously "the great man." But what else, other than pride and pain, did his extremely active public life mean? And what did it accomplish? In sum, because the "if only" lament is so paramount, *Ralph Ellison: A Biography* is suffused with unresolved grievance, as if Ellison's source of angry stoical isolation—his father's desertion to death—doomed him to repeat it, as he became an absent father to a (legitimately) needy younger generation that, in turn, must suffer attachment to a figure unable to gratify them. *Tragedy* is the word both Toni

Morrison and Stanley Crouch use to describe Ellison's later life, and the sense of terrible inevitability, even a Greek necessity, it imparts makes the word apt as both a personal and collective judgment.

In classical Freudian terms, melancholy is what occurs when the work of mourning cannot be completed, when the bereft one unconsciously holds on to the lost object, unable to let it go, and the other remains morbidly alive. The lost object that Barbara Foley clings to is a heroic proletarian character—Leroy—that Ellison invented early in composing *Invisible Man* only to excise before publication. She dubs him "the invisible man within *Invisible Man*" (Foley 13). The uncompleted work of mourning manifested in an idealizing "if only" presides implicitly over Foley's exhaustive and fascinating examination of Ellison's ur-text housed in the Library of Congress. Foley valuably brings to light Ellison's early drafts but, unfortunately, makes them her sole critical lens for assessing the published novel. She judges *Invisible Man* as a monument of missed opportunities and she now asks us to see it as a "conflicted and contradictory text bearing multiple traces of his struggle to repress and then abolish the ghost of his leftist consciousness and conscience" (7). One doesn't even need to read between the lines; for Foley, a good deal of political bad faith attends Ellison's struggle, from which he emerged that flattest of stick figures: postwar cold warrior who published "a far less humane and anti-racist novel than it might otherwise have been" (23). If only Ellison had retained the key figure of the early drafts—Leroy, the kingly proletarian Promethean radical, organic intellectual, merchant seaman, interracial union organizer whom Ellison had invented as his protagonist's secret sharer, the "black face of negation" that kept the naive narrator honest. With Leroy retained (instead of what remained of him, the kingly doomed Tod Clifton), then *Invisible Man* would have been a novel that Marxists would revere and Ellison could be spoken of in the same hushed tones with which one invokes Paul Robeson. Instead, the published *Invisible Man* "beckons the world's people away from anti-colonial rebellion and socialism" to become cheerleaders for American cold war liberal pluralism, whereas Robeson, advocate of proletarian internationalism, sacrificed a great career and incurred persecution because he urged African Americans to become "leading participants in the world-historical process that would free all dispossessed people from their chains" (Foley 348).

Foley concludes with a pitch for the contemporary relevance of the urtext *Invisible Man*: "Invisible man's original plan for expanding his own and others' humanity, suitably updated" for the twenty-first century, "continues to require serious consideration. That we have witnessed over the past decade the readiness of not one but two black secretaries of state to affirm the imperatives of Wall Street, ... and have since then elected a black president who looks through and past the 'black face of negation' [Leroy's phrase] staring back at him both at home and abroad, indicates the need for fundamental systemic change—not simply change we can believe in. ... As Leroy urged, we cannot afford to file and forget" (349). Thus Foley's efforts at resurrecting the true Marxist king that Ellison created and destroyed end on a wistful note of nostalgia for what might have been had Leroy been our guide. Indeed, he had hoped to be president. Foley's disappointment is the bitter irony of seeing black Americans attain great power yet refuse, like Ellison, to get with the Marxist program. When blacks betray their assigned political identity, when they cannot be counted on to fulfill the world historical mandate of political liberation that they bear, evidently, as a birthright, then "fundamental systemic change" is required. Brother Jack could not have said it better. Foley's necessitarianism inscribes the black subject as a preordained revolutionary subject; if deviation occurs, disappointment is inevitable. To be sure, Foley's disappointment is not Rampersad's; whereas he regrets the selfishness of Ellison's self-possession, she regrets that he and his novel grew beyond his thirties Marxism. But for both critics Ellison remains stubbornly alive in his power to betray, still the seductive imago inducing gnawing frustration.

Foley's implied linkage of Ellison and Obama is worth pausing over (and it is worth noting that two essays in the present collection, by Bryan Crable and John Callahan, examine this linkage in detail.) In college Obama read *Invisible Man* so often he wore out his copy. One thing that connects these men—both inward, detached, even distant, intellectuals—is a capacity to incite the highest hopes and the deepest disappointment. A certain ambiguity about race loyalty also is present—many have commented on Obama's preference, even alleged deference, to white Ivy League advisers. "A History of Disappointment" is the title of a recent Jackson Lears essay on Obama's life, the title referring to the legacy of the grandiose, gifted, self-destructive father of the future president, a largely absent father whom his son idealized. After Obama senior drank himself to death, dying in a car wreck at forty-six, his son eventually had to come to grips with the bitter reality of his father's failures and disgrace. In the wake of his father's quick exit as well as his mother's busy career and remarriage, the son was left to rely on himself. Lears depicts Obama as an "isolato" trapped in a circle of disappointment, recoiling from its parental embodiment but as president producing it in his cautious, even timid, leadership style. And, in turn, that style is another imprisonment, manifested in the imperative "to never be angry regardless of the offense" (Lears 13)—a pacifying strategy that is mandatory for black professionals to "soothe race consciousness among whites," a strategy that, wrote Ta-Nehisi Coates in a thoughtful *Atlantic* essay, is "part of Obama's genius."

Not surprisingly, Obama's remarkable autobiography, *Dreams from My Father*, is unlike any politician's memoir: it exudes melancholy from start to finish, as well as an unsentimental acuteness of judgment, even about those closest to him. Obama's public life as community organizer coexisted with an emotional solitude. On the eve of announcing his candidacy in 2006, Obama declared: "I'm not Bill Clinton. I don't need this [the cheering crowds]. I don't need anything" (Lears 13). Conquering neediness in himself, or disguising it in cool detachment, Obama, like Ellison, aroused it in others, particularly the need to project fantasies of momentous liberating possibility, as if invited to do so by the reserve of Obama's proud autonomy comprised of a palpable intelligence and gravitas. But as father in chief he proffers no invitations and instead often seems frustratingly diffident and detached. *Why can't he show some passion, some heat, why has he turned the presidency into a seminar*... these soon became familiar laments, as his reluctance to love and nurture (*feel your pain*) made disappointment inevitably the dominant reaction of many on the left and right, notwithstanding his empathic candor about the death of young Trayvon Martin ("If I had a son, he would look like Trayvon") or his public tears when discussing the massacre in Sandy Hook.

I am not denying, by the way, the many legitimate political reasons for feeling disappointed in the president; nor, for that matter, the legitimate reasons for being disappointed in Ellison; but these reasons have not been my concern here. Rather, my focus has been on the less rational dynamics of disappointment—a fixation on the "if only," the sad yearning for more and for the might have been that seems, for many, to define their relation to these two men. How to get past this melancholy dwelling in the unappeasable, which breeds the need to allegorize and fantasize? Perhaps this recognition will help: Ellison and Obama are flawed, mature adults of great gifts, one gift of which is a refusal of the pleasures and consolations of easy affirmation, the Gatsby-like mirror of ideal reflection. In glad-handing America, and especially in its political culture, the refusal of glibness, of backslapping bonhomie, and of the compulsive need to be agreeable always flirts with career failure and induces anxiety in others. At its heart, Obama's political success has been built on an audacious commitment to avoid or minimize demagoguery, a stance embodied in the detachment of his composed and collected demeanor. Given their refusal of the insulation of pseudo-warmth, self-possession and rational deliberation are never without risks; but if that detachment also creates a space to allow others to think for themselves, then it becomes a moral force worth respecting. After all, "Be your own father," says that canny wise man, the Vet.

"HOW MANY LIGHTBULBS DOES IT TAKE TO SCREW IN A BLUES SINGER?"
The French Revolution, King Louis Armstrong, and the Futuristic Jungleism of Jazz

STEVEN C. TRACY

In the prologue of *Invisible Man*, Ralph Ellison gathers a variety of seemingly disparate symbols related to revolutionary ideas and liberating performances. Here at the beginning and end of the novel, the figure of Louis Armstrong, the trope of the Bastille and French Revolution, and the notion of transgressive performances coalesce to point to Ellison's prediction of future social successes rooted in so-called primitive responses to the world. However, not only are these responses in many ways not primitive; they are also downright postmodern and futuristic. A close examination of Armstrong's recorded performance of the Andy Razaf song "(What Did I Do to Be So) Black and Blue?" will help illuminate the futuristic jungleism of jazz as it continues to resonate thematically and stylistically in Ellison's writings, as well as in African American literature and culture.

I

The location of the unnamed main character at the outset, also the denouement, of the novel is of course extremely important. Not only does it set the work in the context of such literary ancestors as Fyodor Dostoevsky and

Richard Wright, but it also places the protagonist in a liminal space horizontally (on the outskirts of Harlem) and vertically (underground but not *of* the ground—not dead, alive).[1] There is a certain artistic liminality as well, one that Ellison wrote about and defended all his life. From the epigraphs quoting Herman Melville and T. S. Eliot; the references to Edgar Allen Poe; the allusions to Miguel de Unamuno, Dostoevsky, and Wright; and the importance of the black preacher, the trickster Jack-the-Bear, and Louis Armstrong, it is clear that Ellison is writing from a space both black and white, American and international, literary, philosophical, folkloristic, and musical.

The protagonist himself names it "a border area" (IM 5) in recognition of its anomalous position, where all rules are off, and a kind of "lawlessness" that is both liminal and transgressive vies for legitimacy. The protagonist also occupies a sort of liminal position between God and man. That is, in a world where African Americans are frequently denied humanity, both in the world of the novel and in the twenty-first-century world of continuing inequities in housing, pay level, school achievement, and health care, the protagonist asserts his manhood, his self. In the first five sentences, he uses the words *I am* five times, calling attention not only to his manhood, but also to his very existence, an existence that is frequently erased due to what he refers to as *invisibility*. However, the assumption of the power to assert his existence, to claim humanity, in a society that seeks to deny it through this condition of invisibility, is the assumption of enormous power. It recalls the power of the initial power-who-names-things, the I-AM-THAT-I-AM, the Word of the beginning.[2] Thus the space is invested with vast symbolic meaning and power, though qualified by its anomalous position: "a man of substance, of flesh and bone" (3), like Shakespeare's Shylock, but a self-naming purveyor of the Word as well. He is trapped in a prison created by the state, scheming to storm the citadel at the propitious moment. Even in a post-Obama world where African Americans are elected to public office, the numbers are frequently so low, and the ability to alter the system significantly is so low, that the likelihood of success is low, even though there is value in the effort and, perhaps, an illusory encouragement that the system itself, the system Peter Wheatstraw carts the changing blueprints for, can be changed.

The protagonist, of course, denies that he is in a tomb or womb, but he does not deny that he is in *both*. Such an idea captures the complicated nature of his position and his voice. He is simultaneously burying himself in his revelation while he is creating himself in the action of speaking. For some, the notion of speaking as action is absurd, but given the restrictions on speech and speaking platforms for African Americans and other American minorities, what seems inactive becomes an action of great import. Indeed, the protagonist becomes a speechifier for the Brotherhood, notably at the eviction of the old black couple. The speech itself produces a response to the physical eviction itself. The paradox is that the action is controlled and perverted by the Brotherhood, which implies that meaningful action is not necessarily produced by speech. Rather, it must be thoughtful, organized, empowered group speech that directs the action.

The hole is described by the protagonist as a place of hibernation, "a covert preparation for a more overt action" (IM 13). While this lends a very serious air to the function of the hole, it simultaneously suggests something humorous as well, connected as the notion of hibernation is with the bear, suggested by Ellison's reference to Jack-the-Bear in the prologue. Is the situation action or inaction, serious or humorous, womb or tomb? Well, it seems to be in a border area that contains them all. Is this serious literature, or comic folklore, or both? The questions that crop up in relation to the nature of the text suggest that, as influenced as Ellison was by his modernist heroes Eliot, Hemingway, Joyce, and others, his is a postmodernist extension of their experimentation. It extends from their notions of discontinuity, the importance of myth and ritual, and the desire for regeneration (itself not a death or birth, but something of a hybrid combination) to the manifestations of such elements in African American culture as well.

However, recognizing African American "modernism" as part of the Zeitgeist of the time does not mean that Ellison's use of the elements of African American culture is modernist. Indeed, the protagonist mocks novelistic conventions in a most postmodernist manner. By mocking "Hollywood-movie ectoplasms" as unreal, he insists upon the questioning of whether storytelling is a serious realistic act. By recalling the fantastic tales of Edgar Allan Poe, he evokes a genre that necessitates the suspension of disbelief in order to invest in the story. In one sense, the protagonist has it wrong here. By and large, Poe's stories are not "peopled" by ghosts or fiends. Rather, they are haunted by the minds of narrators or characters or both. This is where the pun on *spook* becomes apparent. A term of derision for African Americans, it rescues the author from the inaccurate statement of the narrator, suggesting that the "spook" is not a ghost but a figment of white folks' imaginations. When he says "bear with me" (IM 14) at the end of the prologue, he calls attention to the simultaneous artificial seriousness and tragic humor of his words: Jack-the-Bear presides over the ambience of the chapter.

Quite clearly, in postmodernist fashion Ellison is embracing discontinuities and recognizing the heterogeneity, hybridity, and impurity that characterizes the postmodern world. Not only is this apparent from the heterogeneity of the hole, which is illuminated by and filled with liminality, and the hybridity of the voice, which speaks in local, national, and international tones; Ellison also takes pains to establish that the notion of "purity," frequently championed as an ideal, is in fact illusory and oppressive, and that its antonym is not impurity, as it is frequently understood to be in racist ethos, but heterogeneity itself. Furthermore, by using a variety of styles—absurdist, naturalistic, existential—and accepting and championing the validity of pop and mass art, seeing it as less distant from "high" art than thought by mainstream critics, Ellison brings to his art a postmodernist attitude that emphasizes the uses to which African American art can be put.

II

Ellison's ultimate exemplar of the revelatory trickster African American artist is Louis Armstrong, and Armstrong's work is truly an exemplar of what I call "Futuristic Jungleism," after a recording by Irving Mills. Mills was the white manager of black bandleader Duke Ellington, for whom Ellison wrote an essay, "Homage to Duke Ellington on his Birthday," citing Ellington's "aura of mockery" (CERE 683), similar to his characterization of Louis Armstrong's tricksterism. The term actually encompasses the three major elements of African American "hot music"—a catchall term for the overlapping nature of the genres of African American music bridging into the 1920s. For example, Fats Waller was a ragtime piano player who accompanied various blues singers such as Ada Brown, Rosa Henderson, Alberta Hunter, and Monette Moore. He also recorded jazz with Tom Morris and Red Allen, and white players Eddie Condon and Gene Krupa in the 1920s. One could make similar statements about Jelly Roll Morton and James P. Johnson, and jazz cornetist Johnny Dunn even employed all three piano players at two sessions in the space of thirteen days! Of course, we can see hot music in work songs, spirituals, game songs, and field hollers, plus some other, earlier ancestors, but the sometimes undifferentiated reference to hot music frequently encompassed the genres of ragtime, blues, and jazz, often with reference to two or three of the genres, sometimes with negligible association to any. In one of his series of recorded interviews with Alan Lomax, "When the Hot Stuff Came In," Jelly Roll Morton asserts that "the hot stuff came in 19-2," qualifying that "there was another style of hot music that came before—ragtime" (Morton). Perhaps the etymology of the word *hot* with this meaning, combined with the stereotypical association of earthy or unbridled sexuality with African Americans, explains it: *hot*, as a term meaning to act in a fashion that is passionate or sexually stimulating, goes back at least as far as Chaucer (Calt 128). The looseness with which this music overlappingly developed and the casual way that the terms for various genres were interchanged at the time demonstrate the ways the music represented hybrid mixes or ragtime or jazz genres to make relevant musical, social, political, and aesthetic points. This kind of hybridity gave birth to rhythm and blues in the 1940s, soul and funk in the 1960s and '70s, and the rap music that samples a variety of genres and embraces the heterogeneity of individual stylistic creation. A hallmark of African American music, it continues to operate in the artistic endeavors of contemporary musical artists. As a passionate and discerning student of jazz, Ellison was certainly aware of such elements and developments in the music, and indeed, as Robert O'Meally points out, Ellison wove elements of blues, gospel, sermons, and toasts "through the fabric" of his novel (O'Meally, *Craft* 78).

A title of a jazz recording by the Mills Blue Rhythm Band in 1931 (led by Duke Ellington's manager, Irving Mills) captures the racial and aesthetic tensions and the spectrum of attitudes and possibilities for African American music at the time: "Futuristic Jungleism." Rooting jazz in the jungle experience exposes the racist primitivism of attitudes among whites, and even some blacks, of the time. Often thinking of Africans as savage and backward, some people seeking basic and visceral thrills took recourse to jazz as an approximation of what it would be like to be earthy and impulsive. Rather than suppressing all of their desires as prescribed by the oppressive and empty society whose shortcomings had been exposed by industrialization and a war of a previously unimagined intensity and destructiveness, they partook in the vicarious thrill of pretending to be earthy and impulsive in the steamy Harlem nights, while returning to their inhibitions in the chilly dawns. Getting back to the "real" person behind societally based pretensions brought many people, white and black, face to face with implications for African American society that not only swung ominously in that old direction, but also ripped a path to the future. If the jungle and the future are both frightening—"Jazz Frightens Bears" read a 1928 *New York Times* headline—they are also infinitely bewitching as well. If society becomes "new" by "regressing" to the jungle, then the jungle is not only contemporary, but also futuristic for the avant-garde in terms of how they envision the "progress" of art. Futuristic jungleism.

"Futuristic Jungleism" refers to the ways that African American music was treated paradoxically as both savage and visionary in the minds of mainstream Americans responding to popular prejudices, and also in works of modernist figures such as Pound, Eliot, Picasso, and Diaghilev. Exploring the various ways in which primitivism was described and discussed, and the transformative elements borrowed from African American hot music, lays a solid groundwork for characterizing the time in which the material emerged and the context out of which Ellison's *Invisible Man* emerged. A comprehensive examination of the 1920s provides bridges between the disciplines of folklore, ethnomusicology, classical and pop musical history (including piano rolls and sheet music), visual art, pop culture, performance studies, and American and African American literary studies of the 1920s that illuminate how these contradictory notions sat uneasily side by side.

On the one hand, African Americans were considered by many white Americans to be not many years out of the jungle, with an atavistic connection that made them the stereotypical "other." The characterization of African Americans as beasts and rapists on the one hand, and childlike simpletons on the other, encompassed the attitudes that whites held toward and employed against blacks in the 1920s. The music itself was jungle music—primitive, passionate, associated with sex, elemental, even immoral. The dispersal of African American music in a variety of ways, including its dissemination in tent shows, sheet music, and piano rolls, as well as in the work of classical composers such as Dvořák, Antheil, Stravinsky, Gershwin, Schulhoff, and Suesse, however, suggests both a mainstream as well as an intellectual viability. The music's connection to popular bandleaders and artists such as Paul Whiteman, piano-roll purveyors Zez Confrey and Pauline Alpert, and Al Jolson, Sophie Tucker, Marion Harris, and Annette Hanshaw, as well as its use by country music singers such as Emmett Miller and Jimmie Rodgers and its appearance in cartoons and other media such as Betty Boop cartoons, represents the rather visceral and "jungle" side of the music.

But when classical composers and musicians began looking for the new gesture, the future of classical music, the reflection of the modern temperament and milieu, they also turned to the revolutionary aspects of jazz to point to the future. In this, white artists "sampling" African American music were regressive, transgressive, and progressive. They were in some liminal space between past and future, regressing toward sociocultural taboos of the past, transgressing racial boundaries, moving on the path to obliteration in the progressive future. There is, perhaps, no better gesture and genre to serve Ellison's purposes in *Invisible Man*, with its references to Trueblood's stereotypical "black" behavior, liminal raids by the unnamed protagonist, and voice that speaks for American society at large, as suggested in the final lines of the novel.[3]

Armstrong, as the most revolutionary jazz figure of his era, was truly the man who transformed American culture. The idol of many jazz performers who employed a diversity of instruments, he was the serious jazz musician who was a pop performer, the man who blended high and pop art into a pleasing heterogeneous mix of old-time African American work songs and field hollers, avant-garde jazz, minstrelsy, and schmaltz with a mile-wide grin. Armstrong's iconization by Ken Burns and Wynton Marsalis in the 2001 documentary series *Jazz*, along with the ascendancy of Marsalis, the neotraditionalist whose hybrid and high-profile recordings with artists such as Willie Nelson and Bela Fleck and the directorship of Jazz at Lincoln Center make him the best-known jazz performer of the era, demonstrate how the influence of an Armstrong can stretch from the beginning of the twentieth century into the twenty-first, his recordings still instructing countless students in the art and aesthetic of jazz. His seemingly effortless invention and Faustian-grasping virtuosity, along with a tricksterish wit and laconic manner, made him seem to be the paradoxical "untutored" genius. Actually, Armstrong *was* tutored, in feeling, virtuosity, and manner, by the rich African American woodshedding tradition of experience, hard work, mother wit, and knowledge of the difference between education and intelligence, which helped you listen to valuable officially un-honored voices. That bespeaks both a futuristic jungleism and a postmodernism that Ellison the writer could—and did—admire and use as a template for his own writing and intellectual outlook.

Ellison emphasized many of these elements related to Armstrong in his essays, where Armstrong was the most frequently mentioned jazz performer. In a 1958 rejoinder to Irving Howe, Ellison affirms Armstrong's powers as a trickster, "whose clownish license and intoxicating powers are almost Elizabethan" (CERE 106). His 1964 address "Hidden Name and Complex Fate" describes the "range of allusion" of T. S. Eliot's *The Waste Land* to be "as mixed and as varied" as that of Armstrong (CERE 203), just as he compares the "artful juxtapositioning of earlier styles" of these two figures in "On Bird, Bird-Watching, and Jazz" (CERE 259). And in a most explicit statement of Armstrong's revolutionary manner in "Remembering Richard Wright," he compares Wright and Armstrong: "He was well aware of the forces ranked against him, but in his quiet way he was as arrogant in facing up to them as was Louis Armstrong in a fine blaring way" (CERE 668). Ellison saw himself as heir to the jazz tradition, and believed in the tradition and individual talent thesis that Eliot adopted, even if he could have found that as a source in West African aesthetics. Thus, while Ellison illuminates Armstrong, Armstrong also illuminates Ellison, and both point to a futuristic postmodernism that partakes of the jungle stereotype that was associated with jazz in the 1920s.

III

Which brings us back to that illuminated hole of Ellison's protagonist. Ellison clearly does not want to depict his protagonist as being "in the dark" about himself, especially since the end is in the beginning, the experience is had, Robin is picked clean and has learned a lesson. When he proclaims that he has illuminated the blackness of his invisibility (IM 13), he affirms the substance of the culture that goes willfully unseen. By doing so, he acknowledges a sociopolitically constructed prison, as well as his substantive retort to his jailers. It is a retort that is socially transgressive: "Black is . . . an' black ain't" (IM 9). It is full of possibility (IM 156), as the Vet says, paradoxically existing and not, affirmative and negative, an excuse for the imprisonment, but not a valid explanation.

The physical illumination underground, of course, comes from a different source, and it is here that a small detail opens up the prologue and helps define both the condition of the protagonist and the role of Armstrong in providing a path for transcendence. In his quest to make the Monopolated Light and Power Company pay for his condition—"light confirms my reality, gives birth to my form" (IM 6), he proclaims—he wires his hole with 1,369 lightbulbs of the old, expensive type, to *steal* that which helps him say "I am," and prove it (although the condition of the "inner eyes" of the viewer, as he says earlier, can still render him invisible [IM 3]). Most interesting from an interpretive standpoint here is the number of bulbs Ellison has chosen for the illumination. It is quite a large number, in keeping with the intent, but an odd number to light upon randomly. But the number is not a random number. Most recently, Adam Bradley has suggested that the number makes reference to the Harlem numbers racket in both *Invisible Man* and Ellison's subsequent novel, plausible enough in that it fits well with Ellison's sense of signifying wordplay with "folk idioms," evoking its associations with "excrement" in the Harlem dream book (Bradley 3). Eric Sundquist emphasizes such wordplay in folk idioms such as spirituals, slave songs, street-vendor songs, folktales, and the vernacular language of the folk, all reflecting important elements dealing with mobility, tricksterism, orature and creativity, self-determination, and self-identity (*Cultural Contexts* 115–44). However, Ellison seems to have more historically revolutionary acts in mind, and the "numbers" explanation of 3-6-9 representing excrement really does not account for the millennial number (literally and figuratively, since it suggests the coming of a happy time when the old regime, signified by the new creation, will fall): number one. Still, Ellison may well be combining both folk and historical symbolism, continuing a pattern to which Barbara Foley calls attention in her discussion of his interview responses, "stress[ing] the connections between Negro folklore and transhistorical patterns of myth and ritual" (79).

In keeping with the author's intention to illuminate the state prison of invisibility, and to project revolutionary transgressive acts in response to such villainy, Ellison has chosen to evoke the initiation in 1369 of the building of the Bastille, the fortress and state prison in Paris. Begun in that year under the direction of Hugues Aubriot, the Bastille became the symbol of absolutism and the exercise of complete and utter control and despotism. What better symbol to evoke, albeit very subtly, than the Bastille in a text that explores the ways in which absolute power and control can choose to deny the existence and even visibility of someone or something, the existence of which can be confirmed by a simple lightbulb—or 1,369? Of course, this evocation of the beginning of construction of the Bastille also contains the seeds of its ending as well: the absolutism associated with the edifice made it the symbol that needed to be destroyed as a gateway to the larger revolution. Indeed, the insurrectionary storming of the Bastille in 1789 marked the beginning of the French Revolution, the same year that the US Constitution was ratified and George Washington was elected president—the climactic events of the American Revolution. The upheaval of this revolutionary era is reflected in Ellison's text, and though 1789 comes in its waning days, it marks an important year in the events of what historians call the Enlightenment—exactly what Ellison is attempting to discuss (with a pun on "enlighten" for lagniappe!). In fact, given Ellison's radical period preceding the publication of *Invisible Man*, it is quite reasonable to associate the French Revolution with his own popular front journalism and espousing of and striving with proletarian radicalism in the 1930s and 1940s, even if, arguably, the French Revolution was a bourgeois revolution later taken up by the proletariat under bourgeois leadership.[4]

Further, the idea of absolutism had connotations before the Enlightenment that carried over obliquely into the Enlightenment and are reflected in *Invisible Man*. Previously, an absolute form of government connoted a government untainted, pure, or free from elements foreign to its nature. The notion of purity, as in a kind of absolute separateness or sovereignty, surely applies to the notion of absolute monarchy. Such a fear of hybridity, or aversion to "pollutants," itself turns up in the absolute white world of the novel. This is most obviously the case in the Liberty Paints episode, where the purity of Optic White Paint is trumpeted, even in the face of the black material that is the guts of the paint itself (IM 196–218). The fact that Ellison associates absolutism with liberty in the world of the novel, and then reveals that the relationship is illusory, reinforces the point that the exploration of mixed, liminal spaces contradicts notions of absolutism. Thus, Ellison produces a postmodern signifying on this major strain in modernism.

Other insurrectionary acts of the early 1790s included the storming of the Tuileries and the imprisonment of the reigning monarch King Louis XVI, leading to the election of the National Convention, a legislative body named after the American Constitutional Convention of 1787. It is no coincidence that, after his reference to the 1,369 lightbulbs illuminating his hole, the evocation of the Bastille and French Revolution, and the overthrow and imprisonment of the monarch Louis XVI, Ellison has his protagonist evoke his jazz monarch—the heir apparent to Joe "King" Oliver, named "King of Zulus" in the 1949 Mardi Gras, which James Lincoln Collier points out was "[a]mong New Orleans blacks ... a great honor" (IM 31)—Louis Armstrong, often dubbed King Louis or the King of Jazz (his 1949 "coronation" of Armstrong came roughly halfway in between when Ellison started and published the novel). It is futuristic jungleism projected into the bebop era of jazz, when musicians rebelled against previous notions of jazz's aesthetics and purpose, even as they built on the revolutionary advances of people such as Armstrong. This King Louis, however, is on the side of the insurrection. He represents the uncommonness of the "common man." When Ellison writes, "Louis bends that military instrument into a beam of lyrical sound" (IM 8), he recognizes that Armstrong demonstrates his own martial prowess (Ellison acknowledges that Armstrong "was taught to play a rather strict type of military music" in New Orleans in an essay on Alain Locke [CERE 443]), his revolutionary fervor, even as he ignites a different kind of revolution, more subtle, more nuanced, more aesthetic, as well as social, political, and cultural. It is multivocal; it surrounds and overwhelms. For example, the protagonist listens to five versions of the Armstrong recording of "(What Did I Do to Be So) Black and Blue" for auditory, visceral, and social reasons. He wants to hear the vibrations of the music in the sound; he wants to explore the emotional experience and response to the condition of blackness and blueness, finally named and proclaimed in public; and he wants to hear and see how the jazz performer translates the technique, feeling, and idea into a social statement that transgresses boundaries in such subtle and nuanced ways. In Armstrong's "slightly different sense of time" and the "nodes" he has the wit and genius to perceive and execute, we hear the clearing of a musical ground and the projection of what will become the formative influence on American music in the future, even now, all these years after Armstrong. By forcing his audiences to listen and *hear* in a different way, one attuned to African American aesthetics and sociocultural understanding, all in a music that seemed to many white and middle-class black listeners to be echoes of a primitive jungle mentality, Armstrong and his hot cohort set the world on futuristic fire.

IV

The song "(What Did I Do to Be So) Black and Blue?" was the composition of Andrea Razakkeriefo, a descendant of Madagascar's royal family and semipro pitcher in the Negro Leagues who turned songwriter and, partnering with some of the great ragtime and jazz performers of the time, became a prolific songwriter under the name Andy Razaf. The genesis of the song is a mini-tragicomedy in itself. In 1929, one of the financial backers of the Hot Chocolates revue approached Razaf with a suggestion for a song. Now such an event would not have been so momentous except that the "benefactor" was Arthur Flegenheimer, a.k.a. Dutch Schultz, known as a "short-tempered, murderous mobster" (Singer 216). His suggestion also came at the point of a gun. The suggestion? Schultz wanted a humorous song, sung by an African American, about how hard it was to be black! Razaf decided to comply, but with a postmodern signifying twist on Schultz's demand—presenting the song in terms of social stratification within the black community, rather than between whites and blacks. When dark-skinned Edith Wilson performed the song on an all-white stage, dressed in a white negligee and "swaddled deep in white bedclothes" (Singer 217), the audience responded with laughter, a perhaps stunned recognition of the frank and groundbreaking nature of the lyric, and ultimately a standing ovation, the latter of which Razaf felt had saved his life (Singer 219). Balancing precipitously on the high wire, the hushed crowd deciding whether to provide a safety net in case the aerial artist slipped and lost his footing in the mobster's mind, Razaf wrote a masterpiece. As Barry Singer points out, Razaf is a "deft" lyricist, making use of early minstrel references and disarming his audience before producing "his most telling lines" from behind the intraracial illusion of stanza one (Singer 219). The composition was a groundbreaking protest song, given the tenor of the times, even if a bit equivocal, and certainly confrontational, though the confrontation was softened by certain stereotypical references—again, a "jungleistic" veneer fronting a "futuristic" truth. And, in a very real sense, it was a storming of a state prison by a beleaguered entity that aimed at the overthrow of an oppressive system.

However, Ellison's allusion to Louis Armstrong's version of "(What Did I Do to Be So) Black and Blue?" goes beyond the mere cleverness of the title, which evokes the treachery and rough treatment faced by African Americans in slavery and the Jim Crow era, the bruising cleverly alluding to African American skin color and both the synonym for sadness and the popular African American musical genre known as the blues. Armstrong recorded the tune with his Hot Five on July 22, 1929, three days after he recorded a version of Fats Waller's "Ain't Misbehavin'" with his orchestra. But Armstrong most certainly *was* misbehaving as he picked up and transformed the Razaf song into something somewhat different from the work performed earlier by Ethel Waters, signifying upon Razaf's signification on Dutch Schultz.

In the Armstrong version, the song begins with a four-bar solo keyboard introduction on a celesta or harpsichord, which lends a light, airy, dreamlike quality to the work, almost like a fantasy, the sweetness of which will be belied by the lyrics. However, rather than foreground the lyrics, Armstrong's arrangement takes a different track. The next four bars of the intro feature the entry of the band chording behind the high-pitched, virtuosic playing of the trumpet, at first with syncopated quarter notes, and then with a powerful, rushing display of rhythmic genius that seems to be rushing excitedly to the melody, as if there is some central visceral point to be made in both the style and articulation of the melodic phrases. But it is to the melody without the words just yet. Instead, Armstrong demonstrates his lyrical mastery, invention, and revolutionary rhythmic style before the lyrics enter—an idea that would certainly not be lost on Ellison, himself a music major and trumpeter with acquaintances from the Kansas City jazz tradition. Armstrong's solo confronts, indeed storms, the bastion of American racism. What this accomplishes, in part, is to focus listeners on the supreme power and mastery of the black performer rather than on the lamenting of the disadvantages of blackness that the original lyrics emphasize. Rather than humor, Armstrong evokes awe and admiration from an audience because of the surprises he produces in his variations, improvisations, and grace notes and phrases. Each of the familiar half-line phrases alters slightly or extensively the rhythmic expression of the melody, turning it, as the vernacular saying goes, "every which way but loose." Not only does this produce a variety and nuance to the phrases, but it lends different voices to the expression—a kind of group expression springing from the mind of the individual. In a sense he "re-dresses" the song in an outfit of mastery and vigor, as the song attempts to redress the situation that necessitated its message.

"What did I do?" Armstrong asks. Just listen to what I—we—have done, and do, and will do. We have not done anything to be despised and rejected, scorned and beaten—black and blue. But the power and strength and skill and genius of blackness, and the sweet ability of the blues to assuage the feelings of sadness and longing and disappointment and determination inherent in being blue—these we have created from a black and blue tradition that will rise and dominate and define the music of America in profound and overwhelming ways for generations to come.

Lest we miss the importance of this emphasis on the stylistic transformation of the song, it should be pointed out that the vocal does not enter until 1:33 in the recording—just as the recording is over halfway done. And with sixteen seconds' worth of music following the vocal at the end of the song, the complete lyric is subordinated in both space (delayed entry) and time (less the instrumental elements) to the lead voice of the trumpet, followed by another voice from the trombone, and finally an orchestrated reworking of the melody by the horn section—essentially making it a multivocal, individual and group, call-and-response template for African American artistic and sociopolitical expression—the very essence of Ellisonian aesthetics.

When Armstrong does begin to sing the lyrics, the difference from what Razaf wrote as well as what Waters sang is marked. First, Armstrong skips the entire first stanza of Razaf's song. Since Armstrong and the band has played a stanza instrumentally, one might assume that that first lyric stanza has been replaced by the instrumental performance, particularly since the time limitations of a 78 RPM record would not have allowed Armstrong to sing an additional stanza on one side of the record, and his instrumental prowess prompted fans to expect at least an instrumental break on his recordings. However, since Razaf wrote three stanzas, of which Armstrong sings only one, it seems more likely that Armstrong is either making a technological concession or deliberately altering the structure and meaning of the song. Still, he would have had to make a choice as to what to eliminate, and in this case the choice to eliminate stanza one erases the intraracial meaning of the song and allows the song to become implicitly a song that explicitly confronts interracial discrimination.

This makes the song much more revolutionary and racially confrontational. However, it also creates a situation of deniability; if questioned, the time restraints of the technology could be invoked to explain and ameliorate the interracial confrontation produced by the elimination of stanza one. Ellison himself practices a bit of this kind of "partial transcription" himself: in the section dealing with the blueprint man, he has Wheatstraw sing everything but the final line of a well-known traditional blues stanza. Though Ellison leaves out the line, he does count on discerning readers, familiar with jazz, to understand the strategic joke. While the singer describes the *surface* "ugliness" of his "baby"—an issue that has been emphasized for the protagonist by a number of people, including the Vet—the protagonist uses the lyric to emphasize her practical physical skills—which transcend mere surface—as well as his devotion: "I love my baby better than I do myself" (IM 173). Here, though, Ellison stops, four bars short of the end of the twelve-bar blues stanza. What does he leave out? The lyric in the original recording continues, "Come to find out she was loving somebody else." It is a lyric that doubles back on itself. The singer is clearly proud that he has looked beneath surface beauty to the woman's skill in loving, only to find out that he has not looked deeply enough. The lyric doubly reinforces Ellison's point—but only if we have the mother wit and knowledge of the jazz tradition to understand it.

The stanza that Armstrong does sing is a combination of stanzas two and three in the Razaf composition. As he begins, he retains the lyrics of the beginning of stanza two, with a very important change. The conventions of the empty bed and hard bedsprings that occur in blues songs of the time remain, and so does the minstrel reference to old Ned. However, Armstrong switches the reference to Ned to the beginning of the second line, and replaces "Pains in my head" with "Wish I was dead" in the climactic position of the couplet before the refrain. This emphasizes a death wish that was not expressed in the complete Razaf lyrics. What Armstrong *has* eliminated here is the sentiment from the Razaf complete version in which the speaker questions why he was born. Of course, there is an essential difference. To question why you are born implies an absence of purpose to your existence. The wish to be dead suggests conditions in the world that produce this kind of a depression. Armstrong thus strengthens the idea that something in the world has produced untenable conditions; in this case, interracial racism. Interestingly, Armstrong does retain the rhyming word for "born" in the lyric he sings, "scorn," though it rhymes with nothing else in his version. This emphasizes the absence of the "Why was I born?" sentiment.

While Armstrong sings these lyrics in a clear and vigorous manner, the lyrics of the bridge are more problematically performed. The performance on record reveals an Armstrong articulating in a very loose, almost mumbling fashion the words "I'm white inside." This is a part of the lyric that was meant to argue the essential identical nature of all races. However, the idea is stated in "white-privileging" and Western symbolic terms: to be "white" inside is to suggest that despite your inferior blackness "outside," inside is as good as white folks. There is still that old "jungle" veneer to overcome. Understandably, given the virulence of white racism at the time, many blacks would have felt that to be white inside was not a positive condition. What was supposed to be well-meaning phraseology was in fact a Eurocentric insult. What Armstrong does here in performance is de-emphasize the attractiveness of that designation by reducing in vigor and clarity the articulation of those words. Furthermore, when he continues with the line "'Cause I can't hide what is in my face," he changes the word *on* to *in*, making it less superficial, deeper, as if there is a stronger and richer tradition and inherent strength in the blackness. Even more importantly, Armstrong does not even sing the word *face*. He starts, but skips off into a joyous, scat-like celebration of an element of African American culture by replacing the superficial look with a deeper expression of culture. He sings that he can't hide it, but the irrepressible nature of African American invention and improvisation turns the unsatisfactorily stated sentiment of the lyric into a rollicking jubilee—a time of liberation and rejoicing in black culture. And he *avoids* referring to his face to complete the sentiment—he *does* hide it! What did he do to be so black and blue, Armstrong asks, but the protesting is also a boundary-crossing celebration. As Ellison says, Armstrong makes "poetry out of being invisible" (IM 8)—in this case through a signifying re-take on Razaf's lyric.

Armstrong removes certain biblical or religious elements from the complete lyric as well. The centuries-old racist notion that blacks were the ancestors of Ham who, having seen his father Noah naked, was "marked" with what racist adherents inferred was black skin, is excised by Armstrong, likely because it seems to lend credence to the racist notion of blackness as a curse. It makes perfect sense, then, for Armstrong to remove "My only sin is in my skin," which, even though it can be taken ironically, as it should be, is of a piece with the racist ideology supporting black inferiority. In *Invisible Man*, Ellison himself undercuts black religious inferiority in the sermon where the preacher intones paradoxically yet powerfully that "black is ... an' black ain't." (IM 9). As if to emphasize his signifying reading of Razaf's lyrics, Armstrong returns as instrumentalist at the very end of the song, picking up the cue from the saxophonist and building to a virtuoso high note to place his exclamation point on the altered sentiments of the song.

The aesthetic, talent, and persona of Louis Armstrong, early-generation jazz performer extraordinaire, provided Ralph Ellison with the example of an ancestor whose voice, most frequently transmitted in the oral tradition, still resonates heavily with blacks and whites in the twenty-first century. In fact, the increasing acceptance of the legitimacy and value of the oral tradition is in part due to the influence of African American music. It has caused scholars in the twenty-first century to continue to examine the operations of the oral tradition, to discern its particular strengths, and to teach the understanding of those strengths to new generations of children. Jazz has demonstrated how a revolution in thought and style and subject matter, a true political revolution, can come from an oral tradition falsely considered to be apolitical or merely primitive jungleistic entertainment. It has demonstrated how the creations of the subjected helped to democratize America, or at least push it further in that direction. As those boundaries continue to fall in the twenty-first century, the contributions of writers like Langston Hughes and Ralph Ellison to the transformation of American society through their championing of culture and employment of new artistic aesthetics themselves help transform American society into the more heterogeneous, hybrid, diverse society it was supposed to be when the country was established over two hundred years ago. And the subtle strategies and intelligences that we now discover in the reputed jungleism of African American music suggests that scholars of the future will have much more to learn from the limitations of seeing jungleism where futuristic ideas reign.

How many lightbulbs does it take to screw in a blues singer? 1,369.

NOTES

1. Fyodor Dostoevsky, *Notes from Underground* (1864), and Richard Wright, *The Man Who Lived Underground* (1945).

2. Gen. 1; Exod. 3:14a: "And God said unto Moses I AM THAT I AM"; John 1:1: "In the beginning was the Word, and the Word was with God, and the Word was God" (Authorized [King James] Version [AV]).

3. "And it is this which frightens me: Who knows but that, on the lower frequencies, I speak for you?" (IM 581).

4. Two essays Ellison wrote for the Communist journal *New Masses* are "A Congress Jim Crow Didn't Attend (May 14, 1940)" and "The Way It Is (October 20, 1942)" (CERE 13–26 and 310–19, respectively).

CONCLUSION
Ralph Ellison in the Twenty-First Century

"THAT PAUSE FOR CONTEMPLATION"
A Centennial Meditation on Ralph Ellison

JOHN CALLAHAN

I

To invoke time in a straight line is a dangerous way to commemorate Ralph Ellison's centennial. Hubris is a preening force, which invites a boomerang from nemesis if we forget that in 1946, a mere year after Ellison wrote *Invisible Man*'s astounding first sentence ("I am an invisible man"), he made a case for any novel's reliance on the fluid, protean relationship between artist and reader. "Once introduced into society," he wrote in "Twentieth-Century Fiction and the Black Mask of Humanity," "the work of art begins to pulsate with those meanings, emotions, ideas brought to it by its audience, and over which the artist has but limited control" (CERE 94). The flux and flow Ellison describes recalls Invisible Man's claim that invisibility "gives one a slightly different sense of time, you're never quite on the beat. Sometimes you're ahead and sometimes behind. Instead of the swift and imperceptible flowing of time, you are aware of its nodes, those points where time stands still or from which it leaps ahead" (IM 8).

For Ellison, time is multiple, malleable, its flow interrupted by experience at sudden unpredictable points. *Invisible Man* is a case in point. During its life in print the book has been a reminder of time's ability to stand still and leap ahead, for readers and its author. Thirty years after its publication, Random

House asked Ellison to write an introduction to the thirtieth-anniversary edition of his novel. He complied, though not without grumbling about *time* lost from his still-unfinished second novel. The piece has the hybrid rhetorical form of a meditation that is also a tall tale about the origins of *Invisible Man* between conception and birth. At times the extended introduction has the feel of an act of "antagonistic cooperation" between Ellison and what he calls in the first and last paragraphs "a most self-willed and self-generating piece of fiction ... a most willful, most self-generating novel" (IM vii, xxiii).

In the early 1980s Ralph Ellison was not the only reader possessed by *Invisible Man*. Strangers, some close by, others distant, were also engaged. When they finished, some put the book away; others fingered its pages until ink and paper were smudged and worn. Ralph did not know that one of those readers was a preoccupied undergraduate at Columbia, a young man he might have passed on his daily walk down Riverside Drive—a jogger of black and white parentage who was reading and rereading *Invisible Man* as he sought to solve his own riddle of American identity....

One blue spring day in the early 1980s, Ralph Ellison walks south through Riverside Park tuned to some inner frequency. Presently, a tall slender black man jogs toward him. Ralph senses the young man thinking; his novelist's eye catches a frown crease the brown face before a dazzling outright grin breaks out on the jogger's face as they pass on the path. Several times a week the undergraduate runs north past Ellison's 730 Riverside Drive apartment house all the way to Trinity Church, and back to Broadway and 110th Street. In his back pocket is his scruffy, beat-up copy of "Invisible Man."

The young jogger likes to read while he drinks coffee. Like the narrator of the novel he carries with him, he has talent as an orator, and aspires to become a leader, maybe a writer too, once he sorts out his identity as a person of two races. For several months "Invisible Man" has been part of his mind, lining out his desire to become truly a black American. He likes having the book handy after his run when he stops in a coffee joint near Columbia and smokes a cigarette—one of the Djarums whose Indonesian blend of cloves and tobacco takes him back to Jakarta where he lived for a while as a boy with his mother and half-sister. Face to face briefly with the young man, Ellison spots his intensity and admires the easy lope of his stride before he resumes brooding about the novel-in-progress he's more and more desperate to finish. Like apparitions, his two principal characters burst into his mind: the Reverend Alonzo Hickman, formerly and partly still a jazzman, along with the orphaned baby boy he'd named Bliss and raised like a son until the boy flees his blackness, reinvents and renames himself, and ends up as the doomed, race-baiting Senator Adam

Sunraider. By the time Ralph emerges from his reverie, the young jogger has gone past, arms pumping easily up and down his sides.

Without breaking stride, the jogger passes Ralph, words from the book in his back pocket sounding in time to the beat of his heart: "America is woven of many strands. I would recognize them and let it so remain.... Life is to be lived, not controlled; and humanity is won by continuing to play in the face of certain defeat." In his mind's eye the jogger sees the face of the older man he's just passed. He remembers the crescent-shaped scar under his eye and thinks the man looked like the kind of old-school guy who could tell him something about how to be black and American. Who knows, maybe he's even read "Invisible Man."

For a moment the jogger slows down, wishing he'd stopped to speak to the older man as he was never able to speak to his own father. Ahead a seagull swoops over the Hudson, cawing away in an angry, bebop riff. As the jogger increases his pace, he conjures a line from "Invisible Man" he has yet to unriddle: "Our fate is to become one, and yet many" (IM 577). His strides lengthen as Invisible Man's words sound on a frequency that belongs to him as well as to the man he's just passed in the park who, having written "Invisible Man" decades before, is now consumed with the fate of other characters he pursues through the familiar, unfamiliar labyrinth of America....

The foregoing, of course, is a conceit of mine. As far as I know, no such actual encounter happened, though it could have. Ralph Ellison's daily walks took him through terrain that was prime jogging territory for Barack Obama while he was coming of age at Columbia. Shedding *Barry* for *Barack* as soon as he arrived in New York from Southern California by way of Hawaii, the young Obama joined the ranks of countless others who tapped into *Invisible Man*'s frequencies in order to decipher their own stories and create identities authentic enough to find their individual way in the labyrinth.

As it happens, Obama's crisis of racial identity went back to his high school years in Hawaii. There, as he would later write in his remarkable autobiography, *Dreams from My Father* (1995), he read African American literature, including *Invisible Man*, and "kept finding the same anguish, the same doubt; a self-contempt that neither irony nor intellect seemed able to deflect" (*Dreams* 86). Later, in New York in the early '80s, according to his friend, Mir Mahboob Mahmood, young Obama "carried and at every opportunity read and reread a fraying copy of Ralph Ellison's *Invisible Man*. It was a period during which Barack was struggling deeply within himself to attain his own racial identity, and *Invisible Man* became a prism for his self-reflection" (Maraniss 453).

Fast-forward to 2008, when inflammatory excerpts from the Reverend Jeremiah Wright's sermons went viral on cable TV and the Internet, and put Senator Obama's presidential campaign in mortal jeopardy. Against the advice of his advisers, Obama wrote and delivered in Philadelphia's Constitutional Hall a speech called "A More Perfect Union." The examples of "racial stalemate" and stereotype he used flowed largely from a "peculiar disposition" and "construction" of American "inner eyes." Like Ellison's Invisible Man, Senator Obama put his voice and mind and presence to work using his invisibility to achieve visibility through the written and the spoken word.

The intriguing hit-and-miss quality of the connection between Ralph Ellison and Barack Obama recalls a hunting story Ellison liked to tell about his boyhood in Oklahoma. "After bringing down a rabbit or quail, men would proclaim in voices that throbbed with true American optimism, 'A hit, my boy, is history!' But if they missed and the quarry got away, they'd stare at the sky or cover and say, 'A miss, my boy, is a mystery'" (CERE 856). History and mystery, hit and miss: these words link the hunter's pursuit of game with the individual's hunt for identity and the citizen's (and leader's) pursuit of American democratic equality. Ellison, though drawn to mystery, fumed at "misses in our attempts to achieve our democratic commitments that are so embarrassing that we have a tendency to assign our failures to the world of mystery" (CERE 856). To the end of his life Ellison did not swerve from the conviction that American writers "are challenged to take individual responsibility for the health of American democracy. It is their role to transform the misses of history into hits of imaginative symbolic action" (CERE 856–57).

II

These days, the American task of transformation to which Ellison referred is even more urgent. Our first black president is also a writer who often carries out his obligation to perfect the union by affirming in the contemporary life of the nation what Invisible Man called the *principle* asserted in the founding documents of the Declaration of Independence and the Constitution. Yet after Barack Obama's election and reelection as president of the United States, there continues to be implacable resistance to him on grounds that he is somehow *alien* ("I wish this president would learn how to be an American" raged the former governor of New Hampshire, John Sununu [CNN]), invisibility has taken on a subtler, perhaps even more insidious cast in the unfolding new century than was the case in the last.

With *Invisible Man* the novel in its seventh decade and the centennial of Ralph Ellison's birth underway, time seems simultaneously to stand still and leap ahead. Surely these *nodes* of time are complementary; each calls for what Ellison described as "that aura of a summing up, that pause for contemplation of the moral significance of the history we've been through" (CERE 821). Ellison's life spanned most of the twentieth century, from his birth in 1913 or '14 to his death in 1994. As writer and citizen, he cast one eye on the nineteenth century through the prism of the Civil War even as he anticipated the accelerating impacts of the digital age on personality in the twenty-first century with the other. At his death he had published three books: *Invisible Man* (1952), *Shadow and Act* (1964), and *Going to the Territory* (1986). In the twenty years since his death, six posthumous volumes have appeared: *Conversations with Ralph Ellison* (1995), *The Collected Essays of Ralph Ellison* (1995), *Flying Home and Other Stories* (1996), *Juneteenth* (1999), *Trading Twelves: The Selected Letters of Ralph Ellison and Albert Murray* (2000), and *Three Days before the Shooting...* (2010). Presently a volume of Ellison's selected letters from 1933 to 1993 is in preparation with publication anticipated in 2016.

Separately and together, the posthumous volumes heighten the power of *Invisible Man* and bring the full achievement of Ellison's essays, short fiction, interviews, and soon, I believe, his letters beyond the intimidating shadow cast by his now-classic novel. The *Collected Essays of Ralph Ellison* bring into the light previously uncollected or unpublished pieces like "February" (1955), "A Congress Jim Crow Didn't Attend" (1940), "Tell It Like It Is, Baby" (1956/1965), "Indivisible Man" (1970), "Commencement Address at the College of William and Mary" (1972), "Address to the Harvard College Alumni" (1974), "Roscoe Dunjee and the American Language" (1972), "On Being the Target of Discrimination" (1989), "Notes for Class Day Talk at Columbia University" (1990), and, last but not at all least, Ralph's story of his grandfather, "Big Alfred" Ellison in "Address to the Whiting Foundation" (1992). These and most other essays stand as separate pieces on their merits at the same time that they illuminate and extend the full range of Ellison's oeuvre.

In previously unpublished stories like "A Party down at the Square," "The Black Ball," and, now, in the second edition of *Flying Home and Other Stories* (2012), "A Storm of Blizzard Proportions" we witness Ellison take up the challenge of what he called "the most insidious and least understood form of segregation... that of the word" (CERE 81). These stories bear witness to Jim Crow and African American responses at crucial intersections between personality and history such as the life of Jack Johnson and the Spanish

Civil War. Certainly, *Juneteenth* and *Three Days before the Shooting . . .* lift Ellison's forty years of work on his ambitious second novel out of the back alleys of rumor into volumes accessible to Ellison's readers. Finally, *Trading Twelves: The Selected Letters of Ralph Ellison and Albert Murray* offers a singular correspondence between two of the most gifted American writers of the twentieth century, and also a down payment on the rich, multifaceted treasure of Ellison's letters to follow.

"'Dem's years,'" Invisible Man's grandfather said, mocking his grandson's subjugation to time. In search of a node when time stood still *and* leaped ahead for Ralph Ellison, one could do worse than choose the evening of January 27, 1953, when he delivered his address at the National Book Award ceremony honoring *Invisible Man*. Of the many worthy talks by winners of the award, Ellison's "Brave Words for a Startling Occasion" stands at the pinnacle. Therein he boldly asserts that "if I were asked in all seriousness just what I considered to be the chief significance of *Invisible Man* as a fiction, I would reply: *its experimental attitude,* and its attempt to return to the mood of personal moral responsibility for democracy which typified the best of our nineteenth-century fiction" (CERE 151; emphasis added). Yet Ellison did not begin *Invisible Man* looking for a new form. Rather, trying to tell the story he wanted to tell, he became aware that "the forms of so many of the works which impressed me were too restricted to contain the experience which I knew." His challenge writing *Invisible Man* was to present America in the grip of Jim Crow during the story Invisible Man tells in the narrative proper; then, in the prologue and epilogue, have his rabble rouser turned writer hint at a country teetering on the cusp of change, poised to leap toward integration. Unfortunately (fortunately, really), neither the "so-called novel of manners," the "tight, well-made Jamesian novel," nor the "hard-boiled novel, with its dedication to physical violence, social cynicism and understatement" fit his purposes (CERE 151, 152).

Like Thomas Kuhn's scientist in *The Structure of Scientific Revolutions*, Ellison starts out looking to existing paradigms to solve his problem; when none fits his needs, he adopts an *"experimental attitude."* In the case of *Invisible Man*, he seizes upon the vernacular tradition of American speech—"a mixture of the folk, the Biblical, the scientific and the political"—and the improvisatory form of jazz. "To attempt to express that American experience which has carried one back and forth and up and down the land and across, and across again the great river, from freight train to Pullman car, from contact with slavery to contact with a world of advanced scholarship, art and science, is simply to burst such *neatly understated forms of the novel asunder*" (CERE 152; emphasis added).

To clarify his theme, Ellison looked back to "our classical nineteenth-century novelists" as writers who "took a much greater responsibility for the condition of democracy and, indeed, their works were imaginative projections of the conflicts within the human heart which arose when the sacred principles of the Constitution and the Bill of Rights clashed with the practical exigencies of human greed and fear, hate and love." In his address he weaves his "dream of a prose which was flexible, and swift as American change is swift, confronting the inequalities and brutalities of our society forthrightly, yet thrusting forth its images of hope, human fraternity and individual self-realization." He also asserts that "what has been missing from so much experimental writing has been the passionate will to dominate reality as well as the laws of art," which for him remains "the true source of the experimental attitude" (CERE 152–53). Finally, in words that echo *Invisible Man*'s persistent question, "And could politics ever be an expression of love?" (IM 452), Ellison links the tough work of citizenship with human intimacy. "The way home we seek is that condition of man's being at home in the world, which is called love, and which we term democracy" (CERE 154). The quest for the way home is Ellison's quest: as a person, a boy and man, writer and citizen, American and African American.

We see how this is so a year later in a letter written to his teacher at Tuskegee, Morteza Sprague, after Ellison heard word of the *Brown v. Board* decision announced on the radio. Immediately he stakes out territory that he fitfully explored in stories and essays before *Invisible Man* that would continue to be his domain through forty years of labor on the novel he never finished, as well as in countless essays, interviews, addresses, and letters. "Well, so now the judges have found and Negroes must be individuals, and that is hopeful and good," he writes, adding that he is now in 1954 "writing about the evasion of identity which is another characteristically American problem which must be about to change." Bringing the letter to a close, he raises a metaphorical glass to the task ahead: "Anyway, here's to integration, the only integration that counts: that of the personality" (Ellison, Letter to Morteza Sprague 39). Plainly, for Ellison the quest for integration is profoundly social and of society. At the same time the truest, deepest integration he had in mind is a profound, recurring matter requiring each individual to answer the same questions: "What's inside you, brother; what's your heart like? What are your real values?" (CERE 739).

Character after character in his fiction, and the Ralph Waldo Ellison of the essays, interviews, and letters, pursues that integration of the personality he rightly identified as the crux facing the country at the time of *Brown v. Board*. It is a crux that sixty years later poses questions of justice and equality, which have troubled American consciousness in different and myriad guises from the nation's founding to the present. What, after all, was the dream of young Ralph Ellison and his boyhood friends in Oklahoma when they dreamed of becoming Renaissance men if not forthright integration of the personality? Their models, Ellison was quick to point out, were not "judges and ministers, legislators and governors" in Jim Crow Oklahoma; they were jazzmen. "Like Huck," Ellison recounts, "we observed, we judged, we imitated and evaded as we could the dullness, corruption and blindness of 'civilization.'" For "it was no more incongruous," he wrote later, "in this land of incongruities, for young Negro Oklahomans to project themselves as Renaissance men than for white Mississippians to see themselves as ancient Greeks or noblemen out of Sir Walter Scott" (CERE 52, 55).

Ellison's fluid, contingent ideal resembles his later idea of the territory as "an ideal place, ever to be sought; ever to be missed but always there" (from Ellison's inscription in my copy of *Going to the Territory*). After the success of *Invisible Man*, he returned to Oklahoma City for the first time since the summer of 1935, and wrote Albert Murray that the old territory's "still a town where the eyes have space in which to travel, and those freights still making up in the yard sound as good to me as ever they did when I lay on a pallet in the moon-drenched kitchen door and listened and dreamed of the time when I would leave and see the world" (*Trading* 51).

Young man Ellison's journey began in 1933, and his first stop was Tuskegee Institute in the black belt of Alabama. There "on the lower frequencies" of *The Waste Land* he heard the blues-toned chaos of T. S. Eliot's hometown St. Louis as well as the sounds of the broken universe of Europe at the end of World War I. Eliot's use of demotic speech and a blend of vernacular with high modernist idioms convinced Ellison that he had absorbed more of black American style than Eliot acknowledged when he characterized his old American self as merely that of "a small boy with a nigger drawl" (T. S. Eliot's letter to Herbert Read in 1928 [Baskett 150]). Ellison's reference points for *The Waste Land* were the breaks and improvised multiple takes of Louis Armstrong's jazz classic "Chinatown," as well as the whistles and shrieks from freight trains he heard rolling out of the yards in Deep Deuce, the black neighborhood of Oklahoma City. There, he lay on his pallet four blocks from Slaughter's dance hall and heard Jimmy Rushing sing the blues and Oran "Hot Lips" Page, Lester

Young, and Count Basie "upset the entire Negro section of the town" as they blew their horns into the night (CERE 269).

No wonder that, as boy and man, Ellison identified America as a nation improvised and a country whose culture was improvisatory. No wonder that in *Invisible Man* voice and form join in a succession of improvisations and a collage of voices backed by Invisible Man's bass line on the lower frequencies of invisibility. Writing his memoir (and Ellison's novel), Invisible Man becomes a writer: "Who knows but that, on the lower frequencies, I speak for you?" (IM 581). Ending with an ironic rhetorical question, Invisible Man tells his readers, *you may not see me, but I'll sure as hell make you hear my voice.* In a moment of reverberation, time stands still and then leaps ahead—for readers as they seek to sort out their own visibility and invisibility, and for Ralph Ellison as he extends his narrator's question into a different American time about to flow in new fits and starts in the shifting world after *Brown v. Board*.

III

While in residence at the American Academy in Rome from 1955 to 1957, Ellison sought with some method and a little melancholy madness to bring his novel-in-progress into clear focus. Judging from the manuscripts and copious notes left behind in his papers, he seems to have done so partly by writing an elusive essay, which, at this twenty-first-century remove, seems a companion to the astonishing May 19, 1954, letter he wrote Morteza Sprague in response to *Brown v. Board*. Called "Tell It Like It Is, Baby," the essay was triggered by a 1956 letter from Virgil Branam, a close friend of Ralph's since their boyhoods as "Renaissance Men" in Oklahoma City, and, as Eric Sundquist elaborates elsewhere in this volume, a likely starting point for the character Cliofus in the unfinished second novel. "Dear Uncle Raf," Branam began, "Have you read about those cracker senators cussing out the Supreme Court and all that mess? Let me hear what a home-boy done gone intellectual thinks when he's away from the Apple and all the righteous studs.... How's the writing going? Do you find it makes a difference being over there? Tell a man how it is" (CERE 29). (Ellison wisely used parts of Branam's letter as epigraph to "Tell It Like It Is, Baby" when the *Nation* published it in its 1965 centennial issue.) Branam of course was riffing on the infamous 1956 Southern Manifesto. Signed by an overwhelming majority of Southern senators and congressmen, the document pledged unyielding defiance to the Supreme

Court's unanimous decision ruling "separate but equal" unconstitutional and integration the law of the land.

Ellison stopped work on his second novel to draft the essay. Written nine years later, his preface calls "Tell It Like It Is, Baby" something he was "unable to complete.... I simply could not organize the various elements—literary, political, psychological, personal—into the complex, meaningful whole, which my sense of reality and my concern with fiction demanded. But I could not forget the essay." The preface tells how Ellison's anger over the Southern Manifesto of 1956 dovetailed with certain of his "most non-political preoccupations," such as the death of his father when he was three, and his deep, almost personal sense of injury at "the horror generated by the Civil War and the tragic incident which marked the reversal of the North's victory" (Lincoln's assassination). A stranger in the old world of Italy, Ellison felt intensely drawn to the swiftly changing center of gravity back home in America, especially the accelerating civil rights movement. Perhaps most intriguing, the difficult rhetorical literary issues that frustrated Ellison writing the essay seem very close to ones he faced and failed to resolve in the forty years of work behind and ahead of him on the second novel he would never finish.

In 1978, responding to "The Historical Frequencies of Ralph Waldo Ellison," an article I had written on the connections between his essays and *Invisible Man*, Ellison wrote thanking me for "having restored ['Tell It Like It Is, Baby'] to a place in [his] working memory." He went on to explain the ambivalent kinship he felt toward the essay: "What's more," he said, "I now realize just why I forgot it: After I had given it to a usually insightful friend to read, his exasperated response had been, 'Well, I read it, but what the hell *is* it?' So rather than try to spell it out for him—and for myself—I simply banished it from memory." He then mentions matters of rhetoric and literary form crucial to what he had attempted to work out in "Tell It Like It Is, Baby," and perhaps also later on in "The Little Man at Chehaw Station" (1977) as well as other ambitious essays such as "Going to the Territory" and "An Extravagance of Laughter"—issues left unresolved and unsolved in his immensely ambitious unfinished second novel. In any case, regarding "Tell It Like It Is, Baby," Ellison wrote in 1978: "I simply banished it from memory. And this, perhaps, because I was aware that when one attempts to mix literary modes in the interest of making disparate materials into *rhetorical* wholes one runs the risk of leaving *structural* holes—YET! I knew also that most of my essays tend to be somewhat 'mammy-made' or eclectic, so my friend's annoyed reaction led me to conclude that the piece was a total failure" (Ralph Ellison to the author, 17 January 1978; emphasis added).

Ellison's statement is cryptic enough for one to say, as his friend did of "Tell It Like It Is, Baby," "what the hell *is* it?" What does it mean? Yet his terms—*literary modes, disparate materials, rhetorical wholes, structural holes*—have an uncanny relationship to thematic and technical matters he tapped into in "Tell It Like It Is, Baby"—depths he was beginning to sound in the novel he had interrupted to write the troublesome essay in the first place. For example, his preoccupation with that American "evasion of identity" he wrote of to Sprague in the immediate wake of *Brown v. Board* becomes a painful complement to "the orphan's loneliness" at the heart of "Tell It Like It Is, Baby." Ellison splices into this frequency in relation to the anger and loss he felt for years, and perhaps still felt, about his father dying when he was three. In both essay and novel Ellison finds in his own experience as well as in the fictional character of Bliss/Sunraider ties between the death of a father and the murder of President Lincoln, whom slaves and, increasingly with time, many white Americans came to see as a historical Father Abraham. In the midst of a passage about the meanings of his own father's death, Ellison poses a question at the quick of the father-son relationship developing between Hickman and Bliss in the second novel: "*But what quality of love sustains us in our orphan's loneliness; and how much is thus required of fatherly love to give us strength for all our life thereafter?*" (CERE 35).

Like the question at the end of *Invisible Man*, the one in "Tell It Like It Is, Baby" is profoundly rhetorical. Its petals open slowly, revealing questions that seem insoluble riddles. The qualitative flows into the quantitative. In Ellison's case the burden handed to memory by the contingency of death must have been staggering, especially if one thinks of the heroic cast given to Lewis Ellison by his widow Ida as well as his three-year-old, surviving son. Although his mother sustained him, young Ralph conjured apparitions of his father that, when they vanished, left him angry and bitter. As he went through changes and his identity shifted accordingly, his father's real time remained fixed and static. From Rome in "Tell It Like It Is, Baby," Ellison confronts again and again the nightmare of living with his loss and takes somewhat to heart the Vet's advice to Invisible Man: "Be your own father, young man" (IM 156).

Nine years later in New York in 1965 Ellison completes both the essay and the episode in his second novel in which Reverend Hickman midwifes a boy child into the world and names him Bliss. From the get-go Bliss is an orphan, yet Hickman becomes a father to him. However, the actual and surmised marks of race intervene. Bliss seeks his absent mother, who he knows is white; come adolescence, he cannot accept Hickman as "the dark daddy of flesh and word" (*Juneteenth* 264). "Heart mysteries" there, Yeats wrote in "The Circus Animals' Desertion." Yet in Book II or *Juneteenth*, Bliss, self-made into Senator Adam Sunraider, the race-baiting senator from a New England state, mortally wounded in an assassination by *his* unacknowledged son, summons Hickman and only Hickman to his hospital bed. There, with Hickman as his guide, Bliss/Sunraider struggles to undo "the evasion of identity" that has brought him to the edge of the underworld. Here Ellison revisits on a grand, tragicomic scale in the second novel the personal, racial, and national themes of the essay he almost completed, put aside, then some nine years later, finished for its own sake and as a prelude to mining further the richest veins of his novel-in-progress.

IV

As if to recapitulate *Invisible Man* at the same moment he hears the second novel buzzing in his head, Ellison's 1953 "Brave Words for a Startling Occasion" had deftly invoked the Greek god Proteus, the shape-shifter who could and did change into all manner of shapes to stave off unwelcome questions. "For the novelist," Ellison wrote, "Proteus stands for both America and the inheritance of illusion through which all men must fight to achieve reality" (CERE 154). In *Invisible Man* the confidence man Rinehart is Ellison's Proteus figure. In one of his disguises he is Reverend B. P. Rinehart, *Spiritual Technologist*; elsewhere Ellison reveals these initials to stand for Bliss Proteus. In "Ralph Ellison in His Labyrinth," Eric Sundquist examines the numerous stunning guises in which Proteus and the protean theme turn up in *Three Days before the Shooting* .... Sundquist also identifies and brilliantly analyzes the formal crux and conflict embodied in the unfinished totality of Ellison's immense work. "In a novel that ran the risk of giving way to protean tale-telling without end—in which the very idea of plot progression appears to have been set aside in favor of relentless improvisation—Cliofus, appropriately, has the last words" (Sundquist, this volume).

Did "protean tale-telling without end" come to vanquish the "plot progression" of the second novel? Perhaps so, but there is also abundant evidence that Ellison, true to his role as novelist, struggled to hold in check his impulse toward protean tale-telling run wild. For example, in James

Allan McPherson's "Indivisible Man," written in collaboration with Ellison in 1969–70, Ellison contributed a perspective that has the ring of authenticity and truth about where matters stood with the novel-in-progress some twenty-five years before his death. The passage I have in mind, written by McPherson in reportorial third-person prose, leads to a few direct remarks from Ellison to McPherson. (I should note that Ellison approved the final text the *Atlantic* published in December 1970.) By then the trauma of the November 1967 fire at the Ellison summer home in the Berkshires, which destroyed precious revisions of the second novel, seems to have abated enough that "he is presently in the process of revising again," a view supported by publication of the "Night-Talk" episode in 1969—a dazzling piece full of "relentless improvisation" that *also* advanced the plot. For his part, McPherson reports on the current state of the novel-in-progress in carefully balanced prose before yielding to Ellison's voice: "He has enough typed manuscripts to publish three books, but is worried over how the work will hold up as a total structure. He does not want to publish three separate books, but then he does not want to compromise on anything essential. 'If I find that it is better to make it a three-section book, to issue it in three volumes, I would do that as long as I thought that each volume had a compelling interest in itself'" (CERE 391).

In the context of the second novel, it is worth remembering, as Adam Bradley points out in his superb study, *Ralph Ellison in Progress*, that "by the summer of 1950, Ralph Ellison had an 868-page manuscript of *Invisible Man* with no conclusion" (Bradley 178)—no prologue and no epilogue either. Over the next year and a half working with his editor, Albert Erskine, Ellison cut and revised his first novel down to 612 pages, including shaping a prologue and epilogue out of existing passages and adding salient new ones. If the immense archive of manuscripts and notes in the Ellison Papers at the Library of Congress is a full, accurate record, Ellison did not do for his second novel the sort of full-scale, plot-driven revision he accomplished with *Invisible Man*. At the same time, it is clear from the related narratives compiled in *Three Days before the Shooting . . .* why Ellison apparently considered multivolume publication. The two narratives he titled simply Book I and Book II are in typescript: Book I, dated 1972 in Fanny Ellison's hand, and Book II, revised and expanded in subsequent years "until at least 1986, when, according to Mrs. Ellison's handwritten note, her husband took the latest, most complete typescript to their rebuilt summer home in Plainfield" (TD 233*).* The break between Book I and Book II is a clean, sharp, appropriate transition to the flashback, which begins Book II. Even considering the unfinished state of Books I and II at Ellison's death, one can imagine a single long book or two medium-length volumes; though whether the latter option would have met Ellison's criterion of "each volume [having] a compelling interest in itself" is a tougher call.

In some ways the computer-generated manuscripts indicate serious revision of motive, character, and form. For example in the old typescript version of "Song of Innocence," published by the *Iowa Review* (Spring 1970), the white reporter McIntyre goes to Oklahoma to unravel the mystery of Senator Sunraider's past. In the computer version composed from 1988 to 1992, Ellison sends Reverend Hickman instead. Ellison last revised the computer files comprising the narrative of Hickman in Washington, DC, in July 1993. (The beginning of this narrative is a recapitulation, revision, and expansion of passages of the prologue in the typescript version of Book I, published as the opening section of "And Hickman Arrives" in *Noble Savage* in 1960.) Most of these Hickman-centered files were reworked and revised from typescripts dating back as far as the 1950s. Overall, writing on his computer, Ellison seems to have paid more attention to tinkering with particular scenes and passages than to addressing how "the work will hold up as a total structure" (CERE 391). Ellison's multitudinous notes are rich and suggestive *pensées* if not blueprints offering specific if provisional solutions to problems of form, sequence, motive, and plot posed by the novel in his mind. Yet he never seems to have set about with the fierce determination on display with *Invisible Man* of 1950–51 to fill in one way or another the "structural holes" resulting from his attempts to "mix literary modes" in order to shape his "disparate materials into rhetorical wholes."

From 1970 on, Ellison's apparent indecision and inaction on these formal, technical fronts highlight Sundquist's question of whether he and his principal characters Hickman and Bliss/Sunraider (and the redoubtable Cliofus from the Oklahoma narrative) were trying to hold Proteus fast as they question his different avatars about the riddle of form, or let him go with a wink and a nod, knowing he would reappear over and over again in yet another guise of the trickster. In the latter case there would have been no finished book in the conventional sense, and the novel could have gone on and on, breaking off instead of coming to a considered halt. Recalling the rhetorical question, which concludes but in some sense does not end *Invisible Man*— "Who knows but that, on the lower frequencies, I speak for you?"—perhaps "that pause for contemplation," which Ellison was seeking in 1982, turned into a wish merely for a sense of an ending rather than something that could be called the end.

V

Perhaps the end of the Ellison centennial is a propitious moment (and year) for Ellisonian time both to stand still and leap ahead. Invisible Man may have had it right. Perhaps invisibility "gives one a slightly different sense of time" so that "you're never quite on the beat. Sometimes you're ahead and sometimes behind" (IM 8). Perhaps by absorbing and brooding on "nodes of time" in *Invisible Man* and *Three Days before the Shooting* . . . (and the notes and drafts pertaining to both works), scholars might yet hold the Proteus in Ellison fast long enough to learn whether during his later years he set aside his earlier quest to set "relentless improvisation" flowing hand in hand with a "plot progression" capable of rounding off his epic novel. Perhaps in the drafts and notes—look to the notes, the notes, the notes—there is not one but various endings challenging readers to put up or shut up as the last paragraph of *Invisible Man* did and still does with its single sentence: "Who knows but that, on the lower frequencies, I speak for you?" (IM 581)

As we ponder the riddles of Ellison's fiction, it might also be wise to "slip into the breaks and look around" at drafts of essays such as "Tell It Like It Is, Baby" (1956/1965), "The Little Man at Chehaw Station" (1977), "Going to the Territory" (1979), and "An Extravagance of Laughter" (1985). Perchance Ellison solved in these essays or even in *Leaving the Territory* the unfinished riotous draft of a memoir in his papers, the riddle he posed in his 1978 letter about how to "mix literary modes" to create true "rhetorical wholes" from those "disparate materials," which fascinated him in whatever writing he did, including his protean improvisational letters.

And of course, like the notes, there are the letters. As I work on editing them with Marc Conner, sixty years of incredibly various, multifaceted correspondence tell me that although there are biographies of Ellison, first in importance Arnold Rampersad's, there is no *biography* yet—at least none whose purpose is to discern, in Ellison's 1954 words, "the only integration that counts: that of the personality" (Ellison, Letter to Morteza Sprague 39). Nonetheless an editor is an invisible man and has his choice of guises. In my case, editing Ralph's letters, the daemon I'll follow is not Proteus but another character who, often passed over, underneath his mask possesses certain protean lineaments along with a sudden, astonishing, game- and life-changing centripetal force.

For my daemon I'll take the yokel in *Invisible Man*. Against the prize-fighter and "the smart money," the yokel's only chance was "to slip into the breaks and look around." Doing so, Invisible Man tells us, he "simply stepped inside of his opponent's sense of time." The point is clear. Because the yokel dared step inside his opponent's "sense of time," the "unheard sounds came through, and each melodic line existed of itself, stood out clearly from all the rest, said its piece, and waited patiently for the other voices to speak" (IM 8, 9). Like the little man behind the stove at Chehaw Station, behind his mask the yokel stands for what Ellison, taking his cue from Ralph Waldo Emerson, insisted on: "consciousness, consciousness, *consciousness*. And with consciousness, a more refined conscientiousness" (CERE, 429).

Is there a better charge to those of us fortunate enough to bear Ellison's flame into the possibilities of this turbulent new century?

WORKS CITED

Abrahams, Roger D. "A Flying Fool." *Afro-American Folktales: Stories from Black Traditions in the New World*. New York: Pantheon, 1985. 280–81.
Adell, Sandra. *Double-Consciousness/Double Bind: Theoretical Issues in Twentieth-Century Black Literature*. Urbana, University of Illinois Press, 1994.
Agiesta, Jennifer, and Jon Cohen. "Fewer Americans Think Obama Has Advanced Race Relations, Poll Shows." *Washington Post*, 18 January 2010. Web. Washingtonpost.com. 27 April 2010.
Allfree, Claire. "Gillian Slovo's New Play 'The Riots' Looks for the Truth behind UK Unrest." *Metro*, 16 November 2011. Web. http://metro.co.uk/2011/11/16/gillian-slovos-new-play-the-riots-looks-for-the-truth-behind-uk-unrest-222362/. 11 March 2014.
"All God's Chillen Had Wings." *The Book of Negro Folklore*. Ed. Langston Hughes and Arna Bontemps. New York: Dodd, Mead, 1958. 62–65.
Apel, Dora. "Just Joking? Chimps, Obama and Racial Stereotype." *Journal of Visual Culture* 8, no. 2 (2009): 134–42. *EBSCO Host Communications and Mass Media Complete*. Web. 20 February 2012.
Arana, Marie. "He's Not Black." *Washington Post*, 30 November 2008. Web. Washingtonpost.com. 27 April 2010.
Artuso, Kathryn Stelmach. *Transatlantic Renaissances: Literature of Ireland and the American South*. Newark: University of Delaware Press, 2013.
Baldwin, James. "Everybody's Protest Novel." *Partisan Review*, June 16, 1949, 578–85.
Barnes, Marian B. "The Ibo Landing Story." *Talk That Talk: An Anthology of African-American Storytelling*. Ed. Linda Goss. New York: Touchstone, 1989. 139–40.
Barthes, Roland. *Roland Barthes*. Trans. Richard Howard. New York: Hill and Wang, 1977.
Baskett, Sam S. "T. S. Eliot as an American Poet." *Centennial Review* 26, no. 2 (Spring 1982): 147–71.
Beavers, Herman. "Documenting Turbulence: The Dialectics of Chaos in *Invisible Man*." *Ralph Ellison and the Raft of Hope: A Political Companion to "Invisible Man"* Ed. Lucas E. Morel. Lexington: University Press of Kentucky, 2004. 193–217.

Bellah, Robert N., Richard Madsen, William M. Sullivan, Ann Swidler, and Steven Tipton. *Habits of the Heart: Individualism and Commitment in American Life*. New York: Harper and Row, 1985.

Billups, Andrea, and David R. Sands. "Obama Term Expected to Be Post-Racial." *Washington Times*, 9 November 2008. Web. Washingtontimes.com. 20 February 2010.

Bittle, William E., and Gilbert Geis. *The Longest Way Home: Chief Alfred C. Sam's Back-to-Africa Movement*. Detroit: Wayne State University Press, 1964.

Blackwell, Ken. "Post-Racial Preference America." *National Review Online*, 10 November 2008. Web. NationalReview.com. 20 February 2010.

Bloom, Harold. *The Anxiety of Influence: A Theory of Poetry*. Oxford: Oxford University Press, 1973.

———. *How to Read and Why*. New York: Scribner, 2001.

———. "Introduction." *Ralph Ellison's "Invisible Man": Modern Critical Interpretations*. New ed. New York: Infobase, 2009. 1–6.

———. "Introduction." *Ralph Ellison: Modern Critical Views*. New ed. New York: Infobase, 2010. 1–3.

———. *A Map of Misreading*. Oxford: Oxford University Press, 1975.

Bohn, Kevin. "Gun Sales Surge after Obama's Election." CNN, 11 November 2008. Web. CNN.com. 27 April 2010.

Bowen, Zack. "Ulysses." *A Companion to Joyce Studies*. Ed. Zack Bowen and James F. Carens. Westport, CT: Greenwood Press, 1984. 421–557.

Bradley, Adam. *Ralph Ellison in Progress: From "Invisible Man" to "Three Days before the Shooting...."* New Haven, CT: Yale University Press, 2010.

Brophy, Alfred L. "*Invisible Man* as Literary Analogue to *Brown vs. Board of Education*." *Ralph Ellison and the Raft of Hope: A Political Companion to "Invisible Man."* Ed. Lucas E. Morel. Lexington: University Press of Kentucky, 2006. 119–41.

Bruccoli, Matthew. *Some Sort of Epic Grandeur: The Life of F. Scott Fitzgerald*. Rev. ed. New York: Carroll and Graf, 1993.

Buchwald, Dagmar. "'Let 'em Swoller You till They Vomit or Bust Wide Open': Doing the Parasite between Chaos and Control in Ralph Ellison's *Invisible Man*." *Amerikastudien/American Studies* 45, no. 1 (2000): 73–90.

Buell, Lawrence. *The Dream of the Great American Novel*. Cambridge, MA: Harvard University Press/Belknap Press, 2014.

Burke, Kenneth. *Attitudes toward History*. Berkeley: University of California Press, 1984.

———. "I, Eye, Ay—Emerson's Early Essay on 'Nature': Thoughts on the Machinery of Transcendence." *Sewanee Review* 74, no. 4 (Autumn 1966): 875–95.

———. "Letter to Kenneth Burke." *Kenneth Burke Papers*. State College: Pennsylvania State University Press, 1945.

———. *Permanence and Change: An Anatomy of Purpose*. Berkeley: University of California Press, 1984.

———. *The Philosophy of Literary Form: Studies in Symbolic Action*. Berkeley: University of California Press, 1984.

Butler, Robert J. "Dante's *Inferno* and Ellison's *Invisible Man*: A Study in Literary Continuity." *The Critical Response to Ralph Ellison*. Westport, CT: Greenwood Press, 2000. 95–106.

———. "Ellison's 'Black Eye': Transforming Pain into Vision." *The Critical Response to Ralph Ellison*. Ed. Robert J. Butler. Westport, CT: Greenwood Press, 2000. 141–48.

———. "Probing the Lower Frequencies: Fifty Years of Ellison Criticism." *A Historical Guide to Ralph Ellison*. Ed. Steven C. Tracy. Oxford: Oxford University Press, 2004. 233–60.

———. "Review of *Ralph Ellison* by Arnold Rampersad." *African American Review* 42, nos. 3–4 (2008): 759–61.

Calderone, Michael. "Matthews: 'I Forgot He Was Black Tonight for an Hour.'" *Politico*, 27 January 2010. Web. Politico.com. 27 April 2010.

Callahan, John F. "'American Culture Is of a Whole': From the Letters of Ralph Ellison." *New Republic*, 1 March 1999, 38–39.

———. "Ellison's *Invisible Man*." *Ralph Ellison's "Invisible Man": A Casebook*. Ed. John F. Callahan. New York: Oxford University Press, 2004. 287–319.

———. "Ralph Waldo Ellison, Francis Scott Fitzgerald, and 'The Dark Fields of the Republic.'" *F. Scott Fitzgerald Review* 1, no. 1 (2002): 122–39.

Calt, Stephen. *Barrelhouse Words: A Blues Dialect Dictionary*. Urbana: University of Illinois Press, 2009.

Campbell, Joseph. *The Hero with a Thousand Faces*. Princeton, NJ: Princeton University Press, 1973.

Canetti, Elias. *Crowds and Power*. New York: Farrar, Straus and Giroux, 1982.

Carter, Paul. "Ambiguous Traces, Mishearing, and Auditory Space." *Hearing Cultures: Essays on Sound, Listening, and Modernity*. Ed. Veit Erlman. 2004. Repr. Oxford: Berg, 2005. 43–63.

Carter, Stephen L. *The Violence of Peace: America's Wars in the Age of Obama*. New York: Beast Books, 2011.

Cassuto, Leonard. "*A Father's Law*, 1950s Masculinity, and Richard Wright's Agony over Integration." *Richard Wright: New Readings in the 21st Century*. Ed. Alice Mikal Craven and William E. Dow. New York: Palgrave Macmillan, 2011. 39–54.

Cavendish, Dominic. "The Riots: Duo Who Turned a Crisis into a Drama." *Daily Telegraph*, 8 November 2011. Web. http://www.telegraph.co.uk/culture/theatre/theatre-features/8877272/The-Riots-duo-who-turned-a-crisis-into-a-drama.html. 6 November 2015.

CBS News. "Obama's Racial Identity Still an Issue." CBS Interactive, 27 November 2007. Web. CBSNews.com. 27 April 2010.

———. "Post-Racial USA? Not So Fast." CBS Interactive, 15 November 2008. Web. CBSNews.com. 27 April 2010.

Certeau, Michel de. *The Practice of Everyday Life*. Trans. Steven Rendall. Berkeley: University of California Press, 1984. Kindle ed.

Chambers, Ross. *Room for Maneuver: Reading Oppositional Narrative*. Chicago: University of Chicago Press, 1991.

Clifford, James. *Routes: Travel and Translation in the Late Twentieth Century*. Cambridge, MA: Harvard University Press, 1997.

CNN. "Romney Surrogate Apologizes for Saying Obama Should 'Learn How to Be an American.'" CNN, 17 July 2012. Web. politicalticker.blogs.cnn.com. 12 October 2015.

Coates, Ta-Nehisi Paul. "Fear of a Black President." *Atlantic*, 22 August 2012. Web. TheAtlantic.com. 12 April 2014.

——. "Is Obama Black Enough?" *Time*, 1 February 2007. Web. TIME.com. 27 April 2010.

Conner, Marc C. "'Leaving the Territory': Ralph Ellison's Backward Glance." *Modernism and Autobiography*. Ed. Maria DiBattista and Emily O. Whitman. New York: Cambridge University Press, 2014. 113–24.

——. "The Litany of Things: Sacrament and History in *Invisible Man*." *Ralph Ellison and the Raft of Hope: A Political Companion to "Invisible Man."* Ed. Lucas E. Morel. Lexington: University Press of Kentucky, 2004. 171–92.

——. "Reading Ralph Ellison: A Hidden Name and Complex Fate." *South Atlantic Review* 73, no. 4 (Fall 2008): 146–53.

——. "To Utter the Holy: The Metaphysical Romance of *Middle Passage*." *Charles Johnson: The Novelist as Philosopher*. Ed Marc C. Conner and William R. Nash. Jackson: University Press of Mississippi, 2007. 57–81.

Consentino, Donald. "Who Is That Fellow in the Many-Colored Cap? Transformations of Eshu in Old and New World Mythologies." *Journal of American Folklore* 100, no. 397 (1987): 261–75.

Crable, Bryan. *Ralph Ellison and Kenneth Burke: At the Roots of the Racial Divide*. Charlottesville: University of Virginia Press, 2012.

Crane, Gregg. "Ralph Ellison's Constitutional Faith." *The Cambridge Companion to Ralph Ellison*. Ed. Ross Posnock. Cambridge: Cambridge University Press, 2005. 104–20.

Csikszentmihalyi, Mihaly. *Flow: The Psychology of Optimal Experience*. New York: Harper and Row, 1990.

Deren, Maya. *Divine Horsemen: The Living Gods of Haiti*. New Paltz, NY: McPherson, 1983.

DeVeaux, Scott K. *The Birth of Bebop: A Social and Musical History*. Berkeley: University of California Press, 1997.

Devlin, Kimberly. *Wandering and Return in "Finnegans Wake."* Princeton, NJ: Princeton University Press, 1991.

Dewey, John. *Art as Experience*. 1934. Repr. New York: Perigree Books/G. P. Putnam's Sons, 1980.

DiBattista, Maria. *First Love: The Affections of Modern Fiction*. Chicago: University of Chicago Press, 1991.

Dickstein, Morris. "Ralph Ellison, Race, and American Culture." *Ralph Ellison's "Invisible Man": A Casebook*. Ed. John F. Callahan. Oxford: Oxford University Press, 2004. 125–47.

Dietze, Rudolf F. "Ralph Ellison and the Literary Tradition." *History and Tradition in African-American Culture*. Ed. Gunter H. Lenz. Frankfurt: Campus Verlag, 1984. 18–29.

Dimaggio, Anthony. "Transcending Racism?" *Counterpunch* 14, no. 16 (November 2008). Web. Counterpunch.org. 20 February 2012.

Dodd, Lynda G. "Presidential Leadership and Civil Rights Lawyering in the Era before *Brown*." *Indiana Law Journal* 85, no. 1599, art. 14 (2010): 1599–1657. Web. http://www.repository.law.indiana.edu/ilj/vol85/iss4/14. 16 June 2015.

Dorson, Richard M. "Colored Man in Heaven." *American Negro Folktales*. Greenwich, CT: Fawcett, 1956. 178–80.

Douglass, Frederick. "The Meaning of July Fourth for the Negro (July 5, 1852)." *Pre–Civil War Decade, 1850–1860*. Vol. 2. *The Life and Writings of Frederick Douglass*. Ed. Philip S. Foner. 5 vols. 1950. Repr. New York: International, 1975. 181–204.

———. "Oration in Memory of Abraham Lincoln (April 14, 1876)." *Reconstruction and After.* Vol. 4. *The Life and Writings of Frederick Douglass.* Ed. Philip S. Foner. 5 vols. 1955. Repr. New York: International, 1975. 309–19.

Drehle, Von. "The Five Faces of Barack Obama." *Time,* 21 August 2008. Web. TIME.com. 27 April 2010.

Du Bois, W. E. B. *The Souls of Black Folk: Essays and Sketches.* 1903. Repr. Greenwich, CT: Fawcett, 1961.

———. *Writings.* Ed. Nathan Huggins. New York: Library of America, 1986.

Dundes, Alan. "Preface." *Mother Wit from the Laughing Barrel: Readings in the Interpretation of Afro-American Folklore.* Ed. Alan Dundes. Englewood Cliffs, NJ: Prentice Hall, 1973. xv–xvi.

Dyson, Michael Eric. *I May Not Get There with You: The True Martin Luther King, Jr.* New York: Free Press, 2000.

Ealy, Steven D. "'A Friendship That Has Meant So Much': Robert Penn Warren and Ralph W. Ellison." *South Carolina Review* 38, no. 2 (2006): 162–72.

Eddy, Beth. *The Rites of Identity: Religious Naturalism and Cultural Criticism of Kenneth Burke and Ralph Ellison.* Princeton, NJ: Princeton University Press, 2003.

Edwards, Brian T. "Ralph Ellison and the Grain of Internationalism." *Globalizing American Studies.* Ed. Brian T. Edwards and Dilip Parameshwar Gaonkar. Chicago: University of Chicago Press, 2010. 115–34.

Egerton, John. *Speak Now against the Day: The Generation before the Civil Rights Movement in the South.* Chapel Hill: University of North Carolina Press, 1994.

Eliot, T. S. "Gerontion." *The Complete Poems and Plays, 1909–1950.* San Diego: Harcourt Brace Jovanovich, 1971. 21–22.

Ellison, Ralph. *The Collected Essays of Ralph Ellison.* Ed. John F. Callahan. 1995. Repr. New York: Modern Library, 2003.

———. Ellison Papers. Manuscript Division, Library of Congress, Washington, DC.

———. "Flying Home." *Flying Home and Other Stories.* By Ralph Ellison. Ed. John F. Callahan. New York: Random House, 1996. 147–73.

———. *Going to the Territory.* 1986. Repr. New York: Vintage, 1987.

———. "Hidden Name and Complex Fate." *The Collected Essays of Ralph Ellison.* New York: Modern Library, 1995. 189–209.

———. "In a Strange Country." *Flying Home and Other Stories.* By Ralph Ellison. Ed. John F. Callahan. New York: Random House, 1996. 137–46.

———. *Invisible Man.* New York: Random House, 1952. New York: Vintage, 1989. New York: Modern Library, 1992.

———. *Juneteenth.* Ed. John F. Callahan. New York: Random House, 1999.

———. Letter to Kenneth Burke, 23 November 1945. TS. Kenneth Burke Papers, Pattee Library, Pennsylvania State University, State College.

———. Letter to Morteza Sprague, 19 May 1954. In John F. Callahan, "'American Culture Is of a Whole': From the Letters of Ralph Ellison." *New Republic,* 1 March 1999, 38–39.

———. *Living with Music: Ralph Ellison's Jazz Writings.* Ed. Robert G. O'Meally. New York: Modern Library/Random House, 2001.

———. "Ralph Ellison's Territorial Vantage." *Living with Music: Ralph Ellison's Jazz Writings*. (1976 interview by Ron Welburn originally published in *The Grackle: Improvised Music in Transition* [1977–78]). Ed. Robert G. O'Meally. New York: Modern Library/Random House, 2001. 15–33.

———. *Shadow and Act*. New York: Random House, 1964.

———. *Three Days before the Shooting . . . : The Unfinished Second Novel*. Ed. John F. Callahan and Adam Bradley. New York: Modern Library, 2010.

Ellison, Ralph, and Albert Murray. *Trading Twelves: The Selected Letters of Ralph Ellison and Albert Murray*. Ed. John F. Callahan and Albert Murray. New York: Modern Library, 2000.

Ellison, Ralph, William Styron, Robert Penn Warren, and C. Vann Woodward. *Conversations with Ralph Ellison*. Ed. Maryemma Graham and Amritjit Singh. Jackson: University Press of Mississippi, 1995. 141–72.

Engeman, Thomas. "*Invisible Man* and *Juneteenth*: Ralph Ellison's Literary Pursuit of Racial Justice." *Ralph Ellison and the Raft of Hope: A Political Companion to "Invisible Man."* Ed. Lucas E. Morel. Lexington: University Press of Kentucky, 2004. 91–104.

Erlmann, Veit. *Hearing Cultures: Essays on Sound, Listening, and Modernity*. Oxford: Berg, 2004.

Etzioni, Amitai. *The Spirit of Community: The Reinvention of American Society*. New York: Simon and Schuster, 1993.

Ewers, Justin. "Obama and Race Relations: Civil Rights Leaders Aren't Satisfied." *US News and World Report*, 30 April 2009. Web. USNews.com. 20 February 2012.

Fenn, Peter. "Barack Obama Should Worry about the Enthusiasm Gap." *US News and World Report*, 9 March 2012. Web. USNews.com. 20 February 2012.

Ferris, Marc. *Star-Spangled Banner: The Unlikely Story of America's National Anthem*. Baltimore: Johns Hopkins University Press, 2014.

Fitzgerald, F. Scott. *The Great Gatsby*. 1925. Repr. New York: Scribner, 1992.

———. *Tender Is the Night*. 1934. Repr. New York: Scribner, 1995.

Foley, Barbara. *Wrestling with the Left: The Making of Ralph Ellison's "Invisible Man."* Durham, NC: Duke University Press, 2010.

Frank, Joseph. "Ralph Ellison and a Literary 'Ancestor': Dostoevski." *New Criterion* 2 (September 1983): 140–52.

Franklin, John Hope. *The Color Line: Legacy for the Twenty-First Century*. Columbia: University of Missouri Press, 1993.

Frost, Robert. "The Gift Outright." *The Poetry of Robert Frost*. Ed. Edward Connery Lathem. New York: Holt, Rinehart and Winston, 1969. 348.

Garrido, Jon. "Enthusiasm for Obama Is Gone: Hispanics, Latinos, Liberals and Independents Must Look for Another." *Solidarity USA*, 12 January 2011. Web. SolidarityUSA.org. 20 February 2012.

Gates, Henry Louis, Jr. *Figures in Black: Words, Signs, and the "Racial" Self*. New York: Oxford University Press, 1989.

———. *The Signifying Monkey: A Theory of Afro-American Literary Criticism*. New York: Oxford University Press, 1988.

Gibson, Donald B. "Wright's Invisible Native Son." *American Quarterly* 21, no. 4 (1969): 729–38.

Gillespie, Dizzy, and Al Fraser. *To BE, or Not . . . to BOP*. Minneapolis: University of Minnesota Press, 1979.

Gilman, Sander L. *Franz Kafka, the Jewish Patient*. New York: Routledge, 1995.

Gioia, Ted. *The Birth (and Death) of the Cool*. Golden, CO: Speck, 2009.

Goethe, Johann Wolfgang von. *Faust: Part One*. Trans. David Luke. Oxford: Oxford University Press, 1987.

Goodwyn, Frank, and Grace Greenwood. *The Magic of Limping John: A Story of the Mexican Border Town*. New York: Farrar and Rinehart, 1944.

Guelzo, Allen. *Lincoln's Emancipation Proclamation: The End of Slavery in America*. New York: Simon and Schuster, 2004.

Guterl, Matthew Pratt. *The Color of Race in America: 1900–1940*. Cambridge, MA: Harvard University Press, 2001.

Harrison, Jane Ellen. *Epilogemena to the Study of Greek Religion*. Cambridge: Cambridge University Press, 1921.

Hayles, Katherine N. *Chaos and Order: Complex Dynamics in Literature and Science*. Chicago: University of Chicago Press, 1991.

Hegarty, Paul. *Noise/Music: A History*. London: Continuum, 2007.

Homer. *The Odyssey*. Trans. Robert Fitzgerald. Garden City: Anchor, 1963.

———. *The Odyssey*. Trans. T. E. Lawrence. 1932. Repr. New York: Signet, 1999.

———. *The Odyssey*. Trans. W. H. D. Rouse. 1937. Repr. New York: Signet, 1999.

Howe, Irving. "Black Boys and Native Sons." *Twentieth Century Interpretations of "Invisible Man."* Ed. John M. Reilly. Englewood Cliffs, NJ: Prentice Hall, 1970. 100–102.

Hsu, Hua. "The End of White America?" *Atlantic*, January–February 2009. Web. TheAtlantic.com. 20 February 2012.

"Inauguration Jubilation Spreads across the Country." CNN, 20 January 2009. Web. CNN.com. 27 April 2010.

"Inside Obama's Sweeping Victory." Pew Research Center, 5 November 2008. Web. Pewresearch.org. 20 February 2012.

"It's Official: Obama Is Black." MSNBC, 3 April 2010. Web. MSNBC.com. 27 April 2010.

Jackson, Lawrence. *Ralph Ellison: Emergence of Genius*. New York: John Wiley and Sons, 2002.

———. "Ralph Ellison's Politics of Integration." *A Historical Guide to Ralph Ellison*. Ed. Steven C. Tracy. New York: Oxford University Press, 2004. 171–206.

Jacobson, Matthew Frye. *Whiteness of a Different Color: European Immigrants and the Alchemy of Race*. Cambridge, MA: Harvard University Press, 1998.

James, Rawn, Jr. *The Double V: How Wars, Protest, and Harry Truman Desegregated America's Military*. New York: Bloomsbury Press, 2013.

Jarrett, Michael. *Drifting on a Read: Jazz as a Model for Writing*. Albany: State University of New York Press, 1999.

Johnson, Charles. "The End of the Black American Narrative." *American Scholar* 7, no. 3 (Summer 2008): 32–42.

———. "The End of the Black American Narrative." *Best African American Essays*. Ed. Gerald Lyn Early. New York: Ballantine, 2010. 111–22.

———. "The King We Need: Teachings for a Nation in Search of Itself." *Shambhala Sun* 13, no. 3 (2005): 41–50.

———. "National Book Award Acceptance Speech." *TriQuarterly* 82 (Fall 1991): 208–9.

———. "A Phenomenology of the Black Body." *Michigan Quarterly Review* 32, no. 4 (Fall 1993): 599–614.

———. "Whole Sight: Notes on New Black Fiction." *Callaloo* 22 (Autumn 1984): 1–6.

Johnson, James Weldon. *The Autobiography of an Ex-Coloured Man*. New York: Hill and Wang, 1960.

Johnson, Lyndon B. "Commencement Address at Howard University: 'To Fulfill These Rights.'" *Public Papers of the Presidents of the United States: Lyndon B. Johnson 1965: Containing the Public Messages, Speeches, and Statements of the President*. Ed. US GPO. Washington, DC: US Government Printing Office, 1966. 635–40.

Jones, Chris. "An Invisible Man, Visibly in Pain." *Chicago Tribune*, 22 January 2012. Web. http://articles.chicagotribune.com/2012-01-22/entertainment/ct-ent-0123-invisible-man-review-20120122_1_ralph-ellison-invisible-man-court-theatre. 11 March 2014.

Jonsson, Patrik. "After Obama's Win, White Backlash Festers in US." *Christian Science Monitor*, 17 November 2008. Web. CSMonitor.com. 27 April 2010.

Joyce, James. *Letters of James Joyce*. Vol. 3. Ed. Richard Ellmann. New York: Viking, 1966.

———. *Ulysses*. The Corrected Text. Ed. Hans Walter Gabler. New York: Random House, 1986.

Kass, Leon. *The Beginning of Wisdom: Reading Genesis*. New York: Simon and Schuster, 2003.

Kerényi, Karl. "The Trickster in Relation to Greek Mythology." *The Trickster: A Study in American Indian Mythology*. Ed. Paul Radin. New York: Schocken, 1972. 173–91.

Kesler, Charles R. *I Am the Change: Barack Obama and the Crisis of Liberalism*. New York: Broadside Books/HarperCollins, 2012.

King, Martin Luther, Jr. "I Have a Dream." *I Have a Dream: Writings and Speeches That Changed the World*. Ed. James M. Washington. San Francisco: Harper, 1992. 101–6.

———. "Letter from Birmingham Jail." *Why We Can't Wait*. By Martin Luther King Jr. New York: Signet, 2000. 85–112.

Knopf, Terry Ann. *Rumors, Race, and Riots*. New York: Transaction, 2006.

Krasner, David. *American Drama 1945–2000*. Oxford: Blackwell, 2006.

Krebs, Justin. "Obama's Enthusiasm Gap Is a Major Problem." WNYC, 16 July 2010. Web. WNYC.org. 20 February 2012.

Kuhn, David Paul. "White Support for Obama at Historic High." *Politico*, 24 October 2008. Web. Politico.com. 20 February 2012.

LaBelle, Brandon. *Acoustic Territories: Sound Culture and Everyday Life*. London: Continuum, 2010.

Lears, Jackson, "A History of Disappointment." *London Review of Books* 34, no. 1 (2012): 10–13.

Levitt, Morton P. *Modernist Survivors: The Contemporary Novel in England, the United States, France, and Latin America*. Columbus: Ohio State University Press, 1987.

Lewis, R. W. B. *The American Adam: Innocence, Tragedy, and Tradition in the Nineteenth Century*. Chicago: University of Chicago Press, 1955.

———. "Eccentrics' Pilgrimage." *Hudson Review* 6, no. 1 (Spring 1953): 144–50.

List, Robert N. *Dedalus in Harlem: The Joyce-Ellison Connection.* Washington, DC: University Press of America, 1982.

Litwack, Leon. *Trouble in Mind: Black Southerners in the Age of Jim Crow.* New York: Knopf, 1988.

Locke, Alain. "Harlem: Dark Weather-Vane." *Survey Graphic* 25, no. 8 (August 1936): 457. Web. http://newdeal.feri.org/survey/36457. 23 December 2014.

Lukács, Georg. *The Theory of the Novel.* Trans. Anna Bostock. 1920. Repr. Cambridge, MA: MIT Press, 1971.

Mackey, Nathaniel. *Bedouin Hornbook.* Charlottesville: University of Virginia Press, 1988.

Mailer, Norman. "The White Negro: Superficial Reflections on the Hipster." *Dissent* (Fall 1957). Web. https://www.dissentmagazine.org/online_articles/the-white-negro-fall-1957. 6 November 2015.

Mamet, David. *Three Uses of the Knife: On the Nature and Purpose of Drama.* New York: Vintage, 2007.

Manning, Susan. *Modern Dance, Negro Dance: Race in Motion.* St. Paul: University of Minnesota Press, 2006.

Maraniss, David. *Barack Obama: The Story.* New York: Simon and Schuster, 2012.

Marlowe, Christopher. *Doctor Faustus.* Ed. Sylvan Barnet. New York: Signet, 2010.

Marshall, Paule. *Praisesong for the Widow.* New York: Dutton Obelisk, 1983.

Marvin, Thomas F. "Children of Legba: Musicians at the Crossroads in Ralph Ellison's *Invisible Man*." *American Literature* 68, no. 3 (1996): 586–88.

"maud, n. 1." *OED Online,* March 2014. Web. OED.com. 11 May 2014.

Maxwell, William J. "Creative and Cultural Lag: The Radical Education of Ralph Ellison." *A Historical Guide to Ralph Ellison.* Ed. Steven C. Tracy. New York: Oxford University Press, 2004. 59–83.

McCarthy, Patrick. "The Structures and Meanings of 'Finnegans Wake.'" *A Companion to Joyce Studies.* Ed. Zack Bowen and James F. Carens. Westport, CT: Greenwood Press, 1984. 559–632.

McWhorter, John. "Racism in America Is Over." *Forbes,* 30 December 2008. Web. Forbes.com. 12 October 2015.

Media Matters. "Matthews: Does Obama 'Connect with Regular People' or Just African-Americans and College Grads?" *Media Matters for America,* 2 April 2008. Web. MediaMatters.org. 20 February 2012.

Melnick, Jeffrey P. *A Right to Sing the Blues: African Americans, Jews, and American Popular Song.* Cambridge, MA: Harvard University Press, 1999.

Melville, Herman. *The Confidence-Man: His Masquerade.* Ed. Harrison Hayford. Evanston, IL: Northwestern University Press/Newberry Library, 1984.

———. *Moby-Dick; or, The Whale.* Ed. Harrison Hayford, Hershel Parker, and G. Thomas Tanselle. Evanston, IL: Northwestern University Press, 1988.

Métraux, Alfred. *Voodoo in Haïti.* Trans. Hugo Charteris. London: Deutsch, 1959.

Mitchell, W. J. T. "Obama as Icon." *Journal of Visual Culture* 8, no. 2 (2009): 125–29. *EBSCO Host Communications and Mass Media Complete.* Web. 20 February 2012.

Morel, Lucas E. "America's First Black President? Lincoln's Legacy of Political Transcendence." *Lincoln Reshapes the Presidency*. Ed. Charles M. Hubbard. Macon, GA: Mercer University Press, 2003. 120–52.

———. "Ralph Ellison's Democratic Individualism." *Ralph Ellison and the Raft of Hope: A Political Companion to "Invisible Man."* Ed. Lucas E. Morel. Lexington: University Press of Kentucky, 2004. 58–90.

———, ed. *Ralph Ellison and the Raft of Hope: A Political Companion to "Invisible Man."* Lexington: University Press of Kentucky, 2004.

———. "Recovering the Political Artistry of *Invisible Man*." *Ralph Ellison and the Raft of Hope: A Political Companion to "Invisible Man."* Ed. Lucas E. Morel. Lexington: University Press of Kentucky, 2004. 1–21.

Morton, Jelly Roll. *Jelly Roll Morton: The Complete Library of Congress Recordings by Alan Lomax*. Rounder 11611-1888-2. CD.

Murray, Albert. *The Blue Devils of Nada: A Contemporary American Approach to Aesthetic Statement*. New York: Pantheon, 1996.

Musil, Robert. *The Man without Qualities*. 2 vols. Trans. Sophie Wilkins and Burton Pike. New York: Knopf, 1995.

Muyumba, Walter. *The Shadow and the Act: Black Intellectual Practice, Jazz Improvisation, and Philosophical Pragmatism*. Chicago: University of Chicago Press, 2009.

Myers, Andrew H. "Resonant Ripples in a Global Pond: The Blinding of Isaac Woodard." American Studies Association conference exhibit, 16 November 2002. Web. http://faculty.uscupstate.edu/amyers/conference.html. 16 June 2015.

Nagourney, Adam. "Obama Wins Election; McCain Loses as Bush Legacy Is Rejected." *New York Times*, 4 November 2008. Web. NYTimes.com. 27 April 2010.

Nancy, Jean-Luc. *Listening*. New York: Oxford University Press, 2010.

National Public Radio. "Democratic Convention Made History." National Public Radio, 30 August 2008. Web. NPR.org. 27 April 2010.

———. "Gun Shop Owner Links Ammo Shortage to Obama." National Public Radio, 7 April 2009. Web. NPR.org. 27 April 2010.

Obama, Barack. *An American Story: The Speeches of Barack Obama*. Ed. David Olive. Toronto, ON: ECW Press, 2008.

———. *The Audacity of Hope: Thoughts on Reclaiming the American Dream*. New York: Three Rivers Press, 2006.

———. "Barack Obama 2004 Democratic National Convention Keynote Address—American Rhetoric." *Barack Obama 2004 Democratic National Convention Keynote Address—American Rhetoric*. American Rhetoric, 2004. Web. AmericanRhetoric.com. 20 February 2012.

———. *Dreams from My Father: A Story of Race and Inheritance*. 1995. Repr. New York: Three Rivers Press, 2004.

O'Brien, John. "An Interview with Ralph Ellison (1972)." *Conversations with Ralph Ellison*. Ed. Maryemma Graham and Amritjit Singh. Jackson: University Press of Mississippi, 1995. 222–34.

O'Meally, Robert G. *The Craft of Ralph Ellison*. Cambridge, MA: Harvard University Press, 1980.

———, ed. *Living with Music: Ralph Ellison's Jazz Writings*. New York: Modern Library, 2001.

———. "The Rules of Magic: Hemingway as Ellison's 'Ancestor.'" *Speaking for You: The Vision of Ralph Ellison*. Ed. Kimberly W. Benston. Washington, DC: Howard University Press, 1990. 245–71.

Parrish, Timothy. "Ralph Ellison, Finished and Unfinished: Aesthetic Achievements and Political Legacies." *Contemporary Literature* 48, no. 4 (2007): 639–64.

———. *Ralph Ellison and the Genius of America*. Amherst: University of Massachusetts Press, 2012.

Paulson, William R. *The Noise of Culture: Literary Texts in a World of Information*. Ithaca, NY: Cornell University Press, 1988.

Pelton, Robert D. *The Trickster in West Africa: A Study of Mythic Irony and Sacred Delight*. Berkeley: University of California Press, 1980.

Podhoretz, Norman. "What Happened to Ralph Ellison?" *Commentary*, July–August 1999, 46–58.

Porter, Horace A. *Jazz Country: Ralph Ellison in America*. Iowa City: University of Iowa Press, 2001.

Porter, Kenneth. "The Flying Africans." *Primer for White Folks*. Ed. Bucklin Moon. Garden City, NY: Doubleday, 1946. 171–76.

Posnock, Ross. "Introduction." *The Cambridge Companion to Ralph Ellison*. Cambridge: Cambridge University Press, 2005. 1–10.

Proust, Marcel. *Remembrance of Things Past*. 3 vols. Trans C. K. Scott Moncrieff and Terence Kilmartin. New York: Random House, 1982.

Puchner, Martin. *The Drama of Ideas: Platonic Provocations in Theater and Philosophy*. Oxford: Oxford University Press, 2010.

Purcell, Richard. "The Enigma of Arrival; or, When Should We Have Read Ralph Ellison's *Three Days before the Shooting* . . . ?" *boundary 2* 39, no. 3 (2012): 169–89.

Putnam, Robert D. *Bowling Alone: The Collapse and Revival of American Community*. New York: Simon and Schuster, 2000.

Rampersad, Arnold. *Ralph Ellison: A Biography*. New York: Alfred A. Knopf, 2007.

Rankine, Patrice. *Ulysses in Black: Ralph Ellison, Classicism, and African American Literature*. Madison: University of Wisconsin Press, 2006.

Rawick, George P. *From Sundown to Sunup: The Making of the Black Community*. Westport, CT: Greenwood Press, 1972.

Remnick, David. *The Bridge: The Life and Rise of Barack Obama*. 2010. Repr. New York: Vintage Books/Random House, 2011.

Rogin, Michael Paul. *Subversive Genealogy: The Politics and Art of Herman Melville*. Berkeley: University of California Press, 1985.

Rosenberg, Jonathan. *How Far the Promised Land? World Affairs and the American Civil Rights Movement from the First World War to Vietnam*. Princeton, NJ: Princeton University Press, 2006.

Rourke, Constance. *American Humor: A Study of the National Character*. 1931. Repr. New York: New York Review Books, 2004.

Rovit, Earl H. "Ralph Ellison and the American Comic Tradition." *Wisconsin Studies in Contemporary Literature* 1 (1960): 34–42.

Rowley, Hazel. "The Exile Years? How the 50's Cultural Wars Destroyed Richard Wright." *Bookforum*, December–January 2006. Web. http://www.bookforum.com/archive/dec_05/rowley.html. 6 November 2105.

Rueckert, William H. *Kenneth Burke and the Drama of Human Relations*. 1963. Repr. Berkeley: University of California Press, 1982.

Samuels, David. "The Changeling: The Content of Obama's Character." *Harper's*, September 2012, 29–39.

———. "Invisible Man: How Ralph Ellison Explains Barack Obama." *New Republic*, 22 October 2008, 22–27.

Saslow, Eli. "The 17 Minutes That Launched a Political Star." *Washington Post*, 25 August 2008. Web. TheWashingtonPost.com. 20 February 2012.

Schechner, Richard. *Environmental Theatre*. 1974. Repr. Milwaukee, WI: Applause Theater and Cinema Books, 2000.

Schuyler, George S. *Black No More*. 1931. Repr. New York: Macmillan, 1971.

Silverman, Billy. "Racist Obama Email: California NAACP Demands Apology from OC GOP Official (Updated)." *Huffington Post*, 18 April 2011. Web. TheHuffingtonPost.com. 20 May 2014.

Singer, Barry. *Black and Blue: The Life and Lyrics of Andy Razaf*. New York: Schirmer Books, 1992.

Skerrett, Joseph T., Jr. "The Wright Interpretation: Ralph Ellison and the Anxiety of Influence." *Speaking for You: The Vision of Ralph Ellison*. Ed. Kimberly W. Benston. Washington, DC: Howard University Press, 1990. 217–30.

Smith, Shawn Michelle. "Obama's Whiteness." *Journal of Visual Culture* 8, no. 2 (2009): 129–33. EBSCO Host Communications and Mass Media Complete. Web. 20 February 2012.

———. *Photography on the Color Line: W. E. B. Du Bois, Race, and Visual Culture*. Durham, NC: Duke University Press, 2004.

Stein, Rob. "Race Gap Persists in Health Care, Three Studies Say." *Washington Post*, 17 August 2005. Web. http://www.washingtonpost.com/wp-dyn/content/article/2005/08/17/AR2005081701437.html. 6 November 2015.

Stepto, Robert B. *From behind the Veil*. Urbana: University of Illinois Press, 1979.

Sullivan, Andrew. "Goodbye to All That: Why Obama Matters." *Atlantic*, December 2007. Web. TheAtlantic.com. 20 February 2012.

Sundquist, Eric J. *Cultural Contexts for Ralph Ellison's "Invisible Man."* Boston: St. Martin's Press, 1995.

———. "'We Dreamed a Dream': Ralph Ellison, Martin Luther King, Jr., and Barack Obama." *Daedalus* 140, no. 1 (Winter 2011): 108–24.

Szalay, Michael. "Ralph Ellison's Unfinished Second Skin." *American Literary History* 23, no. 4 (Winter 2011): 795–827.

Thomas, Pete. "Barack Obama Hastens Gun, Ammo Sales; Sarah Palin First in Line?" *Los Angeles Times*, 11 November 2008. Web. LosAngelesTimes.com. 20 February 2012.

Thompson, Robert Farris. *Flash of the Spirit: African and Afro-American Art and Philosophy*. New York: Random House, 1983.

Thomson, George. *Aeschylus and Athens: A Study in the Social Origins of Drama*. London: Lawrence and Wishart, 1946.

Tindall, William York. *A Reader's Guide to "Finnegans Wake."* New York: Farrar, Strauss and Giroux, 1969.
Turner, Victor. *From Ritual to Theatre: The Human Seriousness of Play.* New York: PAJ, 2001.
Von Frank, Albert J. "Frost's 'The Gift Outright.'" *Explicator* 38, no. 1 (Fall 1979): 22–23.
Walker, Julia A. 2005. *Expressionism and Modernism in the American Theatre: Bodies, Voices, Words.* Cambridge University Press. Web. Wales.com. http://www.wales.com/en/content/cms/English/About_Wales/Wales_Fact_File/WelshNationalAnthem/WelshNationalAnthem.aspx. 30 December 2014.
Wallace, Charles. "The New American Divide." *Wall Street Journal,* 21 January 2012, 1–5.
Warren, Kenneth W. "Chaos Not Quite Controlled: Ellison's Uncompleted Transit to Juneteenth." *The Cambridge Companion to Ralph Ellison.* Ed. Ross Posnock. Cambridge: Cambridge University Press, 2005. 188–200.
———. "Ralph Ellison and the Problem of Cultural Authority: The Lessons of Little Rock." *Ralph Ellison and the Raft of Hope: A Political Companion to "Invisible Man."* Ed. Lucas E. Morel. Lexington: University Press of Kentucky, 2004. 142–57.
———. *So Black and Blue: Ralph Ellison and the Occasion of Criticism.* Chicago: University of Chicago Press, 2003.
———. *What Was African American Literature?* Cambridge, MA: Harvard University Press, 2011.
Warren, Robert Penn. *Who Speaks for the Negro?* New York: Random House, 1965.
Washington, Booker T., W. E. B. Du Bois, and James Weldon Johnson. *Three Negro Classics: Up from Slavery; The Souls of Black Folk; The Autobiography of an Ex-Coloured Man.* Ed. John Hope Franklin. New York: Avon, 1965.
Watkins, Mel. *On the Real Side: Laughing, Lying, and Signifying—the Underground Tradition of African-American Humor That Transformed American Culture, from Slavery to Richard Pryor.* New York: Simon and Schuster, 1994.
Watts, Jerry Gafio. *Heroism and the Black Intellectual: Ralph Ellison, Politics, and Afro-American Intellectual Life.* Chapel Hill: University of North Carolina Press, 1994.
Weiner, Rachel. "AP: Many Insisting That Obama Is Not Black." *Huffington Post,* 14 December 2008. Web. TheHuffingtonPost.com. 16 May 2014.
Weiss, Hedy. "Hypnotic 'Invisible Man' Illuminates a Figure in the Shadows." *Chicago Sun-Times,* 22 January 2012. Web. http://www.suntimes.com/entertainment/weiss/10132261-452/hypnotic-invisible-man-illuminates-a-figure-in-the-shadows.html. 11 March 2014.
West, Hollie. "Ellison: Exploring the Life of a Not-So-Invisible Man." *Washington Post,* 19, 20, 21 August 1973. 2–10.
Wideman, John Edgar. *Fatheralong: A Meditation on Fathers and Sons, Race and Society.* New York: Random House, 1994.
Williams, Daniel. "Emlyn Williams and Ralph Ellison." *Beyond the Difference: Welsh Literature in Comparative Contexts.* Ed. Alyce von Rothkirch and Daniel Williams. Cardiff, UK: University of Wales Press, 2004. 132–46.
———. "The Invisible Man's Welsh Routes: Ralph Ellison in Wartime Wales." *Black Skin, Blue Books: African Americans and Wales, 1845–1945.* Ed. Daniel Williams. Cardiff, UK: University of Wales Press, 2012. 208–52.

Williams, Juan. *Eyes on the Prize: America's Civil Rights Years 1954–1965.* New York: Penguin, 1988.

———. "Obama's Color Line." *New York Times,* 30 November 2007. Web. NYTimes.com. 27 April 2010.

Winant, Gabriel. "White Voters and Obama's Slide in the Polls." *Salon.com.* 14 September 2009. Web. Salon.com. 20 February 2012.

Wolven, Scott. "TNG Interview with John Callahan." *New Guard Literary Review* 2 (2011): 306–18.

Woodruff, Paul. *The Necessity of Theater: The Art of Watching and Being Watched.* New York: Oxford University Press, 2010.

Wright, Richard. *Native Son.* With an introduction by Arnold Rampersad. New York: Harper Perennial Modern Classics, 2005.

———. *White Man, Listen!* New York: Harper Perennial, 2008.

X, Malcolm, and Alex Haley. *The Autobiography of Malcolm X.* New York: Grove, 1966.

Yeats, William Butler. *The Autobiography of William Butler Yeats.* New York: Collier, 1967.

Young, Harvey. *Embodying Black Experience: Stillness, Critical Memory, and the Black Body.* Ann Arbor: University of Michigan Press, 2010.

Zarrilli, Phillip B. "Toward a Phenomenological Model of the Actor's Embodied Modes of Experience." *Theatre Journal* 56 (2004): 653–66.

ABOUT THE CONTRIBUTORS

HERMAN BEAVERS is associate professor of English and Africana studies at the University of Pennsylvania, where he teaches courses in African American literature and creative writing. He is the author of *Wrestling Angels into Song: The Fictions of Ernest J. Gaines and James A. McPherson* (1995) and *A Neighborhood of Feeling* (1986). He has just completed the monograph *Changing the Order of Things: Geography and the Political Imaginary in the Fiction of Toni Morrison*.

ROBERT BUTLER is a professor of English at Canisius College. He has published widely in American and African American literatures. His books include *Richard Wright's "Native Son": The Emergence of a New Black Hero* (1991), *The Open Journey in Contemporary African American Fiction* (1998), *The Critical Response to Ralph Ellison* (2001), and *The Richard Wright Encyclopedia* (2008).

JOHN CALLAHAN is the retired Morgan S. Odell Professor of Humanities at Lewis and Clark College. He is the literary executor for Ralph Ellison. He is the author of *In the African-American Grain: The Pursuit of Voice in Twentieth-Century Black Fiction* (1988) and editor of *The Collected Essays of Ralph Ellison* (1995), *Flying Home and Other Stories* (1996), *Juneteenth* (1999), *Trading Twelves: The Selected Letters of Ralph Ellison and Albert Murray* (2000), and *Three Days before the Shooting . . .* (2010).

MARC C. CONNER is the Ballengee Professor of English and provost at Washington and Lee University. He is the editor of *The Aesthetic Dimensions of Toni Morrison* (2000), *Charles Johnson: The Novelist as Philosopher* (2007), and *The Poetry of James Joyce Reconsidered* (2012).

ABOUT THE CONTRIBUTORS

BRYAN CRABLE is professor of communication and director of the Waterhouse Family Institute for the Study of Communication and Society at Villanova University in Villanova, Pennsylvania. He is the editor of *Transcendence by Perspective: Meditations on and with Kenneth Burke* (2014) and the author of *Ralph Ellison and Kenneth Burke: At the Roots of the Racial Divide* (2012).

STEVEN D. EALY is a senior fellow at Liberty Fund, Inc., an Indianapolis-based educational foundation, where he has been based since 1993. Previously he was a professor of political science at Armstrong State University in Savannah, Georgia. He has published on Robert Penn Warren, Ralph Ellison, Eric Voegelin, the philosophy and history of American philanthropy, and constitutional interpretation. Currently he is working on a comparison of characters and stories common to the Bible and the Qur'an.

LENA HILL is associate professor of English and African American studies at the University of Iowa. She is the author of *Visualizing Blackness and the Creation of the African American Literary Tradition* (2014) and the coauthor of *Ralph Ellison's "Invisible Man": A Reference Guide* (2008).

LUCAS E. MOREL is the Class of 1960 Professor of Ethics and Politics and head of the Politics Department at Washington and Lee University. He is the editor of *Ralph Ellison and the Raft of Hope: A Political Companion to "Invisible Man"* (2004) and *Lincoln and Liberty: Wisdom for the Ages* (2014), and author of *Lincoln's Sacred Effort: Defining Religion's Role in American Self-Government* (2000).

TIMOTHY PARRISH is professor of English at Virginia Polytechnic University. He is the author of *Walking Blues: Making Americans from Emerson to Elvis* (2001), *From Civil War to Apocalypse: Postmodern History and American Fiction* (2008), and *Ralph Ellison and the Genius of America* (2012), and editor of *The Cambridge Companion to American Novelists* (2013).

ROSS POSNOCK is Anna Garbedian Professor of the Humanities at Columbia University. Among his books are *Color and Culture: Black Writers and the Making of the Modern Intellectual* (1998) and the forthcoming *Renunciation: Acts of Abandonment by Writers, Philosophers, and Artists* (2016).

PATRICE RANKINE is professor of classics and dean for the Arts and Humanities at Hope College in Holland, Michigan. He is author of *Ulysses in Black: Ralph*

Ellison, Classicism, and African American Literature (2006) and *Aristotle and Black Drama: A Theater of Civil Disobedience* (2013).

GRANT SHREVE is a PhD candidate at Johns Hopkins University. He specializes in nineteenth- and twentieth-century American literature and has published articles in *American Literature* and *Leviathan: A Journal of Melville Studies*.

ERIC J. SUNDQUIST is the Andrew W. Mellon Professor of the Humanities at Johns Hopkins University. His books include *King's Dream* (2009), *Strangers in the Land: Blacks, Jews, Post-Holocaust America* (2005), and *To Wake the Nations: Race in the Making of American Literature* (1992).

STEVEN C. TRACY is professor of Afro-American studies at the University of Massachusetts, Amherst. He has authored, edited, coedited, or provided introductions for thirty books, provided more than seventy-five contributions to book publications edited by others, and written over fifty CD liner notes. A singer–harmonica player, he has opened for B. B. King, Muddy Waters, Sonny Terry and Brownie McGhee, Canned Heat, and others, and has recorded with blues groups and the Cincinnati Symphony Orchestra.

INDEX

Page numbers in *italics* refer to illustrations.

absolutism, 302–3
acousmatic sound, 87–89, 94
Adell, Sandra, 60–61
affirmations, 180–81, 187
affirmative action, 146, 255–56
African American exceptionalism, 156–65
African American folktales, 132–35, 157
African American literature, 16; black protest literature, 40; Butler on, 52–53; Johnson, C., on, 52; new directions in, 51–52; Warren, K., on, 32n7, 51
African American narrative: Johnson, C., on, 6, 32n8, 52; victimization in, 52
African Americans: black body and, 63–64, 71–72, 85, 88; black culture, 145; black students, 253–54; experience of, 6–9, 203, 205–6, 212, 255, 259n9; fetishization of, 97n5; life of, 8–9, 170–71, 203; self-made black American, 144–50; tradition for, 8, 205; unarmed blacks, 35n26
alienation, 245–46
All the King's Men (Warren, R. P.), 280n23, 283n41
America: connectedness and individualism in, 21; Ellison on, 5, 12; founding of, 20, 51, 143, 151–56, 160–61; founding ideals, 252; George Washington paintings and moral compromise of, 151–56; in "In a Strange Country," 246, 248–51; post-Obama, 295; post-racial, 25, 101–2, 103, 108, 113n6; progress in, 22–23
American Academy in Rome, 321–22
American Adam (Lewis), 118–19, 176
American Adam figure, 172, 175, 176, 190n7
American culture, 9–10, 145
American exceptionalism, 43, 156–65
American experience: black experience in relation to, 205–6; complexity of, 6–7, 10, 176
American flag, 60, 132, 159, 236; in "In a Strange Country" (Ellison), 249–50
American history: American present and, 202, 205–6, 212–16; fiction and, 203, 205, 206
American national anthem, 249–51, 256
American novelists, 5, 32n6, 203
anger, 287–88
Anna Livia Plurabelle (Joyce), 182–83, 192n16
apocalyptic future, 230
appearances, 103–4, 110
Ara, Konomi, 16
Arendt, Hannah, 45, 53n1
Armstrong, Louis: Beavers on, 75–76, 78–79, 89, 94–95; on beboppers, 96n1; French Revolution, Louis XVI, and,

302–3; futuristic jungleism and, 297–301; Parrish on, 197–98; as trickster, 300; "(What Did I Do to Be So) Black and Blue?," performed by, 303–9
art: Black Arts movement, 144, 145, 159; Hill, L., on, 143, 149–56; *Landscape with the Fall of Icarus*, 161, 161–62; paintings, of George Washington, 152–56, *153*, *154*; religion and, 158–59, 161–63; Shreve on, 236–37
artistic form, 58–59
artistic purity, 56
artists: *The Collected Essays of Ralph Ellison* on, 7; Conner on, 177–78; responsibility of, 6–7
Artuso, Kathryn Stelmach, 191n8
"Atlanta Exposition Speech," 263, 268, 270–71
Aubriot, Hugues, 302
Audacity of Hope (Obama), 20–21, 22
Auden, W. H., 162
auditory knowledge, 80, 82–83

Baker, Houston, 285
Bakhtin, Mikhail, 58
Beavers, Herman: on acousmatic sound, 87–89, 94; on Armstrong, 75–76, 78–79, 89, 94–95; on beboppers, 75–78, 94–95, 96nn1–2; on Creelman, 84–86, 98n11; on disillusionment, 91–93; on flow, 89–91; on hearing and space, 79–80, 83–84; on *Invisible Man*, as noisy text, 82–83; "The Noisy Lostness: Oppositionality and Acousmatic Subjectivity in *Invisible Man*," 24, 75–98; on oppositional behavior, 78–79, 89, 94–95; on public addresses, 84–88, 89–91; on social responsibility, 90; on sound studies, 79–83; on underground, 81–82, 83; on visuality, 88; on Washington, B. T., 84–86, 89–90, 98n11
beboppers, 75–78, 94–95, 96nn1–2. *See also* jazz

Bellow, Saul, 34n15
Berry, Abner, 43
Bible, 187–88; Book of Job, 279n4; Romans, 267, 280n12
biblical fathers, 168, 187–88
Bill of Rights, 5, 51
biographical fathers, 168
birth, 184
Black Arts movement, 144, 145, 159
black body, 63–64, 71–72, 85, 88
"Black Boys and Native Sons" (Howe), 44
black culture, 145
black eye, 251
black president, 23. *See also* Obama, Barack
black protest literature, 40
black students, 253–54
Blakey, Art, 97n5
Bliss/Sunraider (character): Conner on, 187–88; death of, 228–29; Gatsby compared to, 173–75; Hill, L., on, 151, 164; Parrish on, 204, 207–16; race and, 204, 207–8, 215, 225–26; Rinehart and, 209–10; Sundquist on, 117–22, 125, 128–29, 131–38, 140n12, 141n17; tragedy of, 222–31
Bloom, Harold, 171, 178, 190n5
body, 24; black, 63–64, 71–72, 85, 88; pain and, 63; race and, 71–72, 74n26; Rankine on, 62–65; riots and, 69; sound and, 88; theater and, 62–63
"Body and *Invisible Man*, The: Ralph Ellison's Novel in Twenty-First-Century Performance and Public Spaces" (Rankine), 24, 55–74. *See also* Rankine, Patrice
"Book of America" (Ellison), 213
Book of Job, 279n4
Bowen, Zack, 180
Bradley, Adam, 11, 13, 15, 239n1; on computer sequences, 31n2; on contemporary relevance, 31n3; on father figures, 165n1; *Ralph Ellison in Progress: From "Invisible Man" to "Three Days before the Shooting . . .*", 17, 325

bravery, 252–53, 255–56
"Brave Words for a Startling Occasion" (Ellison), 120, 324–25
Brockway, Lucius, 89
Brophy, Alfred, 53n1
Brown, Lloyd, 43–44
Brown v. Board of Education, 27, 45, 121, 144; Parrish on, 206–7; Shreve on, 219
Buchwald, Dagmar, 93, 98n13
Buell, Lawrence, 32n6
Burke, Kenneth, 17, 102; Crable on, 241n10; on dialectical transcendence, 232–33; Ellison and, 105–6, 110–11, 113n10; on transformation, 232
Burns, Ken, 300
Butler, Robert: on African American literature, 52–53; on civil rights movement and *Invisible Man*, 44–46; on complaints against Ellison's writing, 43–44; on critical bias, 39–40; on fairly assessing Ellison, 42–53; on integration, 50–51; "*Invisible Man* and the Politics of Love," 23–24, 39–54; on narrative against Ellison, 40–42; on nonviolence and Christian love, 46–51; on Wright, R., 45–46

Callahan, John, 11–12, 13, 15, 30, 121; on computer sequences, 325–26; on Fitzgerald and Ellison, 176; on letters, 327; *Ralph Ellison's "Invisible Man": A Casebook*, 16; on "Tell It Like It Is, Baby," 321–23; "That Pause for Contemplation: A Centennial Meditation on Ralph Ellison," 313–28; on *Three Days before the Shooting . . .*, 325–26; on time, 313–14, 317, 327
Cambridge Companion to Ralph Ellison (Posnock), 16
Cameron, David, 70–71
Cameron, Roger, 192n16
Canetti, Elias, 121
Carter, Paul, 79–80
Cassuto, Leonard, 45–46

Castiglione, Baldassare, 77
catharsis. *See* tragic catharsis
Cayton, Horace, 288–89
Certeau, Michel de, 91–92, 93
Chambers, Ross, 78, 88
Chandler, Dana C., Jr., 159
change: progress and, 22–23; technological, 4; violent, 35n26
chaos, 210
characterization, 117–18
Chehaw Station, 7, 328
"Chiefly about War Matters" (anonymous), 260
Christian love, 44, 46–51
citizenship, 247, 257n6, 259n13, 319; father figures relating to, 145–47, 149, 151–56; Hill, L., on, 151–56, 157, 164
civic pollution, 224–25
Civil Rights Act of 1964, 6
civil rights movement, 6, 27; Bill of Rights and, 51; Butler, on *Invisible Man* and, 44–46; Ellison's involvement in, 44–46, 53n1; Freedom Riders, 45; integration and, 50–51; Little Rock Nine and, 20; Parrish on, 171; student sit-ins, 45; urban riots and, 45; Wright, R., and, 45–46
Civil War, 203, 205, 212–13
classical tragedy, 220, 223–24
Cliofus (character), 136
Cold War liberalism, 43
Collected Essays of Ralph Ellison, The, 11; on artist, 7; on man at Chehaw Station, 7, 328; on territory of hope, 3
color, 25
color blindness, 103, 110–11
colorlessness, 110–12
color line, 101, 109, 129, 197; in modernity, 198; Morel on, 252–53
Communist Party, 39; self-reliance and, 147; Wright, R., and, 42, 146
community, 21
computer sequences: Bradley on, 31n2; Callahan on, 325–26; dialectical

transcendence in, 231–39; mythology in, 234; scapegoating in, 235–36
connectedness: human interconnectedness, 271, 274; individualism and, 21
Conner, Marc, 11–12; on artists, 177–78; on Bliss/Sunraider, 187–88; "Father Abraham: Ellison's Agon with the Fathers in *Three Days before the Shooting . . .*," 26, 167–93; on Faulkner, 168–72, 190n6; on Fitzgerald, 172–77; on Joyce, 177–86; on literary fathers, 168–72; on patriarchs, sacrifices, and covenants, 186–89; on Rampersad, 33n11; on "Tell It Like It Is, Baby," 26, 167–68; on visibility, 177–78; on Wright, R., 168–69
conscience, 148–49
Constitution, 5, 22; Douglass on, 270; slavery and, 270
constitutional faith, 239
covenants, 186–89
Crable, Bryan: on Burke, 241n10; on colorlessness, 110–12; on invisible and visibility, 103–10; "*Invisible Man* in the Age of Obama: Ellison on (Color) Blindness, Visibility, and the Hopes for a Postracial America," 25, 99–114; on Obama, 100–110; on post-racial America, 25, 101–2, 103, 108; on racial binarism, 99–101, 108–10; *Ralph Ellison and Kenneth Burke: At the Roots of the Racial Divide*, 17
Crane, Gregg, 239n1
creative writing, 147–48
Creelman, James, 84–86, 98n11
cripples, 121–27, 134, 136
critical bias, 39–40
crossroads, 129–30
Crouch, Stanley, 289
Csikszentmihalyi, Mihaly, 90–91
cultural balance, 51, 54n3

Declaration of Independence, 5; Douglass on, 268–70; equality and individual rights in, 21; ideals of justice in, 54n2; Obama on, 20
democracy, 197; novel form relating to, 219, 220, 224
democratic faith, 20, 256
DeVeaux, Scott, 96n2
devil, 130, 134–35, 281n33
dialectical transcendence: Burke on, 232–33; in computer sequences, 231–39
dialogic consciousness, 233–34
DiBattista, Maria, 180
Dickstein, Morris, 178
discipline, 8–9, 35n26
discrimination, 246
disempowerment, 92–93, 178
disillusionment: Beavers on, 91–93; with Obama, 102
diversity: of American culture, 10, 21, 52; of American experience, 6; of identity, 111–12; of whiteness, 246; of backgrounds and occupations, 248
Donaldson, Jeff, 159
Dostoevsky, Fyodor, 294–95
Douglass, Frederick, 132; on Constitution, 270; on Declaration of Independence, 268–70; Grandfather and, 266, 271–72; public addresses by, 268–70; slavery, 268–70; "What to the Slave Is the Fourth of July?," 268–70
dramatic stage theater, 62–63
Dreams from My Father (Obama), 19, 21, 292
Du Bois, W. E. B., 99, 197; Posnock on, 287–88
Dunham, Stanley Ann, 20
Dvinge, Anne, 143
Dyson, Michael Eric, 103

Ealy, Steven D.: on Grandfather, 262–68, 271–78; "Invisible Man's Grandfather and the American Dream," 28, 260–84; on narrator of *Invisible Man*, 261–62; on religion, 266–67; on Romans, 267, 280n12; on tricksters, 261–62

Eddy, Beth, 240n4
Edwards, Brian, 31n4
Eliot, T. S., 12; "Gerontion," 136; *The Waste Land*, 186
Elkins, Stanley M., 146
Ellington, Duke, 297
Ellison, Ralph: affinities between Obama and, 18–19, 21–23, 315–16; on America, 5, 11; background on, 3–4, 40–41; beginning of career, 40; on black president, 23; Burke and, 105–6, 110–11, 113n10; Butler, on fair assessment of, 42–53; in civil rights movement, 44–46, 53n1; contemporary moment and, 17–23; criticisms against, 285–93; death of, 4; Emerson, Ralph Waldo and, 190n5; expanding Ellison canon, 9–17; falsification by, 40–41; Fitzgerald and, 172–77; in historical context, 42–43; on home, 3–4; on identity, 19–20; interpretive studies of, 15–17; after *Invisible Man*'s success, 320–21; Joyce and, 177–86; major complaints against, 40–41, 43–44; mission of, 5; most important fact about, 196–97; narrative against, 40–42; on novel form, 57–58, 220; in our time, 23–31; on self-made black American, 144–50; in twenty-first century, 4–31; understanding, 195–98; on visibility, 104, 105; white critical establishment and, 40–41, 43–44; Wright, R., and, 40, 146–48, 165n7, 165n8, 168–69; as writer, 195–97, 203. *See also specific topics; specific works*
Emerson, Ralph Waldo, 11, 18; Ellison and, 190n5
Emperor Jones, 60
Engeman, Thomas, 181–82
Enlightenment, 302–3
environmental theater, 62
epic, 195; *Invisible Man* as, 68; novel form compared to, 58
E pluribus unum (Out of many, one), 8, 21, 35n26, 100, 137–38

equality, 20, 77, 103, 202, 249
escape, 263–64
Eshu-Elegba, 129–31
ethnicity, 9; Posnock on, 10
Etzioni, Amitai, 54n3
"Extravagance of Laughter, An" (Ellison), 134–35, 140n11, 175
eyes, 105–7, 211

faith, 20, 239
falsification, 40–41
"Fantasy of a Blackless America, The" (Ellison), 21
fate, 267, 280n13
"Father Abraham: Ellison's Agon with the Fathers in *Three Days before the Shooting . . .*" (Conner), 26, 167–93. *See also* Conner, Marc
father figures: biblical fathers, 168, 187–88; biographical fathers, 168; Bradley on, 165n1; citizenship relating to, 147, 149, 151–56; Fitzgerald and, 172–73; Lincoln as, 160–61, 167, 180–82, 187; literary fathers, 168–72; Moynihan Report relating to, 144; patriarchs, sacrifices, and covenants, 186–89; political ideology relating to, 163–64; "The Politics of Fatherhood in *Three Days before the Shooting . . .*" on, 25–26, 142–66; Posnock on, 288–89; in "Tell It Like It Is, Baby," 167, 181, 189
Faulkner, William, 26; Conner on, 168–72, 190n6; *Go Down, Moses*, 170–71; Parrish on, 169, 212; Rampersad on, 169
Faust (Goethe), 135, 141n14
feedback loop, 91
female voice, 183–85
fetishization, 97n5
fiction: American history and, 203, 205, 206; protest, 8; "Why Do We Read Fiction?" on, 276–77. *See also* novel form
Finnegans Wake (Joyce), 178, 182–85

Fitzgerald, F. Scott, 26; Callahan on, 176; Conner on, 172–77; father figures and, 172–73; *The Great Gatsby*, 173–76; *The Last Tycoon*, 176; *Tender Is the Night*, 172–73
flow, 89–91
"Flying Africans, The" (folktale), 132–33
"Flying Home" (Ellison), 133, 134–35
Flying Home and Other Stories (Ellison), 11
Foley, Barbara: Howe and, 287; on Leroy, 290–91; on letters, to Wright, R., 165n7; on patriotism, 259n13; Posnock on, 286, 290–92; *Wrestling with the Left: The Making of Ralph Ellison's "Invisible Man"*, 16–17, 23–24, 29, 39, 43
folktales, 132–35, 157
folk wisdom, 156–57, 159
Franklin, John Hope, 100
freedom, 49, 51, 154, 256, 260–61
Freedom Riders, 45
French Revolution, 302–3
Freud, Sigmund, 286, 290
Frost, Robert, 135–36
futuristic jungleism, 294, 297–301

genre: artistic form and, 58–59; Rankine on, 70–72
"Gerontion" (Eliot), 136
Gibson, Donald, 39
"Gift Outright, The" (Frost), 135–36
Gillespie, Dizzy, 77, 78
Gioia, Ted, 77, 96n4
Go Down, Moses (Faulkner), 170–71
Goethe, Johann Wolfgang von, 135, 141n14
Goodwyn, Frank, 135, 141n13
gossip, 183
Grandfather (character): background on, 263; deathbed words of, 262–68, 272–73, 275; Douglass and, 266, 271–72; Ealy on, 262–68, 271–78; on fate, 267; humanity of, 276; lessons of, 263–65; liberal arts and, 265; love and, 276; political philosophy of, 265; on religion, 266–67; "trouble" of, 267; Washington, B. T., and, 263, 265–66, 271–72
Great Britain, 269
Great Gatsby, The (Fitzgerald), 173–76
Green, Paul, 56
Guelzo, Allen, 191n13

Hammons, David, 159
Haverford Statement, 219
Hawthorne, Nathaniel, 260
healing, 282nn36–38
hearing: auditory knowledge, 80, 82–83; cultures, 80; listening and, 79–81, 85–86; space and, 79–80, 83–84
Hemingway, Ernest, 192n17
hero: mythology of, 177–78, 218–19; in tragedy, 220–21, 225–31
heroism, 8
Heroism and the Black Intellectual (Watts), 39
Hersey, John, 119, 143, 205, 212
Hickman (character): Callahan on, 323–24; "Hickman in Georgia & Oklahoma," 151–52, 209, 215, 232, 233–34; "Hickman in Washington DC," 33n10, 157–58, 175, 232–33; Hill, L., on, 143–44, 150–51, 157–65; Parrish on, 210–16; Sundquist on, 119, 122–23, 125–28, 131–32, 137, 138
Hill, Lena, 16; on African American exceptionalism, 156–65; on art, 143, 149–56; on Bliss/Sunraider, 151, 164; on citizenship, 151–56, 157; on Ellison and self-made black American, 144–50; on Hickman, 143–44, 150–51, 157–65; on Leroy, 156–57; on Millsap, 151–55; "The Politics of Fatherhood in *Three Days before the Shooting . . .*," 25–26, 142–66; on secretary, 157–58; on uncreated conscience, 148–49; on visuality, 143; on Woodridge scene, 148–50; on Wright, R., 146–48
Hill, Michael, 16
Historical Guide to Ralph Ellison, A (Tracy), 16

historical precipice, 200–201
home, 3–4, 58, 203, 252, 319
hope, 3–9, 22, 182, 249
Howe, Irving, 33n11, 192n17, 219; "Black Boys and Native Sons," 44; Posnock on, 285–86; Rampersad, Foley, and, 287; "The World and the Jug" and, 8, 58, 285–86
"'How many lightbulbs does it take to screw in a blues singer?': The French Revolution, King Louis Armstrong, and the Futuristic Jungleism of Jazz" (Tracy), 29–30, 294–309
Hughes, Langston, 41, 192n17
human boundary and transcendence, 174–76
human interconnectedness, 271, 274
humanity, 276
humor, 247
Hurston, Zora Neale, 41

Icarus myth: *Landscape with the Fall of Icarus* and, *161*, 161–62; *Three Days before the Shooting . . .* and, 25, 117–18, 131–35, 140n6
identity: American, 207; Ellison on, 19–20, 259n9; Obama on, 19, 34nn19–20, 315; Parrish on, 208–9; politics, 10; racial, 99, 114nn11–12; Sundquist on, 121–22, 128–29; white, 205
ideological commitments, 42–43
ideological formulas, 6–7
implicit morality, 224, 234–35
"In a Strange Country" (Ellison): America in, 246, 248–51; American flag in, 249–50; black eye in, 251; music in, 247–51; national conflict in, 250; private club in, 247–48; race, alienation, and, 245–46; religion and, 249; Wales in, 246; Welsh oppression in, 248–49; "What America Would Be Like without Blacks" and, 251–52; Yanks in, 247
"'In a Strange Country': The Challenge of American Inclusion" (Morel), 27–28, 245–59. *See also* Morel, Lucas

inclusion, 22–23, 27–28; challenge of, 246; Morel on, 256
individualism, 21
information theory, 79, 89–90
integration, 44, 140n10, 204, 319; Butler on, 50–51, 53, 54n3; Callahan, on Ellison and, 319–20; civil rights movement and, 50–51; cultural balance and, 51, 54n3; King on, 47, 50–51; of music, 247–48, 252; of personality, 240nn2–3; Shreve, on Ellison and, 219–23; "What America Would Be Like without Blacks" relating to, 251–52
intellectual suppression, 149–50
internationalism, 31n4
Interpretive studies, 15–17
intimacy, 226–27
invisibility: as auditory knowledge, 80–82, 93–95; Beavers on, 93; *Invisible Man* and, 208, 295, 301, 321; Obama and, 18, 316; visibility and, 103–10
Invisible Man (Ellison): adaptation of, by Jacoby, 16, 24, 55, 56–57, 62–67; Butler, on civil rights movement and, 44–46; contemporary relevance of, 31n3; cultural significance of, 55–56; *Dreams from My Father* relating to, 19; as epic, 68; lessons learned by Invisible Man, 275–78; narrative in, 19; narrator of, 261–62; *Native Son* relating to, 46–47; as noisy text, 82–83; nonviolence and Christian love in, 44, 46–51; novel form and, 318–19; Obama and, 19, 291–92, 315; paradox of, 196; readers of, 5; reviews of, 39, 43–44; sermon in, 254–55; setting of, 294–97; thirtieth-anniversary edition of, 313–14; violence in, 48–49. *See also specific topics*
"*Invisible Man* and the Politics of Love" (Butler), 23–24, 39–54. *See also* Butler, Robert
"*Invisible Man* in the Age of Obama: Ellison on (Color) Blindness, Visibility,

and the Hopes for a Postracial America" (Crable), 25, 99–114. *See also* Crable, Bryan
"Invisible Man's Grandfather and the American Dream" (Ealy), 28, 260–84. *See also* Ealy, Steven D.
Isaac (from Old Testament), 187–88

Jackson, Lawrence, 16, 233
Jack-the-Bear (character), 261–62
Jacobson, Matthew, 99
Jacoby, Oren, 16, 70. *See also Invisible Man*
James, Henry, 4
jazz, 8, 32n9, 248; beboppers, 75–78, 94–95, 96nn1–2; futuristic jungleism of, 294, 297–301; "'How many lightbulbs does it take to screw in a blues singer?': The French Revolution, King Louis Armstrong, and the Futuristic Jungleism of Jazz" on, 29–30, 294–309; "Noisy Lostness, The: Oppositionality and Acousmatic Subjectivity in *Invisible Man*" on, 24, 75–98; Parrish on, 198; popularity of, 77–78; race and, 77–78, 298–99; sexuality and, 297–98; unfinished narrative relating to, 199
Jim Crow, 126–27, 268
jogger, 314–15
Johnson, Charles, 7–8, 30–31, 145, 170; on African American narrative, 6, 32n8, 52
Johnson, Lyndon, 134, 140n10, 145
Jones, Chris, 64
Joyce, James, 26; *Anna Livia Plurabelle*, 182–83, 192n16; Conner on, 177–86; Ellison and, 177–86; *Finnegans Wake*, 178, 182–85; *A Portrait of the Artist as a Young Man*, 177–78; Rankine on, 191n9, 192n14; *Ulysses*, 178, 179–80
Juneteenth (Ellison), 11, 14, 34n12, 136, 190n3, 193n20
justice, 35n26, 52n2, 241n6, 274, 283n38

Kellman, Jerry, 19
Kennedy, John F., 141n15

King, Martin Luther, Jr., 134; *Why We Can't Wait*, 47, 50–51
Kirkland, Avon, 16

LaBelle, Brandon, 80, 82–83; on acousmatic sound, 87
Landscape with the Fall of Icarus (painting), *161*, 161–62
"Landscape with the Fall of Icarus" (Williams, W. C.), 162
language, 107–8, 184–86
Last Tycoon, The (Fitzgerald), 176
law, 272, 274, 281n33; Ellison on, 46
Lee, William, 151–56, 166n16
Le Mire, Noël, *152*, 152–53
Leroy (character): Foley on, 290–91; Hill, L., on, 156–57; Shreve on, 236; Sundquist on, 125–27, 130–31
letters, 11–12, 46, 123, 146–47, 165n7; Callahan on, 327. *See also* Murray, Albert; *specific works*
Levitt, Morton, 178–79
Lewis, R. W. B., 25, 118–19, 175, 176; on American Adam figure, 190n7
liberal arts, 265
Lincoln, Abraham, 120, 140n10, 191n13; Callahan on, 176; Ealy on, 273; Ellison on, 179–80, 191n13; as father figure, 160–61, 167, 180–82, 187; in *The Last Tycoon*, 176; Parrish on, 210–12, 215; religion and, 181–82
List, Robert, 192n14
listening, 79–81, 85–86
literary fathers, 168–72
literary influence, 168–72, 184
literary tradition, 196
Little Rock Nine, 20
Litwack, Leon, 203
Locke, Alain, 69
Louis XVI (King), 303
love, 276; challenges of, 173–75; Christian, 44, 46–51; necessary for community, 21; politics and, 21–22, 36n27, 44, 52–53

Lowenstein, Daniel, 257n6
Lukács, Georg, 57–59

Mackey, Nathaniel, 79, 97n6
Malcolm X, 19, 35n21, 133
Mandela, Nelson, 281n35
Man for All Seasons, A (Bolt), 274
Man without Qualities, The (Musil), 27, 200–201, 202
Marley, Bob, 133
Marsalis, Wynton, 300
Martin, Trayvon, 292
Marx, Bill, 65, 66
Marxism, 291
masks, 121, 126–27, 130
Masses and Mainstream (Brown), 43–44
Matthews, Chris, 103
McElroen, Christopher, 16, 55, 66, 70
McEwen, Lauren, 65
McIntyre (character): Parrish on, 204; Sundquist on, 123–25
McKnight, Reginald, 6
McPherson, James Allan, 13, 324–25
Melnick, Jeff, 97n7
Mills, Irving, 297
Millsap (character): Hill, L., on, 151–55; Parrish on, 209
minorities, 252–53
minstrelsy, 127–29, 139n5
modernism, 24, 200, 296–97
modernist narrative, 178–79; *The Man without Qualities* as, 201; Parrish on, 198, 200–201
modernity, 179–80; color line in, 198
More, Thomas, 274
Morel, Lucas, 16, 181; on affirmative action, 255–56; on American flag, 249–50; on bravery, 252–53, 255–56; on color line, 252–53; on humor, 247; "'In a Strange Country': The Challenge of American Inclusion," 27–28, 245–59; on inclusion, 256; on music, 247–51, 252; *Ralph Ellison and the Raft of Hope*, 16, 53; on

"What America Would Be Like without Blacks," 251–52
Morrison, Toni, 31n5, 133, 286; on victimization, 32n8
Morton, Jelly Roll, 297
mourning, 290
"Mourning and Melancholy: Explaining the Ellison Animus" (Posnock), 28–29, 285–93
Moynihan Report, 144
Murray, Albert, 46, 94–95, 118, 123, 181, 230–31, 274; in *Trading Twelves: The Selected Letters of Ralph Ellison and Albert Murray*, 11
music, 75–77; in "In a Strange Country," 247–51; integration of, 247–48, 252; Morel on, 247–51, 252; record players, 83; sound studies and, 79–83. *See also* jazz
Musil, Robert: German translations of, 217nn2–3; *The Man without Qualities*, 27, 200–201, 202
Muyumba, Walter, 239n1
Myrdal, Gunnar, 144
mythology: in computer sequences, 234; of hero, 177–78, 218–19

NAACP. *See* National Association for the Advancement of Colored People
Nancy, Jean-Luc, 80–81
narrative: of African Americans, 6, 32n8, 52; in *Dreams from My Father*, 19; against Ellison, 40–42; female voice, 183–85; in *Invisible Man*, 19; modernist, 178–79, 198, 200–201; national, 194–95; in *Three Days before the Shooting . . .*, 13–14; unfinished, 4, 10, 11, 198–200, 206, 215–16. *See also* African American narrative
National Association for the Advancement of Colored People (NAACP), 45
National Book Award, 7, 15, 100, 120
national conflict, 250

national narrative, 194–95
Native Son (Wright, R.), 39, 42; *Invisible Man* relating to, 46–47; Rankine on, 59–60
Negro Freedom Movement, 219
Noble Savage, The (Bellow), 34n15
No Future without Forgiveness (Tutu), 282n38
"Noisy Lostness, The: Oppositionality and Acousmatic Subjectivity in *Invisible Man*" (Beavers), 24, 75–98. *See also* Beavers, Herman
nonviolence, 44, 46–51
novel form: democracy relating to, 219, 220, 224; Ellison on, 57–58, 220; epic compared to, 58; *Invisible Man* and, 318–19; Lukács on, 57–59; Rankine on, 57–60; theater compared to, 59–60

Obama, Barack, 4; affinities between Ellison and, 18–19, 21–23, 315–16; appearance of, 103–4, 110; *Audacity of Hope*, 20–21, 22; on community, 21; Crable on, 100–110; on Declaration of Independence, 20; disillusionment with, 102; *Dreams from My Father*, 19, 21, 292; election of, 18, 100–101, 103, 109, 114n12; on *E pluribus unum*, 21; family of, 101, 109, 114n13; on father's race, 34n19; on founding of America, 20; on identity, 19, 34nn19–20, 315; *Invisible Man* and, 19, 291–92, 315; Kellman on, 19; Parrish on, 18, 34n18; political strategy of, 34n18; Posnock on, 286, 291–92; post racial America and, 101–2, 103, 108; racial binarism relating to, 109–10; reelection campaign of, 25, 101–2; Samuels on, 18, 34n19; visibility of, 104–6; Wright, Jeremiah, relating to, 21–22, 316
O'Brien, John, 135
Oedipus, 130
Oklahoma City, 320
Old Testament, 187–88. *See also* Bible

O'Meally, Robert, 298
O'Neill, Eugene, 60
oppositional behavior, 78–79, 89, 94–95
orphan's loneliness, 172–73, 174, 186–89

pain, 8, 287; body and, 63; humor and, 247; punishment and, 289
paradox, 196
Parker, Charlie, 96n2, 97n5, 246
Parrish, Timothy, 4–5, 12; on Armstrong, 197–98; on Bliss/Sunraider, 204, 207–16; on *Brown v. Board of Education*, 206–7; on civil rights movement, 171; on Ellison's importance, 17–18; on Faulkner, 169, 212; on Hickman, 210–16; on identity, 208–9; on jazz, 198; on Lincoln, 210–12, 215; on McIntyre, 204; on Millsap, 209; on modernist narrative, 198, 200–201; on Musil, 200–201, 202; on national narrative, 194–95; on Obama, 18, 34n18; on Proust, 195, 199, 202; on race, 203–4, 207–8; *Ralph Ellison and the Genius of America*, 17; "Ralph Ellison's *Three Days*: The Aesthetics of Political Change," 27, 194–217; on reading *Three Days before the Shooting . . .*, 198–200; on Rinehart, 209–10; on sacrifice, 215; on Severn, 207–8; on "Tell It Like It Is, Baby," 210; on tricksters, 209–10, 213; on understanding Ellison, 195–98; on unfinished narrative, 198–200, 206, 215–16; on violence, 206–8; on Wright, R., 169
past, 202, 205–6, 212–16; in *All the King's Men*, 283n41
patriarchs, 186–89
patriotic responsibility, 158–59, 162
patriotism, 159, 249, 259n13
Paulsen, William, 84
perceptions, 107–8
Pilgrims, 260–61, 272n2
Plessy v. Ferguson, 126–27, 268
Podhoretz, Norman, 169, 190n3

Poe, Edgar Allan, 296
poems, 123
police officers, 35n26, 69, 257n1
political development, 25–26
political ideology, 163–64
politics: love and, 21–22, 36n27, 44, 52–53; Wright, R., and, 41–43, 45–46
"Politics of Fatherhood in *Three Days before the Shooting . . . , The*" (Hill), 25–26, 142–66. *See also* Hill, Lena
Porter, Kenneth, 132–33
Portrait of the Artist as a Young Man, A (Joyce), 177–78
Posnock, Ross, 4, 9–10, 12, 100; on Baker, 285; *Cambridge Companion to Ralph Ellison*, 16; on criticisms against Ellison, 285–93; on Du Bois, 287–88; on father figures, 288–89; on Foley, 286, 290–92; on Howe, 285–86; "Mourning and Melancholy: Explaining the Ellison Animus," 28–29, 285–93; on Obama, 286, 291–92; on Rampersad, 286–89
post-civil rights era, 18
posthumous publications, 11–12, 317–18. *See also specific works*
postmodernism, 296–97
post-Obama America, 295
post-racial America, 25, 101–2, 103, 108, 113n6
Pound, Ezra, 12
power, 295; disempowerment and, 92–93, 178; relationships, 91–93
present, 202, 205–6, 212–16
primitivism, 299
principle, 268, 272–73, 316
progress, 22–23
protean tale-telling, 324–25
protest fiction, 8
Proust, Marcel: Parrish on, 195, 199, 202; on past and present, 202
public addresses: acousmatic sound and, 87–88; Beavers on, 84–88, 89–91; by Douglass, 268–70; flow and, 89–90; speaking and, 295–96; by Washington, B. T., 84–86, 89–90, 98n11, 263, 268, 270–71
punishment, 289
Putnam, Robert, 54n3

race: Bliss/Sunraider and, 204, 207–8, 215, 225–26; body and, 71–72, 74n26; color and, 25; conscience of, 148; Dyson on, 103; jazz and, 77–78, 298–99; Morel on, 245, 253, 259n9; Obama on, 21–22, 34n20, 35n22, 36n30; Parrish on, 203–4, 207–8; performance of, in contemporary theaters, 56; Rankine on, 70–72; theater and, 56, 71–72; tragic catharsis and, 225; visibility, invisibility, and, 103–10; Washington, B. T., on, 270–71; "(What Did I Do to Be So) Black and Blue?" on, 308–9
race of life argument, 140n10
race relations, 99, 113n2, 113n4; Sundquist on, 129
racial binarism, 99–101, 108–10
racial essentialism, 10
racial exclusion, 83–84
racial provocation, 8
Ralph Ellison: A Biography (Rampersad), 16, 31n5
Ralph Ellison: An American Journey (Kirkland), 16
Ralph Ellison and Individuality (Ara), 16
Ralph Ellison and Kenneth Burke: At the Roots of the Racial Divide (Crable), 17
Ralph Ellison and the Genius of America (Parrish), 17
Ralph Ellison and the Politics of the Novel (Rice), 16
"Ralph Ellison and the Problem of Cultural Authority: The Lessons of Little Rock" (Warren, K.), 53n1
Ralph Ellison and the Raft of Hope (Morel), 16, 53

Ralph Ellison: Emergence of Genius (Jackson), 16
"Ralph Ellison in His Labyrinth" (Sundquist): *Three Days before the Shooting...* and, 25, 117–41. *See also* Sundquist, Eric
Ralph Ellison in Progress: From "Invisible Man" to "Three Days before the Shooting..." (Bradley), 17, 325
Ralph Ellison's "Invisible Man": A Casebook (Callahan), 16
Ralph Ellison's "Invisible Man": Reference Guide (Hill and Hill), 16
"Ralph *Ellison's Three Days before the Shooting...* and the Implicit Morality of Form" (Shreve), 27, 218–42. *See also* Shreve, Grant
"Ralph Ellison's *Three Days*: The Aesthetics of Political Change" (Parrish), 27, 194–217. *See also* Parrish, Timothy
Rambo, Mary (character), 156–57
Rampersad, Arnold, 5, 10, 29; Conner on, 33n11; on Faulkner, 169; Howe and, 287; on *Juneteenth*, 34n12; Posnock on, 286–89; *Ralph Ellison: A Biography*, 16, 31n5; Rankine on, 71
Rankine, Patrice: on adaptation of *Invisible Man*, 56–57, 62–67; on body, 62–65; "The Body and *Invisible Man*: Ralph Ellison's Novel in Twenty-First-Century Performance and Public Spaces," 24, 55–74; on genre, 70–72; on Jacoby's *Invisible Man*, 62–67; on Joyce, 191n9, 192n14; on *Native Son*, 59–60; on novel form, 57–60; on race, 70–72; on Rampersad, 71; on riots, 61, 65–70; on theater, 60–65; *Ulysses in Black: Ralph Ellison, Classicism, and African American Literature*, 16
Razaf, Andy, 29, 294, 304–5, 307. *See also* "(What Did I Do to Be So) Black and Blue?"
Reagan, Ronald, 145

record players, 83–84
religion, 230; art and, 158–59, 161–63; Book of Job, 279n4; Ealy on, 266–67; Grandfather on, 266–67; "In a Strange Country" and, 249; Lincoln and, 181–82; Old Testament, 187–88; religious sermon, 254–55; Romans, 267, 280n12; in "(What Did I Do to Be So) Black and Blue?," 308–9
remembering, 206
Remembrance of Things Past (Proust), 195
Remnick, David, 288
Rice, William, 16
Rinehart (character), 117–18, 209–10
Ringgold, Faith, 159
riots: body and, 69; civil rights movement and urban riots, 45; Rankine on, 61, 65–70; in theater, 70
Riots, The (Slovo), 55, 61–62, 70
Romans, 267, 280n12
Roosevelt, Franklin, 140n10
Rueckert, William, 224–25

sacred documents, 20, 54n2, 280n31
sacrifice, 158–60; covenants, patriarchs, and, 186–89; Parrish on, 215; Shreve on, 219, 226–27, 229, 237–39; Theseus myth and, 219; tragic catharsis and, 226–27, 229
sacrificial sons, 158–59, 162–63, 188
sacrificial violence, 219, 220, 229–35, 241n6
Samuels, David, 18, 34n19
Savage, Edward, 152–54, *154*
scapegoating, 229, 235–37
Schechner, Richard, 62
scholarly trends, 9
Schultz, Dutch, 304
secretary (character), 157–58
segregation, 206
Selected Letters of Ralph Ellison, The (Ellison), 11–12
self-destruction, 49
self-made black American, 144–50
self-reliance, 147

sermon, 254–55
setting, 294–97
Severen (character), 226, 241n5
Severn (character), 207–8
sexuality, 128; jazz and, 297–98
Shadowing Ralph Ellison (Wright, John), 16
Shank, Barry, 157
Shreve, Grant: on art, 236–37; on Bliss's tragedy and Ellison's failure of resolution, 222–31; on Book I, 222–23, 240n2; on Book II, 223, 226–27; on *Brown v. Board of Education*, 219; on civic pollution, 224–25; on dialectical transcendence, computer sequences, 231–39; on implicit morality, 224; integration and Ellison, 219–20; on Leroy, 236; on mythology of hero, 218–19; "Ralph Ellison's *Three Days before the Shooting* . . . and the Implicit Morality of Form," 27, 218–42; on sacrifice, 219, 226–27, 229, 237–39; on Severen, 226, 241n5; on Theseus myth, 218–19; on tragedy, 220–31; on tragic catharsis, 224–27
Shull, Linwood, 257n1
sickness, 215
Skerrett, Joseph, 168
slavery, 212–13; Constitution and, 270; for Douglass, 268–70; freedom intertwined with, 260–61; Pilgrims and, 260–61, 272n2; for Washington, B. T., 268
Slavery: A Problem in American Institutional and Intellectual Life (Elkins), 146
Slovo, Gillian, 55, 61–62, 70
Smith, A. C., 64–65
So Black and Blue: Ralph Ellison and the Occasion of Criticism (Warren, K.), 16
socialization, 264–65
social realism, 8
social responsibility, 90
Socrates, 264
sound: acousmatic, 87–89, 94; body and, 88; studies, 79–83
space, 79–80, 83–84

speaking, 295–96
Sprague, Morteza, 45, 193n18, 220, 319
sprezzatura, 77, 96n4
stoic heroism, 8
street theater, 62
student sit-ins, 45
suffering, 162
Sundquist, Eric: on African American folktales, 132–35; on Bliss/Sunraider, 117–22, 125, 128–29, 131–38, 140n12, 141n17; on characterization, 117–18; on Cliofus, 136; on cripples, 121–27, 134, 136; on crossroads, 129–30; on Eshu-Elegba, 129–31; on Frost, 135–36; on Goethe, 135, 141n14; on Hickman, 119, 122–23, 125–28, 131–32, 137, 138; on Icarus myth, 117–18, 131–35, 140n6; on identity, 121–22, 128–29; on Legba, 129–30; on Leroy, 125–27, 130–31; on McIntyre, 123–25; on minstrelsy, 127–29, 139n5; on race relations, 129; "Ralph Ellison in His Labyrinth," 25, 117–41; on Rinehart, 117–18; on tricksters, 124–25, 129–30
Szalay, Michael, 165n4

tactics, 93, 98n12
technological change, 4
"Tell It Like It Is, Baby" (Ellison), 11; Callahan on, 321–23; on classical form, 223–24; Conner on, 26, 167–68; father figures in, 167, 181, 189; Parrish on, 210
Tender Is the Night (Fitzgerald), 172–73
territory, of hope, 3–9
"That Pause for Contemplation: A Centennial Meditation on Ralph Ellison" (Callahan), 313–28
theater: body and, 62–63; dramatic stage, 62–63; environmental, 62; novel form compared to, 59–60; performance of race in, 56; race and, 56, 71–72; Rankine on, 60–65; riots in, 70; street, 62
Theseus myth, 218–19
Thompson, Robert Farris, 130

Thomson, George, 226
Three Days before the Shooting . . . (Ellison), 4, 5, 8, 10, 11; African American folktales relating to, 132–35, 157; anatomy of, 13–14; background on, 12–13; Callahan on, 325–26; characterization in, 117–18; computer sequences of, 14–15, 31n2, 231–39, 325–26; cripples in, 121–27, 134, 136; crossroads in, 129–30; Eshu-Elegba in, 129–31; "Father Abraham: Ellison's Agon with the Fathers in *Three Days before the Shooting . . .* " and, 26, 167–93; "Hickman in Georgia & Oklahoma," 151–52, 209, 215, 232, 233–34; "Hickman in Washington DC" section of, 33n10, 157–58, 175, 232–33; Icarus myth and, 25, 117–18, 131–35, 140n6; minstrelsy and, 127–29, 139n5; narrative in, 13–14; political development in, 25–26; "The Politics of Fatherhood in *Three Days before the Shooting . . .*" and, 25–26, 142–66; "Ralph Ellison in His Labyrinth" and, 25, 117–41; "Ralph Ellison's *Three Days before the Shooting . . .* and the Implicit Morality of Form," 27, 218–42; "Ralph Ellison's *Three Days*: The Aesthetics of Political Change" and, 27, 194–217; reading of, 198–200; secretary, 157–58; time span of, 212; tricksters in, 124–25, 129–30; typescripts of, 13–15; as unfinished narrative, 198–200, 206, 215–16. *See also specific characters*
Till, Emmett, 231, 246
Tillich, Paul, 280n13
time, 212, 313–14, 317, 327
Tindall, William York, 183
Tracy, Steven: *Historical Guide to Ralph Ellison, A*, 16; "'How many lightbulbs does it take to screw in a blues singer?': The French Revolution, King Louis Armstrong, and the Futuristic Jungleism of Jazz," 29–30, 294–309; on power, 295; on setting, 294–97; on underground, 302

Trading Twelves: The Selected Letters of Ralph Ellison and Albert Murray (Ellison), 11
tradition: African American, 8, 205; literary, 196
tragedy, 172, 176–77, 289–90; of Bliss/Sunraider, 222–31; classical, 220, 223–24; hero in, 220–21, 225–31; Rueckert on, 224–25; Shreve on, 220–31
tragic catharsis: Eddy on, 240n4; race and, 225; sacrifice and, 226–27, 229; Shreve on, 224–27; Wright, R., relating to, 225
transcendence, 174–76
transformation, 232
tricksters: Armstrong as, 300; Ealy on, 261–62; Jack-the-Bear, 261–62; Parrish on, 209–10, 213; Sundquist on, 124–25, 129–30
Truth and Reconciliation Commission, 274, 282nn36–37
Tutu, Desmond, 274–75, 282nn36–38
twenty-first century: "The Body and *Invisible Man*: Ralph Ellison's Novel in Twenty-First-Century Performance and Public Spaces," 24, 55–74; Ellison and contemporary moment, 17–23; Ellison in our time, 23–31; Ellison's meaning for, 4–9; new understandings of Ellison in, 9–17

ubuntu concept, 274–75, 282n38
Ulysses (Joyce), 178, 179–80
Ulysses in Black: Ralph Ellison, Classicism, and African American Literature (Rankine), 16
unarmed blacks, 35n26
uncreated conscience, 148–49
underground: Beavers on, 81–82, 83; Tracy on, 302
unfinished narrative, 4, 10, 11, 198–200, 206, 215–16
United States citizenship, 151–56
urban riots. *See* riots

victimization, 7–8, 236, 237–38; in African American narrative, 52; by identity politics, 10; Morrison on, 32n8
violence: breaking cycle of, 274; in *Invisible Man*, 48–49; Parrish on, 206–8; sacrificial, 219, 220, 229–35, 241n6; as self-destruction, 49
violent change, 35n26
visibility: colorlessness and, 110–12; Conner on, 177–78; Ellison on, 104, 105; invisibility and, 103–10; of Obama, 104–6
visuality, 88, 143
Voting Rights Act of 1965, 6

Wales, 246; national anthem of, 257n8; Welsh oppression, 248–49
Wallace, Charles, 54n3
Waller, Fats, 297
Warren, Kenneth, 31n3, 231; on African American literature, 32n7, 51; "Ralph Ellison and the Problem of Cultural Authority: The Lessons of Little Rock," 53n1; *So Black and Blue: Ralph Ellison and the Occasion of Criticism*, 16; *What Was African American Literature?*, 32n7; "Why Do We Read Fiction?," 276–77
Warren, Robert Penn, 45, 129, 159; *All the King's Men*, 280n23, 283n41
Washington, Booker T.: "Atlanta Exposition Speech," 263, 268, 270–71; Grandfather and, 263, 265–66, 271–72; public addresses by, 84–86, 89–90, 98n11, 263, 268, 270–71; on race, 270–71; slavery, 268
Washington, George, 151–56, 153, 154
The Waste Land (Eliot), 186
Watts, Jerry Gafio, 44; *Heroism and the Black Intellectual*, 39
Weiss, Hedy, 64–65
Welsh oppression, 248–49
"What America Would Be Like without Blacks" (Ellison), 240n3, 251–52
"(What Did I Do to Be So) Black and Blue?," 294, 303–9

"What to the Slave Is the Fourth of July?" (Douglass), 268–70
What Was African American Literature? (Warren, K.), 32n7
white critical establishment, 40–41, 43–44
white identity, 205
white liberal intellectuals, 240n2
white-privileging, 308
white supremacy, 287–88
"Why Do We Read Fiction?" (Warren, R. P.), 276–77
Why We Can't Wait (King), 47, 50–51
Wideman, John Edgar, 133
Williams, Juan, 101, 103
Williams, William Carlos, 162
Wilson, Edith, 304
Wilson, Ivy, 166n16
Woodard, Isaac, 257n1
Woodridge scene, 148–50
Worker, The (Berry), 43
"World and the Jug, The" (Ellison), 8, 58, 285–86
Wrestling with the Left: The Making of Ralph Ellison's "Invisible Man" (Foley), 16–17, 23–24, 29, 39, 43. See also Foley, Barbara
Wright, Jeremiah, 36nn28–30; Obama relating to, 21–22, 316
Wright, John, 16
Wright, Richard: Butler on, 45–46; civil rights movement and, 45–46; Communist Party and, 42, 146; Conner on, 168–69; Ellison and, 40, 146–48, 165n7, 165n8, 168–69; *Native Son*, 39, 42, 46–47, 59–60; Parrish on, 169; politics and, 41–43, 45–46; tragic catharsis relating to, 225

Yanks, 247
Yeats, William Butler, 121
Yerby, Frank, 41
Young, Harvey, 60

www.ingramcontent.com/pod-product-compliance
Lightning Source LLC
Chambersburg PA
CBHW030603230426
43661CB00053B/1823